New Spain, New Literatures

HISPANIC ISSUES • VOLUME 37

New Spain, New Literatures

Luis Martín-Estudillo
Nicholas Spadaccini
EDITORS

Vanderbilt University Press
NASHVILLE, TENNESSEE
2010

© 2010 Vanderbilt University Press
All rights reserved
First Edition 2010

This book is printed on acid-free paper

The editors gratefully acknowledge assistance
from the College of Liberal Arts and the
Department of Spanish and Portuguese Studies
at the University of Minnesota.

The complete list of volumes in the
Hispanic Issues series begins on page 297.

Library of Congress Cataloging-in-Publication Data

New Spain, new literatures / Luis Martín-Estudillo, Nicholas Spadaccini, editors.
p. cm.—(Hispanic issues ; v. 37)
Includes bibliographical references and index.
ISBN 978-0-8265-1723-4 (cloth : alk. paper)
ISBN 978-0-8265-1724-1 (pbk. : alk. paper)
1. Spanish literature—20th century—History and criticism. 2. Spanish literature—Minority authors—History and criticism. 3. Cultural pluralism in literature. 4. Literature and society—Spain—History—20th century. 5. Politics and literature—Spain—History—20th century.
6. Cultural pluralism—Spain.
I. Martín-Estudillo, Luis.
II. Spadaccini, Nicholas.
PQ6072.N495 2010
860.9'0064—dc22
2010021336

HISPANIC ISSUES

Nicholas Spadaccini
Editor-in-Chief

Antonio Ramos-Gascón and Jenaro Talens
General Editors

Nelsy Echávez-Solano and Luis Martín-Estudillo
Associate Editors

Eric Dickey, Adriana Gordillo, and Kelly McDonough
Assistant Editors

*Advisory Board/Editorial Board
Rolena Adorno (Yale University)
Román de la Campa (University of Pennsylvania)
David Castillo (University at Buffalo)
Jaime Concha (University of California, San Diego)
Tom Conley (Harvard University)
William Eggington (Johns Hopkins University)
Brad Epps (Harvard University)
Eduardo Forastieri-Braschi (Universidad de Puerto Rico, Río Piedras)
*Ana Forcinito (University of Minnesota)
David W. Foster (Arizona State University)
Edward Friedman (Vanderbilt University)
Wlad Godzich (University of California, Santa Cruz)
Antonio Gómez-Moriana (Université de Montréal)
Hans Ulrich Gumbrecht (Stanford University)
*Carol A. Klee (University of Minnesota)
Eukene Lacarra Lanz (Universidad del País Vasco)
Tom Lewis (University of Iowa)
Jorge Lozano (Universidad Complutense de Madrid)
Walter D. Mignolo (Duke University)
*Louise Mirrer (The New-York Historical Society)
Mabel Moraña (Washington University in St. Louis)
Alberto Moreiras (University of Aberdeen)
Bradley Nelson (Concordia University)
Michael Nerlich (Université Blaise Pascal)
*Francisco Ocampo (University of Minnesota)
Miguel Tamen (Universidade de Lisboa)
Teresa Vilarós (University of Aberdeen)
Iris M. Zavala (UNESCO, Barcelona)
Santos Zunzunegui (Universidad del País Vasco)

Contents

Introduction:
    Contemporary Spanish Literatures: Enduring Plurality
    Luis Martín-Estudillo and Nicholas Spadaccini   ix

PART I
New Mappings / New Cartographies

1   On Rivers and Maps:
    Iberian Approaches to Comparatism
    Enric Bou   3

2   Peripheral Being, Global Writing:
    The Location of Basque Literature
    Mari Jose Olaziregi   27

3   Galician Writing and the Poetics of Displacement:
    Ramiro Fonte's *A rocha dos proscritos*
    Kirsty Hooper   43

4   Memory and Urban Landscapes
    in Contemporary Catalan Theater
    Jennifer Duprey   61

5   The New Capital of Spanish Literature:
    The Best Sellers
    Maarten Steenmeijer   81

PART II
Institutions and Literatures

6   A Hispanist's View of Changing Institutions,
    or About Insects and Whales
    Randolph D. Pope   99

7	Political Autonomy and Literary Institutionalization in Galicia	
	Dolores Vilavedra	117
8	Tensions in Contemporary Basque Literature	
	Jon Kortazar	135
9	The Persistence of Memory: Antonio Gamoneda and the Literary Institutions of Late Modernity	
	Jonathan Mayhew	149

PART III
Challenging Identities

10	The Curse of the Nation: Institutionalized History and Literature in Global Spain	
	Gonzalo Navajas	165
11	Postmodernism and Spanish Literature	
	María del Pilar Lozano Mijares	183
12	African Voices in Contemporary Spain	
	Cristián H. Ricci	203
13	From Literature to Letters: Rethinking Catalan Literary History	
	Stewart King	233
14	The Space of Politics: Nation, Gender, Language, and Class in Esther Tusquets' Narrative	
	Laura Lonsdale	245

Afterword:
Regarding the Spain of Others: Sociopolitical Framing of New Literatures/Cultures in Democratic Spain
Germán Labrador Méndez — 261

Contributors — 277

Index — 281

◆ Introduction

Contemporary Spanish Literatures: Enduring Plurality

Luis Martín-Estudillo and Nicholas Spadaccini

It is common knowledge that Spain's transformation during the last several decades from an authoritarian, centralist State with a homogeneous population into a democratic, plurinational, and multicultural society has also been marked by a thriving cultural production, which highlights "difference" as a major asset. To a great extent, one might consider this shift a historical novelty, as the Spain of the 1930s also saw efforts to reaffirm its inherent plurality only to be undermined by institutional forces for whom the stability of the national project depended on the suppression of linguistic, religious, and ideological singularities. During the last few decades we have witnessed the opposite dynamic. While the Franco regime conceptualized the Spanish nation from rigid schemes of identity understood as sameness, which at best relegated internal differences to the role of folkloric manifestations, the discourse of a "plural" state based largely on its own linguistic and cultural diversity has been embraced by many in democratic Spain. The institutional modernity and flexible identity that have come to characterize the country have been facilitated by new social and political realities, as well as by new economies and organizations—the result of interconnected processes in recent history which have been reflected on, and influenced by, a vibrant cultural scene in which literature still plays a defining role.

The present project is an attempt to describe and to analyze the dynamics of the lettered field in contemporary Spain, taking into account a period that is roughly identified with the post-Franco era. In one way or other, the literature of democratic Spain can be seen, at the same time, as the product of both old and new institutional practices and as a challenge to an established set of institutions, being perhaps first among them its own canonical status. Understanding this complex reality requires the raising of issues that are at the center of current debates in Spain and elsewhere. Among them are the emergence of minoritized literatures; the question of multilingualism and identity; the relationships between culture and institutions (including new ones, such as those being shaped by new technologies or those emerging from Spain's regional governments); the negotiation of historical memories; the connections between migrations and the redefinition of nationhood; and the impact of global commercial and cultural trends on local symbolic systems.

The very notion of "Spanish literature" has been altered by the redefinition of the political landscape that followed the end of the dictatorship, a conjunction which favored the growing recognition of the nation's composite (and sometimes contradictory) nature. The process of decentralization and devolution carried out since the approval of the 1978 Constitution has had a strong impact on cultural policies and practices. Functions formerly held by the State were transferred to the regional governments, which established new and wide nets of patronage. This is especially evident in the case of Catalonia, the Basque Country, and Galicia, three entities with their own languages and differentiated traditions, with strong nationalist movements. In those areas, the connections between history, language and identity, as well as their symbolic mediations through discourses such as literature, are common topics in public debates. While literature is still seen as an instrument of national affirmation, its resonance among the various nationalities shows that the project is no longer limited to that of a nation-state united around a predominant language and culture. The literary work of demystification of the so-called "eternal" or "sacred" Spain, which was at the core of the artistic projects of Spanish-language authors such as Luis Martín-Santos, a Basque, or Catalan writer Juan Goytisolo, has found a less virulent but probably more effective counterpart in the work of Catalan, Basque, and Galician-language writers for whom identitary issues are an important part of their reflections. Their ongoing questioning of national identities, which in many cases takes an internationalist turn, is also animated by the recent arrival of an unprecedented influx of immigrants from Latin America, Africa, and Eastern Europe who have brought along their own perspectives.

At the same time, the State and other institutions such as the publishing industry have redefined their position in the cultural sphere through dynamics of centralization and diversification. The State has done so by launching projects and institutions conceptualized as an auxiliary branch of foreign policies. This kind of "cultural diplomacy" is aimed at propagating a certain image of the nation outside of Spain. The Cervantes Institute is a case in point. Interestingly, institutions at the sub-statal level are not only replicating that model, but are even surpassing it in terms of relative spending, thanks to the power that they have accumulated to develop their own policies, organizations and projects in fundamental symbolic areas such as education and the arts. Thus, the role of public regional institutions in the establishment or strengthening of literary systems, the dissemination of vernacular literatures, and their incorporation in pedagogical settings through grants and other types of more or less direct patronage can hardly be overestimated.

One wonders how such policies play out within the Basque Country, Catalonia, and Galicia, and what their ultimate goals are. Writing in a minoritized language has at least a double function: one which is directed toward an inner market and is geared toward the self-preservation of memory and identity; another that is aimed at the outside, so as to be perceived as different (thus reinforcing the idea of diversity within a unity). The interests of regional governments to support their vernacular literatures, and with them their differentiating symbolic systems, must also be seen as a complement to their own efforts for increasing self-government. This is usually done regardless of the political inclinations of the writers whose works are presented, in one way or another, as conforming a "national" literature (see Kortazar in this volume). Some authors, however, insist on going beyond this type of localist identification as they see themselves working within a plural Spain that is also part of larger communities: the European Union, the world republic of letters, and so on. Significantly, the tensions connected with the overlapping movements of national affirmation and globalization have prompted a variety of cultural phenomena, which often have destabilizing effects on traditional structures. Such is the thrust of Hooper's essay (in this volume) on Galician-language poet Ramiro Fonte. In Hooper's view, while Fonte, a long-time expatriate, criticized the institutional settings of Galician literature from the outside, he was unable to move beyond them conceptually. In contrast to his poetry, Hooper points to the current critical rereading of the most canonical of Galician authors, Rosalía de Castro, whose work is now seen as containing traits that are destabilizing to the very idea of a national literature, whose foundation she helped to cement.

At the same time as authors and critics rethink literature along new identitarian mappings generated by global dynamics, the publishing world has also seen opposing movements of centralization and diversification. While big media conglomerates such as PRISA and Planeta have absorbed many smaller presses and have become international entities with strong interests in the entire Spanish-speaking world, there are also new independent publishers venturing in the marketplace with specialized objectives; with an attachment to the traditional role of the book; and/or with an eye toward the opportunities presented by the new conditions of distribution and consumption of literature via the Internet.

The innovations and flexibility of a variety of media through which literature is disseminated are ratified by the changing approaches from which these new literatures are studied both within and outside Spain. The evolving problematic alluded to by several essays in this volume, has not always been met with adequate responses from the literary disciplines. One might say that the weight of a philological tradition based on the predominance of canonical Spanish-language works not only limited, to a certain extent, the aggiornamento of Spanish literary studies, but also impacted on the production, mediation, and reception of texts. Yet, it could also be argued that Hispanism, as a discipline, has been affected by the new cultural landscape generated by the changing social and political realities of contemporary Spain, as well as by the changing practices of literary studies which, during the last forty years, have been energized by new theoretical orientations and the rejection of master narratives. One thinks not only of poststructuralism and deconstruction, but of postcolonial and cultural studies, approaches which, in one way or another, resonate throughout this volume (see especially Ricci).

The reactions, or the lack thereof, of institutions and individuals who try to make sense of the literature produced within this new context marked by these extraordinary political, social, and cultural changes are highlighted by Pope (in this volume), who points to the voluminous production of narrative fiction on a yearly basis and the virtual impossibility for professors of literature to account for it in their courses under present institutional settings and restrictions. While the profession has become increasingly aware of this dilemma, as seen in a somewhat greater emphasis on synchronic approaches to different issues and a movement toward greater interdisciplinary and collaborative work, university structures are not always sufficiently flexible to account for dynamic changes in the contemporary cultural and social landscape. Pope also emphasizes the importance of popular culture for an understanding of contemporary narrative and poetry, viewing it as a way of capturing student attention and of stimulating an appreciation of related literary texts. His concern over the vastness of our object of study is made even more evident by the explosion of literary production in languages other than Spanish within Spain and the concurrent need to consider its "national literatures" as inherently multilingual.

A redefinition of the practices of Hispanism, with an eye toward the recognition of the diverse literary traditions of Iberia on an equal, non-hierarchical level, is highlighted by Enric Bou (in this volume), who argues for the importance of comparatist approaches. Thus, his essay focuses on the metaphor of rivers and maps, which allows for a discussion of alternative conceptions of identity and an examination of power relations between interacting—rather than opposing—entities, such as self and other, center and periphery, and inside and outside. Bou also works from the assumption that Hispanism deals with a multicultural, multilinguistic reality, and overcomes the question of the connections between language and identity to look at broader issues of common interest.

Linguistic diversity, the single most remarkable feature of the Spanish literary sphere of the democratic period, poses a challenge for contemporary Hispanism. Yet, it also provides a great opportunity for its own renewal and strengthening within a diversified academic field in which "difference" is emphasized and celebrated. The reconfiguration of the Spanish literary system in line with the political and societal changes that have allowed for a full development of what may be understood as a multilingual nation (or even a "nation of nations") can be seen as an actualization of current tendencies toward multiplicity, a central feature of global cultural movements. However, one must be aware of important differences within this process. Although the three major languages other than Spanish (Catalan, Basque, and Galician) suffered severe restrictions in their use during the dictatorship, the fact is that the Catalan literary system was the best prepared to resist the blow of a Castile-centered type of nationalism promulgated by the Franco regime. When the dictatorship imposed itself and instituted the repression of linguistic diversity, Galicia and the Basque Country had much less developed systems of their own, so it was not until the recovery or reconstitution of high degrees of self-rule and the subsequent promulgation of laws that supported their respective languages, that there arose an infrastructure in support of the institutionalization of their literatures.

In the case of the Basque language, even the question of a valid standard was a matter of controversy among its most educated and influential speakers, well into the late 1960s. Olaziregi (in this volume) provides an overview of the current state of Basque literature after grounding it in an historical landscape dominated by marginality until the emergence of nationalism at the end of the nineteenth century. Nationalism brought with it an increased awareness of the importance of the connections between language and nation and the relevance of literary representation for the forging of a collective identity. Yet, as Olaziregi points out, views on these issues among Basque intellectuals varied. For Gabriel Aresti, for example, the Basque language was a crucial aspect of Basque identity, surpassing other considerations such as ethnicity, while for Jorge Oteiza, the focal point of identity was not the Basque language, but an aestheticized imaginary with prehistoric origins.

The infrastructure needed for the full development of a Basque literary system was created only after the process of devolution following the recovery of democratic freedoms in the 1970s. Interestingly, with the change in juncture the resistance that was shown against the monolithic identitarian model of Francoism was to shift inward, as some of the most prominent Basque writers felt a need to question the kind of rigid identitarian discourse promoted by certain nationalist sectors, both Basque and Spanish (see Olaziregi and Kortazar in this volume). Authors such as Ramón Saizarbitoria and Bernardo Atxaga seem to embrace postmodern notions of identity, with an emphasis on multiplicity and hybridity. Yet they are cognizant that embracing otherness from an understanding of the self, implies a recognition of one's historical and linguistic roots. Atxaga, for instance, envisions a future for Basque literature on the basis of a dialogue with, and an appropriation of, different traditions.

In Galicia, the telling case of Manuel Rivas's canonization is also explained by his ability to synthesize and agglutinate the different views on identity held there, as well as by his social and linguistic commitment (see Vilavedra in this volume). At the same time it is important to note that Rivas's work would be unthinkable within a systemic vacuum. Vilavedra (who also happens to be one of Rivas's translators into Spanish) establishes a chronology of the constitution of a literary structure in Galician, beginning with the passage of the Statute of Autonomy in December of 1980, and the creation of the Association of Galician Writers, followed by the passage of the Law of Linguistic Normalization (1983) and its impact on the institution of literature in Galicia, and the establishment's recognition of women narrators in the year 2000.

The kind of legislative and institutional actions that Vilavedra notes had crucial consequences for the stabilization of indigenous literary institutions within Catalonia, Galicia, and the Basque Country, and was to have an impact on the subsequent proliferation of publishing houses and the production of textbooks in their respective languages. Thus, while Catalonia already had important publishing structures (some of the major Spanish-language publishers were, and still are, based in Barcelona) and the commercial viability of texts in Catalan is fairly established, to the point that even books written originally in Spanish are translated into that language, Galician and Basque literatures face comparable challenges in trying to forge a wide readership for books published in those languages.

As previously argued, the traditional disciplinary settings of Hispanism within Spain and elsewhere (including the United States) do not facilitate the kind of engagement with the linguistic plurality found within Spanish literature. It could even be argued that it might be easier to approach such complexity from the outside; in courses taught in languages other than Basque, Catalan, Galician, or Spanish, courses in which all the texts would be read in translation.

Paradoxically, in the struggle to define and reaffirm identity at the infrastatal (regional or national, depending on the case) level against the centralist background of Francoism, some institutional impulses have tended to suppress internal diversity by defining identity in conjunction with language. Along these lines, King and Lonsdale (see their respective essays in this volume), question the link between literature and nation-building, a link which was created with notable success in Catalonia, especially from the nineteenth century on, when the cultural movement known as the *Renaixença* (Renaissance) favored the formation of a Catalan canon tied to language. The idea is that this limited notion is subject to question in the current context of globalization in that it does not fully engage with the realities of Catalonia as both a multicultural and a multilingual society. Thus, once Catalan literature in Catalan is translated, say, in German—as was the case for the Frankfurt fair noted by King—does it mean that it should no longer to be considered "Catalan"? What place within that tradition would be occupied by authors such as the Moroccan-Amazigh Laila Karrouch and Najat El Hachmi (see Ricci in this volume), or by Esther Tusquets, a daughter of the Barcelona bourgeoisie who writes in Spanish (see Lonsdale in this volume)? The work of these and other writers point to Catalonia as a complex entity, rather than a purified construct of a wishful nationalist imaginary supported by a network of governmental cultural institutions. The same can be said of the many writers in Galicia and the Basque Country who shift between languages, including major authors such as the above-mentioned Manuel Rivas and Bernardo Atxaga, whose significance for Galician and Basque letters can hardly be overvalued.

Language is just one ingredient in the issue of identity, which nowadays cannot possibly be boiled down to just one element. The drive to achieve a cohesive picture around a single language, as promoted for a variety of reasons by certain institutions, gives rise to contradictions; essentialist policies tend to replicate the very models which non-centralist intellectuals have tried to escape: namely, the hegemonic project of Castile, from the early modern period to Ortega y Gasset's fixation with a center. Navajas (in this volume) reflects on this generalized movement away from the center, not only in geographical terms, but also in ideological, subjective terms. Navajas argues that, for some artists who are presently working in Spain, "the national reference is seen as an obstacle in the consideration of the only significant goal for art: the search for the creation of powerful links among human beings separated precisely by the traditional communal bounds of the fatherland, family, and language." The work of many of the African authors who write from, and on, Spain now touches on those issues from fascinating perspectives (see Ricci in this volume).

In contrast with the strong ties between language and identity showcased by those authors and institutions seeking to establish a 'national literature,' or by those attempting to challenge that very same category from within, authors of bestsellers see language as a vehicle of communication which supports their projects of speaking to a global market (see Steenmeijer in this volume). This literature is conceptualized as a commodity, unattached of preoccupations of identitary, linguistic, or cultural nature. It thus speaks to a global "consumer public," rather than to specific national readerships. Thus, one can understand the reticence of the critical establishment in Spain (in both the press and academia) to consider this type of literature as being worthy of attention beyond its socio-economic dimensions and the fact that these writers were born in Spain. Ironically, when the traditional division between high-, mid-, and low-brow culture has long been dismissed by academics who privilege cultural studies, these novels continue to be absent from most reading lists dealing with contemporary Spanish literature. This might be explained by the fact that these kinds of formulaic texts often lack the sort of specificity and identitarian problematics which would serve to connect them more closely to the different Spanish literary and cultural traditions.

Another topic which recurs throughout the volume and is closely tied to the questioning of identity is that of the literary treatment of the past. In a previous volume of *Hispanic Issues*, Christine Henseler and Randolph Pope observed that, in Spain "by the late eighties a significant part of a new young society is not only enjoying different material conditions, political structures, and freedoms, but the luxury of forgetting the past and being able to concentrate in living an exuberant, consumerist, drug-imbued, sex-abundant life" (xiv). However, during those years this tendency overlapped with a less noticeable, but still significant, interest to look into the recent history of Spain from a literary lens. It is fair to say that the question of cultural memory and the issue of human rights are now at center stage in many of the debates that are taking place within Spanish society. The pressures for the recovery of the experiences that the dictatorship tried to obliterate, and which during the Transition to democracy were only partially vindicated for the sake of national reconciliation, were to grow significantly during the 1990s, and have reached their paroxysm during the last few years. The present-day debates involve not only politicians and lawyers, but also intellectuals and writers, many of whom have dealt with these very issues for decades, and, most especially, since Spain's Transition to democracy.

On might recall that, for different reasons, the Transition had been promoted both within and outside of Spain as a communal success. The canonized narrative of its unfolding tells the story of a few heroes (with King Juan Carlos and Prime Minister Adolfo Suárez in the lead roles) who dismantled the dictatorship from within in the presence of an audience formed by an expectant and rather passive people. This characterization, which was distrusted from the start by some of those who were critical of the establishment, now finds wider resonance in various sectors of Spanish society. Moreover, civic groups, intellectuals, and foreign institutions, among others, have been playing an active role in the configuration of a different social landscape and have added urgency to the call for a revision of the established account of the process. It has also been argued that while the political system was transformed, many of the social and cultural structures which characterized Francoism are still in place. Thus, the so-called Transition to democracy did not provide closure to fundamental issues and, furthermore, set a symbolic system which was far from satisfactory for many. The disillusionment of many who had hopes of a greater renewal in Spain following the change in regime, overlapped with the international context of generalized crisis (social, economic and epistemic), which was to mark postmodernity (see Lozano in this volume).

The revision of Spain's recent history is an encompassing feature of Spanish contemporary narrative in all of its linguistic manifestations. A massive number of texts dealing with a history, which seemed to have begun on or circa April 14, 1931 (the day of the proclamation of the Second Republic), have occupied the attention of critics and readers alike. What stands out from those texts is the need to work through, recover, and protect the memories of those who had been silenced, not only by the Franco regime, but also by a political elite which, for the most part, decided that it was convenient to ignore a long history of governmental crimes and oppression. Many of the cultural products that have elicited the most interest share an emphasis on the importance of remembering, or better, of *commemorating*: to remember along with others, collectively, reaching beyond one's own memories and thus knitting a collective net where one can situate existence and give it meaning beyond the shallow presentness and tendency to the oblivion, which characterized Spain's precipitous run to high modernity. The significance of this issue transcends the confines of the narrative genre (see Mayhew in this volume), as seen in the recent canonization of poet Antonio Gamoneda, whose work deals with the issue of historical memory. His recognition and success might well be due to the fact that, in addition to the notion of bearing witness through the testimonial voice in his poetry, the latter offers a symbolic treatment of the relationships between past and present. His adherence to modernist aesthetics runs parallel to his preoccupation with the recovery of a forgotten past, which contrasts with the project of those associated with the "poetry of experience."

The present volume reveals the richness and complexity of the many voices that have risen in Spain since its Transition to democracy, voices which project a rich kaleidoscope of views about identity within a vast and fragmented political and social landscape in which writers of fiction, poetry and drama of different backgrounds and experiences come to grips with issues of language and identity, human rights, urban planning, immigration, and social justice, among others. They do so by engaging tradition and often expressing aesthetic and ideological dissidence. This is shown in the essay by Duprey (in this volume) dealing with Catalan theater and the re-writing of ancient Greek myths to get at conflicts dealing with contemporary issues of memory. The theoretical/critical approaches that are brought to bear on the topic of this volume are quite varied, yet they complement one another in delving into the complexities of current discussions about identity and related issues, at a time when people and capital move in various directions, from within and outside of Spain. A democratic, multilingual Spain, fully engaged in the European and global arenas, with a substantial percentage of its population constituted by immigrants from Africa, Latin America, and Eastern Europe is no longer the Spain of the Transition to democracy. This new Spain produces new literatures and other manifestations of culture which are only partially indebted to its recent past, as they often leave aside their own traditions to engage with the infinite voices of a world in constant flux. It is no longer sufficient to hold onto the old canon of contemporary, post-civil war writers which has fed academic curricula and research agendas for the last few decades; it is time to open critical pathways which can reveal, and reflect upon, the complexity of a cultural system increasingly characterized by an enduring plurality.

Work Cited

Henseler, Christine, and Randolph D. Pope. "Introduction: Generation X and Rock: The Sounds of a New Tradition." *Generation X Rocks: Contemporary Peninsular Fiction, Film, and Rock Culture*. Ed. Christine Henseler and Randolph D. Pope. *Hispanic Issues* Vol. 33. Nashville: Vanderbilt University Press, 2007.

Part I

New Mappings / New Cartographies

◆ 1

On Rivers and Maps:
Iberian Approaches to Comparatism

Enric Bou

For many years, scholars have studied the case of Spain, and even the entire Iberian Peninsula, as a separate entity within the confines of Europe.[1] Countries such as Portugal and Castile, that were once leaders in the transformation of the Western world, opening up new and poignant ways of relationship with the Other, have become modern nations which, because of their eccentricity, are commonly depicted as failing to fulfill the requirements of the Northern European paradigm. The ways of colonialism and the access to modernity have been, for these countries, everything but an easy path. Thus, scholars (some within the context of Europe, others within the framework of globalization and colonialism) have used terms like "alternative," "marginal," and "peripheral" to portray the Iberian experience.[2] Though well-intended, this kind of approach only stresses the original sin of the accuser: "Let the one without sin cast the first stone." Recent studies, such as John H. Elliott's *Empires of the Atlantic World* (2007), teach us many lessons. For one thing, they show that colonialism and its aftermath is a convoluted history in which there are only losers, particularly among the "discovered." When discussing general historical and cultural movements, Elliott portrays in dazzling ways the many oddities related to time and space. The complications introduced by the effects of time-lag are further amplified by the effects of fragmentation, and by the complex dialogue between center and periphery, which is the unpredictable implication in the colonizing society of its creation of parallel worlds, similar but extremely different. This mirror effect can be further developed if we turn the tables and look at just the case of Castile and Portugal—or, even better, the entire Iberian Peninsula—from such a perspective. By this I mean looking at the study of cultural issues from a multicultural and plurilinguistic perspective, which allows us to shift paradigms and challenge preconceptions.

In recent years we have witnessed an unfathomable general reassessment of what it means to study culture/literature in the Iberian Peninsula, as has been suggested by several studies.[3] Tensions connected with the overlapping movements of national affirmation and globalization have provoked different perspectives, new ways of looking at old issues. What was once depicted as a backward and lagging area in Europe, has, in recent years, been looked at very differently. Issues of multiplicity and cultural difference have been revalued as something positive and as potential sources of inspiration and reformulation for the tortuous, unresolved, postcolonial narratives of former major players, such as the UK or France. Not too long ago, Joan Ramon Resina inquired in non-rhetorical terms: "What would happen if Hispanism were conceived as a supranational discipline in which the various cultures of the Iberian peninsula (including the Portuguese) could be studied in a non-hierarchical relation to each other?" (114). However, this poignant question has not yet been satisfactorily answered.

Here I propose a reflection on comparative literature in the Iberian Peninsula, which takes into account this emerging drive for the redefinition of Hispanism. I will do this through the reading of two motifs, rivers and maps, as a way of presenting a different version of Comparatism, one more akin to issues of center and periphery, otherness and non hierarchical assumptions. This approach is not exactly a "humanistic geography." Although this project owes much to that field, it is not by any means inscribed in that tradition. Rather, it is indebted to the idea of restoring and making explicit the relation between knowledge and human interests. In this article I want to emphasize a goal I have in common with geographers: "to explore how worlds, places, landscapes, meanings, and human experiences are socially constructed and help constitute specific cultural contexts" (Adams, Hoelscher, and Till XVI). In fact, what I pursue is both a reflection on Comparatism and the discussion of two practical cases, which provide lessons on how to read in a non-centripetal way.

Claudio Guillén's "Europa: ciencia e inconsciencia," a chapter in his latest book *Múltiples moradas* (1998), suggests a way of "reading" Europe. He explores in a new light some concepts dear to him, such as the combination of unity and diversity, which he deems crucial in a general discussion of Comparatism. He proposes that the conceptualization of "Europe" is aware of and based on the awareness of it as a heterogeneous conglomeration of juxtaposed lands, or unwelded pieces, and that to grasp this multifarious reality requires a plurality of perspectives and definitions as varied as they are uncomfortably accurate: states, nations, countries, autonomies, provinces, communities, nationalities, territories, regions, cantons, shires, jurisdictions, municipalities, towns, counties, towns, hamlets, villages, places (381–82). The reason for this variety of terms lies within a diversity of criteria: geography, history, politics, society, and economy. It is the combination of all these factors what has played a part in an equivocal complicity. He concludes that no political map of the continent suggests the abundance he describes, and that as a place of interspaces, multiplication of countless adjacent fragments, almost infinately divisible, Europe offers the historian not only successive changes but also rhythmic reiterations, recurrent conflictive structures (383).

In his discussion of Europe he also borrows a key idea from Francisco Tomás y Valiente: that our identity does not belong to a single unique entity. On the contrary, we belong to different circles, not as uncommitted individualists, but rather as rational human beings aware of the true complexity of social reality, where every man is a point of intersection between different collective subjects (qtd. in Guillén 403). Moreover, Guillén introduces the idea of dialogue of pluralities, expanding what Edgar Morin proposed in his book *Penser l'Europe*. The French thinker provides some complementary thoughts, particularly that a dialogue of pluralities pushes for change and transformation. What is "important" to note about European culture, according to Morin, is not only its "governing ideas (Christianity, humanism reason, science) but also their opposites." The "genius" of the continent, he writes "does not rest solely in plurality and change, but more precisely in the dialogue between the pluralities that produce the change." He points out that the redeeming qualities of Europe can be found specifically in the "antagonism between the old and the new," and not just in the "production of the new as such" (74). This is important because honoring and exploring this antagonism leads us closer to the concept of enrichment through dialogue and the confrontation of diversity. Although Morin sounds a little bit too optimistic, not taking into account the sheer quantity of blood, pain, and hatred generated by the confrontation of opposite religious, philosophical, and political schools of thought, his concept of a "dialogue of pluralities" may be taken as a good objective for the future. Guillén concludes his essay on a more personal note suggesting that the "complexity we struggle to grasp is best understood as the constant movement and oscillation between concepts and their limits" (426). He warns against "reducing either the multiplicity that makes it possible nor the acts of conscience that tend to differentiate and discover it—in the I, in the world" (426). Albeit an overtly idealistic, almost utopian conceptualization by both Morin and Guillén, the latter's essay gets us interested in conflictive notions, in new ways of reading a continent both as an entity and as the purveyor of a rich literary tradition. Guillén's proposal encapsulates many tools to read a continent, exploring, in fact, the rich literary tradition on which it has been founded, and which goes well beyond the secluded world of conventional comparative literature. By taking Guillén's conflictive notions in the borders of literature a bit further, I wish to pursue a vindication of comparative literature in the Iberian Peninsula.

Drawing Rivers

"Los mismos que expulsaron a los judíos en 1492 nos expulsan a nosotros" (The same people who expelled the Jews in 1492 are expelling us), said Joaquim Xirau in 1939 on his way to exile. For too long the notion of hispanicity has been defined through a politics of exclusions and inclusions, expulsions and executions, censorship and repression, conquest and colonization, and concentration camps and forced labor. Thus, fear and menace have been the *mot d'ordre* among so-called intellectual circles. Rivers provide an illuminating example of the appropriation and (re)definition of space because they have been incorporated into a symbolic geography.

Let's start with the image of a particular river, as portrayed by Italian critic Claudio Magris. In his book *Danubio* (1986), Magris uses Heraclitus' image of the river applied to the Danube in a rather innovative way. For him the Danube represents a consideration of identity. A river, which is primarily a geographical trait, exudes other notions beyond physicality. In fact, certain rivers seem to express an identity, or even a notion of diversity. On the other hand, the case of the Rhine, an iconic German river, offers a conflictive notion. According to Claudio Magris the Rhine is mostly "un mistico custode della stirpe" (28) (a mystic custodian of the stock), whereas the Danube has a much more complex meaning because

> è il fiume di Vienna, di Bratislava, di Budapest, di Belgrado, della Dacia, il nastro che attraversa e cinge, come l'Oceano cingeva il mondo greco, l'Austria absburgica, della quale il mito e l'ideologia hanno fatto il simbolo di una koinè plurima e sovranazionale. . . . Il Danubio è la Mitteleuropa tedesca-magiara-slava-romanza-ebraica, polemicamente contrapposta al Reich germanico. (28–29)

> (This is the river of Vienna, Bratislava, Budapest, Belgrade, Dacia, the circle which, the same way the Ocean surrounded the Greek world, crosses and surrounds Habsburg, Austria, which through myth and ideology has become a symbol for a plural koine. . . . The Danube is the Mitteleuropa German-Magiar-Slavic-Romance-Hebraic, polemically contrasted to the German Reich.)

Precisely because rivers move constantly, they have become a symbol of renovation, a statement against fixation and stillness, contrary to what is identical and cannot be modified. It is very clear, however, that here we are not discussing actual rivers, or their physical aspect. On the contrary, Magris encourages us to speak of a symbolic geography. His characterization of these two rivers allows us to make a distinction between alternative versions of identity. In fact, this image of rivers is useful when trying to find other ways of discussing Hispanicity or Spanishness (españolidad), moving away from the "españolada" in the version portrayed by the Francoist Ministry of Information and Tourism: *Spain is different*, Fraga Iribarne dixit. As is well known, slogans such as "*Spain is different*" wanted to stress bullfights, beaches, and "fiestas" (Kaplan 193). Accordingly, I want to stay away from a notion of hispanicity that is "carpetovetónico," identical, and stationary in character, and to offer, as a substitute, a more open notion, based on variety and abstractness.

In *A Thousand Plateaus* (*Mille Plateaux*) (1980) Deleuze and Guattari propose a concept of alternative space, one which belongs to nomads, living on the fringes of an established—striated—society, a concept which may prove very useful in my discussion of rivers and maps. On the one hand we encounter the walled city-state, closed and with a well regulated spatiality. The second—smooth—kind of space is that of the "bricoleur," the nomad's camp, built with materials at hand, an informal workplace without walls. Smooth space invites roaming, wandering between regions, instead of going from place to place with specific starting and finishing points.

Smooth space is without landmarks, or with landmarks that are too feeble to remain. Rather, trajectory itself becomes a landmark:

> The first aspect of the haptic, smooth space of close vision is that its orientations, landmarks, and linkages are in continuous variation; it operates step by step. Examples are the desert, steppe, ice, and sea, local spaces of pure connection. Contrary to what is sometimes said, one never sees from a distance in a space of this kind, nor does one see it from a distance; one is never "in front of," any more than one is "in" (one is "on . . ."). Orientations are not constant but change according to temporary vegetation, occupations, and precipitation. There is no visual model for points of reference that would make them interchangeable and unite them in an inertial class assignable to an immobile outside observer. (Deleuze and Guattari 493)

Against the well-defined striated space, these authors juxtaposed smooth space. This well-known distinction allowed the diffusion of key concepts such as deterritorialization, which derives from the spatial metaphor. It describes the condition of the "plane of consistency" or "smooth space." Its opposite—territorialization—describes the condition of "striated space." As proposed by these authors, striated space consists of lines between points; smooth space consists of points between lines. Striated space consists predominantly of closed intervals; smooth space of open intervals. Striated space closes off surfaces; smooth space consists of "distributed" surfaces (480–81). To better understand this use of space we could add Henri Lefebvre's spatial triad: the perceived, the conceived, and the lived (33–39). All the rivers, as perceived by writers, use as a starting point, a spatial practice: that is, the production and reproduction of spatial relations between objects and products. The spatial practice of a society secretes that society's space.

Rivers can be related to this sense of space, as they have a dual condition of being, at the same time, smooth and striated. They define, but at the same time, are difficult to define. From a geographical perspective, they set a very clear path, but, likewise, their content (meaning) is difficult to ascertain. They set landmarks and borders, but their significance is transferable. At the same time, rivers can be substitutes, through a synecdochical effect, for an entire country, and can connect points in their path (as in the quote from Magris), thus creating a new identity that goes beyond the limitations of political borders. In Lefebvre's terms, they are crucial for a definition of space. Subsequently when poet Josep Carner evokes a mythical and imaginary France through images of rain and rivers, in his sonnet "Plou" from *Cor quiet* (1925), he summarizes the map of France in a few names of rivers: "París regala deplorablement; / es nega Niça d'aiguarells en doina. / Milers d'esgarrifances d'un moment / punyen Sena, Garona, Rin i Roine" (147) (Paris swamps herself deplorably; / Nice is drowning. / A thousand shivers suddenly / hit Seine, Garonne, Rhine, Rhoine).

When this poem was written, rain had not only a meaning in climatic terms, but also had a "moral" meaning, as it was perceived to provide moments of recollection and reflection. This can also be perceived in a Eugeni d'Ors' 1907 "glosa":

> Oh Pluja! Germana la Pluja, tu no n'ets responsable pas, de les inundacions. Ja hem quedat que la culpa era dels homes que no s'autocanalitzaven.—En canvi a n'a tu, quants beneficis te devem, els homes civils! [. . .] Tu proporciones ocasió a què llegeixin llibres alguns homes que no llegirien llibres. [. . .] Potser per a l'establiment definitiu de la nostra civilitat en convindria això: que plogués—no, tant com ploure, no,—que plovisquegés tres anys de carrera, aquí. . . . Amb això ens estaríem a casa, aniríem als círcols, als salons, als teatres, però no a passejar. [. . .] I després de tres anys ja començaríem a tenir dret, sense perill, al bon sol, i ja ens assemblaríem lo suficient a París per a començar a pensar en assemblar-nos a Atenes. (667–68)

> (Oh Rain! Sister Rain, you aren't responsible for the floods. We already decided that men who don't channel themselves are at fault.—On the contrary, how many benefits do we civilized men owe you! [. . .] You give men who otherwise would not read books ocassion to read them [. . .] Maybe it would be convenient for the definitive establishment of our civility that it would rain—no, not so much rain, no—that it would drizzle here three years straight. . . . If it were so we would stay home, we would go to the gatherings, to the sitting rooms, to the theatres, but we wouldn't go for walks. [. . .] And after three years we would begin, without danger, to have a right to the sun; and then we would resemble Paris closely enough to begin to think about resembling Athens.)

The rivers in Carner's poem are clearly a substitute for the whole of France, but they are also a referent for civility, and, furthermore, a certain model of European civilization. This goal of refinement can be attained through reading and study, and in a rainy climate it is much easier not to be distracted by café life. In the sophisticated mental rewriting of European tradition performed by Catalan "noucentistes," Paris is, among other things, a passport to get to Greece, its classic culture an idealized version of the Mediterranean, a goal very dear to the them ("ens assemblaríem lo suficient a París per a començar a pensar en assemblar-nos a Atenes"). Carner manages to draw a map of France based on parts of its geography: regions (Britanny and Normandy), cities (Paris and Nice), and the four main rivers (Seine, Garone, Rhine, and Rhône), creating a physical, yet imagined version of the whole country.

In a similar way, but with different meaning, Federico García Lorca incorporates two of Granada's rivers in a poem, opposing them to the Guadalquivir, the main Andalusian river. In "Baladilla de los tres ríos" from *Poema del cante jondo* ("Baladilla of the Three Rivers," from *Poem of the Andalusian Song*), we read contrasting versions of Andalusia:

> El río Guadalquivir
> va entre naranjos y olivos,

los dos ríos de Granada
bajan de la nieve al trigo.

¡Ay, amor
que se fue y no vino!

El río Guadalquivir
tiene las barbas granates,
los dos ríos de Granada
uno llanto y otro sangre. (142)

(The River Guadalquivir / goes between orange and olive trees, / Granada's two rivers / flow down from the snow to the wheat. / Oh, love / that went and didn't come! / The River Guadalquivir / has crimson beard, / Granada's two rivers / one tears and the other blood.)

In this way, Lorca indicates how different the Guadalquivir River is from its tributaries, the Darro and the Genil. This is perceived through different notions of vegetation, color, and sorrow, linked to these two rivers, which imply opposite places and states of mind: the planes—Guadalquivir—opposed to the steep descent from Sierra Nevada, as represented by the Darro and the Genil. Metonymically, both rivers are converted respectively into "llanto" and "sangre," two of the most recurrent words in Lorca's poetry and plays. Here we also recognize typical distinctions in Lorca's work: between dry land and the magical, onirical forest, individual freedom and moral constraints, wedding and blood, life and death. The two Granadine rivers are real, as they belong to the realm of geography, but they attain a symbolic status when they confront the Guadalquivir.

Alberto Caeiro, one of Fernando Pessoa's heteronyms, in a poem from *O Guardador de Rebanhos* (1911–12), "O Tejo é mais belo," compared, through a paradox, the powerful Tejo (Tagus) with the nameless minuscule river, which crosses his small town:

O Tejo é mais belo que o rio que corre pela minha aldeia,
Mas o Tejo não é mais belo que o rio que corre pela minha aldeia
Porque o Tejo não é o rio que corre pela minha aldeia.
[. . .]
O Tejo desce de Espanha
E o Tejo entra no mar em Portugal.
Toda a gente sabe isso.
Mas poucos sabem qual é o rio da minha aldeia
E para onde ele vai
E donde ele vem.

E por isso porque pertence a menos gente,
É mais livre e maior o rio da minha aldeia.

(The Tagus is more beautiful that the river that runs through my village, / But the Tagus is not more beautiful that the river that runs through my village / Because the Tagus is not river that runs through my village. [. . .]The Tagus arrives from Spain / And the river Tagus enters the sea in Portugal. / Everybody knows that. / But few know which is the river of my village / And where it goes / And where it comes from. / And because it belongs to fewer people / It is freer and largest the river in my village.)

This reductionism of sorts is useful in exalting small things, in a re-creation of the *aurea mediocritas*, and thus allows the contrast of a lesser known and anonymous local river—which clearly is of immense intimate value to the poet—with a very well-known river of Iberian dimensions. In a way he is expressing a vindication of small things, meaning that identity is closer to anonymous intimate realities, the "terruño," or *petit pays*. The conclusion of the poem stresses this aspect of disparity between the cosmopolitan world and the little familiar corner:

Pelo Tejo vai-se para o Mundo.
Para além do Tejo há a América
E a fortuna daqueles que a encontram.
Ninguém nunca pensou no que há para além
Do rio da minha aldeia. O rio da minha aldeia não faz pensar em nada.
Quem está ao pé dele está só ao pé dele. (53–54)

(Through the Tagus you get to the world. / Beyond the Tagus there is América / and fortune for those who can find it. / Nobody ever thought what it is in addition / to my village's river. My village's river makes you not think about anything. / Who is next to it is next to it.)

Here, the river Tagus has no association with grandeur or connections to other continents. It does not make you think about anything. The river only reminds you that you are there: "Quem está ao pé dele está só ao pé dele." Pessoa's consideration can be related to what Georges Perec wrote about space in *Espèce d'espaces* (1974). His is an idealistic perception of space as immutable, one which creates emotional linkage to points in somebody's life map. He imagines "stable, static, untouchable" (122) places that serve as references for one's personal history. Together with the emblematic artifacts of one's life they comprise "the attic of [one's] childhood filled with unbroken memories" (122). But he realizes immediately that this is an impossible dream because of time's destruction, and that it creates a sense of doubt and a need for marking space. "Those sorts of places," he writes, "don't exist" (122). For Perec, space is always in doubt and he feels the constant "need to demarcate it, designate it" (122). It is never simply given to you, he writes; you must "conquer it" (122). But because these intimate spaces are part of some sort of personal photography collection, one cannot keep them, because they have been destroyed by time. Perec describes his spaces as "fragile"; time has "used them, destroyed them" and "nothing will ever again resemble what it was" (122). He sees "yellowed photos torn around the edges" and he can no longer recognize them (122). That is why writing, as Perec concludes, is one of the few available protocols for saving lost space. He describes writing as a way "to try meticulously to retain something . . . to snatch some snippets from the void that deepens, to leave some part, a groove, a trace, a mark or somekind of sign" (123). A postmodern version of Proust's need for remembrance, these words are a reminder of the fragility of the present, and the need to inscribe in our own intimate landscape a sense of property. It is also a vindication of an intimate reality without big names, those who become recognizers. In this sense it is similar to Pessoa's claim that intimate space—a nameless river—provides a better understanding of one's intimate world, and is much more powerful from a representational point of view. In other words, he puts forward the strength of quasi-anonymity against the power of fame and name recognition.

In yet another poem, "Tresmares" by Gerardo Diego, the poet gives voice to a mountain peak in Cantabria and he converts it into a symbol and birthplace of a certain reductive conception of Iberia:

> Ni una gasa de niebla ni una lluvia
> o cellisca ni una dádiva de nieve
> ni un borbollar de fuentes candorosa
> dejo perderse. Madre soy de Iberia
> que incesante en mi seno nace y dura.
> A los tres mares que la ciñen, corren
> —distintas y purísimas—mis aguas.
> Al Ebro el Híjar, el Pisuerga al Duero
> y el Nansa se despeña. Tres destinos:
> Mediterráneo, Atlántico, Cantábrico.
> Y mi cúspide eterna, bendiciendo
> —vientos de Dios—España toda en torno.
> Prostérnate en mi altar si eres hispano.
> Si de otras tierras, mira, admira y calla. (419)

(Not a thin film of fog nor rain nor / slush nor a downpour of snow / nor innocent spouting fountains / will I let go to waste. I am the mother of Iberia, / that in my breast is born and endures without end. / To the three seas that cradle her, my waters / –distinct and pure-run free. / Hijar to the Ebro, Pisuerga to the Douro / And the Nansa over flows. / Three different seas: / Mediterranean, Atlantic, Cantabric. / And my eternal summit, blessing /—winds of God—Spain all around. / Prostrate yourself at my altar if you are Hispanic. / If a foreigner: look, admire, and shut up.)

While rivers are like "sons," the mountain is an "altar" only for true believers of a very specific origin—"hispano"—and this altar must impose silence and respect on those visitors coming from other countries ("otras tierras"). Here we have shifted the paradigm, since the rivers have become, as was the case in Magris, expression of identity. In fact, rivers in Diego's poem bestow a reductionist version of identity, where only the believers—"hispanos"—have the right to pray, to participate in an identity ceremony. The rest have to watch silently. This poem can be related to another one by Fray Luis de León, "Oda VII-Profecía del Tajo" (Prophecy of the Tagus River), in which the river itself admonishes King Rodrigo because of his love for Cava and his negligence towards the invading Moors. As a result the Tagus river speaks ("el río sacó fuera / el pecho, y le habló desta manera") (The river started speaking this way) and reprimands him for having lost Spain:

¡Ay! esa tu alegría
qué llantos acarrea, y esa hermosa,
que vio el sol en mal día,
a España ¡ay cuán llorosa!,
y al cetro de los Godos ¡cuán costosa! (47)

(Oh! This, your joy, / that sobs engenders, and lovely, / who saw the sun on a bad day, / to Spain; how sensitive! / and on the sceptor of the Goths; how expensive!)

Even in this case we cannot but notice the use of first person in a sort of prosopopoeia, but also the symbolic, rather historical sense of those lines. The river, Tagus, denounces a distressing event in Spanish history, a terrible stain in the country's honor.

Following these lines, André Gide in his *Voyage au Congo* (1927) distinguishes, in an almost ridiculing fashion, between the Belgian and the French margin of Congo River. This is proof of the absurdity of defining countries according to the colonizer's identity (Gide 35). We are in desperate need of establishing bridges, to better launch communication for everybody. In this way, without bridges, rivers only separate.

In her poem "Soledad," from *En las orillas del Sar* (1884), Rosalía de Castro manages to adapt the *locus amoenus* motif to synthesize spiritual values. Opposed to materialism and nature, she defends the heart ("corazón") as a space in which she can dwell:

Un manso río, una vereda estrecha,
un campo solitario y un pinar,
y el viejo puente rústico y sencillo
completando tan grata soledad.

¿Qué es soledad? Para llenar el mundo
basta a veces un solo pensamiento.

Por eso hoy, hartos de belleza, encuentras
el puente, el río y el pinar desiertos.

No son nube ni flor los que enamoran;
eres tú, corazón, triste o dichoso,
ya del dolor y del placer el árbitro,
quien seca el mar y hace habitable el polo. (81)

(A gently flowing river, a narrow path, / a solitary field and a pine forest, / and the old bridge, rustic and simple, / rounding out such pleasant solitude. / What is solitude? To fill the world / one solitary thought is enough. / So today, tired of beauty, you find / the bridge, the river and the pine forest deserted. / Clouds and flowers are not the ones who love; / You are, my heart, sad or happy, / arbiter of pain and pleasure, / the one who dries the ocean and makes habitable the poles.)

Here we recognize a refusal of external landscape and a retreat into inner life. Like Emily Dickinson, Castro prefers an intimate version of nature, one which portrays states of mind, or can be used as a refuge from the world. Also, as in Pessoa's poem, here, too, we come upon a sense of intimacy. Against "puente," "río" and "pinar," metaphors for the external world of nature, the poet finds refuge in her heart ("corazón"), which dries up the sea and makes the pole livable.

Rivers were also present in other definitions of Hispanic identity and they refer to a nearly forgotten chapter in the history of the Franco regime, which includes concentration camps, called with a sinister euphemism "Servicio de Colonias Penitenciarias Militarizadas" (Department of Militarized Penal Colonies). This "service" was responsible for centralizing the Franco regime's use of political prisoners as forced laborers or slaves. Concentration camps had an unintended side effect, as they facilitated the installation of prisoners' families in their vicinity, and thus the spontaneous creation of new towns such as El Palmar de Troya, Dos Hermanas, Los Palacios or two neighborhoods in Seville, Torreblanca, and Bellavista. One of the project's most important effects was the Canal del Bajo Guadalquivir, the so-called Canal de los presos, or "Prisoner's Channel."[4] Interestingly enough this historical fact may be useful to demonstrate the way in which the identity between waterway and people has completely converged to become one and the same identity. In this particular case, each defines the other to the point that they are inseparable: it's not just *a* canal, it is *their* canal, and they are not simply prisoners, they are the prisoner's whose purpose—and very existence—depended on and *became* the canal. Their history and memory are preserved by this waterway.

This brief overview of the many literary examples—in which the metaphor of the river expresses transformation as well as national identity—would not be complete without mentioning the first stanza of the *Deutschlandlied* (Song of the Germans), which was excluded from the National Anthem after the second World War, because of its possible negative allusions to the "Dritte Reich." In the first stanza of that song, rivers were used again to define identity and borders. After the infamous "Deutschland, Deutschland über alles," they used to sing: "Von der Maas bis an die Memel, / Von der Etsch bis an den Belt" (Hoffmann von Fallersleben 274) (From the river Mosel to the Niemen, / From the river Etsch to the Belt"). That is, the four rivers which circled old Prussia, and which used to encapsulate a sense of German identity. Furthermore, in this case, the river motif is a public expression of identity, nationalism, and solidarity, and the river/people definition is consecrated through national discourse, which is circulated, shared, and uttered by all members of the community.

This set of examples provides us with a possible classification of rivers, which maybe useful in my discussion of Hispanism. Going back to Henri Lefebvre's spatial triad (the perceived, the conceived, and the lived) they all use as a starting point a spatial practice, that is, the production and reproduction of spatial relations between objects and products. The spatial practice of a society creates that society's space. In the poems we've examined, spatial practice is introduced by the geographical idea of a river and a particular name associated to it, both physical and conceptual. Such handling by the poet introduces two possibilities. In some cases (Carner, García Lorca, Diego), we come across a representation of space that identifies what is lived and what is perceived with what is conceived. A second tendency is the one in which the river serves as representational space (Pessoa, Castro). This kind of space refers to spaces "lived" directly "through its associated images and symbols and hence the space of 'inhabitants' and 'users' . . ." (Lefebvre 39). These are the lived experiences that emerge as a result of the dialectical relation between spatial practice and representation of spaces.[5] All the rivers evoked here bestow a sense of identity. Some are transformed into a symbol of the national and political, aesthetic and vital dilemmas, whereas, others become an expression of vital obsessions related to intimacy, where name or location is not important. If we go back to the distinction offered by Deleuze and Guattari, the first group is a good example of striated river; in the second one we locate smooth versions of a river.

Reading Maps

A second possibility of reading in smooth or striated ways is provided by maps. As stated by Louis Marin, maps are "the inscription of an essence in the visible" (qtd. in Jacob 30). Therefore, just as rivers may come to symbolize two models of expressing the complexity of national identity, maps can be seen as metaphors for smooth or striated spaces, representing national consciousness. The idea of the map as a cultural construct is further amplified in a seminal book by Benedict Anderson. When discussing his understanding of "Imagined Communities" from an anthropological point of view, he proposes a definition of nation in these terms: "[I]t is an imagined political community—and imagined as both inherently limited and sovereign" (6). He adds that it is imagined because it is impossible that all inhabitants know each other. All nations are limited, because they have finite boundaries, bordering other nations, and none (except for a few radical religions, Christians, Muslims, Communists, among others) can become a nation of planet-wide dimensions. A nation is imagined as sovereign because the concept was born in an era when Enlightenment and Revolutions were destroying the "Ancien Régime," which was based upon divinely ordained, and dynastical principles. It is also imagined from an egalitarian perspective because, as Anderson puts it, "regardless of the actual inequality and exploitation that may prevail in each, the nation is always conceived as a deep, horizontal comradeship" (7). "Nationhood" calls for many ironic situations, almost surrealistic, depending on who (what community) formulates the concept or definition of a given territory: Spanish or British Gibraltar, as opposed to Spanish or Moroccan Ceuta and Melilla; Val d'Aran and Vall d'Aran; Puerto Rico as "Estado Libre Asociado," literally "Associated Free State of Puerto Rico," with its grab bag of misunderstandings, or "independent Puerto Rico," etc.

According to Anderson, colonial rulers created three institutions of power, which were influential in nurturing a sense of nationhood among previously loosely interconnected areas: the census, the map, and the museum. The map had two purposes. On the one hand, historical maps, were conceived as a series of pictures "designated to demonstrate, in the new cartographic discourse, the antiquity of specific, tightly bounded territorial units" (174–5). This sequence of maps would arrange a narrative of the space, with vast historical depth. On the other hand, maps became a sort of "logo," almost a piece of an immense imperial jigsaw, in which each piece could be detached from its context, thus entering "an infinitely reproducible series, available for transfer to posters, official seals, letterheads, magazine and textbook covers, tablecloth, and hotel walls" (175).

I would like to explore different possibilities of map reading, which can be traced to Anderson's proposal. The map of Spain has been read in many contradictory ways. One cannot help but think about the clashing meanings of Spain's supposed resemblance to a bull's hide: "la piel de toro," the base for Salvador Espriu's 1960 rendition of "la pell de brau," in an influential poetry book, which became a symbol of freedom and reconciliation in 1960 (Walters 126). As we can see in the series of maps in the Appendix, it is obvious that there has been a shifting perception according to what maps intend to represent. *Map 1* depicts Roman Hispania, divided into the three provinces at the time of the Principate: Baetica, Lusitania, and Tarraconensis. The division of the territory is extremely different from the one portrayed in subsequent periods, as can be seen in *Map 2* and *3*, where we observe a strong division between Christian and Musulman Kingdoms, showing how the Iberian Peninsula after Roman occupation had become the battleground in a religious war which would last for eight centuries. *Map 4* is drawn one hundred years before the end of the so-called "Reconquest." In this map the emphasis is not only on the division between Christian and Muslim kingdoms, but also on the presence of an Aragonese-Catalan empire in the Mediterranean. *Map 5* portrays Spain at the time of Charles the Fifth, with much emphasis on expansion in Europe and Northern Africa. These four maps are school-book versions of a well-known narrative of reconquest, growth, and unification. This is a narrative, which stresses the existence of foreign and internal enemies, with a hidden problematization of unity.

The unity issue becomes central in *Map 6*, a 1854 map that makes a clear distinction between four different Spains:

1. Castile and Andalusia: "España Uniforme ó Puramente Constitucional que comprende estas treinta y cuatro Provincias de las coronas de Castilla y León, iguales en todos los ramos económicos, judiciales, militares y civiles" ("Uniform or Purely Constitutional Spain which comprises these thirty-four Provinces of the Crowns of Castile and Leon, equal in all economic, judicial, military, and civil branches")
2. Kingdom of Navarre including the Basque Country: "España foral" ("Spain of the Fueros")
3. Crown of Aragón: "España Incorporada ó Asimilada que comprende las once provincias de la Corona de Aragón, todavía diferentes en el modo de contribuir y en algunos puntos del derecho privado" ("Incorporated or Assimilated Spain which comprises the eleven provinces of the Crown of Aragon, still different in the manner of contribution and in some points of private law")
4. Cuba, Puerto Rico and the Philippine Islands: "España colonial" ("Colonial Spain")

This Political map of Spain was drawn in shortly after the First Carlist War, and represents the frontiers according to tax, legal system, and the military situation (Torres Villegas). In this particular case, we realize how important map inscriptions are, proving right that maps' modes of inscription and graphic choices are as fundamental as the content of the textual fragments they use: "Texts organize a space of legibility that constantly interferes with the vision of the map's forms" (Jacob 9). What is remarkable about this map is that read one hundred and fifty years after it was drawn, it still accurately portrays a current political conception of the Iberian Peninsula, particularly of Spain, stressing the unresolved issue of regional and national differentiation.

In another case we confront head-on the thorny issue of linguistic difference. What is disquieting about *Map 7* is the fact that it was published in the 1923 edition of *Enciclopedia Espasa* (vol. 21: 416–17). Even though the text about languages in that volume was supposedly written by eminent linguist Ramón Menéndez Pidal, the accompanying map is full of far-fetched inaccuracies such as the presentation of a linguistic reality which has been static for more than thirteen centuries, and with inscriptions which lead the reader to believe that there is such a thing as "dialectos baleáricos," or a "dialecto valenciano," ancillaries of a "castellano." There is a supralinguistic identity shaped by this "Lengua española," which includes Galician-Portuguese, Basque, and Catalan. Furthermore, there is a suspicious coincidence between linguistic borders and those of main political regions of the time: Andalusia, Aragon, Asturias, Catalonia, Galicia, Leon, and Murcia (Burgueño 173–74).

The last two maps present a contemporary view of the Peninsula. *Map 8* shows the result of the 2008 general elections of the Spanish Parliament. The use of blue and red coloring codes is a reminder of the division of Spain at the Civil War's outset, and an echo of the US system of coloring political maps. *Map 9* is a Meteosat-type image of the Iberian Peninsula. The absence of signs alluding to frontiers, and coloring referring to political divisions, allows the reader to focus on much more important meaningful issues, such as the peninsula's situation vis-à-vis Africa, or the significant impact of global warming, with a crystal clear difference between north and south, that is, between desert zones and humid ones, and also the physical, topographical, geological characteristics of the country in general.

After reviewing these examples of map reading, we realize that we have different possibilities: from the glacial look, allegedly scientific, of sociology, to the manipulations of reality as seen in historical and linguistic maps. This kind of map reading can be traced to Plutarch. When he wrote about the election of the couple Theseus and Romulus, he justified his historical decision to go beyond real facts in geographic terms, making the point that, in the same way, Sosius had added notes on the margins of maps, referring to areas full of "sandy deserts full of wild beasts, unapproachable bogs, Scythian ice, or a frozen sea" (Plutarch 1). The reality depicted in those maps was discredited, or rather, accepted at another level: "I might very well say of those [legendary periods] that are farther off: 'Beyond this there is nothing but prodigies and fictions, the only inhabitants are the poets and inventors of fables; there is no credit, or certainty any farther'" (Plutarch). Likewise, many political maps can be read as pure speculation, created by "inventors of fables," or national narratives. This is so because, as Christian Jacob puts it, "between the map and its referent stands an array of complex relationships of substitution, creation, and intellectual conjecture" (100).

The reading of political maps as fiction is further corroborated by Polish journalist and writer Ryszard Kapuściński, who in his startling book *Imperium* (1993) offered a daunting evaluation of the Soviet Empire, which, unfortunately, can be applied to many others. In that book he reminds us of the absurdity of borders:

> At the approach to every border, tension rises within us; emotions heighten. People are not made to live in borderline situations; they avoid them or try to flee from them as quickly as possible. And yet man encounters them everywhere, sees and feels them everywhere. Let us take the atlas of the world: it is all borders. Borders of oceans and continents. Deserts and forests. [. . .] And the borders of monarchies and republics? Kingdoms remote in time and lost civilizations? Pacts, treaties, and alliances? [. . .] How many victims, how much blood and suffering, are connected with this business of borders! There is no end to the cemeteries of those who have been killed the world over in the defense of borders. Equally boundless are the cemeteries of the audacious who attempted to expand their borders. It is safe to assume that half of those who have ever walked upon our planet and lost their lives in the field of glory gave up the ghost in battles begun over a question of borders. (19–20)

Map 1. Roman Hispania around AD 100, divided into three provinces at the time of the Principate: Baetica, Lusitania, and Tarraconensis.

Map 2. The Iberian Kingdoms in the year 1030 at the beginning of the "reconquest."

Map 3. The Iberian Kingdoms in the year 1210 midway through the "reconquest" wars.

ON RIVERS AND MAPS   19

Map 4. The Iberian Kingdoms in the year 1360 by the end of the "reconquest" wars. Granada is the only remaining "non-Christian" territory.

Map 5. The Iberian Kingdoms and their European controlled territories under Charles V (c. 1550).

Map 6. Political map of Spain in 1854 drawn shortly after the First Carlist War, representing the frontiers according to taxation and legal system, and the military situation.

Map 7. Distribution of "Spanish languages" from 711 to the present according to Enciclopedia Espasa (1923).

Map 8. Election results of the 2008 general elections to the Spanish Parliament (Red = Socialist Party; Blue = Partido Popular).

Map 9. Satellite view of the Iberian Peninsula.

Kapuściński speaks about the absurdity of superimposing geography and politics, and also, from a much more tragic perspective, about violence among human beings goaded by this phenomenon. That is why he concludes: "And our brains? Encoded in them, after all, is an infinite diversity of borders" (20). He was writing in the 1990s, from the other side of the light, at the end of the tunnel, and he was uncovering a daunting chronicle of the Soviet "Gulag," a communist version of the German "Lager" and Spanish "campos de trabajos forzados" (forced labor camps). Kapuściński's condemnation brings into the picture another hidden map of Europe, one that refers to unhappiness and shame, the one depicted by concentration camps.

In this perspective, it is worth mentioning the case of Franz Tunda, the main character in Joseph Roth's novel *Die Flucht ohne Ende* (*Flight without End*). Tunda is an officer in the Austrian Army, and after having been taken prisoner by the Russians in World War I, he survives the Russian Revolution under a false name. He decides to go back to his homeland, but it has disappeared. He has become a man without land. Europe is under a new order, and the Austro-Hungarian Empire has all but disappeared. He decides to go looking for his former fiancée in Berlin and Paris. This second flight allows him to find himself, and particularly to discover a new European spirit. He has become a man without a country, a map, or identity: "Jetzt aber war Franz Tunda ein junger Mann ohne Namen, ohne Bedeutung, ohne Rang, ohne Titel, ohne Geld und ohne Beruf, heitmatlos und rechtlos" (322, 10) (Franz Tunda was a young man without a name, without importance, without rank, without title, without money and without occupation—homeless and stateless).

A similar case is the actual one lived by Claudio Magris. He lost his Trieste, which once belonged to *Mitteleuropa*, and which was taken away, first to become a city in Yugoslavia, and later, after World War II, to be reincorporated into Italy. These are examples of movements on the map, which illustrate the creation of new identities, yet without moving from one's own place, in the way that a river remains the same, though its waters may change.

Discussing the situation of the Armenian people, Kapuściński explained the country's tragic destiny because of its specific geographical position on the map:

> The map, looked at from the south of Asia, explains the tragedy of the Armenians. Fate could not have placed their country in a more unfortunate spot. In the south of the Highland it borders upon two of the past's most formidable powers—Persia and Turkey—Let's add to that the Arabian Caliphate. And even Byzantium. Four political colossi, ambitious, extremely expansionist, fanatical voracious. And now—what does the ruler of each of these four powers see when he looks at the map? He sees that if he takes Armenia, then his empire will be enclosed by an ideal natural border to the north. Because from the north the Armenian Highland is magnificently protected, guarded by two seas (The Black and the Caspian) and by the gigantic barrier of the Caucasus. And the north is dangerous for Persia and for Turkey, for the Arabs and Byzantium. Because in those days from the north and unsubdued Mongolian fury loomed. (47–48)

The case of Armenia provides us with superb and dreadful examples of maps and borders created and used by insatiable human greed, at the service of controlling the Other. In this case, the map is used as a planning tool for wars of invasion, for domination of close-by territory with military purposes. It reminds us vividly of some meanings of Iberian Peninsula maps discussed earlier. In fact, those maps are a very graphic way of representing disparate models of identity, which has been an unvarying issue in Spain from the beginning of modernity. At the onset of the nineteenth century there were violent clashes between the different ways of organizing political life in Spain, from Cádiz to the "Gloriosa," all the way to the Second Republic. Through that century, many voices paid attention to the need of defending a co-existence between a variety of cultures and histories, of rivers and maps. Some versions of Romanticism did much to vindicate forms of diversity. Other versions provoked a fundamentalist governmental theory of the state, which has been the prevailing one.

I mentioned at the beginning a Francoist tourist slogan, "Spain is different." Now, looking at it again, from another perspective, such as the one discussed here, that slogan may not be just another Francoist euphemism like the villainous inscription "Una, grande y libre" (One, great, and free) where only the first adjective was true. Reading rivers and maps in smooth—not striated—terms presents us with another way of being "different." A possible utopist solution to the maladies of Hispanic identity can be found in comparative literature, which can help to establish bridges between cultures. This would be a way of dealing with complexity, similar to the one defended by Guillén, "como movimiento y oscilación continuos entre conceptos-límite, como encuentro de propensiones y fuerzas polares" (understood as the constant movement and oscillation between concepts and their limits, as the meeting of propensities and polar forces). Another comparatist, Antonio Monegal, argues that Hispanism needs "models that are no longer based on the concept of the nation, but on the more complex concept of culture" (24). He proposes maps that are not based on national boundaries that separate "the inside from the outside," but maps that instead acknowledge "the fluctuation of such positions, their character as cultural constructs, simultaneously inside and outside" (24). For Monegal and others, Hispanic studies, in order to progress, must consider the impact of "cultural research" with roots in the "theory of difference" (24). Even the name Spain presents a problem for him, because to understand "what such a name signifies," he writes, "it is necessary to begin by not thinking of Spain as the place of identity but of a difference" (Monegal 24).

The rivers and maps of Europe remind us of so many fights, of so much destruction which has taken place because of the colors of a flag, the names of a piece of land, the sounds of words uttered in a post-Babel world. Set against rivers, which produce identity, or maps, which become symbols, we should be able to read literature as a river and a map, with innovative meanings. We can strive for an idea of smooth identity, not a striated one, following Foucault's call for a society with many heterotopias, as a space for the affirmation of difference, and also as a means of flight from authoritarianism and repression.[6] We need to draw rivers and read maps of another kind, which may allow us to invent a tradition, imagine a community not curtailed by the limitations of lands and borders, of intellectual closeness and repression, but one open to dialogue and diversity, to multiculturalism and multilingualism. Rivers are regional delimiters for geographical, cultural, linguistic, and political reasons. They should not become dividers, but catalysts for establishing bridges. As expressed in anthropology, "in its empirical moments [space] has long acted as a sort of 'clearing' for thinking about the inescapable and troubling spatialisation of human individual and collective experience" (Osborne and Rose 225). A new Iberian Comparatism focused on issues of inclusion and difference, non-hierarchical approaches, and an emphasis on multilinguism would do much to lead Europe on a path towards inclusiveness and respect for the Other.[7] This Comparatism would profit much from such a "smooth" heterotopic perspective, where rivers and maps signal an open way of reading, one based on dialogue, not rigid, exclusionary identity.

Notes

1. Earlier versions of this essay were presented at the conference "Spanishness in the Spanish Novel and Cinema of the 20th-21st Century" (University of North Texas, Denton, March 2008), organized by Cristina Sánchez-Conejero, and the Sociedad Española de Literatura General y Comparada (SELGYC) conference, which was organized by Antonio Monegal and Montserrat Cots (UPF, Barcelona, September 2008). I am most indebted to the feedback and suggestions I received from those audiences and the input from some colleagues who very carefully read my paper: Lluís Quintana, Heike Scharm, and Sara Snider.
2. This is what Susan Friedman implies when she writes, "The association of modernism and modernity with Europe and the United States in the humanities not only excludes nonwestern locations but also contains peripheries within "the West"—including, for example, margins based on gender, race, and geography, namely those of women, ethnic and racial minorities, and locations such as Spain, Portugal, the Balkans and Eastern Europe, Brazil, and the Caribbean" (512). For a thorough discussion of this issue, see a historical interpretation by George Mariscal, regarding particularly the cases of George Ticknor and James Fitzmaurice Kelly (3–6). See also a more contemporary discussion in Delgado; Mendelson; Vázquez, 2007.
3. See, for example, King and Browitt, Varela and Abuín González, Epps and Fernández Cifuentes, Moraña. Once published, the volume coordinated by Fernando Cabo Aseguinolaza, Anxo Abuín González, and César Domínguez Prieto, *A Comparative History of Literatures in the Iberian Peninsula*, may be a landmark.
4. According to Isaías Lafuente political prisoners were responsable for building huge reservoirs such as the ones in Ebro, Benagéver, Entrepeñas, Pálmaces, Mediano, Riosequillo, Revenga, Barasona, Mansilla de la Sierra, González Lacasa, El Cenajo, Torre del Águila, Barrios de Luna, Yesa, San Esteban and Linares, la Real Acequia del Jarama; and also canals in Bajo del Guadalquivir, Bajo del Alberche, Montijo, Jarama, Bárdenas, Monegros, Toro-Zamora, Bierzo, Badarán y Linares del Arroyo (Lafuente 2002).

5. Of course all three spaces are interconnected, as was demonstrated by Edward Soja in *Thirdspace*, with his "trialectis of spatiality," where the spatial and temporal are joined by the social (Soja).
6. "L'hétérotopie a le pouvoir de juxtaposer en un seul lieu réel plusieurs espaces, plusieurs emplacements qui sont en eux-mêmes incompatibles" (Foucault 48).
7. Douwe Fokkema previously made a call of this kind in an early article. See Fokkema.

Works Cited

Adams, Paul C., Steven Hoelscher, and Karen E. Till, eds. *Textures of Place: Exploring Humanist Geographies*. Minneapolis: University of Minnesota Press, 2001.

Anderson, Benedict. *Imagined Communities*. London: Verso Books, 2006.

Burgueño, Jesús. "El mapa escondido: Las lenguas de España." *Boletín de la Asociación de Geógrafos Españoles* 34 (2002): 171–92.

Caeiro, Alberto. *Poesia*. Edição de Fernando Cabral Martins e Richard Zenith. Série Obras de Fernando Pessoa. Lisboa: Assírio and Alvim, 2004.

Carner, Josep. *Poesies escollides*. Barcelona: Edicions 62, 1979.

Castro, Rosalía de. *En las orillas del Sar*. 1884. Ed. Marina Mayoral. Madrid: Editorial Castalia, 1981.

Deleuze, Gilles, and Félix Guattari. *Mille plateaux*. Paris: Editions de Minuit, 1980.

Delgado, L. Elena, Jordana Mendelson, and Oscar Vázquez. "Introduction: Recalcitrant Modernities—Spain, Cultural Difference and the Location of Modernism," *Journal of Iberian and Latin American Studies* 13:2 (2007): 105–19.

Diego, Gerardo. *Obras completas II Poesía*. Ed. Francisco Javier Díez de Revenga. Madrid: Aguilar, 1989.

Elliott, John H. *Empires of the Atlantic World: Britain and Spain in America, 1492–1830*. New Haven: Yale University Press, 2006.

Enciclopedia universal ilustrada. Vol. 21. Madrid: Espasa Calpe, 1923.

Epps, Bradley S., and Luis Fernández Cifuentes, eds. *Spain Beyond Spain: Modernity, Literary History, and National Identity*. Lewisburg: Bucknell University Press, 2005.

Fokkema, Douwe W. "Comparative Literature and the New Paradigm." *Canadian Review of Comparative Literature* 9.1 (1982): 1–18.

Foucault, Michel. "Des espaces autres (conférence au Cercle d'études architecturales, 14 mars 1967)." *Architecture, Mouvement, Continuité* 5 (October 1984): 46–49.

Friedman, Susan Stanford. "Definitional Excursions: The Meanings of Modern/Modernity/Modernism." *MODERNISM/modernity* 8.3 (2001): 493–513.

García Lorca, Federico. *Poema del cante jondo: Romancero gitano*. Madrid: Cátedra, 1977.

Gide, André. *Voyage au Congo suivi de Le retour du Tchad: Carnets de route*. Paris: Gallimard, 2006.

Guillén, Claudio. "Europa: Ciencia e inconsciencia." *Múltiples moradas: Ensayos de literatura comparada*. Barcelona: Tusquets, 1998. 368–426.

Hoffmann von Fallersleben, August Heinrich. *Auswahl in drei Teilen: Lyrische Gedichte*. Vol. 1. Ed. Augusta Weldler-Steinberg. Berlin: Bong and Co., 1912.
Jacob, Christian. *The Sovereign Map: Theoretical Approaches in Cartography throughout History*. Chicago: University of Chicago Press, 2006.
Kaplan, Temma. *Red City, Blue Period: Social Movements in Picasso's Barcelona*. Berkeley: University of California Press, 1992.
Kapuściński, Ryszard. *Imperium*. London: Granta, 1994.
King, Stewart, and Jeff Browitt, eds. *The Space of Culture: Critical Readings in Hispanic Studies*. Newark: University of Delaware Press, 2004.
Lafuente, Isaías. *Esclavos por la Patria: La explotación de los presos bajo el franquismo*. Madrid: Temas de Hoy, 2002.
Lefebvre, Henri. *The Production of Space*. Oxford: Blackwell, 1991.
León, Fray Luis de. *Poesía de Fray Luis de León*. Ed. Antonio Ramajo Caño. Barcelona: Centro para la edición de los clásicos españoles Galaxia Gutenberg, Circulo de Lectores, 2006.
Magris, Claudio. *Danubio*. Milano: Garzanti, 1990.
Mariscal, George. "An Introduction to the Ideology of Hispanism in the U.S. and Britain." *Conflicts of Discourse: Spanish Literature in the Golden Age*. Ed. Peter W. Evans. Manchester: Manchester University Press, 1990. 1–25.
Molinero, C., M. Sala, and J. Sobrequés, eds. *Los campos de concentración y el mundo penitenciario en España durante la guerra civil y el franquismo*. Barcelona: Crítica, 2003.
Monegal, Antonio. "A Landscape of Relations: Peninsular Multiculturalism and the Avatars of Comparative Literature." *Spain Beyond Spain: Modernity, Literary History, and National Identity*. Ed. Brad Epps and Luis Fernández Cifuentes. Lewisburg: Bucknell University Press, 2005. 231–49.
Moraña, Mabel, ed. *Ideologies of Hispanism*. Hispanic Issues Vol. 30. Nashville: Vanderbilt University Press, 2005.
Ors, Eugeni d'. *Glosari 1906–1907*. Ed. Xavier Pla. Barcelona: Quaderns Crema, 1996.
Osborne, Thomas, and Nikolas Rose. "Spatial Phenomenotechnics: Making Space with Charles Booth and Patrick Geddes." *Environment and Planning D: Society and Space* 22.2. 209–28.
Perec, Georges. *Espèces d'espaces 1974*. Paris: Galilée, 2000.
Plutarch. *Lives of Noble Grecians and Romans*. Vol. 1 (Modern Library Series). New York: Random House Publishing Group, 1992.
Resina, Joan Ramon. "Hispanism and Its Discontents." *Siglo XX/Twentieth Century* 14.1–2 (1996): 85–135.
Roth, Joseph. *Flight without End: A Novel*. Woodstock: Overlook Press, 2003.
———. *Die Flucht ohne Ende Werke. Erster Band*. Ed. Hermann Kesten. Köln: Kiepenheuer & Witsch, 1975. 311–421.
Soja, Edward W. *Thirdspace: Journeys to Los Angeles and Other Real-and-Imagined Places*. Oxford: Blackwell, 1996.
Torres Villegas, Francisco Jorge. *Cartografía hispano-científica ó sea los mapas españoles en que se representa bajo sus diferentes fases*. Madrid: Imprenta de don José María Alonso, 1857.

Varela, Anxo Tarrío, and Angel Abuín González, eds. *Bases metodolóxicas para unha historia comparada das literaturas na península Ibérica*. Santiago de Compostela: Universidad de Santiago de Compostela, 2004.

Walters, D. Gareth. *The Poetry of Salvador Espriu: To Save the Words*. Woodbridge, Suffolk: Tamesis, 2006.

2

Peripheral Being, Global Writing: The Location of Basque Literature

Mari Jose Olaziregi

All for Our Country

The state in which the Center for Basque Studies is located, Nevada (USA), has, as its motto, a phrase that applies well to the journey taken by literature written in the Basque language up to the present time: "All for Our Country." At the very least, it highlights the motivations to which many Basque writers ascribe when explaining their choice to use the Basque language, or *euskara*, for their creative work.

It is especially so because, although it is thought that some 3,000 languages will disappear during this century, it seems to be almost guaranteed that Basque will survive, or at least this is what can be deduced from the statements made by David Crystal in his book *The Language Revolution*. Basque meets the sociohistorical criteria listed by Crystal as necessary to ensure survival or, minimally, not to join the list of endangered languages: it is a language that has a number of speakers that is considerable and clearly over 100,000; it has a political infrastructure that, at least in the Spanish Basque Country, defends, subsidizes, and legislates measures for its promotion and standardization; it has a significant television and media presence; and above all, it is clear that, for many Basque speakers, or *euskaldunak*, the Basque language is their most essential mark of identity. These are the characteristics that lead Crystal to include Basque on his Top-10 list of minority languages. But, if the specter of the death of the Basque language has been exorcised, to what needs does creation in Basque respond today? How have sociolinguistic factors determined the evolution of Basque literature? What position does this literature hold in the present-day global literary scene? What has been the evolution of Basque Literature since the death of Franco? These are some of the questions that I will address below.

Beginnings of Literature Written in Basque

The book of poems *Linguae Vasconum Primitiae* (1545), by Bernard Etxepare, marks the beginning of Basque Literature. As Arkotxa and Oyharçabal point out, it is a collection of poems whose paratext already makes clear the international ambition of the poet: the use of Latin for the title and the declaration that it is a work of *primitiae*, first fruits, support this evaluation. Encouraged by the benefits that he saw in the invention of the printing press for the spread of a small literature like ours, Etxepare exhorted, "Euskara, Jalgi Hadi Kanpora!" ("Basque, go forth!"), declaring his strong desire that our language should hold a place in the Republic of Letters. Thus, poetry not only became the founding genre of our literature, but also the genre that would lead the establishment of Basque literature, around 1950, as an autonomous activity within Basque society.

Between these two points in time, there were 400 years of a literary history dominated by pastoral works, a literature led by religious men who, after the Council of Trent, taught the couplet *euskaldun = fededun* (Basque speaker = believer), which had a strong influence on all literary production until the end of the nineteenth century. Clearly, there were extra-literary factors involved in the creation of the body of work in the Basque language. This body of work lacked the most basic infrastructure necessary to establish itself as a developed literary system due to several barriers, such as the difficulty of publishing in Basque (until 1700, three of every four Basque books were published outside of the Basque Country, and there was a notable book, *Peru Abarka*, that took decades before it was finally published in 1880), prohibitions on publishing, and a certain number of lost publications. All of these factors created a situation in which one of the most fundamental elements for the canonization and legitimization of literary texts, education in all its forms, never existed in Basque. The University of Oñati, which was founded in the sixteenth century, and the Royal Seminary of Bergara, which was created under the aegis of the ideas of the Enlightenment, are academic indications of an endemic evil of our literary past: the fact that our rulers, even at the time of the *Fueros* (medieval charters granting special privileges, in this case to the Basque provinces), have never cared about Basque, and certainly not about education or literacy in our language. In the eighteenth century, Basque was declared a patois in the French Basque region, while in the Spanish Basque Country, laws and acts were passed to expand education in Spanish; for example, in 1780, it became obligatory to teach the grammar defined by the Royal Academy of the Spanish Language. The point made by Juan Ignacio Iztueta in his *Guipuzcoaco provinciaren condaira* (*History of the Province of Guipuzcoa*, 1847) is well known: five of every six Guipuzcoans knew Basque, but administration and politics were carried out in Spanish, and therefore, only one-sixth of the population of

Guipuzcoa participated actively in the political life of the time. Thus, political life was foreign to the world of Basque, and literary life as described by Lasagabaster ("La Ilustración" 157) was almost non-existent in the Basque language in the eighteenth century. Furthermore, the authors and works that we now claim as part of our literary history did not belong to any system of Basque literature but to the system of the Church, with its pastoral approach and emphasis on the catechism. The only strictly literary life in the eighteenth century was developed through the Amigos del País (Friends of the Country), in the Royal Basque Society and in the Royal Seminary of Bergara mentioned above, but it was primarily in Spanish.[1]

This brief description of the beginnings of Basque literature reveals a literary scene in which a diglossic situation implies that our literary past suffers from, or meets, many of the characteristics that Antón Figueroa describes in his *Diglosia e texto* (*Diglossia and Text*): the inclusion of non-literary works in our historiography, and of works not originally written in Basque, and the preeminence of folkloric, mythic or ethnographic elements in its assessment. It is, definitively, a literature shaped by the ups and downs of its language, with the result that, until the final third of the twentieth century, it had no full literary system, that is, one with a structure including the production, mediation, receipt, and recreation of consolidated texts.

Euskadi, Basque Homeland

The most definitive event that shaped Basque literary life occurred in the nineteenth century. This was not the curiosity that our land and our language would inspire in linguists like Humboldt, nor the exoticism seen in the language by European artists like Wordsworth, Merimée, and even von Chamisso, but the emergence, under the shadow of Romanticism, of nationalist ideology. Sabino Arana proclaimed that "*Euzkotarren aberria Euzkadi da*," that is, that Euskadi (or Euzkadi, as Arana wrote) is the homeland of the Basques. By 1847, Iztueta had established an equivalence that would be decisive: that between the *Fueros* and the Basque language (Aldekoa 86). Another author, Joseph Agustín Chaho, would establish himself with legends like that of Aitor (1847), precursor of the historical-legendary literature that, encouraged in Spanish by nationalist authors like Goizueta, Araquistáin, and Villoslada, seeped into both poetry and narrative written in Basque. "Aitor's lineage" (Juaristi) would provide the fertile soil in which Basque nationalism would sow the "imagined community" (Anderson) maintained, as are most types of nationalism, by a noble tradition that goes back to time immemorial.

The revocation of foral rights after the Second Carlist War in 1876, unleashed a full-blown cultural revival, *Euskal Pizkundea* (the Basque Renaissance, 1876–1936), the Basque equivalent of the Galician Rexurdimento or the Catalan Renaixença, in which patriotic recognition would stem from recognition of the Basque language. From this point on, the most fundamental purpose of writing in Basque would be to contribute to the creation of the Basque Nation. From the time of the first lettered and literary civilization, the group of Sumerian city-states of Mesopotamia, to modern times and European states like Spain, France, Italy, and Germany (Even-Zohar, "A función da literatura" 445), literature has been used as an omnipresent factor for sociocultural cohesion. This has been the case in the Basque Country as well, where literature has been used to establish an identity and a nation. At this time, through the Juegos Florales (poetic contests), the publication of Cancioneros (collections of songs) and the impetus of philological studies, it was not merely a question of exorcising the specter of the death of the language, but also of developing it into a means of cultured expression appropriate to the times. The *debile principium melior fortuna sequatur* with which Etxepare closed his book in 1545 did not find its true heir until the 1930s, when the poet Xabier Lizardi, in his *Eusko-Bidaztiarena* (*Song of the Basque Traveler*), again pointed out that the task of Basque literature was to transform the rustic language into a language worthy of any sphere (Lertxundi 48).

By this time, literature written in Basque had already begun to create its "Others": specifically, those portrayed in the narrative dealing with local customs that would prevail until the mid-twentieth century, characters that did not fit the stereotype of *euskaldun* = *fededun* = *baserritarra* (Basque speaker = believer = peasant). Consistent with the concept of Nation that arose in the eighteenth century, Basque nationalism, too, was essentialist and met the characteristics, defined in 1882, by the French Orientalist Ernest Renan, among others. The Spanish-speaking immigrants that poured into industrial Basque cities starting in the late nineteenth century, as well as Basque speakers who vigorously denied the Catholic faith and did not follow traditional nationalism, belong to the list of "Others" who would contribute to the fiction of our most representative novelist of the time: Domingo Agirre. In addition to these literary representations, Basque literature would have its more real "Others" in Basque writers who, like Miguel de Unamuno, not only did not write in Basque, but also would dare to predict their own disappearance due to their supposed inability to adapt to modern times. The case of another Basque writer, Pío Baroja, is even more significant because of the high regard he earned from the literary establishment. The celebration of the fiftieth anniversary of his death in 2006, brought not only the organization of conferences and readings in commemoration of his work, but also the publication of translations into Basque of *Zalacaín el aventurero* (*Zalacain the Adventurer*) and *El árbol de la ciencia* (*The Tree of Knowledge*), and a book, *Pío Baroja, 50 urte* (*Pío Baroja, 50 years*), in which literary criticism in Basque would confirm Baroja's warm vision of the Basque world, and the influence that his narrative has had on present-day writers in the Basque language.[2]

Post-symbolist poetry had its greatest expression in the work of José María Agirre (whose pseudonym was Lizardi) and Esteban Urkiaga (pseudonym, Lauaxeta), both nationalists, who participated actively in the *Euzko Pizkundea* that took place during the years of the Second Republic, a time at which nationalist political and cultural activism went hand in hand. Both poets belonged to the Euskaltzaleak (Bascophile Association), which, beginning in 1930, intensified its activities and pursued a type of literary production that would bring prestige to the culture expressed in the

Basque language. Encouraged by the versatile José Aristimuño (pseudonym, Aitzol; see Otaegi), they again tried first and foremost to exorcise the specter of the disappearance of the language and to show that Basque could be the creative language of a quality literature that sought its points of reference in canonic symbolic poets. But neither the language used (Lizardi and Lauaxeta followed the norms dictated by Sabino Arana), nor the chosen manner of expression helped authors reach the small Basque readership whose reading habits in Basque were almost non-existent. The Spanish Civil War, and the subsequent repression with its censorship and ban on publishing in Basque, slowed the clear literary advance that had begun with the poets of the Second Republic. Under the Franco regime's linguistic policies, Basque had no cultural status (Torrealdai, *La censura* 16).

The arrival on the scene of the poet Gabriel Aresti served not only to carry literature written in Basque fully into the modern age, but also to assert that writing in Basque answered needs that surpassed solely nationalist considerations. Aresti's statement that the Basque language was his homeland and a fundamental aspect of the Basque identity was further supported by emphatic declarations such as those he made in 1960: "Basque is a necessity for me. Who says they love bread? Bread is not loved, it is needed. This is how I feel about Basque: I don't love it, I need it" (Aresti 26). These are statements that are significant coming from an *euskaldunberri*, that is, a person whose native language was not Basque, because of the definition assumed by the nationalist ideology. Aresti's prophetic voice was suffused by the Western tradition founded on texts like the Bible and the *Divine Comedy*, texts which Eliot knew how to adapt to the disquiet of modern times. In 1964, Aresti, who in the great Basque metropolis, Bilbao, perceived like none other the diverse and multicultural Euskadi that had been marginalized in Basque literature, published *Harri eta herri* (*Stone and Country*), one of the few books in our recent history that we can honestly say reached Basque readers. This was due in large part to the *klarua* (clear) Basque used by the poet, a Basque nurtured by our classical literature and by the oral tradition. His language was very similar to that which years later, in 1968, the Royal Academy of the Basque Language would promote through the work of the distinguished linguist Koldo Mitxelena.[3]

The Development of the Basque Literary System

In a lecture that he was invited by Basque university students to give in Barcelona in 1966, Aresti stated that the youth of the time was sad and worried (Aresti 71). This youth undoubtedly included the writers that had joined him in creating the publishing house Lur in 1964 in San Sebastian and whose motto was "Lur: Kultura Herriarentzat" (Lur: Culture for the People). But at that time, writing for the people meant publishing an elitist literature, a literature that sought new paths in its efforts to connect with the European trends of the time. Ramón Saizarbitoria, one of its best known members, burst onto the Basque literary scene at the end of the 1960s, publishing experimental novels in the style of the *nouveau roman*, but assuming that he did so for the "national construction" (Etxeberria 103). These were years of cultural militancy during which people bought books in Basque, but were unable to read them for the simple reason that they lacked sufficient linguistic competence (Etxeberria 113), as well as years of militancy and artistic vanguard in which, through influential books like *Quosque tandem* (1963) by Jorge Oteiza, the world would be shown that being Basque meant connecting with the artistic vanguard of the time and with a leftist ideology. Oteiza spoke of Basque style, and of the Basque soul, which, in his opinion, was formed in Neolithic times, but the focal point of his identity was not the Basque language. For this reason, he clashed with Aresti (Aresti 74), and his influence on Basque literature (with the exception of few poets who started to publish in the 1960s, like Lekuona, Gandiaga, and Artze) has not been as resounding as he might have hoped.

Although the arrival of Spanish democracy in 1975 did not bring about a drastic change in Basque literary paradigms, it nevertheless made possible the objective conditions for the consolidation of the Basque literary system. The passing of the Statute of Autonomy (1979) and the Law of Normalization of the Use of the Basque Language (1982) permitted, among other things, bilingual education and assistance for publishing in Basque. With these changes, new publishing houses were established and the number of books published in Basque increased significantly. Between 1876 and 1975, an average of 31.5 books were published each year in Basque, while from 1976 to 1994, the average increased to 660 books per year. At present, some 1500 books are published each year, 59% of which are narrative. This is a significant increase, since only 18.7% of books published between 1876 and 1935 were narratives. The figure rose to 23.8% between 1936 and 1975, and to 48.5% from 1976 to 1996. The Basque literary network now consists of more than 100 publishing houses and approximately 300 writers (85% men, 15% women).

As in contemporary Spanish literature, in Basque literature the novel is also the genre with the greatest impact and literary prestige and, of course, the one that offers the greatest profit for publishing houses. It could be said that the Basque novel of the last three decades has adopted the postmodern premise that states that everything has already been told, but that we must remember it. That is, after the experimental period of the 1970s, the Basque novel seems to have regained its pleasure in simply telling a story. The modern Basque novel displays a clear eclecticism in its influences and literary intertexts, and, although it adopts the techniques of modernism, it enjoys creating parodic and ironic combinations of genres and offering a considerable diversity of typologies.[4]

It is worth noting at this point that the canon of modern Basque literature consists of authors who both followed and subverted the poetic path taken by Aresti. Whether those that worked with Lur (Saizarbitoria, Urretabizkaia, etc.), or those known as the "Literary Autonomy" generation led by the Banda Pott (Failure Group, 1978–1980; Atxaga and Sarrionandia, for example), or those that expanded the spectrum of genres and styles in the editorial boom of the 1980s (Landa, Lertxundi, etc.), or those younger writers who began to publish in the 1990s or at the beginning of the twenty-first century (Epaltza, Zaldua, Cano, Elorriaga, Onederra, Arregi, Meabe, etc.) these authors chose to write in Basque and made the Basque language the focal point of their Basque (and literary) identity. In this sense, I agree with the idea that the arrival of democracy in Spain meant, for minority literatures like Galician or Basque, "the abandonment of its identitary themes and contribute to the reinforcement of the identitary function of language" (Barbeito 24). The biographies of the majority of the previously mentioned Basque writers (Izagirre, Saiizarbitoria, etc.) suggest a language "won" for literature after they had learned or "regained" it (see Etxeberria; Urkiza.) These authors moved in two different spheres: the Basque-speaking sphere of the family, and the Spanish-speaking sphere of public life and education. This created a linguistic schizophrenia that has been problematic in the opinion of some,[5] but that engendered a literary creation inextricably linked to the Basque language.

The desire to break the couplet identifying nationalism with Basque language dominates modern writing in Basque, and it has been given expression in the most recent literature. When the protagonist of the last story of *Gorde nazazu lurpean* (*Let Me Rest*, 2000) by Ramón Saizarbitoria says to his girlfriend, "you are my homeland" (463), and throws the relics of the father of Basque nationalism, Sabino Arana, into the water, he gets rid of the ideological burden inherited from his father and places himself in a position that allows him to live, that is, to accept his castration and face the desire he sees in his girlfriend. The increase in the number of stories that focus on our recent historical past, stories that, in the form of historiographical metafictions or modernized historical novels, deal with events like the Spanish Civil War and postwar period, and the terrorism of ETA (Euskadi ta Askatasuna, Basque Country, and Freedom, a Basque separatist organization that has resorted to terrorism in its fight for Basque independence),[6] is an example of the need felt in Basque literature to reread and *deconstruct* the monological stories that have created exclusive identitarian discourses from different political positions (Basque nationalism, Spanish nationalism.) As Müller asserts, "[m]emory matters" (1). This is a recreation of the past as a factor of identity, a recreation that has had ethical and philosophical consequences, but above all, political ones, since it is obvious that the national communities that have seen their being questioned have found in this recuperation of the historical past an outlet for their previously denied specificity: memory as an antidote to the new utopia of globalization, memory as an anchor to reality and counterpart to hyperreal space, memory, definitively, as the axis of our ethnic maps (Müller 13–18). Paradigmatic novels like *Soinujolearen semea* (*The Accordionist's Son*) by Bernardo Atxaga can be situated in this context. The bombing of Guernica, the terrible executions and disappearances of the postwar period, and the explosion of terrorist violence in the 1960s soar in the sky over Obaba. Again, the restitution of the past has an ethical function in a text by Atxaga, who reminds us that history is a narrative discourse that offers a certain interpretation, one provided, of course, by the winners. In *The Accordionist's Son*, Atxaga again speaks, as he does in *Gizona bere bakardadean* (*The Lone Man*) and *Zeru horiek* (*The Lone Woman*), of exile, of subjects who try to build their home away from home, but here, instead of *heterotopic* spaces (a hotel, a bus), utopias prevail, the possibility of beginning again.

As Gorka Mercero showed, the concept of Nation in Atxaga's novel is not consistent with an essentialist concept, but with a differential one, more similar to contemporary readings like that carried out by Jacques Derrida. The poem that begins *The Accordionist's Son*, "Life and death of words," testifies to this: "This is how / ancient words die: / like snowflakes" but the poet finishes the text by affirming that new words rise to the heavens in the mouth of future generations. Utopia and hope are also present in concepts like *Euskal Hiria* (the Basque City), a city of the future where the coexistence of all Basques is possible . . . in the Basque language ("Otra mirada"). But what has yet to establish itself as the center of a profound debate between Basques is the question of a multiple identity, that is, an identity that incorporates the fact that many languages could dwell in us. Amin Maalouf suggests that it is possible to straddle the fence between two languages and two traditions, to live an extraterritoriality that has established itself as a constituent of an identity, the "In Between" of which Bhabha speaks in *The Location of Culture*. Although it is true that many contemporary Basque writers admit that Spanish or French is also part of their identitarian cartography (Landa, Arkotxa, Zaldua, Elorriaga, etc.), the debate that has recently arisen concerning the publication in Spanish of Mariasun Landa's biography, *La fiesta en la habitación de al lado* (*The Party in the Room Next Door*) has again awakened old ghosts and revealed conceptions that are rigid, and therefore authoritarian, of what writing in Basque involves. The main issue of discussion was the fact that Landa published first her text in Spanish, and then had it translated into Basque. Landa's responded that Spanish also belongs to her and that, in any case, is more relevant to the experiences that she wished to fictionalize, requires no further comment. The future of Basque literature requires acceptance of the fact that, although Basque is the most definitive mark of identity for many of us, the other languages that inhabit us can also become languages of literary creation. To this choice we will have to add a third way in which Basque writers can creolize the Basque language and show their hybrid identity, an identity that, except in stories like *Bi letter* (*Two Letters*) by Atxaga, is not very common in our contemporary literature.

Basque Writing in the Iberian Context:
Translations of Basque Literature

Let us now conclude this reflection on creation in the Basque language with some thoughts on translation, analyzing the function of translated literature (from Basque, into Basque) in our literary system. We have come a long way since the time when Dasconaguerre's lie in claiming that his novel, *Les échos du pas de Roland* (1867), had been translated from Basque was enough to alleviate, though briefly, the anxiety that our literary history lacked a genre (the novel), which was not to have its true birth until 1897. What writer Ramón Saizarbitoria called a "narcissistic hallucination" (*Aberriaren* 21n2) is merely one more episode in the recurring debate on the capacity of the Basque language to create fictional worlds.

The excellent work of Basque translators in the enhancement of a Basque literary language cannot be underestimated. Manuel López Gaseni speaks precisely to this point when he argues that the impact of translated literature can be seen in "the creation of an indigenous literary language, the contribution of literary repertoires previously lacking in Basque literature, and the revival of certain models that were beginning to become outdated." This important function that translated literature has had for literature in the Basque language is consistent with the centrality that Even-Zohar attributes to weak systems ("Polysystem Studies" 47).

In the opinion of Mónica Domínguez, this is the function that translations still have in some literatures of the Iberian sphere, such as the Basque and Galician literatures.[7] In the case of Basque literature, the agreement that Euskal Itzultzaile, Zuzentzaile eta Interpreteen Elkartea (EIZIE; the Association of Translators, Interpreters, and Correctors of the Basque Language, founded in 1987) signed with the Basque Government in 1989, to translate into Basque a collection of works of world literature, the *Literatura Unibertsala* (World Literature) collection, has had a positive influence on the legitimation of the work of the translator in the revival and standardization of the Basque literary language. At the time of this writing, the *Literatura Unibertsala* collection included 135 titles. The same can be said of another collection, *Pentsamenduaren Klasikoak* (Classics of Thought), which came into existence in 1991. This corpus, together with collections of crime novels published by Basque publishing houses such as Igela, Erein, and Elkar, have made available to the Basque reader quality translations of canonical authors like Eliot, Faulkner, Dostoyevsky, Maupassant, Queneau, and Barthes. The Basque literary establishment has recognized the importance that translation has for literature in the Basque language through awards such as the Euskadi Prizes for Translation (first awarded in 1997) and with the creation in 2000 of a program in Translation and Interpretation at the University of the Basque Country. Does this mean to say that translations in the Basque literary system have a centrality that they do not have in other systems?

To date, there has been no rigorous study that would offer trustworthy data on print runs, sales, or processes of canonization. However, the data suggest that translations have a very limited acceptance among Basque readers (Olaziregi, "Aproximación"), and that outside academic circles their real impact is very limited. This is the situation in a context in which cultural consumption in Basque continues to be low: according to *Kultura 07* (Publication of the Observatory of Culture of the Basque Government, November, 2007), 67% of the population of the Autonomous Basque Community do not read a single book, newspaper or magazine in Basque per year. This percentage is as high as 78% in the French Basque country, and 83% in Navarre. Although the last few decades have seen an increase in the number of

Basque speakers, their impact on the consumption of Basque literature has not been as high as it was hoped. This might be due to what writer Anjel Lertxundi describes as "a deficit in the transmission of the language" (Etxeberria 193) or "the crisis of a model of Basque speakers, of readers" (Etxeberria 194). It is highly significant that young Basques who have studied their subjects and materials in Basque through secondary school, have (linguistic) difficulty in reading Basque literature, and that their reading habits in the language decrease toward the end of their secondary education.

To the best of my knowledge, there has been no exhaustive study to date on the translation into other languages of works written originally in Basque. At the present time, the number of titles translated from Basque into other languages is estimated to be approximately 210 (*www.basqueliterature.com*). There is no doubt, however, that since the 1960s, the Basque *intelligentsia* has been convinced of the importance that translation into other languages has for the survival of the Basque language and the professionalization of Basque writers. There has been a very slow increase in the number of titles translated from Basque into other languages, and it was not until the end of the twentieth century that this trend was truly confirmed. Bernardo Atxaga was to mark a turning point in the international image of Basque literature (Olaziregi, *Waking*). His *Obabakoak* (1989), with its translations into 26 languages, marks a milestone in our historiography. Moreover, Atxaga's fame constitutes for many authors a model to follow, even if it has generated a certain anxiety to "homologize" Basque literature and place it on the map of the modern global scene.[8] What seems clear is that the promotion of Basque writing needs a professional and / or institutional infrastructure and should not be left to the scattered success of individual authors. There has been a reliance on direct contact with foreign readers and publishing houses, or on the endorsement of prizes such as Spain's Premio Nacional (National Prize) received by Atxaga and Unai Elorriaga. The case is similar to that of Catalan literature: "(When Catalan identity achieves international status, language, that key historical element, becomes a hindrance, a problem)" (Subirana 260). As an example, we could mention that of the sixteen people who have been awarded the prize "Universal Basque" by the Basque Government since 1997, only one was a Basque writer.

The Basque Government did not fund the translation or promotion of Basque literature until the year 2000, and its presence in forums, such as the Frankfurt Book Fair, has not, as yet, generated the desired curiosity. Other projects and initiatives backed by institutions such as the Committee to Promote Basque Literature, which was created under the aegis of the European organization, Literature Across Frontiers (LAF) in 2005, or the Euskal Idazleen Elkartea (EIE, the Association of Basque Writers, founded in 1982), which launched the Plan for the Promotion of Basque Literature Abroad, also had limited effects in the promotion and dissemination of Basque literature. This is now changing, thanks to the existence of translators with sufficient literary and linguistic competence to translate directly from Basque into other languages. A book series was created for this purpose, in 2004, by the Center for Basque Studies at the University of Nevada, Reno. The success of its first publication, *An Anthology of Basque Short Stories* (2004), has resonated with other translations into Spanish (2005), Russian (2006), and Italian (2007). This case shows that the preeminence of English in the global market can help to overcome the "invisibility" of minority languages such as Basque.

There is no doubt that the Basque literary system is dependent on the central system of the Iberian space, that is, the Spanish system. There is still a need to study the relationships between the different literatures of the Spanish State, and to overcome the "ethnic, linguistic, and cultural homogeneity" (Cabo, "National Canon Formation") which dominates Spanish literary historiography.[9] The data reported by Hooft Comajuncosas are quite remarkable and inspire reflection on the hierarchical relationships and interferences among the various literatures of the Iberian sphere. Hooft Comajuncosas describes the Spanish intercultural space from 1990 to 1998 as very unbalanced due to the dominance of Spanish over the other Iberian languages as a vehicle for translating novels, stories, and poetry written originally in Catalan, Galician, and Basque; Spanish has served as a *lingua franca*. The statistics do not change significantly for the period from 1999 to 2003: the Catalan, Galician, and Basque systems continued translating a great percentage of their works into Spanish (in the case of Basque, as many as 88%, compared with 12% translated from Basque into Catalan or Galician). It is notable that it is the Basque literary system that is most willing to engage in intercultural exchange, that is, the one that translates the greatest percentage of its works into the other languages of the Spanish State. However, the extremely low number of works that are translated from Spanish into the other languages of the Spanish State is particularly striking. While 317 works written in Basque, Catalan, and Galician were translated into Spanish from 1999–2003, only 20 were translated from Spanish into the minority languages.[10]

Despite these data, Hooft Comajuncosas sees a notable trend toward the construction of an intercultural literary space, which is corroborated by the anthologies of poetry and short stories published in the last two decades, and the number of writers who have seen their work published in the various languages of the Spanish State (330). According to him, two Basque authors, Bernardo Atxaga and Unai Elorriaga, are the best example of authors who facilitate the existence of an intercultural space by having their work published in Basque, Catalan, Galician, and Spanish. The practice of translating works into all of those languages is more common in children's and young people's literature. It is tempting to paraphrase Aresti's well-known verse in homage to a socialist from Bilbao, Tomás Meabe ("He is a true Spaniard / who knows the four languages of Spain"), and to disparage the contribution of Basque literature to the creation of an Iberian inter-literary space. Irony aside, the percentages mentioned above reflect the processes of *invisibility* inflicted on the peripheral literatures of the Spanish sphere by the central (Spanish) literature. The problems in the ISBN database in defining the original language of a text, and the omission in the credits of translations of the original title in Basque, are only some of the processes that occur constantly in the case of Basque authors like Atxaga (Hooft Comajuncosas; López Gaseni).

It is worth mentioning the translations into Spanish that Basque publishing houses like Hiru, Erein, Alberdania, and Ttarttalo have produced since the 1990s. While these translations are distributed throughout the Spanish State, they nevertheless find most of their potential readership in the Spanish-speaking Basque community. The comments of Basque authors on the relative lack of interest shown by their fellow citizens toward their work speaks to the relegation of literature written in Basque even in the Basque Country. One can only hope that, in the not-too-distant future, literature written in Basque will establish itself as a more effective means of communication among the different linguistic communities.

Notes

1. With the exception of the traditional Souletine theater, the first documents in the history of Basque theater were the dramatic works of Xabier María Munibe e Idiaquez, Count of Peñaflorida, which included some parts in Basque, and the *Gabonetako Ikuskizuna* (*Christmas Performance*) by Pedro Ignacio Barrutia. It is interesting that in this area dominated by men, Peñaflorida signed the only work that he published entirely in Basque, the *Gabon sariac* (*Christmas Bonus*) of 1792, with a female pseudonym, Luisa de la Misericordia. Was linguistic transgression possible only through a transgression of gender? Basque literature would have to wait until 1804 for the first woman to arrive on the scene, Bizenta Mogel, with her *Ipuin onak* (*Moral Stories*), an adaptation of Aesop's fables. And Bizenta begged pardon in the prologue to her book for daring to publish in a time, and in a context, the Basque context, in which a woman was not supposed to write. Although she was educated under the aegis of the ideas of the Enlightenment, Bizenta did not adopt the destiny assigned to women by certain scholars of the time, the role of maternity (Martín Gaite 263), and thus managed to incorporate, though timidly, the voice of women in an area dominated, despite myths of Basque matriarchalism, by men.
2. This was a matter of settling old debts since, with the exception of critics like Lasagabaster, few studies on contemporary Basque literature have emphasized to such an extent the opportunity lost by Basque narrative of the first half of the twentieth century to dismiss an outdated manner of writing much concerned with local customs, like that of Pereda, and find inspiration in Baroja's realist style, substituting, among other elements, the Manichaean world that prevailed in those narrative universes and incorporating in the Basque narrative universe characters like the fascinating Barojan characters Maribelcha, Teillagorri, and Zalacain (Lasagabaster, *Las literaturas* 279–94).
3. These were not easy years, judging by the arduous debates in the 1950s and 1960s between those who called themselves Bascophiles (followers of Arana's traditional nationalism and supporters of the journal *Euzko Gogoa* [*Basque Soul*]) and the Bascologists (headed by Mitxelena and who would advocate a "live" Basque rather than a

"pure" Basque). For Mitxelena, as for Aresti, being a Basque speaker was more important that being "Basque" in the essentialist sense given by Arana.
4. For a more detailed description of the evolution of Basque Fiction and the present panorama of writers see Olaziregi, "Basque fiction."
5. Ramón Saizarbitoria spoke of a "concealed linguistic disability" (*Aberriaren* 21) with respect to the use of Spanish at certain critical moments of his novel *Hamaika Pauso* (*Innumerable Steps*). The protagonist, Daniel Zabalegui, knows that he will be executed the next day and he decides to write a text. He cannot write it in Basque and remembers the poet Esteban Urkiaga (Lauaxeta), who on the eve of his execution also wrote in Spanish.
6. There are few modern stories that have managed to reflect the painful Basque political reality as Iban Zaldua's story, "Bibliography," does (*An Anthology of Basque Short Stories*). Avoiding a Manichaean approach, Zaldua manages to convey that the Basque reality, like all realities, is a construct of language that allows many readings, as many as the book that becomes the final protagonist of the story. The difference, no doubt, lies in the fact that reality has real victims, victims who have names and who refuse any attempt at fictional distance.
7. In any case, it must be noted that the number of translations of children's and young people's literature continues to be greater than those of what is traditionally considered "literature for adults." Domínguez states that in the 1990s, "the percentage of children's and young people's literature in translation was approximately 50% of the total production of children's and young people's literature in Spain" (16). This percentage has been decreasing and, according to the INE (Instituto Nacional de Estadística, National Institute of Statistics), was 15.28% between 1999 and 2005.
8. Cabo Aseguinolaza sees the same anxiety to reach the world, "or at least Western stature," among Basque academics. As an example, he quotes (incorrectly) the title of the anthology that we published at the Center for Basque Studies: *An American Anthology of Basque Short Stories* (Cabo, n. 5).
9. Researchers like Casas from the University of Santiago de Compostela have begun very promising examinations of concepts such as Even-Zohar's "interliterary system" and Dionyz Durisin's "interliterary community" applied to the Iberian situation (68–97). Other promising work can be found in the reflections in the book coedited by Epps and Fernández Cifuentes. Their volume includes proposals in favor of a new focus that would overcome the monolingual concept of the Spanish State "by delving into either the place of the so-called peripheral languages and literatures (Catalan, Galician, and Basque) or the place of emigrants and exiles in Spanish literary history" (20).
10. Similar numbers are seen in children's and young people's literature (cf. Domínguez).

Works Cited

Abuín González, Anxo, and Anxo Tarrío Varela, eds. *Bases metodolóxicas para unha historia comparada das literaturas da península Ibérica*. Santiago de Compostela: Servicio de Publicaciones de la Universidad de Santiago de Compostela, 2004.

Aldekoa, Iñaki. *Historia de la Literatura Vasca*. Donostia: Erein, 2004.
Altan, Ahmet, et al. *Debout dans Babel: Langues en Europe*. Rekkem (Belgium): Ons Erfdeel vzw, 2007.
Anderson, Benedict. *Imagined Communities*. London: Verso, 1991.
Aresti, Gabriel. *Artikuluak. Hitzaldiak. Gutunak*. Zarautz: Susa, 1986.
———. *Harri eta Herri*. Zarautz: Susa, 2000.
Arkotxa, Aurelia, and Beñat Oyharçabal. "Las primicias de las letras vascas." *www.basqueliterature.com/literatura*. Accessed September 25, 2009.
Atxaga, Bernardo. *Bi letter*. Donostia: Erein, 1984. English: *Two Basque Stories*. Translated by Nere Lete. Reno: Center for Basque Studies-University of Nevada, Reno, 2009.
———. *Gizona bere bakardadean*. Iruñea: Pamiela, 1993. English: *The Lone Man*. Translated by Margaret Jull Costa. London: Harvill Presss, 1996.
———. *Obabakoak*. Donostia: Erein. English: *Obabakoak*. Translated by Margaret Jull Costa. Saint Paul, MN: Graywolf Press, 2009.
———. "Otra mirada." *www.atxaga.org/testuak-textos/otra-mirada*. Accessed September 25, 2009.
———. *Soinujolearen semea*. Iruñea: Pamiela, 2003. English: *The Accordionist's Son*. Translated by Margaret Jull Costa. London: Harvill Press, 2008.
———. *Zeru horiek*. Iruñea: Pamiela, 1995. English: *The Lone Woman*. Translated by Margaret Jull Costa. London: Harvill Press, 1999.
Barbeito, José Manuel, Jaime Feijoo, Antón Figueroa, and Jorge Sacido, eds. *National Identities and European Literatures*. Bern: Peter Lang, 2008.
Barrutia, Pedro Ignacio. "Gabonetako ikuskizuna." *Euskalzale* I. 1897. Vitoria-Gasteiz: Arabako Foru Aldundia, 1983.
Bhabha, Homi. *The Location of Culture*. London: Routledge, 1994.
Cabo Aseguinolaza, Fernando. "Dead, or a Picture of Good Health? Comparatism, Europe, and World Literature." *Comparative Literature* 58.4 (Fall 2006): 418–435.
———. "National Canon Formation as Interliterary Process: The Spanish Case." *Literary Research/Recherche littéraire*: 18 (35). collection.nlc-bnc.ca/100/201/300/ literary_research-ef/n28-n36/old35/ArticlesCabo.htm.
Casas, Arturo. "Sistema interliterario y planificación historiográfica a propósito del espacio geocultural ibérico." *Interlitteraria* 8 (2003): 68–97.
Chaho, Joseph Agustin. *Voyage en Navarra pendant l'insurrection des Basques de 1830–1835*. Paris: Larousse, 1836.
Crystal, David. *The Language Revolution*. Cambridge: Polity Press, 2004.
Dasconaguerre, Jean-Baptiste. *Les échos du pas de Roland*. Paris: Irmin Marchand, 1867.
Domínguez, Mónica. "Las traducciones de la literatura infantil y juvenil en el interior de la comunidad interliteraria específica española (1940–1980)." Diss. Universidad de Santiago de Compostela, 2008.
Epps, Brad, and Luis Fernández Cifuentes, eds. *Spain Beyond Spain*. Lewisburg: Bucknell University Press, 2005.
Etxeberria, Hasier, ed. *Cinco escritores vascos: Entrevistas de Hasier Etxeberria*. Irun: Alberdania, 2002.
Etxepare, Bernard. *Linguae Vasconum Primitiae*. Bordeaux: François Morpain, 1545.

Even-Zohar, Itamar. "A función da literatura na creación das nacións de Europa." *Grial* 31.120 (1993): 441–58.
———. "Polysystem Studies." *Poetics Today* 11.1 (1990): 97–194.
Figueroa, Antón. *Diglosia e texto*. Vigo: Xerais, 1988.
Hooft Comajuncosas, Andreu van. "¿Un espacio literario intercultural en España? El polisistema interliterario en el estado español a partir de las traducciones de las obras pertenecientes a los sistemas literarios vasco, gallego, catalán y español (1999–2003)." *Bases metodolóxicas para unha historia comparada das literaturas da península Ibérica*. Ed. Abuín González Anxo and Anxo Tarrío Varela. Santiago de Compostela: Servicio de Publicaciones de la Universidad de Santiago de Compostela, 2004. 313–33.
Iztueta, Juan Ignacio. *Guipuzcoaco provinciaren condaira*. Donostia: Ignacio Ramon Baroja, 1847.
Juaristi, Jon. *Literatura vasca*. Madrid: Taurus, 1987.
Kultura 07. Observatorio Vasco de la Cultura. Vitoria-Gasteiz: Eusko Jaurlaritza. Kultura Saila, 2007.
Landa, Mariasun. *La fiesta en la habitación de al lado*. Donostia: Erein, 2007.
Lasagabaster, Jesús María. "La Ilustración en la vida literaria vasca del siglo XVIII." *Lapurdum* 9 (2005): 149–57.
———. *Las literaturas de los vascos*. Donostia: Universidad de Deusto, 2002.
Lertxundi, Anjel. *Koldo Mitxelena entre nosotros*. Irun: Alberdania, 2001.
Literatura Uniberstsala. *www.eizie.org/Argitalpenak/Literatura_Unibertsala*. Accessed September 25, 2009.
López Gaseni, Manuel. "Literatura traducida." *www.basqueliterature.com/basque/historia/itzulia*. Accessed September 25, 2009.
Maalouf, Amin. *Identidades asesinas*. Madrid: Alianza, 1999.
Martín Gaite, Carmen. *Usos amorosos del dieciocho en España*. Barcelona: Lumen, 1981.
Mercero, Gorka. "Bernardo Atxagaren Soinujolearen semea: nazioari mugak non ezarri erabakitzearen ezintasuna." *Lapurdum* 11 (2006): 241–70.
Mogel, Bizenta. *Ipui onac*. 1804. Donostia: EEE, 1992.
Mogel, Juan Antonio. *Peru Abarka*. Durango: Julian de Elizalde, 1881.
Müller, Jan-Werner, ed. *Memory and Power in Post-War Europe. Studies in the Presence of the Past*. Cambridge: Cambridge University Press, 2002.
Munibe, Xabier Maria. *Gavon sariac*. 1762. Donostia: Auspoa, 1965.
Olaziregi, Mari Jose. "Aproximación sociológica a los hábitos de lectura de la juventud vasca." *Oihenart* 18 (2000): 79–93.
———."Basque Fiction." *A Companion to the Twentieth-Century Spanish Novel*. Ed. Marta E. Altisent. Woodbridge: Tamesis, 2008. 247–58.
———. *Waking the Hedgehog. The Literary Universe of Bernardo Atxaga*. Reno: Center for Basque Studies and University of Nevada-Reno, 2005.
Otaegi, Lourdes. "Poesía vasca del siglo XX." *www.basqueliterature.com/historia*. Accessed September 25, 2009.
Oteiza, Jorge. *Quosque tandem!* Alzuza: Fundación Museo Jorge Oteiza, 2007.
Pentsamenduaren Klasikoak: www.klasikoak.com. Accessed September 25, 2009.
Saizarbitoria, Ramon. *Aberriaren alde (eta contra)*. Irun: Alberdania, 1999.

———. *Gorde nazazu lurpean*. Donostia: Erein, 2000. Spanish: *Guárdame bajo tierra*. Translated by Fundación Eguia Careaga. Madrid: Alfaguara, 2002.

———. *Hamaika Pauso*. Donostia: Erein, 1995. Spanish: *Los pasos incontables*. Translated by Jon Juaristi. Madrid: Espasa Calpe, 1998.

Serrano Izko, Bixente et al. *Pio Baroja, 50 urte*. Iruña: Ayuntamiento de Iruña, 2007.

Subirana, Jaume. "National Poets and Universal Catalans. Writers and Literature in Contemporary Catalan Identity." *National Identities and European Literatures*. Ed. José Manuel Barbeito, Jaime Feijoo, Antón Figueroa, and Jorge Sacido. Bern: Peter Lang, 2008. 247–66.

Torrealdai, Joan Mari. *La censura de Franco y el tema vasco*. Donostia: Kutxa, 1999.

———. *30 urte liburugintzan: 1976–2005*. Donostia: Jakin, 2007.

Urkiza, Ana. *Zortzi unibertso. Zortzi idazle*. Irun: Alberdania, 2006.

Zaldua, Iban. "Bibliography." *An Anthology of Basque Short Stories*. Ed. Mari Jose Olaziregi. Reno: Center for Basque Studies-University of Nevada, Reno. 2004.

◆ 3

Galician Writing and the Poetics of Displacement: Ramiro Fonte's *A rocha dos proscritos*

Kirsty Hooper

> We are not prompted solely by the defining of our identities,
> but by their relation to everything possible as well—
> the mutual mutations generated by this interplay of relations.
> —Édouard Glissant, *Poetics of Relation* 89

Displacement, whether through forced or economic migration, political exile, or even leisure tourism, is a fundamental feature of modern life.[1] As the quotation at the head of this essay from the Martiniquean scholar Édouard Glissant suggests, one crucial consequence has been the need for scholars and artists to develop a range of innovative critical and creative vocabularies adequate for understanding or representing a phenomenon whose very nature destabilises the comfortable boundaries of nations and their literatures. At the same time, as the example of Galicia and many other non-state communities makes clear, the pull of what Glissant rejects as the Western-Classical model of national-cultural identity remains compelling. A significant body of recent scholarship in Galician cultural theory responds to similar imperatives, as scholars such as Silvia Bermúdez, José Colmeiro, Joseba Gabilondo, Helena Miguélez-Carballeira, Cristina Moreiras-Menor, María do Cebreiro Rábade Villar, or Eugenia Romero seek to relativize and thus to reimagine the structuring concepts of a universalizing—and therefore anything but universal—essence of "Galicianness" based on an unexamined conflation of language, culture, and territory. As I have argued elsewhere, the new cultural formations and productions emerging from movement to and from Galicia have a crucial part to play in this reimagining (Hooper, "New Cartographies"). In their desire to challenge the monolithic thinking that underpins not only Galician writing, but Western concepts of "national" literatures more generally, these scholars share a volition to seek a new critical vocabulary that reflects the new co-ordinates of Galician cultural and civic identity emerging—or, perhaps, being re-oriented or re-discovered—at the start of the twenty-first century.

This essay takes the poetry collection *A rocha dos proscritos* (2005), by the Galician expatriate poet Ramiro Fonte (1957–2008), as a case study for the importance of a critical understanding of displacement in re-examining the co-ordinates of Galician cultural identity. Like many of his fellow Galicians, Fonte spent much of his adult life outside Galicia, first as a teacher of Spanish at the Spanish School in London for almost a decade, and subsequently as director of the Instituto Cervantes in Lisbon, Portugal, a position he held from 2005 until his early death in Barcelona in October 2008. Primarily known as a poet (his first collection of poetry, *As cidades da nada*, was published in 1983), he also published essays and a trilogy of autobiographical novels. The experience of displacement is a key concern in the collection of poetry that is the focus of this essay: *A rocha dos proscritos (Poemas complementarios, 1994–2004)*. The edition of *A rocha* that appeared in 2005 was, as the full title suggests, the culmination of a decade-long poetic project. It comprises three distinct collections: *O cazador de libros* (dated Vigo, November 1994–March 1996), *O detective histórico* (Vigo-Londres, April 1998–February 2001), and *O pasaxeiro inmóbil* (Londres-Vigo, June 2001–December 2004).[2]

For Fonte, a key aim of the project that comprises *A rocha* was to (re)integrate Galician literature into the Western canon, a project that had been fundamental to Galician thought since the emergence of fully-fledged cultural nationalism with the Xeración Nós in the 1920s. As he explained in an interview given at the time of publication:

> As grandes obras que se escribiron en galego dialogan doadamente coas correntes espirituais do seu tempo. Lendo a Rosalía temos a impresión de estar dialogando con Holderlin, con Leopardi. . . . Lendo a Curros, facémolo con Hugo. Se sabemos buscar en Cabanillas atoparemos a certo Baudelaire. (qtd. in Fortes n.p.)

> (The great works that have been written in Galician dialogue effortlessly with the spiritual currents of their time. Reading Rosalía we have the impression of being in dialogue with Holderlin, with Leopardi. . . . Reading Curros, we do so with Hugo. If we know to look in Cabanillas, we will find a certain Baudelaire.)

That Fonte conceived of this project in terms of geographical imagery and metaphors is emphasized in an interview given towards the end of 2007, where he described his objective in writing *A rocha dos proscritos* as having been to expand the boundaries of what he had elsewhere referred to as the "ínsula barataria do sistema literario galego" (Baratarian isle of the Galician literary system) (qtd. in Fortes n.p.):

Fatalmente, un escritor galego, aínda que recibamos grandes obras doutros idiomas, opera nunha paisaxe literaria ás veces moi reducida. Daquela, a min interésame ampliar a paisaxe literaria do que se escribe en galego. (qtd. in Salgado n.p.)

(Fatally, a Galician writer, although we receive great works from other languages, operates in an often very limited literary landscape. For that reason, I'm interested in broadening the literary landscape of what is written in Galician.)

The poet's conception of the collection in terms of space and location can be clearly seen in "Poética," one of the opening group of poems from the first part of the collection *O cazador de libros* which serves as a manifesto: "Nin a pedra do triste, nin a pedra / fermosa dalgún verso modernista / nin *parises* nin íntimas cidades / excluimos desta cartografía" (20, italics in the original) (Neither the rock of sadness, nor the beautiful / rock of a modernist verse / nor *parises* nor intimate cities / do we exclude from this cartography). According to this manifesto or *cartografía*, the canonical poets with whom Fonte dialogues function as co-ordinates around which he can perform a poetic revision of the Galician literary landscape, taking in both the outward-looking urban writings—"parises" of Baudelaire, Benjamin or Cesário Verde, and the inward-looking writings—"íntimas cidades"—of Hugo, Pessoa, Rosalía de Castro or Rubén Darío. This idea is vividly developed in the poem "A rúa Walter Benjamin" (Walter Benjamin Street) (*O detective histórico*), in which the poet tramps the "street" and gazes into the "shop windows" of the Western canon (112).

The preoccupation with spatial and geographical metaphors is unsurprising in the context not only of Fonte's own status as an expatriate or (as he considers himself) an exile, but also of the development of Galician literature, which as Cristina Moreiras-Menor reminds us is the literature of a people in constant movement: "If anything characterizes Galicia, it is precisely its innumerable variety of displaced locations and 'homes'[. . . .] Galicia is the land of emigration, and by virtue of this, it can be found anywhere" (108). Furthermore, the "spatial turn" in cultural and critical theory, impelled by the huge population movements that have characterised the last century and the increasingly global circulation of literary creation, production, dissemination, and reception, means that, as Barney Warf and Santa Arias have written, "geography matters, not for the simplistic and overly used reason that everything happens in space, but because *where* things happen is crucial to knowing *how* and *why* they happen" (1). This does not necessarily imply the creation (or "discovery") of completely new landscapes, for as Robert A. Davidson has observed, "interdisciplinarity has shown that new coordinates are not necessarily *off* the map but *of* the map, that one need not seek out undiscovered country, per se, in order to offer a novel response to the continuing spatialization of disciplines, theory, and lived experience" (3, italics in the original).

This essay explores a part of the cartography (literary and geographical) of *A rocha dos proscritos* that, to borrow Davidson's imagery, is not exactly "undiscovered country," but has remained largely unacknowledged by both poet and critics: London, where much of the collection was written. Focusing on the cycle "Manuscrito en Elsinore," which is part of *O detective histórico*, I explore the connection between the cycle's London location and the two principal discourses of displacement that structure it. On the one hand, there is the discourse of exile embodied in the poet-figure of *A rocha*, depicted as a cosmopolitan *flâneur*, idly exploring the urban streets, or a lonely Romantic exploring "as íntimas cidades." On the other, the discourse of emigration, is represented by the Galician migrants whom the poet meets in London and who are the subject of many of the poems in the cycle. Ultimately, I ask whether these models alone are adequate for representing experiences of displacement that both transcend and question the established bounds of the national space—even one, as Moreiras-Menor reminds us, that itself exceeds national borders.

Exile

As the vast range of critical and creative literature on the topic demonstrates, there are many ways of experiencing displacement and they do not necessarily overlap. Terms such as exile, emigration, and diaspora are attached to different meanings in different temporal and geographical contexts, and the boundaries between them can range from nuanced to impregnable. *A rocha dos proscritos* is, as its title suggests, constructed on the pattern of Romantic exile embodied by Victor Hugo. The cover image of the 2005 edition is a watercolour by Hugo of a sailing boat in the middle of an ocean, struggling against the wind and overshadowed by a looming black cloud. Isolated in the centre of the bottom section of the watercolour (and thus the book's cover) is the single, capitalized word "exil." The collection then opens with a quotation from Walter Benjamin, translated into Galician: "A rocha dos proscritos, desde a cal tódalas tardes contemplaba o océano" (The rock of outlaws, from which every evening he contemplated the ocean.) The quotation is accompanied by a gloss: "WALTER BENJAMIN (a propósito de Victor Hugo e o seu exilio en Jersey)" (7, capitalization in the original) (WALTER BENJAMIN [regarding Victor Hugo and his exile in Jersey]). As Deborah Elise White explains, the French word "proscrit" is fundamental to Hugo's conception of exile as articulated in the collected political writings he published in 1875: "In *Actes et Paroles*, the word that Hugo most often uses to characterize himself (and others) as an exile is 'proscrit': proscribed or banished. As a noun, " 'unproscrit' is a person who has been proscribed or, in other words, an outlaw [. . . .] Hugo's repeated use of it underlines not only the legal character of his banishment, but also its public, published, textual character" (254).

Fonte, of course, was an exile in neither a legal nor a forcible sense, but rather a highly-paid, geographically mobile civil servant (he describes himself throughout as a "mestre mercenario" (161) (mercenary schoolmaster) or "profesor errante" (167) (errant teacher). The "public, published, textual" interpretation of exile that structures

A rocha dos proscritos therefore depends heavily on a distinction between political and ideological exile, as exemplified in Hugo's statement that "exile is not a material thing; it is a moral one" (qtd. in White 262). The poem "Café de artistas" (*O detective histórico*) sets out both the collection's working definition of exile and the context for Fonte's assertion of that status. As the title suggests, the poem plays on a connection between what Fonte had described as the "paisaxe literaria reducida" of Galician letters and the topos of the artists' café as a space for cultural and aesthetic debate. Rapidly summarising several decades of his career, he describes how, starting out, he was an ingénue whose work did not fit the dominant model: "Entre tantos letrados galeguistas, / Non habería publicar eu nada, / Porque a miña verdade só a sabían / Uns versos sen palabras" (97) (Among so many Galicianist men of letters / I wasn't to publish a word / For my truth was known only by / poems without words). The conflict between the politically-committed "letrados galeguistas" and the poet, whose aesthetic project is characterised in the repeated refrain "uns versos sen palabras," enables him to draw a direct connection between his situation and Hugo's, as he is "Proscrito, entre os señores desta vila" (97) (An outlaw, among the gentlemen of this town) who judge his style of poetry to be "nunha mesa da morgue, sempre fría, na brancura dun mármore de lápida" (97) (on a mortuary slab, always cold, on the whiteness of a marble tombstone).

The exile the poet finds is both aesthetic and ideological, as he sees his enemies colonize the empowering—albeit mundane and bureaucratic—spaces of the public sphere: "Eles triunfaron. Nesta Autonomía / Conquistaron xornais, modernas cátedras" (98) (They won. In this Autonomy / They conquered journals, modern professorships). His solution is blunt, reflected in the fractured syntax of the lyric: "Saín de alí. Partín" (98) (I went from there. I left). However, "A pensativa / Musa da miña parte sei que estaba" (98) (The pensive / Muse, I know, was on my side), and he is vindicated by subsequent events. Drawing inspiration from Rosalía de Castro, and the poem, "A xustiza pola man" (An eye for an eye), he takes his revenge by challenging the galeguista co-option of Galician language and culture for the nationalist project, using both towards his own, aesthetic project: "Deixeime aconsellar por Rosalía / E tomei, pola man, xusta vinganza, / Escribindo as palabras desta lingua / Con música de prata" (98) (I allowed myself to be guided by Rosalía / And I took, for an eye, another eye / Writing the words of this language / With silvery music). Now, he says, he has returned to the fold, to find his work has outlived the utilitarian project that drove him out: "Hoxe volvo ó café [. . .] En pago desa morte, teño a vida / Que é a forma máis fermosa da vinganza" (98–99) (Today I return to the cafe [. . .] In payment for that death, I have life / Which is the sweetest form of vengeance).

The poet's self-representation as an ideological exile, driven from Galicia by what he perceives as the utilitarian co-option of culture for political ends, structures the collection and drives his frequently expressed desire to expand the boundaries of Galician literature. This is a formal question too: in his emphasis on classical poetic forms of metre, rhyme, and genre, Fonte is setting himself deliberately at odds with the predominantly experimental tendencies of 1980s and 1990s Galician poetry. As he explains in the poem, "Teoría literaria" ("Literary theory") (*O cazador de libros*), classical forms, already rare in Galicia, are at risk of vanishing: "Medianamente experto / Na arte de rimar: / A tirana vangarda / Xa fixo moito mal" (43) (Averagely expert / in the art of rhyme / The tyrannical avant-garde / Has done a lot of ill). Instead, the poet argues in favor of a poetics based on a balance between distinctiveness and tradition, and on personal experience that simultaneously echoes and tempers the precepts expressed by defenders of the contemporary Spanish "poesía de la experiencia" such as Luis García Montero or Felipe Benítez Reyes (Mayhew, "Avant Garde"), with whom Fonte has sometimes been identified (Bagué Quílez): "A nosa tradición / Debe ser singular, / Máis, non nos enganemos, / Sen ser tradicionais. / E porque a poesía / É cuestión de experiencia, / Da canteira da vida / Sacaremos as pedras" (44) (Our tradition / should be unique / But, let's not deceive ourselves / Without being traditional. / And because poetry / Is a matter of experience / we will take the stones / from the quarry of life). As he explained in an interview given in 2007, this approach won him few admirers in Galicia:

> Non fun entendido e abrín unha liña maldita. A xente traga antes un texto surrealista que non se entende que a rima, que é máis provocadora. *A rocha dos proscritos*, 300 páxinas de poemas formais, recibiron as mellores críticas en España. Aquí non as tivo e houbo quen dixo que eu deixara de ser poeta por aquilo
>
> (I wasn't understood and started down an accursed path. People will swallow an incomprehensible surrealist text before they will something in rhyme, which is more provocative. *A rocha dos proscritos*, 300 pages of formal verse, got the best reviews in Spain. Here it didn't and there were even those who said I was no longer a poet because of it.) (qtd. in Salgado)

This sense of a poet misunderstood and rejected by his "home" audience contributes to the feeling of ideological exile developed throughout the first half of the collection, in particular. Once the poet makes the physical move outside Galicia (a break exemplified in "Poética": "Saín de ali. Partín"), the concept of exile takes on a new dimension, as we will see now in the cycle "Manuscrito en Elsinore." What especially calls our attention in the poems in this cycle is the tension between the figures of exile (embodied in the poet) and emigrant (embodied in the Galician migrants he meets in London), which we might also read in terms of the problem of the relationship between "the poet" and the "ordinary people," and thus of the function of poetry in the world.

Emigration

The poet's self-exile from Galicia and move to London brings him into contact with the community of Galician migrants established there since at least the 1960s and, through them, with a crucial aspect of Galician cultural history. The phenomenon of emigration and the figure of the emigrant have been central to Galician self-representation since the nineteenth century, as we see in the works of Rosalía de Castro, Manuel Curros Enríquez, Ramón Cabanillas or Castelao, and it remains so today. While just fewer than three million people live in Galicia today, another 300,000 Galician-born Spanish citizens live elsewhere in the world. This is a comparatively high rate of migration while the Galician population makes up about 6% of the total population of Spain, Galicians make up some 27% of Spaniards overseas.[3] Perhaps unsurprisingly, emigration has been a central topic in Galician cultural production since the nineteenth century, and its role in the construction of Galician identity has been widely acknowledged although, as I have argued elsewhere, the focus on the vast historical migrations to Latin America has tended to obscure the smaller and more recent movements to London and other Northern European cities (Hooper "Galicia"). The shared origin of both modern Galician cultural production and the Galician lyric tradition of emigration is generally identified with Rosalía de Castro, who, in her poetry collections *Cantares Gallegos* (1863) and *Follas novas* (1880)—widely considered the two foundational works of modern Galician culture—established the markers of Galician identity that remain in force today: language, culture, and territory (often inseparable from emigration, its "dark other").

Interestingly, while Castro provides one of the epigraphs to the first part of the collection, *O cazador de libros*, and appears sporadically through all three parts, it is only in 'Manuscrito en Elsinore' that Fonte really engages with her writing. This cycle of twenty-one poems can be read progressively, as a journey structured by the dialectic between classical models of exile and— for the first time in the collection—traditional Galician models of emigration. The collection opens with "Viaxeiro" (Traveller), in which the poet hails the reader as a recently-arrived traveller: "Viaxeiro que chegas a este lugar de Elsinore, / Deixa toda esperanza ó entrares pola porta" (125) (Traveller who arrives at this place, Elsinore / Abandon all hope on passing through the door). London, the space of exile that is the setting for the cycle, is thus presented through overlapping classical models of liminal spaces between life and death: Hamlet's Elsinore, Dante's Hell, and, later, Orpheus's Underworld, "Orfeo no metro" (Orpheus in the Underground). More specifically, "Elsinore" in the collection represents the Colegio Español where Fonte taught for nearly a decade, as becomes clear in the second poem in the collection, "Bruxas de Elsinore" (Witches of Elsinore), which introduces the Galician migrants for the first time: "E qué imprudentes foron os galegos, / Os nosos emigrantes, e qué cegos / para darvos os corazóns dos nenos" (126) (And how rash were the Galicians, / Our emigrants, and how blind / to give you the hearts of their children). The "bruxas" to whom the emigrants gave up their children's hearts are the teachers and secretaries that people the school; the poet's concern for the children of Galician emigrants will be developed at length later in the cycle (particularly in the title poem [134]). What is striking about these lines is the ambiguous boundary they draw between the poet and the emigrants. On the one hand, the emigrants are described in the third person (he is not one of them), while on the other, he claims them for the collective: they are "our" emigrants.

This ambiguous relationship is further developed in the following poem, "Na National Gallery," in which the poet, wandering alone among the great Classical works of art in London's best known gallery, overhears a conversation between two Galicians, one of them a security guard. The conversation takes place literally against a Classical backdrop, "Ó pé dun grande lenzo do Tiziano / Un deses cadros mestres que o museo / Nas salas principais ten pendurados" (127) (At the foot of a great Titian canvas / One of those masterpieces that the museum / has hanging in the main galleries). Interwoven among the poet's observations and meditations on the works of Titian, Bassano, and Tintoretto are snatches of discussion about the weather in London and Galicia: "Que está chovendo alá, que desde hai anos / non caeu tanta auga desde o ceo" (127) (So it's raining over there, it's years since / so much water's come down from the sky); family anniversaries: "é o cabodano / do seu finado pai este Decembro" (127) (it is the anniversary / of his father's passing this December); their desire to return to Galicia: "A ver se nós volvemos" (127) (Let's see if we make it back); and the local news: " Seica en Clapham mataron outro neno" (128) (Apparently they've killed another kid in Clapham). In contrast to the poet's close attention to the artworks around him, his fellow Galicians are oblivious: "E latrican alleos / á escena deses nobres venecianos, / que, grazas ó pintor, xa son eternos" (127) (And they jabber on oblivious / to the scene of those noble Venetians / who, thanks to the painter, are now eternal). Evidently, a parallel is being drawn between Titian's power to capture his Venetian nobleman forever in a painting and the poet's ability to capture his fellow Galicians in a poem. The subject-object relationship between poet and emigrants serves to draw a further line between the experiences of exile and emigration. The poet wanders about the room, looking at great works of art, while the Galicians remain oblivious to them, and when he eventually leaves the room (stressing his own continued isolation), they remain, stationary as the works of art that surround them: "Na claraboia esvara o ceo do inverno. / Chega a min, mentres parto, solitario / . . . Baixan os ríos cheos" (129) (The winter sky appears through the skylight / As I leave, alone, I hear / '. . . The rivers are swollen').

The poem raises important questions about the representation of emigration, and hierarchies of displacement, in (but not only in) Galician letters. On the one hand, it is important that experiences of emigration that have largely remained invisible are recognised: the emigration to London is one of these (Hooper, "Galicia"). On the other, it is telling that this is the only poem in the collection in which the voices of others are heard, even indirectly, and—crucially—only in fragmented form. The poet-exile interposes himself between the emigrant Galicians and the reader, whether in literal (as in "Na National Gallery") or literary terms, as in the poem "Personaxes secundarios" (Minor Characters), which mediates representations of emigrant Galicians through a process of literaturization: the Colegio Español's two Galician caretakers, Segundo and Marcelino ("Galegos meus, viñeron, xa hai anos / Do norte da Galicia marineira") (137) (My Galicians, they came, years ago / from the seafaring north of Galicia) are re-imagined as Hamlet's gravediggers for whom oblivion is the only means of bearing the unpleasant memories they hold: "O cadáver de Hamlet enterraron / E fécharonlle [sic] os ollos ó de Ofelia, / Fixérono, para iso lles pagaron: / É bo ter a lembranza esquecedeira" (137) (They buried Hamlet's body / and closed the eyes of Ophelia's. They did it, and they were paid for it / It's good to have a forgetful memory). In one sense (and this is clearly an affectionate portrait), the poem expresses solidarity with these forgotten inhabitants of a community whose survival may lie in its very invisibility: "Quen sempre sobrevive nas traxedias / Son estes personaxes secundarios, / Ninguén se acorda deles" (138) (It's always these minor characters / who survive in tragedies / Nobody remembers them). On the other hand, the poet once again draws a distinction between the exile, forging his own path (and writing his own story), and the emigrant who, subject always to the whim (or pen) of others, remains "Agardando toda unha vida enteira / a decisión do autor: 'E cae o pano'" (138) (Waiting a whole life for / the author's decision: "'The curtain falls'").

This particular author's relationship with his "personaxes secundarios" comes to a head in the final poems in the cycle: "A estación de Victoria," "Balada de Portobello Road," "As catro da tarde," and "Adeus," which focus much more closely on the Galician migrants within a broader London context until, in the last of them, the poet finally invokes the poetry of Rosalía de Castro, the canonical Galician poet of exile and emigration.

"A estación de Victoria" provides a vivid reminder that the Galician emigrant community is just one of many groups that have come and gone from the capital over the years. It describes the South London railway station of Victoria, traditionally the nexus for trains between England and the Continent. The Victoria Station of Fonte's poem is not only a space of comings and goings, arrivals and departures, but a space in which multiple temporal planes coexist. This is reflected in the intertwined full rhymes and rhyming couplets that underpin the ABBACCA rhyme scheme, which emphasize the connections at the heart of the poem. The first of these is the triad "historia—Victoria—memoria" in the first stanza: of all London's stations, the poet says, it is Victoria whose history is closest to his heart, "porque a esta estación de tren / todo emigrante xa a ten / gardadiña na memoria" (157) (because this railway station / is squirreled away in the memory / of every emigrant). In this way, he depicts the station as a space that connects the social [hi]story of their arrival at the train station with the intimate memory of that arrival, emphasised through the use of the diminutive, and also suggests he shares in at least some of the emigrants' experience. The Galicians arrive by train from the Continent and, amazed at the hustle and bustle of the "centos de peóns" (157) (hundreds of pedestrians) and flashing neon advertisements, move quickly through the station to their future (emphasised by the consonantal rhyme emigrantes—adiante):

> Uns marchaban, e outros viñan
> E cunha triste maleta,
> Para xogar á ruleta
> Da fortuna (nada tiñan)
> Os galegos emigrantes,
> Que sempre van cara a adiante
> Os seus pasos non detiñan. (158)

> (Some were leaving, and others arriving
> and with a sad little suitcase,
> on their way to play the roulette wheel
> of fortune (they had none)
> the emigrant Galicians
> who always move on forwards
> never paused for a moment.)

While the Galicians move swiftly through the station, in temporal and spatial terms, the poet lingers (now reaffirming his difference from them) and is able to perceive a multi-layered network of experiences: the Victorian philanthropic societies for the protection of fallen women, run by "vellas damas inglesas / envaradas e algo tesas" (157) (elderly English ladies / straight-backed and rather stiff); the soldiers coming and going to wars on the Continent (and the bombs that fell on Victoria itself when the war came closer to home); the explorers and, in an allusion to Conrad's *Heart of Darkness*, the colonialists, among them "quen quixo facer a historia / e estragou a súa memoria, / nas tebras, no corazón / dalgún africano río: / estaba morto do frío / desta civilización" (157) (he who wanted to make history / and smothered his memory / in the shadows, in the heart / of some African river: / he was dead from the cold / of this civilization). Ultimately, the station represents for him the confluence of England's colonial history with the physical spaces of modernity so beloved of his influences Benjamin and Baudelaire, as well as an alternative to the New World for the Galician migrants (158).

The compression of space and time we see in this poem is a characteristic of migrant writing in general, reflecting—as Sandra Ponzanesi and Daniela Merolla remind us in their introduction to *Migrant Cartographies*—the fact that "the compression of space and time is already an integral part of being a migrant" (6). A similar "compression" forms the basis of the poem "Balada de Portobello Road," which represents the Galician community in North London's gritty Portobello Road neighbourhood as one of a number of such communities, along with Portuguese, Jamaicans and Arabs (159). The poem, as its name suggests, is written in the octosyllabic romance metre, giving it a folkloric or traditional air. It begins with two epigraphs, from Lorca's "Seis poemas gallegos" and Castro's *Follas novas*, two of the key works in the traditional corpus of Galician emigration poetry, suggesting that now, at the climax of the cycle, the poet is ready to engage with this enormously powerful lyrical tradition. The Lorca epigraph is a single line from the Andalusian poet's "Cantiga do neno da tenda" by dint of which he is considered part of Galician literature, as one of Galicia's many *alófono*—non-native—poets: "Os galegos paseaban" (159). The whole verse from which the quotation is drawn refers to the disappointment of Galicians migrating to Argentina: "Ao longo das rúas infindas / os galegos paseiaban [*sic*] / soñando un val imposíbel / na verde riba da pampa" (563) (Along the infinite roads / the Galicians were strolling / dreaming of an impossible valley / in the green of the pampas). Fonte weaves a version of this line into the first and last stanzas of his depiction of the Galicians in the gritty north London district of Portobello Road, thus inscribing his own depressing portrait of the horrors and disappointments of emigration not only into a Galician lyric tradition, but, through Lorca, a universal one. Meanwhile the Castro epigraph, from the poem "A disgracia," highlights the inexplicable and inescapable nature of misfortune: "O mal do inferno é fillo, o ben do ceo; / A disgracia ¿de quen?" (159) (Evil is the child of hell, Good of Heaven / Whose child is misfortune?). The combination of the two references sets this "new wave" of migration alongside the traditional, historical migrations to South America, hinting at the inevitable sadness and disappointments inherent to both.

While the overt subject of the poem is the contemporary Galician community of Portobello Road, Fonte extends its reach in time and space, moving between the three temporal planes of past, present and future, and between the spaces of London and Galicia. The first two-thirds of the poem, all written in the present tense, introduce the Galicians as one component of London's ethnic mix, as the poet, walking along the Portobello road, points out the key places in the Galician geography of that part of London: the flyover that casts its shadow over the market, the overhead railway line, "o señor Ramón" and his grocers shop, the "Galicia" café and its tertulia (160), and the Colegio español located at no. 317, where he tries to teach his students poetry that means nothing to them: "¿Entenderán estes versos / Que eu lles poño na pizarra, / Que alí fican, silenciosos / Coma un nome nunha lápida?" (161) (Will they understand these verses / that I write for them on the board, / which lurk there, silently / like a name on a gravestone?). The last third of the poem switches into the future tense, as the poet imagines a forthcoming spring when the gloom and rain that characterize the London winter will lift and he will be reminded of home: "Coas rúas de Portobello / As rúas da miña infancia / Cruzarán os seus destinos" (192) (With the roads of Portobello / the roads of my childhood / Will cross their destinies). "Home" is represented both through the past tense, as the location of his childhood memories, and through the future tense as he imagines the people from his village making their annual pilgrimage up and down Breamo mountain to celebrate the festival of their patron San Miguel (163). The poem ends poised between the three planes, as the poet imagines that its verses will shortly disappear into oblivion, just as those he had tried to teach his pupils at school were wiped clean from the blackboard: "Xa sei que os meses borraron / Os meus versos na pizarra, / E así pasará con estes / Que aquelei nesta balada" (163) (I know the months will erase / My verses on the blackboard / And the same will happen to these ones / which I put in this ballad). Fonte's strategy in this poem (as in "A estación de Victoria) closely mirrors that of English-language writers of postcolonial London, so that John McLeod's description of Bernardine Evaristo's 1997 novel *Lara* could equally have been written of Fonte's poems: "[T]he narrator emphasizes London's links with seemingly remote times and places that stress the city's fortunes as a significant centre of arrival, departure and settlement. On a number of occasions London is described in such a way as to compress its landscape together with those of distant lands" (235).

Where Fonte's work differs from that of a writer such as Evaristo, of course, is that his history, and that of the emigrants he writes about, is not itself tied into London's history. This is reaffirmed in the poem's striking closing image, where the Galicians are compared to the rotting flowers the poet sees on the flower stalls as the market closes for the night:

Nos postos de Portobello
Podrecen as rosas brancas
E os amarelos xacintos,
Esas flores moi románticas
Morren de pena e de frío
E, entre os restos da desgraza,
Aqueloutrados, perdidos,
Estes galegos que pasan (163)

(On the Portobello market stalls
The white roses are rotting
And the yellow hyacinths,
Those very romantic flowers
Die of sorrow and cold
And, among the detritus of misfortune,
Disoriented, lost,
These Galicians, strolling)

"Balada" reveals how the poet's distance from the emigrants is both diminished (in his meditation on his own longing for home) and intensified by his inability to communicate to them through the poetry that is his life's blood, while its final image emphasizes the pull of a Romantic view of emigration characterised by misfortune, melancholy, and *morriña*.

The poet's ambivalence about poetry's relevance to the lives of migrant communities, and especially their children, is strongly expressed in "Balada," where the children he teaches see the poetry they must learn in school as little more than an inscription on a tombstone that has nothing to say to them. In the following poem, "As catro da tarde," he describes his conversations after school with a small Galician boy whose family live in dreadful poverty and whose tales of his life in London are, for the poet, a much more raw expression of the problems of emigration than anything poetry can offer (164–66). The cycle reaches its climax in "Adeus," which describes the poet's thoughts on leaving London. The poem is a modern reworking of one of Castro's most famous poems of emigration, which begins with these words: "Adiós, ríos; adios, fontes; / adios, regatos pequenos; / adios, vista dos meus ollos: / non sei cando nos veremos" (Farewell, rivers; farewell, springs; / farewell, little streams; / farewell, view of my eyes: / I don't know when we'll meet again). Castro's original poem is written in the voice of an emigrant about to leave Galicia and enumerating the things he will miss about his homeland; Fonte's version follows the same anaphoric pattern, but takes as its referent his adopted London: *"Adeus, Támesis de Londres / Adeus, meus cativos tenros; / Lévovos no corazón, / Non sei se volverei vervos"* (167, italics in the original) (Farewell, Thames of London / Farewell, my little ones / I carry you in my heart / I don't know if I will see you again).

A direct connection with Castro and her poem is made in the sixth, seventh, and eighth stanzas of "Adeus," when the poet recalls "[a]s alumnas miñas / Que chorastes ó dicirdes / Os versos de Rosalía" (167) (my [female] pupils / you cried on reading aloud / Rosalía's verses). In the context of the poet's constantly-expressed dissatisfaction with the education available in the Colegio Español for the children of Galician migrants, it is not insignificant that it should be Castro whose words, read aloud, move the girls to tears. Nor is it insignificant, as the following repetition of the first two lines of "Adiós ríos, adiós fontes" reveals, that the very poem that moves them, "porque a vosa historia é / A dese emigrante mesmo" (168) (because your story is / the story of that same emigrant) is the one the poet chooses to gloss at the climax of the cycle. The effect is double-edged: on the one hand, we might read this to be the poet's celebration of Castro's poem as a means by which to unite the two groups whose difficult relationship has structured the cycle: the exile and the emigrant. In this reading, it is Castro's dual location between the Western canon (which allows her to be taught in a Spanish school) and the Galician lyric tradition—like that which the poet attempts to claim for this collection—that gives her words meaning for both the poet and the children of the migrants who, throughout, have remained oblivious to the classical canon. On the other hand, the episode reinforces the poet's self-imposed role as mediator of the Galician migrant experience, this time not mediating the migrant for the reader, but mediating the migrants' own experience back to them through Castro's poetry. The longstanding associations of Castro's poetry with femininity (rather than feminism) and melancholy (rather than social protest) are here reinforced, recalling Marica Campo's lament for a dynamic and confrontational writer who has been canonized "co rostro desfigurado, presentado como unha muller de sensibilidade doentía" (62) (with her face disfigured, presented as a women of morbid sensibility).

Unlike Castro's emigrant, the poet of "Adeus" (and by extension "Manuscrito en Elsinore") is bidding farewell to a temporary home, a transitory location, and he gives no indication of his destination. The emphasis is therefore less on the trauma of uprooting than on resignation to perpetual transit, as we see in the closing stanzas. The penultimate stanza repeats the gloss on Castro's poem with which "Adeus" opened, while the last stanza shifts between an ambiguous nod to the poet's perpetual motion: "Porque partín / Volverei" (173) (Because I left / I will return). The ambiguity lies in the unspecified direction of travel: "volverei" could equally denote resignation at returning to Galicia, or a promise to return to London. The poem's penultimate line suggests a mission accomplished "O mundo vin" (173) (I saw the world), while the last line indicates a lesson learned: "Serei sempre un forasteiro" (173) (I will always be a stranger). The end of "Adeus," and thus of the cycle as a whole, reasserts the poet's self-image as an exile and his essential difference from the emigrants he meets in London. Significantly, while Castro's verse depicts a two-way relationship with the landscape the emigrant is bidding farewell to ("non sei cando nos veremos") Fonte's gives us only the poet's perspective ("non sei se volverei vervos"). This is reinforced when, in the cycle "Sobre o plano de Londres" (part of *O pasaxeiro inmóbil*, the third part of *A rocha*), the poet returns to London but the emigrant community is not mentioned at all.

Diaspora

A rocha dos proscritos makes a connection between "exile" and art and high culture through the poet's expressed desire to (re)integrate Galician literature with the Western canon. While the representation of emigrants is sympathetic and often affectionate, it is also fractured, partial and mediated. Throughout the cycle "Manuscrito en Elsinore," we see the poet moving gradually closer to the emigrants who are part of his life in Elsinore (the Colegio Español) until finally, adopting Castro's poetics, he finds a means of bringing poetry to the children in his charge. Ultimately, however, the transformative effect of Castro's poem is limited to the emigrants; the poet remains alone, forever an exile. The comparison with Castro, the canonical Galician poet of both exile and emigration, is constructive. Both she and Fonte write about emigrants, but there are crucial distinctions between their strategies, which the example of "Adiós" / "Adeus" lays bare: where Castro wrote in popular forms drawn from the oral tradition, Fonte employs classical verse forms which, he admits, alienate Galician readers; where Castro wrote of emigration in the first person, Fonte's poet is always interposed between emigrant and reader; where Castro's poetry was financed, published, and given prestige through the efforts of transnational networks of Galician migrants (Bermúdez, Davies), Fonte's work—despite its overt critique of Galician cultural systems—is published through Galicia's biggest commercial publishing house, Xerais.

Nevertheless, the location and geographical metaphors that structure *A rocha* opens up further possibilities. At a time when, as Ponzaresi and Merolla remind us, the huge and constant population movements around and across continents mean that "literature and art cannot be framed any more within national canons" (8), the city functions as an alternative space for organizing both the experience and representation of identity:

The new cultural dimensions opened up by migration are re-shaping the spaces of identity. Migration . . . forces an operation of hybridisation not only of the metropolitan culture and of the literary representations of cultural difference, but also of the urban landscape and media culture at large. (8)

As we have seen in *A rocha dos proscritos*, what poet-exile and migrants share is precisely a resistance to any such "operation of hybridisation" in their shared focus on the homeland and the (im)possibility of return, their self-legitimisation through the lyric tradition of Galician representations of emigration, their use of the Galician language, and their intra-community solidarity. While the collection appears to establish a hierarchy between exile (agent of elite culture) and emigrant (object of representation), both categories—exile and emigrant—function to strengthen, not challenge, the hegemonic national discourse. In this, they correspond to Nico Israel's definition of exile, which "perhaps most closely associated with literary modernism, tends to imply both a coherent subject or author and a more circumscribed, limited conception of place or home" (3). Importantly, Israel proposes an alternative; "Diaspora," by contrast, aims to account for a hybridity or performativity that troubles such notions of cultural dominance, location, and identity" (3). For Israel the shift from "exile" to "diaspora" can be considered a teleological progression arising from the same set of circumstances as the shift from modernism to postmodernism, colonialism to postcolonialism (3). In this, the shift from "exile" to "diaspora" recalls Glissant's articulation of a shift from "the defining of our identities" (which he identifies with the Western-Classical model of national-cultural identity) to considering identities in terms of "their relation to everything possible as well" (89). What we see in *A rocha dos proscritos* is precisely a resistance to this process, so that despite the volition to expand Galicia's literary landscape, this expansion can occur only within certain parameters.

In conclusion, I return to the comparison between Fonte and Rosalía de Castro that has been present throughout this essay. Fonte is an overtly cosmopolitan writer whose explicitly stated project is to (re)integrate Galician literature into the Western canon. Despite his cosmopolitanism and his regularly expressed discomfort with the hegemonic structures of Galician literature, his project to "aumentar" the boundaries of Galicia's "paisaxe literaria" depends on those boundaries for its existence and prestige. While Fonte's project succeeds in expanding the boundaries of Galicia's literary landscape, its co-ordinates—even its shape—remain fundamentally unchanged. In comparison, Castro—for many years reductively identified as the root of the dominant narrative of Galician national, cultural, and linguistic identity—has recently been reclaimed by scholars critical of scholarship based on unexamined essentialist models. Recent studies by María do Cebreiro Rábade Villar and Joseba Gabilondo, among others, have shown that far from embodying a unitary national essence, Castro can in fact be read as a postnational writer avant la lettre (Gabilondo), forging a new language and subjectivity that destabilise rather than solidify national, cultural or linguistic essences (Rábade Villar).

I asked at the beginning of this essay whether the models of exile and emigrant that structure the progress of "Manuscrito en Elsinore" are adequate for representing experiences of displacement today. The cultural and political consequences of displacement continue to raise very real stakes in Galicia today, but the changing experiences of displacement (whether exile, emigration, leisure tourism, or—increasingly—immigration) are generating new cartographies of identity that cannot simply be mapped onto existing ones. The crucial importance of being open to these new cartographies is poignantly expressed by the London-born, Galician-educated writer Xesús Fraga in his suggestively titled short story collection *A–Z* (2003). As I have argued elsewhere, the opening story of the collection, in which an elderly Galician emigrant in London dies of an easily curable illness because he has never learned enough English to be able to consult a doctor, proposes the eponymous London street map as a model for a new cartography of Galicianness that transcends both the Spanish state and the traditional story of emigration within the Hispanic world ("New Cartographies"). In this light, the statement of Fonte's poet in "Adeus" that he has mislaid his copy of the *A–Z*, "o manual de retórica / para o cidadán poeta" (169) (the rhetoric manual / for the citizen poet), appears, if not a wilful rejection of the dynamic, forward-looking, adaptive identity embraced by the young, bilingual narrator of Fraga's story, then certainly a lost opportunity (or perhaps simply a different set of priorities). Instructively, Fraga's story, too, warns against the fetishization of a romantic notion of exile, as his elderly emigrant—whom everybody reveres as a political exile from Franco's Spain—is finally unmasked as no more than a petty thief fleeing Spanish justice (Hooper, "Galicia").

The importance expressed in Fraga's story, of questioning both cultural models (of language, culture, territory) and fixed identities points at the beginnings of an alternative framework for articulating displacement within a Galician cultural context. The models developed by Glissant, of relationality, or by Israel, of diaspora, are just two examples of critical projects that seek to understand and to represent a phenomenon whose very nature destabilises the comfortable boundaries of nations and their literatures. Fonte's representation of both exile and emigration in *A rocha dos proscritos* demonstrates how these experiences of displacement can ultimately reinforce the very boundaries they apparently transcend. Meanwhile, recent rethinking of Castro's position within Galician literature, and thus the position of Galician literature within wider networks, emphasises the importance not only of finding new co-ordinates of identity, but also, as Robert Davidson reminds us, of re-imagining co-ordinates that are, perhaps, not as fixed as they might appear. A crucial project in Galician Studies now is to continue to develop—and recover—critical and creative vocabularies for representing experiences that transcend the bounds of the national, while at the same time acknowledging its resisting, compelling pull.

Notes

1. I am grateful to my colleagues Diana Cullell and Claire Taylor for their careful comments on this manuscript.
2. The project grew incrementally over a decade: *O cazador de libros*, begun in 1994, was first published alone in 1997; the first edition of *A rocha dos proscritos* (2001) comprised *O cazador de libros* and *O detective histórico*, while the second edition of *A rocha dos proscritos* (2005) contained all three collections.
3. The Instituto Nacional de Estadística gives the population for Galicia on 1 January 2008 as 2,784,169, or 6% of the Spanish total of 46,157,822. The records of the Oficina del Censo Electoral going back to 2002 show that the percentage of Spaniards registered overseas who give their origin as one of the provinces of Galicia is constantly within one percentage point of 27%. (www.ine.es/censoe/censo_cerrado/index.html).

Works Cited

Bagué Quílez, Luis. *Poesía en pie de paz: Modos del compromiso hacia el tercer milenio.* Valencia: Pre-Textos, 2007.

Bermúdez, Silvia. "La Habana para un exiliado gallego: Manuel Curros Enríquez, *La Terra Gallega* y la modernidad nacional transatlántica." *MLN* 117.2 (2002): 331–42.

Campo, Marica. *Memoria para Xoana.* A Coruña: Espiral Maior, 2002.

Castro, Rosalía de. *Cantares gallegos.* Vigo: Juan Compañel, 1863.

———. *Follas novas.* Madrid: La Ilustración Gallega y Asturiana, 1880.

Colmeiro, José F. "Peripheral Visions, Global Positions: Remapping Galician Culture." *Critical Approaches to the Nation in Galician Studies.* Ed. Helena Miguélez-Carballeira and Kirsty Hopper, eds. Special Issue of the *Bulletin of Hispanic Studies* 86.2 (2009): 213–230.

Conrad, Joseph. *Heart of Darkness.* Edinburgh: Blackwood, 1902.

Davidson, Robert A. "Spaces of Immigration Prevention: Interdiction and the Nonplace." *Diacritics* 33.3 (Fall-Winter 2003): 3–18.

Davies, Catherine. "Rosalía de Castro: Cultural Isolation in a Colonial Context." *Recovering Spain's Feminist Tradition.* Ed. Lisa Vollendorf. New York: Modern Language Association, 2001. 176–97.

Fonte, Ramiro. *A rocha dos proscritos (Poemas complementarios, 1994–2004).* Vigo: Edicións Xerais, 2005.

———. *A rocha dos proscritos (Poemas complementarios).* Pontevedra: Deputación Provincial de Pontevedra, Servicio de Publicacións, 2001.

———. *O cazador de libros (Poemas complementarios).* Santiago de Compostela: Sotelo Blanco, 1997.

Fortes, Belén. "Ramiro Fonte: fronte a canóns e ínsulas baratarias." *Tempos Novos* 84 (May 2004). Reprinted at TemposDixital (October 13, 2008). Accessed January 2009. *www.temposdixital.com/?p=618*.

Fraga, Xesús. *A–Z.* Vigo: Xerais, 2003.

Gabilondo, Joseba. "Towards a Postnational History of Galician Literature: Reading Rosalía de Castro's Narrative as Atlantic Modernism." Ed. Kirsty Hooper and Manuel Puga Moruxa. *Contemporary Galician Cultural Studies: Between the Local and the Global.* New York: Modern Language Association, forthcoming.

García Lorca, Federico. *Obras completas.* Ed. Arturo del Hoyo. Madrid: Aguilar, 1978.

Glissant, Édouard. *Poetics of Relation.* Trans. Betsy Wing. Ann Arbor: University of Michigan Press, 1997.

Hooper, Kirsty. "Galicia desde Londres desde Galicia: New Voices in the 21st-century Diaspora." *Journal of Spanish Cultural Studies* 7.2 (2006): 171–88.

——. "New Cartographies in Galician Studies: From Literary Nationalism to Postnational Readings." *Reading Iberia: Theory/History/Identity.* Ed. Helena Buffery, Stuart Davis, and Kirsty Hooper. Oxford: Peter Lang, 2007: 123–39.

Israel, Nico. *Outlandish: Writing Between Exile and Diaspora.* Stanford: Stanford University Press, 2000.

Mayhew, Jonathan. "The Avant-Garde and its Discontents: Aesthetic Conservatism in Recent Spanish Poetry." *Hispanic Review* 67.3 (Summer 1999): 347–63.

McLeod, John. " 'London-stylee!' Recent Representations of Postcolonial London." *Migrant Cartographies* Ed. Sandra Ponzaresi and Daniela Merolla. Lanham, MD: Lexington Books, 2005. 229–38.

Miguélez-Carballeira, Helena. "Alternative Values: From the National to the Sentimental in the Redrawing of Galician Literary History." *Critical Approaches to the Nation in Galician Studies.* Ed. Helena Miguélez-Carballeira and Kirsty Hopper, eds. Special Issue of the *Bulletin of Hispanic Studies* 86.2 (2009): 271–92.

Moreiras-Menor, Cristina. "Galicia Beyond Galicia: 'A man dos paíños' and the Ends of Territoriality." *Border Interrogations: Questioning Spanish Frontiers.* Ed. Simon Doubleday and Benita Sampedro. Oxford: Berghahn Books, 2008: 105–19.

Ponzaresi, Sandra, and Daniela Merolla, eds. *Migrant Cartographies: New Cultural and Literary Spaces in Post-Colonial Europe.* Lanham, MD: Lexington Books, 2005.

Rábade-Villar, María do Cebreiro. "Cultural History and Resistance: The Articulation of Modern Galician Literature." Ed. Kirsty Hooper and Manuel Puga Moruxa. *Contemporary Galician Cultural Studies: Between the Local and the Global.* New York: Modern Language Association, forthcoming.

Salgado, Daniel. "Reivindicando a ética do artesán fronte ao ego do artista (Entrevista con Ramiro Fonte)." *El País Galicia,* December 7, 2007. Accessed December 2008. www.elpais.com/articulo/Galicia/Reivindico/etica/do/artesan/fronte/ao/ego/do/artista/elpepiautgal/20071207elpgal_19/Tes/.

Warf, Barney and Santa Arias, eds. *The Spatial Turn: Interdisciplinary Perspectives.* New York: Routledge, 2009.

White, Deborah Elise. "Victor Hugo's Romantic Exile." *European Romantic Review* 16.2 (April 2005): 253–67.

4

Memory and Urban Landscapes in Contemporary Catalan Theater

Jennifer Duprey

We need a type of theatre which not only releases the feelings, insights, and impulses possible within the particular historical field of human relations in which the action takes place, but employs and encourages those thoughts and feelings which help transform the field itself.
—Bertolt Brecht

In contemporary Catalan theater, memory figures largely as a hermeneutic of the cultural and political processes of the past sixty years. Within these coordinates, it rethinks the past and projects a future inside and outside of Catalonia. The history of drama and performance in Catalonia is intimately related with the memory of a society that has been limited by a series of internal and external conditions especially during the dictatorships of Primo de Rivera (1923–1930) and Francisco Franco, periods in which any expression of Catalan culture was proscribed. New expectations in the world of Catalan culture began to emerge shortly before 1975, the date of Francisco Franco's death, entailing a *canvi de paradigma* (change of paradigm) in the scenic arts. This change is clearly seen, for instance, with the appearance of independent theater companies in Spain during the last years of Francoism. The performances and representations of these companies were in opposition to the dictatorship, and thus provided a reflection of politics in Spain at the time.[1]

Paradoxically, the change of paradigm generated by the creation of independent theater suffers from a limitation: there existed an independent theater, critical of Francoism, with the aim of recuperating Catalan culture, but this theater did not consist of written drama. In fact, the absence of written drama during the sixties had its origins in the late forties. Enric Gallen pointed out that the Catalan scene during these years:

did not show sufficient signs of artistic renewal, with the exception of various isolated attempts by Josep M. de Sagarra—in plays such as *La fortuna de Sílvia (Silvia's Fate)* (1947) and *Galatea* (1948)—to mirror the sort of moral drama that was prevalent in Europe in the late1940s. The publication of Salvador Espriu's important *Primera història d'Esther (The Story of Esther)* in 1948 was, on the other hand, an exceptional event. (17)

At the same time that the theater in France was beginning to be decentralized, and Paolo Grassi with Giorgio Strehler were founding the *Teatro Piccolo di Milano*, professionals in Catalan theater formed in 1949 a board of Management at the *Teatre Romea* of Barcelona. Even so, the general artistic panorama tended to be inward looking and provincial until 1954. The overall impression was that of a regional and rural culture supplied by commercially oriented authors who in the words of Joan de Malniu (the pseudonym of Antoni Ribera): "give us the exact measure of what separates us from European culture, and therefore from Europe" (Gallen, 23).

In the context of the Spanish Transition to democracy, the theatrical scene manifests a kind of regression of what had been accomplished during the sixties in the independent theater. During this period, the political and legal framework that was still in place had been promulgated by Franco; hence, the old and repressive system of censorship had not really disappeared, as seen by the incarceration of the members of the independent company *Els Joglars* in 1977 for their performance of *La torna*, a play that denounced the military. Moreover, despite Spain's "spectacular turn" in its Transition to democracy, it was difficult for Catalan playwrights to perform an essential part of their work: the creation and representation of their dramatic texts. One might say that in the Catalonia of the Transition to democracy, theater began to imitate Spain's political map, and that while remarkable theatrical successes were accomplished based on a politics of social peace, those successes, paradoxically, led to the virtual disappearance from the scene of the Catalan playwright. Within this complex political and theatrical context—referred to in Catalonia as *travessía del desierto* (the journey in the desert)—authors such as Josep Maria Benet i Jornet (the most prolific contemporary Catalan playwright and one of the better known internationally), Jordi Teixidor, Rodolf Sirera, Manuel Molins, and Carles Santos, among others, struggled to claim a space for their creation.

During the first years of the recovery of text-based theater, the vast majority of playwrights were writing about themes that explored the complexities of the human psyche. However, with the passage of time they began to create theatrical texts that at once reflected upon the cultural and social situation of Catalonia and larger questions concerning human predicament. The point of reference and influences for their dramatic proposals were Samuel Beckett, Thomas Bernhard, Harold Pinter, David Mamet, and Bernard-Marie Koltès. In the specific case of Josep Maria Benet i Jornet, one thinks especially of Antonio Buero Vallejo and Bertolt Brecht.

Since the second half of the 1980s, Catalan theater has shown signs of extraordinary diversity and vitality attributable to the demise of the hegemony of non-text based theater and a qualitative change brought to text-based drama by a combination of prestigious private and public institutions within Catalonia. Indeed, the year 1986 can be considered the date of the recovery of text-based drama in Catalonia. Other factors influencing the vitality and diversity of cotemporary Catalan theater have been the funding of certain theater companies and the important role played by the *Sala Beckett*, created in 1988 by José Sanchis Sinisterra for two reasons: to serve as a space for the rehearsals of his *Teatro Fronterizo* (created in 1977), and to promote text-based theater workshops where young Catalan playwrights could develop their talents. The *Sala Beckett*, together with the subsequent appearance of small format theaters—*Teatre Malic*, el *Teatre Tantarantana y Artenbrut*—as well as the reorganization of the *Festival de Teatre de Tàrrega*, as spaces for alternative projects and proposals speak to the richness of contemporary Catalan theater. This richness is also attested to by the fact that The *Teatre Lliure*, the *Sala Beckett*, and the *Teatre Nacional de Cataluya* all formed part of a Catalan and European theatrical forum that promoted exchanges between playwrights from different parts of Europe and, more recently, from Latin America, where Catalan theater is often performed.[2]

Catalan theater's transition from a national context to an international one has also opened a favorable space for reflection about the political, cultural, and ethical issues of our epoch. Sergi Belbel, Josep Maria Benet i Jornet, Beth Escude, Calixto Bieito, Lluïsa Cunillé, Lluís Pasqual, Carles Batlle, and Carles Santos are among a long list of prominent contemporary Catalan playwrights and stage directors whose works have premiered at the Edinburgh and Salzburg Festivals, the *Teatro Piccolo di Milano*, the *Odéon-Théâtre de l'Europe*, the Brooklyn Academy of Music and other important venues in Latin America and the Hispanic Caribbean. Nowadays, contemporary Catalan theater traverses a boundless, limitless theatrical geography.[3]

In this essay I shall examine two plays: Josep Maria Benet's *Olors* (2000) and Jordi Coca's *Antígona* (*Antigone*, 2002). In the first case I explore the cultural significance of ruins in the city of Barcelona; how the ruins have come to materialize the obliteration of Catalan cultural memory, especially in the form of the destruction of material culture caused largely by the logic of the market that was prevalent in the last two decades of the twentieth century. In the second case I examine a contemporary version of the ancient Greek myth of Antigone to consider how the latter's act of defiance against Creon's rule conjures the justice of the act of memory, that is, the memory of the narration, as a poetic figuration, of the violence and injustice perpetrated by Creon.

The two plays studied here were premiered in two of the most important theater venues in Barcelona: the *Teatre Lliure*, founded in 1976 and the *Teatre Nacional de Cataluya* inaugurated in 1996–1997. The *Lluire* began to regularly receive subsidies from the Catalan government and municipality as soon as it opened. In fact, the *Teatre Lliure* is the first independent theater venue that received public subsidies. In terms of its repertoire, the *Lluire* has a cooperative structure—similar to the *Théâtre du Soleil* and the *Teatro Piccolo di Milano*, as well as other theater venues that were born in 1968 in Europe—with the intention of fostering a personal and innovative approach to the texts of universal theater.[4]

Olors: A Landscape of Ruins

Memory is a theme that occupies the dramatic work of Josep Maria Benet i Jornet. In *Olors*, written in 1998 (and premiered on February 24 of 2000, in the *Teatre Nacional de Catalunya* under the direction of Mario Gas)—Benet i Jornet portrays the destruction of the urban space formerly inhabited by the families who reconstructed the city of Barcelona during the postwar period.[5] The play alludes to one of the defining historical changes of contemporary society: the obliteration of cultural memory by means of the disappearance of material culture. The opening of *Olors* takes place in the immediate aftermath of the project of urban reform of the city of Barcelona that began in 1986, and was supposed to finish in 2000. The project included the demolition of houses and patios of El Raval and Ciutat Vella quarters.

The play effectively portrays the cultural meaning of the ruins in the city of Barcelona and the ways in which they materialize a process of destruction of the cultural memory that comprises the logic of the market. This logic is related to an urban policy that seeks homogenous and transparent cities which are gradually turned into disposable ones, cities which, in the words of Xavier Rubert de Ventós, "son el fondo de un sistema que genera un tejido urbano instrumental e indiferenciado" (10) (are the core of a system that generates both an instrumental and undifferentiated urban landscape). Modern ruins are allegorical representations of the historical, fast, and violent changes that a city undergoes. To comprehend the violence of these changes, Svetlana Boym's remarks are worth remembering when she indicates that: "The ruin is not merely something that reminds us of the past, it is also a reminder of the future" (54). Namely, modern ruins are memory of the contingency and the threat of fast destruction.

In *Olors*, the houses of the popular quarter El Raval, where the characters of the trilogy that begins with *Una vella, coneguda olor* and *Baralla entre olors* (Joan, Maria, Mercè, and Manel) lived, are finally destroyed. *Olors* fuses three of the five sensorial senses: smell, sight, and hearing, like different voices from a counterpoint. In the theatrical representation these three senses articulate a tripartite dialogue between history, memory, and the process of decay embodied by that the modern ruins.

In *Olors*, six years have passed since the death of Joan's father, with whom Maria had fallen in love. Mercè, Maria's mother, has memory problems and Manel, the brother, appears destroyed both physically and morally. Maria, who in *Baralla entre olors* loved those dirty patios of the Raval "sucios, descostrados, húmedos; con olor de cocina y colada" (Dirty, old, humid; smelling like kitchen and launder) and that were "llenos de vida" (27) (Full of life), decides to photograph their gradual destruction. The dramatic text opens with the following stage directions about the scenic space:

> Una isla de casas, en el barrio viejo de Barcelona. . . . Galerías, ventanas, cañerías. Abandono total. Ni un signo de vida . . . algunos balcones no tienen puertas y ofrecen a la vista las grietas de sus interiores. Pero además, y sobre todo, los patios parecen heridos, al fondo, por un enorme desgarrón, como si un monstruo hubiera mordido y devorado casas enteras y de algunas hubiera dejado, de momento, restos convertidos en montes de escombros. Quizá reina sobre la brutal herida el perfil amenazador de alguna grúa. (20)

> (An island of houses in the old district of Barcelona. [. . .] Galleries, windows, pipes. Total abandonment. Not a sign of life [. . .] some balconies are bereft of doors and offer the cracks of their interiors. Additionally, and more prominently, the patios seem wounded by an enormous tear, as if a monster had bitten and devoured whole houses, and left the remains of some of them as a pile of debris. Perhaps over the wound reigns the threat of a wrecking ball.)

It is the architecture of the scenic space which, to a great extent, writes and represents the drama. The scenic architecture of *Olors* represents, paradoxicalally, a place with history; the pipes, the irons, the cords, and the holes that we see in the ruins of the patios are at once remainders and reminders of the houses' history in the Raval, remainders that have acquired their own language in the theatrical representation.

These stage directions express market dynamics of destruction and construction since the market designates what is obsolete, so that each new commodification indicates the destruction of what precedes it. In this sense, the logic of the market places the subject in a continuous present that is regenerated with each new commodification. This form of present obliterates cultural memory since in the compression of space and time there is no possibility for the formation of memory.

In the scene, a camera in a tripod figures prominently. In fact, an intense light that alludes to the light of the flash of the camera will mark the changes of scene; the narrative structure of the drama. In his *mise en scène* of *Olors*, Mario Gas added a visual prologue that was not present in Benet i Jornet's original text. To be precise, at the beginning of the representation, images of the city in its different stages of demolition were projected upon the metallic frontal curtain. While the scenic place is illuminated, we see a mature woman on the roof of one of the demolished houses—Maria, the character of *Baralla entre olors*—who observes a photographic reel which, seconds later, will open and expose to the mortal touch of the light. This woman, who watches the patios, their colors, volumes, and edges, expresses with corporal gestures the rage she feels as she witnesses the demolition of the patios she loved. When she decides to photograph again, the noise of a wrecking ball interrupts her work. The noise of this equipment is part of the music of the scenic space. It works like a counterpoint that, at the same time, comments on the dramatic action and attests to the demolition of the patios and the houses of the Raval. The noise has both an integrating function in relation to the totality of the scenic space of *Olors* and a disintegrating one as a manifestation of the destruction. The logic of the market decides which sectors of the city must be demolished in order to be transformed into something new. These are sites that have been designated as being unsuitable, out of place, and obsolete.

While the landscape of houses and patios were the home of Maria's memories, what is left is a landscape of ruins; a memory in ruins. The patios housed secrets, as well as personal and collective histories. They narrated life. They were life that contained life. In contrast, their ruins materialized the violence of an urban project that destroyed material culture and, therefore, cultural memory. The ruins that are left behind attest to an absence and, at the same time, they fuse with it. This absence is not only the one of a place that no longer exists, but it is also the absence of memory.

In the second scene Joan, the architect who works for the company that will construct the square, orders Maria to remove the camera and leave. While looking at Maria's identity card, he declares: "Todo esto sera una plaza" (26) (All of this will be a square) to which she responds in a sarcastic way: "Preciosa, de seguro" (26) (A beautiful one, of course). The houses and the patios of the Raval have been demolished to construct a controlled and impersonal space resembling the new configurations of urban spaces that characterize contemporary cities. A *conditio sine qua non* for the creation of these spaces is the disappearance of places that were full of memories. Joan is the architect who serves this urban policy and, for that reason, agrees with the political administration's idea of an urban community. In *Olors,* Maria takes a position against this type of architect. Ironic, disdainful and finally desperate, she expresses:

> Están los arquitectos creadores. Cultos, sensibles y todo eso. Disponen con auténtico amor, cómo será la vida futura de la gente de la calle, que es la gente que les interesa. Aquí el ámbito comunitario, aquí el ámbito de la privacidad . . . Pero cuidado, ¿eh? No jodamos . . . Espacios sin balcones o, si los hay, con balcones astutamente dispuestos para que no puedas ver la cara del vecino; donde no puedas curiosear la calle y tomar el fresco en camiseta. . . . y sin un sólo rincón para guardar la memoria. Unos arquitectos que . . . trastocan el barrio, lo desfiguran, lo devoran y lo arrasan. Aquí habrá una plaza preciosa. . . . ¡Fuera, una buena limpieza y tendremos una ciudad que no nos dará vergüenza! ¡Quería tanto este barrio, estos patios! . . . Y los han asesinado con asco, sin pensárselo un minuto. No sé si entenderás lo que quiero decir, pero aquí dentro hay casas con una capa de historia a la que no han olido nunca ni el Palacio Güell ni . . . , ¡es igual! En la escalera de casa . . . De esta casa. En la pared de la escalera, mi hermano y yo, pronto hará cincuenta años, grabamos torpemente eso que hoy se llama un graffiti. Todavía está. Una especie de hurí rechoncha y, debajo, unas palabras que decían: "Viva Gilda, viva Catalunya" . . . Ahora se irá a la mierda. Que no quede ninguna memoria. (46–48)

(There exist creative architects. Educated, sensible and all that. They organize, with authentic love, how the future life of the people of the street will be like which are the people who interest them. Here the communitarian space, here the space of privacy . . . But careful, eh? Don't fuck with it . . . Spaces without balconies or, if there are any, with balconies astutely designed so that one cannot see the face of one's neighbor; where one cannot look around the street and take the fresh air in a t-shirt. . . . and without even a corner to store memory. Architects that . . . change and disfigure the neighborhood; they devour and devastate it. Here there will be a beautiful square. . . . Get out, a good cleaning and we will have a city that will not embarrassed us! I loved so much this neighborhood and these patios! . . . And they have assassinated them with repulsion, without thinking a minute about it. I do not know if you would understand what I mean, but there are houses here with a layer of history that hasn't been smell in the Güell Palace nor . . . , it doesn't matter! On the stairs . . . of this house; on the wall of the stairs, my brother and I, soon it will be fifty years, we clumsily drew that which is now called a graffitti. It's still there. A sort of a dumpy goddess, and underneath, words that said: *"Viva Gilda, Viva Catalunya"* . . . Now it will be thrown away to hell. Let there be no memory left.)

Maria criticizes the act of the architect who represents a political order that tends to establish or, rather, to impose a specific type of urbanism. Her critique draws attention to the destructive effects of market imperatives in memory and its even more pervasive effects on material culture: individual places that were noisy, smelled different, and were full of histories through which the subject formed a particular identity. The disappearance of the sounds and aromas of the Barcelonean margins supposes the volatilization of sensorial memory, which is formed by what Nadia Seremetakis identifies as the surplus of production that replaces the particularity and the diversity of the European margins (26–27). The volatilization of the sensorial memory destroys the physical beauty of the buildings in Riera Alta street—of which Benet i Jornet speaks in the Catalan prologue of *Olors*—the scent that emanates from them and the memory of their contours, proportions and textures.

The destruction of the urban margins responds to a project aiming to construct the ideal city, one without mysteries or particular places, with no individual shades, thus bringing sameness everywhere. The urbanism that Joan represents annuls and attenuates, to a high pitch, what is distinctively urban in the city. Paradoxically, as a result, it produces ruins. The urban *topos,* as Manuel Delgado states, "queda en manos de todo tipo de ingenieros, diseñadores, arquitectos e higienistas que aplican sus esquemas y planes políticos de una vida colectiva ideal y transparente a partir de la homogeneización racional de la ciudad" (179–80) (remains in the hands of every type of engineer, designer, architect, and hygienist that apply their schemes and political plans of an ideal and transparent collective life based on the rational homogenization of the city). In order to achieve this collective, transparent life all places considered dangerous, damaging, and sources of disease disappear. Every heterotopia disappears, too. Joan's square project will become embedded in Barcelona's urban texture without having made the smallest reflection on the meaning of the houses and the patios of the Raval in Catalan cultural memory.

Capturing Ruins

When Joan appears on the scene reproaching her for taking pictures of the ruins, Maria cynically answers:

> Sí, fotografiar. Eso hacía. Mi oficio . . . Cada día una foto. A la misma hora. Exactamente . . . El trípode bien sujeto . . . para que enfocara y encuadrara siempre el mismo espacio. La máquina fotográfica bien quieta: un ojo que mira mientras la gran limpieza avanza. (27)

> (Yes, photographing. That's what I was doing. My vocation . . . Every day a photograph; at the same time. Exactly. The tripod held tightly . . . in order to focus on the same spot. The camera, very still: as an eye looking while the great cleansing progresses.)

That is to say, every day is a scene. As an active subject of the *mise en scène*, the camera has become a metronome that measures both the dramatic and scenic times. At the same time, the camera is an active subject that will articulate a cultural process, namely, the process of destruction or the: "gran limpieza que avanza" (46) (the great cleansing that progresses). The camera will capture the forms and reliefs that attest to the loss. Maria's photographs will give an account of a historical process that becomes materialized or that has remained engraved in the ruins.

When Maria places herself in front of the ruins, she experiments the destruction of an urban landscape. Her camera captures holes, bite-marks, and cracks. In this sense, as Roland Barthes suggests, her photographs will catch the *punctum*, the wounds of the ruins; a detail that is a sort of accident that lacerates those who observe them.

The language of photography is a language of events. The camera catches these events and preserves them. Maria will create a visual narrative of the gradual destruction of the houses and the patios, of the serial fabrication of death. If photography always has a point of view since it has an author, Maria's point of view is registering the reality of the devastation of a material culture. Photography has always accompanied death, points out Susan Sontag, for the image that a camera captures is a trace, the remaining of something before the lenses. By means of photography, Maria will create a narrative of the demolition of the patios when it is taking place and, at the same time, will capture what remains of them. In this sense, it could be argued that the images of the ruins in the photographs will be the knowledge, affective, and intellectual, of the loss. Hence, photography and memory create Maria as a subject.

She will record in the photos the forms and the reliefs that attest to the disappearance; the same photos that will remind her of the scents of the spices as well as the sounds of the Maghrebian music coming out of the ruins:

> ¿Sabes lo que he sentido, cada día, aquí, haciendo una foto y vuelta a lo mismo? El olor del polvo de las paredes que se caen. Y además, ya lo ves, a veces, también, olor de especias. Esta música megrebí, fuera de lugar.[6] (46)

> (Do you know what I've been feeling, every day, here, taking a picture, again, and again? The smell of the dust from the collapsing walls. Also, as you can see, sometimes, the smell of spices. This Maghrebian music, out of place.)

Once again, the senses articulate a dialogue between history, memory, and the process of destruction. The scent of dust attests not only to the demolition of the houses, but to the histories and accumulated pain of what was lived in these patios. The scent of spices reminds Maria of her past; the moments lived in the houses that, in *Baralla entre olors*, had the smell of kitchen and launder and were full of life. If the demolition of houses in the Raval leads to the obliteration of cultural memory, photographs, in contrast, will be a support for memory as they are a citation and a sort of proverb. The houses of the Raval contained the past. A past that was engraved in the arch of the windows, in the banisters of the stairs, in the place were Maria and Manel—her brother—wrote a graffiti that said: "Viva Gilda, viva Catalunya." The past of the life in the Raval was carved out in every corner of the patios, in the curve of every border, in the carved relief of its walls.

In their long conversation about the past, Maria and Manel sketch a mental picture of the Barcelona of their youth. She remembers when going for a walk meant amusing oneself by looking at the shop windows of Las Rondas and the Gran Vía: "La vida era eso. Arrimar la nariz al escaparate . . . , apartar la nariz del escaparate" (41) (Life was about that. Bringing your nose closer to the shop window . . . , moving your nose away from the shop window). Manel, in contrast, remembers the Chinese quarter, when he would go out looking for prostitutes: "Parece como si todavía estuviera allí. Los callejones con los letreros. Gomas, lavajes, consulta médica" (42) (It seems as if I was still there. The signs on the narrow streets. Tires, cleansings, and medical consultations). Manel remembers a Chinese quarter filled with noise, laughs, fights, music, dogs, and cats: bars with red lamps, streets crowded with workers, sailors, and soldiers off duty: houses filled with soot, and rooms with the figure of a Sacred Heart that was "el gran amor de las putas" (42) (the prostitutes' great love). He remembers the Chinese quarters when this neighborhood had not yet experienced the volatilization of sensorial memory that the logic of the market produces. This is the picture of Barcelona's past. The picture of its present is the one showing, that which has already disappeared. In Manel's own words: "Gracias a Dios y a su madre de aquella mierda no queda nada" (42) (Thank God and his mother, there's nothing left of that crap). To which Maria responds with irony: "Has retratado Barcelona. ¿Entiendes lo que quiero decir?" (42) (You have pictured Barcelona's image. Do you understand what I'm trying to say?).

At the end of the drama, Maria places herself in front of the camera so as both she and the ruins enter the camera's gaze. Visiting the ruins everyday, Maria has progressively felt the presence of death: "He visto la muerte de refilón" (48) (I just caught a glimpse of death), she says to Joan, as if she had become a specter, too. Immediately, the camera starts to take all the pictures of the reel. With each take, the light of the *flash* illuminates Maria's face, which is reflected, finally, on the ruins. The continuous sound and light of the camera seems to go through Maria's body. In this sense, sound, and light disclose her feelings, and, at the same time, her feelings allow us to perceive the punctual effect—the *punctum*—as well as the destruction and what is ephemeral in the ruins. Sound and light also go through the body of the spectators to the extent that we also feel another form of time. For the sound of time that emerges from the continuous shots the camera is quite different from the sound of time that emerges from the demolition machines. When the camera finishes the reel, a profound silence becomes crystallized and the sky, gradually, becomes dark. We start hearing, immediately, the threatening noise of a wrecking ball.

Antigone: Violence and the Precariousness of Justice

Jordi Coca's *Antigone* (2002)[7]—which premiered in the *Teatre Lliure* of Barcelona in May 2003 under the direction of Ramon Simó[8]—focuses on the silence imposed by Creon in the city and the violence that falls on Antigone, along with the rest of the inhabitants, when she disobeys the tyrant's decree and buries the dead body of her brother, Polynices. The plot develops in a white scenic space with white and black projections of bodies destroyed by the pass of time and actors dressed in colored contemporary costumes. In this dramatic text, Coca develops a theme that was already suggested in Salvador Espriu's *Antigone* (1947): equally responsible are those that use power despotically and those who are capable of exercising influence but remain silent. Accordingly, a fundamental theme in Coca's *Antigone* is the responsibility that we bear for our silence, which has to do with the distance often assumed in relation to the problems of one's collectivity and with the fear that emerges as a consequence of authoritarian forms of power. Therefore, for the Catalan playwright, it is crucial to recover the dialectical nature and political significance of this ancient drama in the context of contemporary Catalan theater.

In his *Antigone*, Coca presents a character who, in disobeying Creon's decree, reclaims a form of justice that is not related to Creon's civil law; that is, a form of justice found behind the silence imposed by Creon on the city and its inhabitants. This alternate justice is based on compassion and vulnerability. The latter is not understood in ontological terms, but epistemologically: a vulnerability that emerges out of the mediations of specific moments and practices that, in turn, constitute moments of recognition, compassion, and understanding in a context of violence. In the case of Coca's *Antigone*, the aforementioned context is defined by war and post-war predicaments. The particularity of the form of justice enacted in Coca's play resides in the act of memory that the city's inhabitants undertake, especially Ismene and the character of the *Noi*, who constitutes the chorus of the play. This act of memory is articulated in the narration of Antigone's political act of defiance and in her ensuing fate as poetic figurations that tell her and Polynices's stories, and thus enmesh Creon's unjust act and his imposition of silence in the city. In this way, both Ismene and the *Noi* will become narrators that negate Creon's silencing act.

Silence

The silence that inhabits the play reverberates powerfully with the contrasting views of Antigone and Creon. For Creon there is only one, supreme good: his univocal idea of civic justice, which his decree expresses. Antigone's claims, however, are not univocal. Her plea on behalf of burying her brother is animated by compassion, vulnerability, and love. She, therefore, adumbrates a different idea of justice for Polynices, one that is outside the demands of Creon's code of civic justice. Marianne Constable's stimulating reflections regarding the possibility of justice are apposite here:

> Silences of justice in the law may allow things to be heard . . . . The silence about justice in the social systems of rules reminds us that in modern law, possibilities of justice lie not in statements of rules themselves, but behind the rules, in the silences where statements of rules run out and responsive action and judgment paradoxically begin anew. (59)

Antigone's claim of justice has nothing to do with what is encapsulated in positivist conceptions of justice in the law. Rather, it reveals the implications for justice, of thinking about its possibilities, precisely at the limits of positive law. An exploration of the non-positivist possibilities of the law supposes finding alternatives to rearticulate the intersections between law and justice in ways that are not reducible to the terms of legal positivism or to the empirical realities of strategic social power. Creon's oppressive silence is related with the citizen's terror and his position of distance regarding the tragic events. The former is reinforced by means of the rhetoric of power he uses to justify his decree:

> El poder ha vingut a les meves mans . . . Per tal de dir-vos clarament la meva voluntat de pau . . . he decidit que un dels dos germans rebi els honors màxims de la ciutat, i que l'altre, *el traïdor, resti insepult a mercè de les feres, ja que ell també va ser una fera per*

a nosaltres. Aquest és un deure que tenim els governants: que cap temor ni cap prudència poruga no ens aturin a l'hora de prendre decisions . . . Aquesta és la meva voluntat, i sé que també es la vostra, perquè és un deure que tenim: *els malvats no poden rebre res del que correspon als homes honestos.* (37–38)

(Power has fallen in my hands . . . to clearly communicate my will of peace. I have decided that one of the brothers receives the maximum honors of the city and that the other, *the traitor, is left unburied at the mercy of wild animals, since he was also an animal to us. This is the right that we governors possess:* that neither fear nor prudence bind us at the time of making decisions . . . This is my will, and I know that it is also yours, because it is the duty we all have now: the evildoers cannot receive what corresponds to honest men.)

This silence signifies the citizen's depoliticization: namely, it is impossible for the inhabitants of the city to take part in political life, to share collective political life and thus retrieve the political identity of the city. In the case of Coca, part of what is at stake is that Creon's silencing act obliterates and impairs the citizens' ability to participate politically. Creon's violence constitutes a remnant of the violence that characterized the civil war, as well as a continuation of it cloaked in the mantle of peace and stability. The latter betrays the falseness of a peace that is only sustained by means of violence. Even so, the idea of peace that emerges from Creon's acts and his rule paradoxically has the effect of rendering peace distant and fragile. Better still, political life is reduced to his decree and justice is solely defined by the terms prescribed in it; a decree that has converted the city itself into a corpse, as it has killed it as a political entity. Creon's decree thus inaugurated a desolated city, whose political death is mostly due to two interrelated reasons: the denial of mourning for Polynices and the imposition of silence. The city that Creon conjures is characterized by a stable order that aims at fostering a sense of identity, however illusionary; a centralized city in which its inhabitants are rendered mute. Aside from Antigone, who questions this silencing, the other inhabitants of the city observe Creon's imposed silence.

This silence has created distance and detachment, since the eyes of the inhabitants of the city have become, in Carlo Ginzburg's phrase, "wooden eyes." This distance, when pushed to extremes, may lead to an absolute lack of compassion, vulnerability, and recognition of the fate of other human beings in contexts of violence, since too great a distance gives rise to indifference. Distance, once cast as indifference, has immense spatial and temporal effects not only inside *Antigone* as a tragic drama, but also in our understanding and recognition, present and future, of the Spanish Civil War and its cultural and political consequences for Catalonia and Spain. Since distance tends to obliterate the interactive relation between the past and the present, it has, at the same time, tremendous effects in the future. Propelled by the collective silence of the rest of the characters, distance serves as a medium through which Antigone's claim of recognition is shattered. The form of recognition that Antigone claims is related to the recognition of the social and political processes leading to the de-humanization, and even de-subjectivization, of human beings, the ways in which their humanity is debased.

The aforementioned distancing is once again discernable in the way in which Creon distances himself from the religious obligation that commands a proper burial to Polynices. Creon, to be sure, has the deepest possible religious obligation to bury the corpse. And yet Polynices was an enemy of the city. And not simply an enemy, but a traitor. Corpses of enemies may be returned to their kin for honorable burial; traitors are not given such consideration. By negating the rites of burial to Polynices, something else is negated: the possibility for dwelling. For those whose bodies are buried, and thus are allowed to dwell, permanence after death is offered, just as their presence in the present is maintained.

Tombs thus become houses, storages of the past in which time itself is stored; they are spaces for dwelling that evolve into sites of memory that provide a sense of continuity between the struggles of the past and the present. As such, they contribute to link the past with the present, the memory of the dead with the lives of the living. Just like a tomb is the place of dwelling afforded to the dead, mourning becomes the process through which the dead, the vanquished, and what has been shattered, or has been forced to disappear, remains. Burial and mourning are two rites that are intimately related to the work of memory, and both are prohibited to Polnicyces by Creon's decree.

In Cocass *Antigone*, the prohibition to bury Polinyces allegorizes this obliteration of the past. Creon thus annihilates the memory of Polinyces, the past that he represents, in the same way that the memory of the Spanish Civil War and the regime that followed it were silenced in Spain during the post war period and in the Transition to democracy.

Memory and Justice

Creon's law stands for the structural organization of violence. It thus represents the violent side of law, and its intrinsic relationship with the legitimating forms of rhetoric that imposes and justifies its use. By confronting this form of structural violence, Antigone inquires whether or not it is possible to conceive justice in a different way. For her, justice resides in the avowal of a form of memory that is different from the memory imposed by Creon. Antigone's avowed memory is linked with the task of the narrator as Walter Benjamin understood it in his essay, "The Storyteller." For Benjamin, the storyteller establishes the ability of individual subjects to exchange experiences through the narration of stories; those lived by them as well as those lived by others. In this way, these stories are known by their listeners, who will then retell them, an act which will constitutes a shared memory. Narrating stories denies and challenges official silences. In Jordi Coca's version of this myth, Antigone ask the *Noi*, Ismene and the guard to go to other cities and tell the story of what has taken place in their city:

Antígona: Salva't. Dona testimoni d'això. Tu i aquest jove que no pot badar boca sereu a la llarga la millor justícia. . . . Ara, tingues coratge i viu. Digues el que has vist . . . Escampa per la ciutat el que es diu en aquesta estança. Sigues la meva memòria. (50–51)

(Antigone: Survive. Bare witness of this. You, and this young men that cannot remain silent, will be the best justice . . . Now have courage and live. Pass on what you have seen . . . . Disseminate around the city what it has been said in this place. Preserve my memory.)

Antigone's call for justice through memory finds expression outside of the space where institutionalized violence operates. Hers is an alternative space in which the idea of the political alluded by Coca is understood beyond the realm of the State, as the social and political life of the city. Antigone is claiming a democratic political life, based on civil and political rights as well as on the citizen's rights to participate politically, that is broken in Spain during the Francoist dictatorship and that the so-called Transition to democracy continued by obliterating historical memory for the sake of a stability that represented the continuation of an imposed silence about the past, whose lineages are found in the authoritarian tradition it was supposed to break from. Under Franco's regime, it was forbidden to question the official history of the recent past, a past characterized by a National Crusade for Catholic Unity and Spanish Identity. By the same token, traces of this obliteration of the past can be discerned during the Transition to democracy, when reflections on the recent past were willfully disavowed, and even repressed. The *Noi*, Ismene and the guard are narrators—in contrast to Creon who is the agent of the State—that will do justice through the stories they tell. In doing so, they will bring about a sense of justice by founding an alternative, shared narrative, against Creon's imposed silence. Their narration will be expressed as noise, as an interference that breaks with the silence. This call for a different form of justice can be found in the words of the narrators, the language of poets, and, for that reason, in the form of justice that lurks from behind the silences of the law, from its interstices.

The idea of justice that Antigone proposes is articulated in the dissemination of her story, of what has taken place, and in the memory of the political act that she has carried on by challenging Creon's edict; a challenge that is in actuality a claim for the opening of a shared political space. Through the stories told about it, Antigone's act will remain alive. Narrative is thus cast as a form of action carried by a subject that seeks to begin something new and different in the world. Storytelling is a narrative act that recreates an experience; a modality of memory and mourning that in turn constitutes what Gillian Rose calls a form of "inaugurated mourning" (12). In contrast to the perpetual melancholy imposed by the State—that condition in which Creon pretends to seclude the inhabitants of the city, thus leaving them immersed in a city in which subjects perish without dying, and neither memory nor mourning is afforded to them—an inaugurated mourning, as Rose puts it, "acknowledges the creative involvement of an action in the configurations of power and law" (12). Stated differently, this form of mourning is a creative, yet gradual process, in which new possibilities of justice that challenge prevalent logics of power are opened. And this is the form of mourning that the storytellers of Coca's Antigone will bring about. In this sense, mourning becomes an act of *poiesis*. All of this, however, unveils the fragility of justice, as it depends on others, those who can narrate the story and will create a memory that disjoints the concept of justice and law of the present. It ultimately depends on the radical negation of the silencing imposed by the State on these storytellers. It is in this precise way that the possibility of a different form of justice depends in the receptivity and understanding of these stories. Against the silence that Creon imposes on the inhabitants of the city, Antigone reclaims the narrative of a collective history that has lived and endured his decrees and violence. Invoking Benjamin once again, "to found a narrative is to grant critical import to experience" (87). But an experience that by nature of its phenomenological expression is fragile and precarious.

At the end of the play, Creon murders Antigone. Unlike Sophocles' Antigone, when the heroine ends up committing suicide, and thus her action suggests defiance by claiming ownership over her own life, Jordi Coca's play appears to end with Creon's ownership of Antigone's life. In being murdered by Creon, Antigone perishes, just like Polynices, yet she does die in a human sense. Against Creon's act, the *Noi*, Ismene, and the guard will bury the corpses of both Antigone and Polynices and grant them a human death insofar as their deaths authorize the narration of a story. Thus, they give an open future to the dead while at the same time they give us a past through poetic figurations in the stories we receive from and about them: poetic figuration carries transformative possibilities as it grant visibility and voice to what is otherwise invisible and silenced. Herein not only resides the importance of the animation of the storyteller's voice and the reception by those that listen to his/her stories, but also another form of justice. Lastly, these stories will become familiar and constitutive of the political legacy that Creon's actions have sought to obliterate in his refusal to bury Polynices's body. These narrations reestablish this legacy insofar as these are the legacy of Antigone's political act. Accordingly, in the play's end Antigone assures Creon that she finds solace in knowing that she leaves behind "entre els altres una llavor fecunda . . . Els teus decrets volen imposar un silenci criminal . . . I d'allò que volies construir, no n'arribaràs a posar ni una sola pedra, perquè la ciutat no són les pedres, són els homes, i els homes parlen" (57–58) (she leaves behind, among the others, a fecund task . . . Your decrees want to impose a criminal silence . . . and of that you wished to construct, you will not get to build a single stone, because the city is not the stones, but made out of men and they speak).

After murdering Antigone, Creon stands in solitude, next to Antigone's dead body. Finally, with resolve, he gazes at her body and spits on it. Creon leaves. Antigone's body is alone, laying on the ground for a few seconds. Creon's victory seems decisive, beyond dispute, as he remains the dominant presence of the drama and the city. Antigone's place at the end of the drama is one of total negation. Yet, as she proclaims right before dying, she has left behind something for the living, the harvest of her political act: the restoration of her memory and Polynices's by means of stories, by the narrations of these fateful events by witnesses. The task consists in challenging silence with narratives of memory. Yet silences also speak: they lend a voice to what has been buried. In this way, Coca's play opens up a space for a dialogue with an open past that makes possible critical reflection on authoritarian legacies and the forms of violence that uphold such authoritarianism. Jordi Coca's *Antigone* ends with this promise; therefore, the closing of the play is hardly the end of the story. Justice, like life, is precarious, but at the same time it is a possibility.

Conclusions

In the two plays analyzed here memory becomes manifest through a dialectical image between past and present. As such, it is about the relationship of these temporal instances not as fix points in time but rather as interactive moments. In terms of its theatrical representations as well as their political and cultural contexts in twentieth-century Catalonia, memory figures as a hermeneutics of the past. These plays allude to the Spanish Civil War, the dictatorship of Francisco Franco, the Transition to democracy, and post-olympic Barcelona. In doing so, these dramatic texts and their performance put into question the projects that remain unfulfilled in Catalonia. For this reason, the attention to the past in contemporary Catalan theater is not motivated by a simple archeological interest, but rather to influence the interpretation and understanding of the present.

In *Olors*, a play that culminates Benet i Jornet's reflections about the city of Barcelona, from the immediate aftermath of Francoist postwar regime to Post-Olympic Barcelona, the link with memory becomes articulated in the staging of the destruction of urban spaces: the patios and houses of El Raval, where the families that reconstructed the city after the war once lived. For this reason, in relation to the idea of a time of cultural memory that will disappear without leaving trace, the play reiterates the necessity of the preservation of cultural memory. In one of its artistic particularities, the link between theater and photography, the relationship between memory and time become crystallized. The possible effectiveness of photography is related to the photographer's ethics as well as a conscience of suffering and destruction. In this sense, the photographer's responsibility is similar to that of the historian in so far as his photographs remember what others will soon forget. This kind of glimpse will (re)construct the past not by ignoring the ruins but by paying attention to them.

In Jordi Coca's *Antigone*, the memory of past injustices provides a singular experience: the refusal to remain deaf to the demands of those that claim or clamor for their rights. The justice that Antigone claims is to be found behind the silence, behind what it is unsaid in Creon's decree. What bestows with wisdom and insightfulness the idea of justice in Coca's play is the invitation to be aware of the hidden side of things, which often time remains invisible. Namely, sides that have been declared insignificant by Official History and by power.

In both the reading and the *mise en scène* of the plays studied here, it is possible to approach the past and capture a moment that fleetingly becomes present. What is a stake is a process of recognition between the reader, the spectator, and the histories that are narrated in the theatrical pieces; a process of recognition that materializes in the relationship between the past and the present by making them coexist in the same space and time, namely, the space and time of the theatrical representation.

In this way, it is possible to understand how an apparently anodyne space as that of the stage is transformed due to this coexistence of temporalities into a lived space, that is to say, a space full of memories. Through this form of recognition contemporary spectators both face and engage in a dialogue with the past and the present of Catalonia. Even while reflecting about the past and the current place of Catalan language and culture, contemporary Catalan theater is not obsessed with national issues. Today, the limits of what delineates the contemporary Catalan stage reach beyond the geographical and political borders of Barcelona and Catalonia.

Notes

1. In Barcelona the following companies appeared: *Adrià Gual, Els Joglars, los Cátaros, el Grup d'Estudis Teatrals d' Horta, L'Escorpí, Comediants y La Claca*. These set of developments brought into being a different theatrical life in the sixties, which was also exemplified by the appearance of professional journals like *Primer Acto*, founded in 1959, and *Yorick* created in 1965. Additionally, in the 1970s a seminal institution for the study of the art of theater like the *Institut del Teatre* was founded.
2. Additionally, in 2002, the *Teatre Nacional de Catalunya* initiated a new project called the "T-6," under the supervision of Sergi Belbel, with the intention of fostering and staging the work of six Catalan playwrights every year.
3. For a more detailed discussion about the recent projects and the international recognition of contemporary Catalan Theater, see Sharon Feldman, "Catalunya Invisible: Contemporary Drama in Barcelona."
4. The *Teatre Nacional de Catalunya* is a public theatre in Barcelona created by the Department of Culture of the Catalan Government and its construction took place from 8 November 1991 to 1996. The theater was designed by the Catalan architect Ricardo Bofill. On November 12, 1996 it opened with Tony Kushner's *Angels in America*, directed by Josep Maria Flotats in the *Sala Tallers*. Its official inauguration, however, took place on September 11, 1997 with the *mise en scène* of *L'auca del senyor Esteve* written by Santiago Rusiñol. On December 17, 1997 the *Líneas de actuación para el Teatre Nacional* (Aesthetics of Theater) were elaborated and approved by a group of collaborators, as well as by the *Consejo de Administración del Teatre Nacional de Catalunya* (The Board of Directors) and the *Mesa de Coordinación Teatral* (The Committee of Theatrical Coordination). Representatives of the Department of Culture and professional sectors

such as the impresario *Adetca*, the company *Ciatre* as well as the *Associació d'Actors i Directors Professionals de Catalunya* (Association of Professional Actors and Directors of Catalonia) constituted this latter organization. For a more detailed discussion about the institutionalization of theater in Barcelona, see Lourdes Orozco, "Del CDG al TNC: evolució del teatre institucional a la ciutat de Barcelona."

5. The scenic designer was Joan Berrondo and the actors were Rosa Maria Sardà, Pere Arquillué, Carme Molina, Joan Anguerra, and Rosa Boladeras.

6. There is a corpus of plays in contemporary Catalan theater that have recently dealt with this significant issue of contemporary Catalan society. *Olors* is one of the plays that allude to the multicultural and pluriracial realities of Catalonia as well as to the memory of immigration in Catalonia in the twentieth century. Immigration emerges as an important theme in the Catalan novel in the sixties. This emergence occurs simultaneously with the creation of autonomous neighborhoods populated by immigrants in Catalonia. In contrast, immigration finds expression in contemporary Catalan theater during in the nineties, primarily as a response to the debates about illegal immigration during this decade. The first play about Maghrebian immigration, *Abú Magrib* (1992), written by the Valencian playwright Manuel Molins, is a play that narrates a young Maghrebian's story of voyages in western Europe. Manuel Molins' work was soon followed by Ramon Gomis' *El mercat de les Delícies* (1993), a play which deals with the relationship between two young immigrants from north Africa who were shipwrecked on a beach on the Andalusian coast; Ignasi Garcia Barba deals with immigration in his plays *A trenc d'alba* (1997) and *Camino de Tombuctú*. Moreover, Sergi Belbel in his play *Forasters* (2004) narrates the history of a Catalan family—in the mid-sixties and forty years later—and their relationship with two families of *nouvinguts*, that is, immigrants, the first one from Andalucia; the second Maghrebian. *Temptació* written by Carles Batlle (2004) relates the story of a Moroccan woman and her father in rural Catalonia. Enric Nolla Gual in *Tratado de Blancas* alludes to aspects of immigration even if this theme is not central in his theatrical texts. Finally, Juan Pablo Vallejo, a Colombian playwright exiled in Catalonia, reflects about the phenomenon of immigration in his play *Patera* (2003).

7. Jordi Coca is the author of well-known narrative works: *La japonesa* (1992); *Dies meravellosos* (1996); *De nit, sota les estrelles* (1999); and *Sota la pols* (2001). His first dramatic text is *Platja Negra* written in 1999. *Antígona* is his second play. Today, Coca is the artistic director of the *Teatre Lluire*.

8. The actors were Daniela Feixas as Antígona; Manel Barceló as Creont; Marc Homs as the Noi; Alícia Pérez as Ismene; Albert Pérez as Tirèsies; and Xisco Segura as the Guard.

Works Cited

Barthes, Roland. *Camera Lucida: Reflections on Photography*. Trans. Richard Howard. New York: Hill and Wang, 1982.
Batlle, Carles. *Temptacio*. Barcelona: Proa, 2004.
Belbel, Sergi. *Forasters*. Barcelona: Proa, 2004.

Benet i Jornet, Josep Maria. *Olors*. Barcelona: La Avispa, 2002.
Benjamin, Walter. "The Storyteller." *Illuminations*. Ed. Hannah Arendt. New York: Schocken Books, 1968.
Boym, Svetlana. *The Future of Nostalgia*. New York: Basic Books, 2001.
Coca, Jordi. *Antígona*. Pròleg, Jordi Malé. Barcelona: Proa, 2002.
———. *De nit*. Barcelona: Proa, 1999.
———. *Dies meravellosos*. Barcelona: Edicions 62, 2002.
———. *La japonesa*. Barcelona: Proa, 2007.
———. *Sota la pols*. Barcelona: Proa, 2001.
———. *Sota les estrelles*. Barcelona: Proa, 1999.
———. *Platja Negra*. Barcelona: Proa, 1999.
Constable, Marianne. *Just Silences: The Limits and Possibilities of Modern Law*. Princeton, N.J.: Princeton University Press, 2005.
Delgado Ruíz, Manuel. *El animal público*. Barcelona: Anagrama, 1999.
Espriu, Salvador. *Antigone*. Barcelona: Aletheia, 2007.
———. *Primera Història d'Esther*. Barcelona: Proa, 2005.
Feldman, Sharon. "Catalunya Invisible: Contemporary Drama in Barcelona." *Arizona Journal of Hispanic Cultural Studies* 6 (2002): 269–88.
Gallen, Enric. "Catalan Theatrical Life (1939–1993)." *Contemporary Catalan Theater: An Introduction*. Ed. David George and John London. London: The Anglo-Catalan Society, 1996.
———. *El teatre a la ciutat de Barcelona durant el règim franquista (1939–1954)*. Barcelona: Institut del Teatre, 1985.
Garcia Barba, Ignasi. *A trenc d'alba*, Barcelona: Premio Teatro Breve, 1996.
———. *Camino de Tombuctú*. *Tablado Iberoamericano*. No. 4. México: Puebla, 1997.
George, David, and London, John, eds. *Contemporary Catalan Theater: An Introduction*. London: The Anglo-Catalan Society, 1996.
Ginzburg, Carlo. *Wooden Eyes: Nine Reflections on Distance*. Trans. Martin Ryle and Kate Soper. New York: Columbia University Press, 2001.
Gomis, Ramon. *El mercat de les Delícies*. Barcelona: Lumen, 2006.
Molins, Manuel. *Abú Magrib*. Alzira: Edicions Bromera, 2002.
Orozco, Lourdes. "Del CDG al TNC: Evolució del teatre institucional a la ciutat de Barcelona." *De la transició a l'actualitat: Primer simposi internacional sobre teatre català contemporani*. Barcelona: Institut del Teatre, 2005: 495–519.
Rose, Gillian. *Mourning Becomes the Law: Philosophy and Representation*. Cambridge: Cambridge University Press, 1996.
Rubert de Ventós, Xavier. *De la modernidad*. Barcelona: Península, 1980.
Sagarra, Josep Maria de. *La Fortuna de Silvia*. Barcelona: Selecta, 1998.
———. *La Galatea*. Barcelona: Proa, 1998.
Seremetakis, Nadia. "The Memory of the Senses." *The Senses Still: Perception and Memory as a Material Culture in Modernity*. Ed. Nadia Seremetakis. Chicago: University of Chicago Press, 1994.
Sontag, Susan. *Regarding the Pain of Others*. New York: Picador, 2003.
Vallejo, Juan Pablo. *Patera*. *Primer Acto* 302 (2003): 25–55.

♦ 5

The New Capital of Spanish Literature: The Best Sellers

Maarten Steenmeijer

"Nosotros no somos nada en el mundo, y las voces que aquí damos, por mucho que quieran elevarse, no salen de la estrechez de esta pobre casa" (84) (We are nothing in this world, and whatever we say here, as much as we want to elevate our voices, does not leave the narrowness of this poor house). With this sentence taken from Benito Pérez Galdós' prologue to Clarín's 1901 edition of *La Regenta*, the author laments the marginal position occupied by Spanish literature in what Pascale Casanova was to call "the world republic of letters" in a book by the same title. In this excellent study, the French critic and sociologist revitalizes this concept in relation to the imaginary of the Enlightenment, redefining it as a "literary universe relatively independent of the everyday world and its political divisions" (xxi). Echoing Pierre Bourdieu's ideas, Casanova views the world republic of letters not as an open space of intellectual exchange, but as a closed one dominated by power relations, processes, and mechanisms:

> This world republic of letters has its own mode of operation: its own economy, which produces hierarchies and various forms of violence; and, above all, its own history, which, long obscured by the quasi-systemic national (and therefore political) appropriation of literary stature, has never really been chronicled. Its geography is based on the opposition between a capital, on the one hand, and peripheral dependencies whose relationship to this center is defined by their aesthetic distance from it. (11–12)

For many centuries, as Pérez Galdós implies in the quote registered above, Spain's position in the international literary space has been marginal at best. This is further illustrated by the fact that the author's magnum opus, *Fortunata y Jacinta*, which embodied nineteenth-century Spanish realism, took more than 100 years to be translated into French (1980) and English (1986).[1] Moreover, Galdós' 1901 observation did not lose its currency in the course of the twentieth century. With few exceptions, notably Miguel de Unamuno, José Ortega y Gasset, and Federico García Lorca, contemporary Spanish literature was widely unknown overseas, and was even less known during the Franco era. Julia L. Ortiz-Griffin and William D. Griffin observed that "for most of the world, the history of Spanish literature began with Cervantes and ended with Lorca" (78).

During the ostracizing, retrogressive, and nationalist Franco regime that propagandized isolationism with impunity, little was done to conceal the insignificant position of Spanish literature within the international literary arena. Having published *Los cipreses creen en Dios* (The Cypresses Believe in God), the beginnings of a trilogy that would become an authentic best seller, in 1955 José María Gironella wrote an article whose title expressed an unmistakable diagnosis: "Why Is the World Unfamiliar with the Spanish Novel?" In 1964, Antonio Iglesias Laguna prepared a study whose title also synthesized the lack of prestige that Spanish literature held in the world: *Why Is Spanish Literature Not Translated?*

In 1963 a young Peruvian's first novel, written in Paris, had been published in Spain after receiving the prestigious Biblioteca Breve Prize in the previous year. I refer to Mario Vargas Llosa's *La ciudad y los perros* (The City and the Dogs), which made history with the advent of the Spanish American *boom* novel. The spectacular phenomenon of this new Spanish American literature was to occupy a primordial space in the center of the literary world thanks to Gabriel García Márquez, Mario Vargas Llosa, Carlos Fuentes, Julio Cortázar, and other major figures like Jorge Luis Borges, Alejo Carpentier, Octavio Paz, and Pablo Neruda. Casanova maintains that,

> In the twentieth century they managed to achieve an international existence and reputation that conferred on their national literary spaces (and, more generally, the Latin American space as a whole) a standing and an influence in the larger literary world that were incommensurate with those of their native countries in the international world of politics. (38–39)

As is well known, Spain—and Barcelona in particular—had a decisive role in the inception of the *boom*. During the height of the Franco period, a literary climate had developed in Barcelona thanks in part to the infrastructure established by editor Carlos Barral and literary agent Carmen Balcells (among others), one which enabled the new Spanish American literature to be published, distributed, and exported on a large scale. The contrast between the position of Spanish American literature and contemporary Spanish literature could not have been more pronounced (see Marco and Gracia). The new Spanish American novel that invaded Spain in the 1960s, to later conquer Europe, contrasts with the poor state of things at home. In the words of author and critic José María Guelbenzu,

> La novela hispanoamericana nos hizo descubrir que el lenguaje que estamos hablando aquí está medio muerto; y quienes nos están enseñando a hablar son Carpentier, Borges, Cortázar, y esto es un golpe muy fuerte. Aquí en España no se habla el idioma

madre, sencillamente se habla el idioma sin más; somos lingüísticamente lentos y pesados como hipopótamos. En todo caso, es el *empleo* que los latinoamericanos hacen del castellano [. . .] el que nos puede ayudar a nosotros mucho, quiero decir, su capacidad de utilizarlo, el pluralismo con que lo hacen, la precisión que buscan. (qtd. in Marco and Gracia 132)

(The Spanish American novel made us discover that the language we speak is half-dead and those who are teaching us to speak are Carpentier, Borges, Cortázar. This is a painful blow. Here in Spain the mother tongue is not spoken; it is simply the language that is spoken. Linguistically we are as slow and as heavy as hippopotamuses. In any case, it is the Latin Americans' use of *castellano* [. . .] that can very well help us. That is, their capacity to use it, the pluralism with which they speak, and the precision that they seek.)

The historical, political, and cultural circumstances claimed *ad nauseam* to explain, lament, and justify the deplorable state of Spanish literature were in fact fallacies. If Spanish American authors had been capable of writing such brilliant and pioneering literature in circumstances comparable to those of Spain's poverty, repression, and isolation, why did Spanish authors continue to espouse a stagnant literary program, such as social realism and its variants, that had dominated post-war Spanish narrative?

This sad but true story does not end here. For if Spanish writers justified themselves by arguing that life was substandard with Franco, only a few years would pass after the dictator's death before they would be compelled to admit that the situation had only minimally improved with democracy. Jordi Gracia reminds us in *La llegada de los bárbaros* that in 1979 the prestigious literary magazine *Camp de l'Arpa* surveyed the opinions of literary editors to map out their position with regards to the state of democratic culture. Gracia notes that, "Unanimously, the diagnosis was very disheartening." Those surveyed

> no rehuyeron caracterizar el presente como uno—otro—de los momentos más estériles de la cultura española. Los adjetivos se repartieron sin ambages: desde negarle la existencia—'no está en situación alguna,' dice Moura—hasta ser 'anémica' (Lacruz), 'desastrosa' (Bruguera), 'descorazonadora' (Esther Tusquets), 'sin vitalidad ni brillantez' (Juan Grijalbo) o en 'situación de marasmo,' según Herralde. (153)

(They did not shy away from characterizing the present as just one of many sterile moments of Spanish culture. The adjectives used to describe such moments were employed without hesitation. Some, such as Moura, even denied its existence, saying, 'It's not in any situation.' Others described it as 'anemic' (Lacruz), 'disastrous' (Bruguera), 'disheartening' (Esther Tusquets), 'without vitality or brilliance' (Juan Grijalbo) or being in a 'state of paralysis,' according to Herralde.)

At the risk of converting this set of self-criticism into a collection of self-flagellations, I would call attention to the revealing title of an article published only two decades ago in the literary magazine *Quimera*: "Is Spanish Literature Boring?" (Bada).

For some decades now, the perception of Spanish literature has changed. At present no one would agree with the depressing diagnosis cited above. In fact, plenty of examples point to Spanish literature having a presence both worldwide and in Spain. Arturo Pérez-Reverte's adventure novels have not only penetrated the North American book market, but have also taken root in Hollywood through the cinematic adaptations of some of his novels by film directors Jim McBride and Roman Polanski. It is also worth noting the surprising success of Javier Marías' novels. The German translation of *Corazón tan blanco* sold 1,200,000 copies and was praised by Marcel Reich Ranicki, the prestigious and powerful critic and host of the literary program "The Literary Quartet," as the best and most important novel he had read in many years.

To properly illustrate the idea and scale of this phenomenon, it is important to keep in mind that this success is not limited to literature written in Spanish, as illustrated, for example, by the fact that the first novel of Catalan anthropologist Albert Sánchez Piñol, *La pell freda* (2002), was translated into thirty languages. Sánchez Piñol's novel is only the tip of the iceberg. Catalan literature is creating a respectable presence worldwide and reached a key point in 2007, when Catalan culture was the honored guest at the Frankfurt Book Fair. Additionally, thanks to authors such as Manuel Rivas and Bernardo Atxaga, Galician and Basque literature continue in Catalan's footsteps, though at a great distance.

Nonetheless, it is clear that authors who write in Spanish dominate the field. It would be pretentious to offer an exhaustive list here of the authors who have been widely translated in the last decades. I shall limit myself to mentioning perhaps the most important: Eduardo Mendoza, Rosa Montero, Arturo Pérez-Reverte, Almudena Grandes, Javier Marías, Antonio Muñoz Molina, Rafael Chirbes, and Enrique Vila-Matas. I think that it would be fair to consider Eduardo Mendoza's *La ciudad de los prodigos* as the novel that finally initiated the *boom* of the new Spanish narrative in the world republic of letters. One should ask, however, if the term *boom* is appropriate to describe the diffusion and reception of recent Spanish narrative compared with that of Latin America during the 1960s and 1970s. My view is that if extensive translation is one of the major criteria, the description is justified and the boom of the Spanish literature is comparable to that of Spanish America.

To have a more complete idea of the position of Spanish literature in the world republic of letters, one must make clear that while the number of translations is impressive, its reception is not. No Spanish author, with the exception of Javier Marías, has the sufficient prestige or literary capital (to use Casanova's term), to qualify as a modern classic. The difference with Spanish American narrative is pronounced if one considers that contemporary Spanish American literature forms part of the literary canon and that the average reader of "good literature" is familiar with the names of Borges, Cortázar, Fuentes, García Márquez, and Vargas Llosa and has probably read some works of these authors consecrated in the world republic of letters. The same would be impossible to affirm for contemporary Spanish literature. As demonstrated in a recent monograph published by *Quimera* (Grohmann and Steenmeijer), the diffusion and reception of Spanish literature differs considerably in countries such as France, Italy, Holland, Germany, Great Britain, and the United States. One might mention, for example, the great resonance that Rafael Chirbes' work has had in Germany, while noting that in a country such as Holland, he has had much less of an impact. At the same time, it is also the case that he is virtually unknown in the English-speaking world.

With this less than spectacular reception in mind, how does one explain that in the last decades so much contemporary Spanish literature has been translated? One important factor, though not a decisive one, is Spain's strong economic and political position in the world. The latter view has been prominently discussed in international newspapers (see for example the "Special Report" of *Time* [March 8, 2004] that introduced on the front page with the following words: "In the arts and architecture, business and foreign affairs, food, and sports [. . .] Spain rocks!"). One should also note that Spain has a remarkable image in foreign countries which has been captured in international media public announcements to promote tourism: "Smile! You are in Spain." Spain is no longer Galdos' nineteenth-century "pobre casa" (poor house) or as it was during the Franco era. Spain has become a wealthy, modern, and democratic country while at the same time remaining exotic: this New Spain represents for most foreigners the hybrid promise of hospitality, hedonism, and modernity.

Another important factor to consider is that Spain has a very professional and competitive literary and editorial infrastructure at its disposal. Though Spain is known for its small readership, this should not detract from the fact that it is among the most industrious countries with regards to book production and distribution. Publishing houses continue opening new markets in Spain, Latin America, and in the United States, where Spanish is its second most spoken language. Additionally, new markets are sought where the Spanish language is highly esteemed among students and professionals.

One would be remiss not to mention the literary agencies that since the revolution led by Carmen Balcells in the 1960s have continued to expand and contribute to the current presence that contemporary Spanish literature enjoys abroad. Another substantial factor, and in some cases decisive, are translation and publication subsidies for authors of Spanish literature. Since 1984 such grants are distributed by the *Dirección General del Libro, Archivos y Bibliotecas del Ministerio de Cultura.* This type of important economic assistance covers translation expenses, which in turn saves foreign publishing houses substantial operating costs, thus making the publication of Spanish literature more attractive, competitive, or put differently, privileged. However, this competitiveness is economic rather than literary, one that can lead to short-sightedness, anomalies, and misunderstandings. Let us consider the way that Antonio Muñoz Molina's work has been widely translated into Dutch: to date, eight titles which include some of his most celebrated novels, such as *Beatus Ille, El invierno en Lisboa, El jinete polaco,* and *Plenilunio,* and minor works such as *Carlota Feinberg.* Nonetheless, one could not submit that he has achieved literary importance in Holland given the fact that his books have received few and not very enthusiastic reviews by Dutch newspapers and that they have had meager sales. Why then, has De Geus continued to publish Muñoz Molina's work? Is it because of its loyalty to, or confidence in, him as an author? Or is it perhaps a love for his literature? Surely, if these were the only motives, the standard would have been to promote two or three of his books rather than eight. It is my opinion that the Spanish government has had an important role in facilitating the translation of Muñoz Molina's works into Dutch by taking upon itself much of the economic risks. The case of Álvaro Pombo is even more illustrative: all six of his novels that have been translated into Dutch (all published by the small publishing house Menken, Kasander & Wigman) received subsidies from the Spanish Ministry of Culture.

Given the above considerations, the massive success of *La sombra del viento,* by Carlos Ruiz Zafón, is surprising, as it has sold two million copies in Spain and more than nine million abroad. When the work appeared in 2001, it was the first novel for adults by an author who was completely unknown in the literary circuit. Planeta promoted the novel without grandiose expectations: the publisher did not organize a publicity campaign and would have been happy if it had sold the first print run of four thousand copies. In the beginning, the media barely noticed Ruiz Zafón's novel. Yet it was to become a huge success, as readers were attracted to it exponentially through word of mouth (which is in reality the ultimate publicity a book can receive). Emili Rosales, Ruiz Zafón's editor (and author of *La ciutat invisible,* a novel which in the shadow of *La sombra del viento* became a considerable success in France, Italy, Germany, and Holland) accurately noted:

> [*La sombra del viento*] es un long-séller que se ha ido construyendo al ritmo de los lectores, pues sus ventas oscilan en unas ondas que coinciden con el tiempo medio que se tarda en leer el libro: es decir, una ola de personas lo leen y luego lo recomiendan, provocando un incremento de ventas, y así sucesivamente. (Ayén 37)

> ([*La sombra del viento*] is a long-seller constructed to the rhythm of readers, for its sales oscillate in waves, which coincide with the average time readers need to read the book. That is, a wave of people read it and then recommend it, provoking an increase in sales, and the same process is repeated time and again.)

The German literary agent Alexander Dobler, whose clientele resides in Germany, Holland, and Scandinavian countries, recalls that initially Ruiz Zafón's novel did not generate a lot of interest abroad. Editors in those countries were doubtful of its forthcoming success given the translation, the editorial costs, and the overall investment involved with the publication of such a voluminous work. Dobler affirms, "Het was geschreven door een auteur die niemand kende en wiens naam ook nog eens moeilijk uitspreekbaar was voor noorderlingen. Het kostte me uiteindelijk een jaar om het boek in het hoofd en hart van mijn cliënten te praten" (Hoeniet 52) (It was a book written by an author that no one knew and whose name was difficult to pronounce for Northern Europeans. All in all, it took me a year to convince my clients). When a German edition was published in 2003, the novel was well received by the media, was widely reviewed, and became a commercial success. Soon thereafter, it received extraordinary praise in the Frankfurt Book Fair from Joschka Fischer, the Minister of Foreign Affairs ("Sie werden alles liegen lassen und die Nacht durch lesen!" [You will leave everything that you are doing and keep on reading all night long]), and became one of the most successful best sellers of the new century.

The reception of Ruiz Zafón's novel in Holland was similar to its reception in Spain. The Dutch version appeared in the fall of 2004, and in the first few months, contrary to the great expectations of the translator (Nelleke Geel) and the publisher, only a few thousand copies were sold. However, in 2005 due to the fascinating and vital role of word of mouth publicity, sales increased astronomically, and continue to grow. *La sombra del viento* turned out to be more than a best seller: it is concurrently a *steady-seller*, and, in the words of Emili Rosales, a long-seller. To date, more than 700,000 copies have been sold in Holland. To have a clear idea of the implications of this figure, one only needs to consider that the fact that the translated works of Vargas Llosa, which includes his narrative and essays, have sold 250,000 copies in Holland in a period that spans more than four decades. *La sombra del viento* is without a doubt, the first true world, or if you prefer, global success for contemporary Spanish literature. Ruiz Zafón's novel is well-known, sold, and read on a massive scale. It is in every bookstore, kiosk, airport, and nightstand. It achieved what no other modern Spanish literary work had managed to achieve before: to form part of a collective global memory. To put Ruiz Zafón's success into perspective, it would be more appropriate to compare the accomplishment of his novel with that of Dan Brown's *The Da Vinci Code*, rather than to the reception of Arturo Pérez-Reverte's novels (the first writer of democratic Spain to achieve the status of an international best-selling author).

Unlike Ruiz Zafón (and of course Brown), Pérez-Reverte has not achieved the same authorial status abroad. In Holland for example, the author of *La tabla de Flandes* continues being an unknown writer who is under-sold, though seven of his works have been translated into Dutch. Among these is *El sol de Breda*, a novel from the Alatriste series whose action takes places in the Netherlands. As such, one would think that it would be more popular with Dutch readers. This is not the case. To celebrate and promote the publication of the Dutch translation and generate publicity, Peréz-Reverte was invited to Breda to "return" the key to the city to its mayor. A similar key was given to General Spinola in 1625 as portrayed by Velázquez in his famous painting *The Surrender of Breda* (which appears on the cover of the Dutch edition of *El sol de Breda*). Pérez-Reverte's visit, I insist, made little difference: the staged presentation generated little publicity and his book sales were as meager as those of his other Dutch translations.

It seems appropriate to link the difference of reception between *La sombra del viento* and Arturo Pérez-Reverte's novels with yet another, perhaps more intrinsic divergence. Pérez-Reverte's novels vindicate historical and cultural signs of identity that are profoundly rooted in the Mediterranean's millennial patrimony (enmeshed with literary ambition fervently defended by its author, though not always confirmed by the critics). Pura Fernández maintains: "El autor se aparta de la literatura fungible o, según sus propias palabras, de la "literatura desechable," la de los autores anglosajones de *best seller*, porque éstos no se nutren "de una imaginación que cuenta con tres milenios de historia narrativa" (43) (The author distances himself from throwaway literature, or according to his own words, 'disposable literature,' like that of English speaking best-selling authors, given that they are not nourished 'by an imagination that has three millennia of narrative history').

In contrast, Carlos Ruiz Zafón draws inspiration from another source. In 1993, he moved to Los Angeles to earn a living as a screen writer and a teen novelist. It was there where he also wrote his first adult novel, *La sombra del viento*. His residence in the United States had a profound effect on *La sombra del viento*, whose plot, sequences, and images are indebted to Hollywood's stereotypical cinema. Thus the reader finds a young hero who confronts precarious situations which he is always able to overcome unharmed. As expected, there are heroes and villains, vulgar sex and pure love, violence, much dialogue, many cliffhangers for climactic tension, and numerous one-liners for comedy. However, *La sombra del viento* is not just Hollywood entertainment. It is also an ode to literature and the text as a place of memory which is fore grounded in the novel's opening plot: the Cemetery of Forgotten Books, the protagonist's (Daniel Sempere) obsession for the work and life of Julián Carax, and the numerous references to a specific literary canon (Charles Dickens, Victor Hugo, Umberto Eco, Gabriel García Márquez, among others). *La sombra del viento* oscillates between high and low culture.

Though there are apparent divergences with respect to their literary sensibilities and stylistic elaborations, I do not deem it unwise to underscore the similarities between *La sombra del viento* and *The Da Vinci Code* (the contemporary best-seller paradigm) with respect to the hybrid character of both novels: the manner in which they combine the cultural tradition of the Old World, and the narrative strategies borrowed from popular culture such as the detective novel and certain Hollywood cinema.

In the case of Javier Sierra's *La cena secreta* (The Secret Supper), its affinity with *The Da Vinci Code* is even more prominent as evidenced by the important role of Da Vinci's *The Last Supper* in both novels though much more emphasized and elaborated in Sierra's novel than in Brown's. While the action in Brown's novel takes place in modern times, *La cena secreta* is a historical novel in which Leonardo da Vinci plays a decisive role and is an essential character. It is important to bring to the fore that the relation between the two novels is one of affinity, and not one of influence. When *The Da Vinci Code* was published in 2003, Javier Sierra had been working on his novel for several years. However, this does not imply that the success of *La cena secreta* is not indebted to Brown's novel. Sierra explained to me:

> Johanna Castillo [agente literaria] leyó *La cena secreta* en Nueva York en una noche y decidió apostar por ella con un adelanto astronómico de 500.000 dólares. En este tiempo Simon & Schuster, antiguos editores de Dan Brown (publicaron todos sus libros, excepto *El código Da Vinci* que editó Random House con el éxito que conocemos), estaban buscando una obra con la que llenar el hueco dejado por Brown. (personal communication June 27, 2008)

> (Johanna Castillo [literary agent] read *The Secret Supper* in New York one night and decided to risk an astronomical advance of $500,000. At this time Dan Brown's previous publishers, Simon & Schuster [they published all his books except *The Da Vinci Code* which was published by Random House with well-known success], were looking for a work to fill the void left by Brown.)

According to Sierra, it was of utmost importance that:

> cuando me pidieron apoyo para las fases iniciales de marketing 'in house' (dentro de la Editorial) del libro, yo les envié un video profesional en el que, en inglés, yo mismo les presentaba el libro y les hablaba del alcance de la historia de *La cena secreta*. Aquel video, diferente a las grabaciones domésticas de autores frente a una cámara que estaban acostumbrados a ver, les animó y les convenció de que tenían un buen material en las manos.

> (When they asked for my support in the book's initial 'in house' marketing phases I sent them a professional video in English in which I presented the book and spoke of the historical significance of *The Secret Supper*. That video was different from the usual homemade recordings by other authors. It enticed them and convinced them that they had good material in their hands.)

Johanna Castillo's and Simon & Schuster's confidence in the novel was shared by the translator, none other than the writer and bibliophile Alberto Manguel, who without a doubt imbued the novel with his own prestige. It would not take long for their confidence to be justified for in spring of 2006, the novel was launched in the North American market with a print run of 370,000 copies. *La cena secreta* soon became an absolute success. It was the first book originally written in Spanish to be highly ranked on the *The New York Times* best-sellers list.

La sombra del viento and *La cena secreta* belong to a new subgenre distinguished as best seller, historical novel, or more specifically, religious thriller, revelation novel, or *thracul* (*thriller histórico religioso aventurero cultural*: cultural adventurous religious historical thriller).[4] Another thracul published in the United States that same spring with similarly impressive circulation was Matilde Asensi's *El último Catón* with a first print run of 100,000 copies. As with *La cena secreta*, it was received as a novel that emulates *The Da Vinci Code* despite the fact that Asensi's original version had been published in 2001, two years before Brown's novel. However, the comparison of *La cena secreta* and *El ultimo Catón* with *The Da Vinci Code* did not prove to be detrimental to the alleged (even though unauthentic) imitators, given that some North American critics judged Sierra and Asensi's novels to be superior narratives and better documented than Brown's.[5]

Ruiz Zafón, Sierra, and Asensi have opened up the international market for the Spanish thracul. Others writers have followed in their footsteps: Emilio Calderón (*El mapa del creador*), Esteban Martín and Andreu Carranza (*La clave Gaudí*), Juan Gómez-Jurado (*El espía de Dios*), and Ildefonso Falcones, whose novel *La catedral del mar* was launched in 2008 in the North American market with much success. It was received with great interest and emphasized as a serious novel, similar to, or even superior to Ken Follett's *Pillars of the Earth*. It was argued that "Follett merely describes the medieval mind-set to a modern audience; Falcones enters it, complete with its acceptance of brutality and embrace of religious sensibility" (*The Washington Post* 2008).

For lack of space, it is not feasible to go into depth here regarding the possible explications for the world success of the thracul. I limit myself to the lucid words of the Dutch philosopher Ger Groot who links the surprising popularity of the genre in the West to a sociocultural phenomenon of extraordinary scope:

> Religion has become secularized in a manner not foreseen by philosophers and sociologists. Religious beliefs have not been substituted by scientific ideas, nor has devotion been compensated by a hedonism lacking in metaphysical emotions. Religion has slipped into daily life. It is everywhere, barely visible, yet, commonplace.

Historical-religious novels—which trace back to Umberto Eco's founding novel of the genre, *The Name of the Rose*—are often read not as fictions, but as revelations. They divulge truths that confront the institutionalized dogma of Christian religions, and in particular Catholicism. They offer alternative histories and "secret" knowledge repressed during centuries of religious institutionalizations. In this way they concurrently satisfy religious, or if you prefer, metaphysical needs and inscribe themselves into the critical and individualistic discourse of modernity, combining the best of two worlds.

In what follows, I am interested in commenting on another question: how do we explain that it is precisely in Spain where so many well-versed authors in this new sub-genre are competing in the center of the world republic of letters? In the first place, it is necessary to comment on the professionalization of the Spanish editorial publishing world, which follows the North American model, by considering the sale of the product as more important than the product itself. The author loses the romantic aura of genius to be converted in an artisan, or if you prefer, an artist that should provide products that perform well in a market dominated by competition and profit. The author's words are no longer sacred by definition. They can or perhaps should be polished, adapted, crossed out, or further developed if the editor deems that such corrections will facilitate greater accessibility to readers.

The inception of Ildefonso Falcones' *La catedral del mar* illustrates that this may not only include the correction of minor details in the form of minimal editorial interventions. In 2002, he began to write a novel which he later revised in the Ateneo School of Writing. Subsequently, he sent his manuscript to six publishing houses and, thereafter, found out that no one was interested in his narrative debut. Through the mediation of a friend of a friend, his book was placed in the hands of literary agent Sandra Bruna, and through her, it reached Ana Liarás, editor at Grijalbo. Between the three of them they prepared his first novel which became a national, and later, an international best seller. As Sandra Bruna specifies: "([E]l libro) necesitaba retoques. Nosotras le recomendamos recortar unas sesenta páginas y mejorar las partes en las que flojeaba. Su editora colaboró también con él perfilando algunos personajes, simplificando episodios" (Azancot) ([The book] needed finishing touches. We recommended that sixty or so pages be reduced and that some weak sections of the novel be further developed. Its editor also collaborated in shaping certain characters and simplifying episodes). Falcones similarly characterizes the revision process: "Trabajamos mucho con el libro los tres, porque al recortar la extensión tuve que cambiar algo el argumento, di más empuje a algunos personajes, aunque sin alterar la trama" (Azancot) (All three of us worked a lot on the book because by reducing its total length I had to change the narrative somewhat, giving more force to some of the characters without altering the plot).

The big changes in the editorial world are illustrative of the great cultural change that has come about in a democratic Spain. The ostracism, self-complacency, and conservatism defended during centuries by dominant institutions gave way to openness, flexibility, and curiosity. It seems to me that the mentality of the contemporary Spaniard has much in common with its North American counterpart. Both feel an insistent and irresistible obsession to prove or justify their existence, to take the initiative, to show off, and to continuously renovate themselves. This may have its origin in the problematic link with the modern tradition of the Old World felt by both countries. To use a forceful term, both countries have a complex. North Americans have the sensation that their historical roots are short and incomplete, while Spaniards believe that theirs are politically incorrect due to the anomalous trajectory they traveled for centuries in a continent replete with modernization. The two countries feel, in some way, that they are handicapped Europeans. One could add that contemporary Spaniards are more than the new European brothers of the Americans due to Spain's profound historic roots.[6] This observation elucidates how authors such as Javier Sierra, Ildefonso Falcones, and Julia Navarro form part of a new generation that is able to take advantage of the best of both worlds: a new mentality of vitality, flexibility, and curiosity stimulated them to play with the historical and cultural discourses transmitted within the traditional model.

Moreover, today's readers, as Javier Sierra posits, "feel the need to return to a more magical perception of reality [. . .] Spain is a country with a rich history [. . .] and when it comes to looking for the origins of Western civilization, it is natural that all eyes turn to Europe and the Mediterranean, the very heart of where it all started" (Montejo). Tom Colchie, Ruiz Zafón's literary agent in the United States, adds yet another argument: "American literature is becoming less and less interesting as a direct result of the industrialization of literature through workshops. [. . .] This is pushing editors to look elsewhere for new, more exciting things" (Montejo).

Given the above discussion, I do not consider it to be an exaggeration to conclude that thanks to its best-selling authors, Spain is settling down in the world republic of letters. Given the success of thraculs, Spanish literature is finally living its long-awaited and anticipated international boom. This (r)evolution has hardly been a motive for the Spanish literary establishment to celebrate. Now that the best seller is news, literary critics, like it or not, have no choice but to review Carlos Ruiz Zafón's new novel, *El juego del ángel* (The Angel's Game) but, on the other hand, the literary press continues to close its doors to an author like Javier Sierra. The literary supplement of *El Mundo*, the daily to which Sierra periodically contributes, insists on not reviewing his novels. In the United States, however, thraculs are worthy of being commented on and reviewed with intent and dignity in such prestigious newspapers as *The New York Times*, *The Chicago Tribune*, *The Los Angeles Times*, and *The Washington Post*. It goes without saying that the less than generous treatment given to these authors in their own country is bothersome to them: "Aquí la literatura es un gueto de mediocridad y pretensión" (Here literature is a ghetto of mediocrity and pretentiousness), grumbled Carlos Ruiz Zafón during the 2008 Madrid Book Fair. (*El País* May 30, 2008). Even Arturo Pérez-Reverte is still bothered by the presumed elitism of Spanish literary critics despite his success in many foreign countries and regardless of the critical and academic recognition his work enjoys in Spain.[7]

It's not difficult to pass judgment on thraculs working from a certain critical-literary imaginary and institutionalized paradigms. I would add that this should not detract from the fact that authors such as Carlos Ruiz Zafón, Javier Sierra, Julia Navarro, and Matilde Asensi have broken barriers by inscribing Spanish letters at the center of the world republic of letters with the type of narrative that Pascale Casanova has denoted as "world fiction" (171). This is to say:

> Productions [that] have created a new composite measure of fictional modernity. Restored to current taste are all the techniques of the popular novel and the serial invented in the nineteenth century: between the covers of a single volume one can find a cloak-and-dagger drama, a detective novel, an adventure story, a tale of economic and political suspense, a travel narrative, a love story, a mythological account, even a novel within the novel. (171)

Departing from other criteria than the established ones, one could affirm that the horizon of the narrative of Javier Sierra and company is broader than that of much of the Spanish literature that is considered to be "serious." The thracul exemplifies the ease with which its authors incorporate scientific, historiographic, cultural, and literary knowledge in their novels. Given these characteristics, Spanish thracul authors have proven themselves to be capable of amassing literary capital that appears to be conquering and establishing a stable position in the center of the world republic of letters. This achievement is not to be underestimated, for it would be the first time since the Golden Age that a consistent and coherent Spanish literary corpus achieves such an accomplishment.

Notes

1. In 1926, an Italian translation of *Fortunata y Jacinta* was published as *Fortunata e Giacinta: Storia di due Donne maritate* (Firenze: Adriano Salani Editores); the first German edition, *Fortunata und Jacinta: 2 Geschichten von Ehefrauen* (Zürich: Manesse), was published in 1961.
2. The presence and prestige of Spanish American literature continued to be dependent in great measure to the consecrated values of the boom (García Márquez, Vargas Llosa, Fuentes). Only one new value competes with them in terms of success and presence (though not in literary prestige): Isabel Allende. As is well-known and was highlighted in Madrid's 2008 Book Fair (Cruz), post-boom literature has not secured the commercial success and literary prestige on the same scale as García Márquez and company. The most commented post-*boom* author is without a doubt Roberto Bolaño. Notwithstanding the numerous translations and critical commentary of his corpus, there is an abyss between the impact of his work and that of García Márquez et al.
3. Ruiz Zafón is also the author of four teen novels that have come to be known after the success of *La sombra del viento*: *El príncipe de la niebla* (1993), *El palacio de la medianoche* (1994), *Las luces de septiembre* (1995), and *Marina* (1999).
4. See also, among others, Ferrero, Galán, and Winston Manrique.
5. "Javier Sierra's take on Da Vinci is much sharper, more focused and more rewarding. This is partly because Sierra is a better writer and largely because his story makes more sense" (*New York Daily News* May 26, 2006); "Asensi's research is much better than Brown's, and her writing is better, too." (*The Calgary Herald* May 27, 2006).
6. In *El antiamericanismo español*, Alessandro Seregni affirms that, according to a 2004 survey, "the Spanish people, second to the Turks, sympathizes less with the United States" (277). John Hooper synthesizes some of the historical reasons for this rejection based on different ideological levels: "The US prompts grim historical memories among many Spaniards. Traditionalists recall that it was the US that put an end to the Spanish empire in 1898, wiped out its fleet and deprived it of Cuba, Puerto Rico and the Philippines. Progressives remember it was Washington that helped Franco out of his international isolation in exchange for military bases in Spain. And due to its close ties with Latin America, Spaniards have tended to be more aware than other Europeans of the ugly sides of US foreign policy there" (75–76). Above all, this resentment refers to the United States' political power and not necessarily to its mentality, way of life, or

North American culture, as stated by Hooper: "Spaniards tend not to expect from the state the sort of cushioning which is regarded as normal in the rest of Western Europe. They look astonished when you say it, but of all the societies in Europe, theirs is the one where attitudes to the role of the state are closest to those in the United States" (81).

7. See also Pérez-Reverte's speech delivered at the Second "Cita internacional de la literatura" celebrated in 2008 in Santillana del Mar, where there are two discursive arguments: a passionate praise for "classic" narrative and a vicious diatribe against certain literary ideals that dominated the era in which he published his first novels: "Durante algún tiempo se nos quiso imponer una idiotez victimista que, además, es mentira: la literatura difícil, minoritaria y poco leída era la única que valía la pena. La otra era prescindible y superficial, culpable de la facilona vulgaridad de contar cosas (como si contar cosas fuera fácil) y de ser bien acogida por el ciego y necio vulgo" (163) (For some time we were to be branded with victimism, which was a lie: difficult minority literature was read little, yet it was the only literature deemed worthwhile. The other was dispensable and superficial, guilty of narrating with improper simplicity [as if storytelling were easy], and of being accepted by the blind and vulgar). This speech is replete with spears thrown at representatives that follow a particular literary program: como "algunos pajilleros de la vacuidad inane, capaces de elogiar, o incluso de escribir, novelas cuyo fascinante argumento es, precisamente, la imposibilidad de escribir una novela" (169–70) (some of the idiotic shallow jerk-offs capable of praising or even writing novels, whose fascinating argument is precisely the impossibility of writing a novel). "Hablo de quienes olvidan, o ignoran, un principio elemental que ya apuntaba Stevenson: si un presunto novelista no tiene nada que contar, por muy bello estilo que maneje, lo mejor es que se calle. Que cierre la boca, que deje las saturadas mesas de novedades de las librerías en paz, y se vaya a hacer puñetas" (164) (I am speaking about those who forget or choose to ignore the basic principle that Stevenson called our attention to: if a would-be novelist had nothing to say, regardless of his stylistic beauty, it would be better that he not even open his mouth. He should keep it shut and refrain from adding weight to the already heavy and saturated bookstore shelves. Let him go to Hell). "Para saber qué siente un don Nadie recién divorciado viajando en metro no necesito leer trescientas páginas donde un pelmazo juega a ser novelista masturbando a la perdiz. Me basta con divorciarme y tomar el metro" (170) (I don't need to read 300 pages by a masturbating bore that plays novelist to know what it's like for a recently divorced Mr. Nobody to take the train. I'd rather divorce my wife and take the train).

Works Cited

Asensi, Matilde. *El último Catón*. Barcelona: Planeta, 2001.
Ayén, Xavi. "Radiografía de un éxito literario." *La Vanguardia* November 26, 2002.
Azancot, Nuria. "Genuino sabor americano: La búsqueda del best seller reinventa el oficio de editar en España." *El Cultural*. March 31, 2006.
Bada, Ricardo. "¿Es aburrida la literatura española?" *Quimera* 43: 12–17.

Brown, Dan. *The Da Vinci Code*. New York: Random House, 2003.
Calderón, Emilio. *El mapa del creador*. Barcelona: Roca, 2006.
Casanova, Pascale. *The World Republic of Letters*. Trans. M.B. DeBevoise. Cambridge: Harvard University Press, 2004.
Cruz, Juan. "Los 37 lectores de Borges." *El País*. June 14, 2008.
Falcones, Ildefonso. *La catedral del mar*. Barcelona: Grijalbo, 2006.
Fernández, Pura. "El pacto de Ulises: Pérez-Reverte circunda de nuevo el Mare Nostrum." *Dossier bestseller español* (2006) 41–47.
Ferrero, Jesús. "Novela de revelación." *El País*. September 2, 2006.
Follett, Ken. *Pillars of the Earth*. New York: Morrow, 1989.
Galán, Lola. "Y la fórmula es: Historia, emoción y laboratorio. La intriga y los enigmas religiosos se dan cita en las obras de la nueva generación de autores de 'best sellers' españoles." *El País*. May 21, 2006.
Gironella, José María. *Los cipreses creen en Dios*. Barcelona: Planeta, 1954.
———. "¿Por que el mundo desconoce la novela española?" *Estudios Americanos* 10 (1955): 139–66.
Gracia, Jordi. "Después de la tormenta, 1973–1982." *La llegada de los bárbaros: La recepción de la narrativa hispanoamericana en España, 1960–1981*. Ed. Joaquín Marco and Jordi Gracia. Barcelona: Edhasa, 2004. 153–63.
Grohmann, Alexis, and Maarten Steenmeijer. *Dossier bestseller español*. *Quimera* 273 (July–August 2006): 23–66.
Groot, Ger. "Nieuwe bijbels tegen de kerk." *Trouw*. December 23, 2006.
Hoenjet, Hans. "Geschiedenis van een kaskraker." *HP/De Tijd*. March 30, 2007.
Hooper, John. *The New Spaniards: Second Edition*. London: Penguin Books, 2006.
Iglesias Laguna, Antonio. *¿Por qué no se traduce la Literatura Española?* Madrid: Editora Nacional, 1964.
Manrique, Winston. "Dios se convierte en 'best seller': El revisionismo de los símbolos cristianos y novelas con trasfondo religioso llenan las librerías." *El País*. February 20, 2006.
———. "Enganchados al 'thriller' histórico." *El País*. February 22, 2007.
———. "La fórmula del secreto." *El País*. September 2, 2006.
Marco, Joaquín, and Jordi Gracia, eds. *La llegada de los bárbaros: La recepción de la narrativa hispanoamericana en España, 1960–1981*. Barcelona: Edhasa, 2004.
Marías, Javier. "Elke Wehr, traductora literaria." *El País*. July 5, 2008.
Martín, Esteban, and Andreu Carranza. *La clave Gaudí*. Barcelona: Plaza & Janés, 2007.
Montejo, Andrea. "Why They Do It Better: Spain and the Historical Novel." *Críticas*. January 6, 2007.
Muñoz Molina, Antonio. *Beatus Ille*. Barcelona: Seix Barral, 1986.
———. *Carlota Fainberg*. Madrid: Alfaguara, 1999.
———. *El invierno en Lisboa*. Barcelona: Seix Barral, 1987.
———. *El jinete polaco*. Barcelona: Planeta, 1991.
———. *Plenilunio*. Madrid: Alfaguara, 1997.
Ortiz-Griffin, Julia L. and William D. Griffin. *Spain and Portugal Today*. New York: Peter Lang, 2003.

Pérez Galdós, Benito. *Fortunata y Jacinta*. Edición de Francisco Caudet. Madrid: Cátedra, 1985.

———. "Prólogo." *La Regenta I*. Leopoldo Alas "Clarín." Edición de Gonzalo Sobejano. Madrid: Castalia, 1986.

Pérez-Reverte, Arturo. "La mochila de Jim Hawkins." *Lecciones y maestros: II Cita internacional de la literatura en español 16, 17 y 18 de junio de 2008*. Ed. Mario Vargas Llosa, Javier Marías, Arturo Pérez-Reverte. Fundación Santillana/Universidad Internacional Menéndez Pelayo, 2008.

———. *El sol de Breda*. Madrid: Alfaguara, 1998.

———. *La tabla de Flandes*. Madrid: Alfaguara, 1990.

Ruiz Zafón, Carlos. *El juego del ángel*. Barcelona: Planeta, 2008.

———. *La sombra del viento*. Barcelona: Planeta, 2001.

Sánchez Piñol, Albert. *La pell freda*. Barcelona: La Campana, 2002.

Seregni, Alessandro. *El antiamericanismo español*. Madrid: Síntesis, 2007.

Sierra, Javier. *La cena secreta*. Barcelona: Random House Mondadori, 2004.

Vargas Llosa, Mario. *La ciudad y los perros*. Barcelona: Seix Barral, 1963.

Part II

Institutions and Literatures

6

A Hispanist's View of Changing Institutions, or About Insects and Whales

Randolph D. Pope

> Perhaps you do not know that most of our professors live on Germany, England, the Orient, or the North like insects on a tree and like the insect they become an integral part of it, taking their worth from their subject.
> —Balzac's dedication of *Cousin Bette*

Balzac's dedication of his 1846 novel about envy and revenge, *Cousin Bette*, to Michele Angelo Cajetani, Prince of Téano, comes from a generous motivation, since it wishes to celebrate a scholar, a "learned commentator of Dante" who had revealed to him "the marvelous framework of ideas on which the greatest Italian poet constructed his work" (3), so the wondrous image of professors as insects on a tree is not meant negatively, but simply as a reminder that in a realist perspective our subject confers value to our work. The French novelist noted that Italy had not received from his compatriots the attention it merited, and we in turn observe that Spain is absent from the scholarly forest he envisions, while it includes Germany, England, the Orient, and even a generic North. Not much has changed in this aspect, since the literature from Spain still is often slighted in the accounts given in other, not Peninsular, European academic circles, as well as in the United States.[1]

Reading that "like the insect they become an integral part of it," I wonder about this "it" and its configuration by Balzac as a stately tree, allowing for the slow change of ages and generations, but still steady, rooted, and faithful to its designation as oak, willow, or ash. The changes in the government, political practice, and daily life in Spain, the strengthening of her diverse languages and regions, the changes in the means of production and distribution of literature, the internationalization of daily communication, the new approaches in literary theory, the reconfiguration of the offerings of academic departments in the US, and the relatively new conversion of universities into for-profit businesses, are just a few of the factors that have altered, or should have altered, not just the relation of Hispanists in the US to Spanish institutions—Spain being the *it* of which we are integral parts—but the concept itself of what constitutes an institution and how it operates. I will focus mainly on only one point of this changed nature: the increase in size of our subject matter and the strategies that have emerged to cope with it.

The production of literature, even if limited to the traditional genres of the novel, poetry, drama, and essay has by far exceeded the possibility of any one person to read it. In the yearly report of cultural activities produced by the Spanish Ministerio de Cultura we read that 69,893 books received an ISBN in 2002, while in the year 2006 the number had increased to 77,330. Of these, 13,063 in 2002 and 15,162 in 2006 were classified under "Creación literaria." If we assign a modest extension of 150 pages to each of these books for 2006 we are faced with 2,274,300 pages to enjoy reading. At an average rate of 2 minutes per page we would need 75,810 hours. Dedicating twelve hours a day to this task, it would take a conscientious critic 6,317.5 days, or over 17 years, to be able to make a statement about the creative books production of 2006, that included all the evidence, provided, of course that this critic had a portentous memory and had not dozed over a few thousand lines. Therefore, in order to practice our discipline we must arbitrarily slice away certain sectors, such as translations or science fiction. The problem, of course, is that both of those areas are a vital part of literature as it is experienced by real readers when they enter into any bookstore. As I am writing this essay in December of 2008, the website of the Casa del Libro reports that the bestsellers are two books by Stieg Larsson, three by Stephenie Meyer, and one each by John Boyne, José Saramago, Fernando Savater, Henning Mankel, and Tami Shem-Tov. Of these writers only one writes in Spanish, Savater, whose novel *La hermandad de la buena suerte* received the Premio Planeta 2008, but garners only three stars out of five from the six readers who have evaluated it, while Meyer's novels about vampires obtains a solid five stars from 289 visitors to the webpage. A student who focused exclusively on the literature originally written in Spanish would reduce his task to one tenth of the bestsellers but would probably reach wrong conclusions as to what are the true interests of most readers in Spain today.

The institutions that study literature have in general not kept up with the openness of the institutions that produce it. They remain disjointed into departments of Spanish, Italian, French, and so on, populated by specialists in Spanish, Italian, and French literature, each one clinging to a particular period, genre, or even author, seldom recognizing that the contemporary world is more fluid, interpenetrated, and dialogical than the strict and austere disciplines. It is true that much of the work done by individual scholars is interdisciplinary and comparative, but the pressure is to specialize in one or two areas, fearful of the superficial and anxious by the sheer vastness of the material. Furthermore, our institutions isolate their members by assigning to each of them a larger or smaller pigeonhole, seldom shared, and often competitive. When it is a labor of Sisyphus to keep up with the publications in one's own assigned area, how can one read with the free curiosity of real readers or novelists? If one spends most of the year surrounded by superb colleagues who, nevertheless, have very little knowledge of one's field, how are we to share information about what is worth while studying? Contacts become virtual, a sort of academic Second Life, brief encounters at conferences, sprinkles of e-mails, and a few exchanged offprints, while at home communication is either through the elevated region of theory, or the points of contact offered by the canonical figures. This insularity is intensified in Spanish universities by a level of inbreeding far surpassing most other nations.[2]

A different challenge for scholars is described in a 2002 article in *Publishers Weekly* as follows:

> Two buildings in Barcelona contain the world headquarters of Spanish publishing groups that largely determine what people will be reading tomorrow not only in Spain but in Argentina, Mexico, Chile, Colombia, and Venezuela, not to forget large swaths of Miami, Los Angeles, and New York City. One of these buildings belongs to Planeta, Spain's leading book publisher, and a contender for first place in the publishing cities of Latin America as well. The other to Bertelsmann—shared by Bertelmann Direct's astonishing Círculo de Lectores club (astonishing because it combines an upscale catalogue with a viable business) and the Random House Mondadori congeries of general trade houses. (Lottman 34)

"Largely determine" is a prudent way of expressing the enormous power of these publishing giants, since their capacity to determine absolutely is kept in check by numerous other publishing houses in Spain, Latin America, and now the United States. Nevertheless, as the subtitle of a 1997 article in *Publishers Weekly* affirmed, "The world-class Spanish-language groups with buying power are still based in Barcelona and Madrid" (Lottman 35). Grupo Planeta has forty publishing houses in twenty-eight countries, and recently bought the French publishing Group Editis for around 300 million dollars. When Planeta pushes Carlos Ruiz Zafón's *El juego del ángel*, or Mondadori Ken Follet's *World Without End*, in Spanish called *El mundo sin fin*, the results are tremendous and international. *El juego del angel*, as reported its website on December 1, 2008, "arrasa en Alemania" (is a huge hit in Germany), where it has become the number one bestseller, while Follet's novel follows his first one, *The Pillars of the Earth*, published in Spanish translation in 1989, and reportedly the most read novel by Spaniards according to the Federación del Gremio de Editores. Therefore, confidently, the first edition of *El mundo sin fin* was of 525,000 copies. In April of this year, another novel about cathedrals, *La catedral del mar* by Ildefonso Falcones, had already sold 1.7 million copies.

The international success of such novels would not be worrisome if their economic success were not accompanied by a phenomenon brought about by another proliferation with similar magnitude and international reach: the availability of books on the internet. I am sure that I am not the only professor to have noticed that students are reticent to buy textbooks when they can find ways to import them into their computers. Alan Deyermond in an engaging 2005 article, "The Books of SEMYR: Reflections on Scholarly Publishing in the New Millennium," laments the fact that in Great Britain both students and faculty are buying fewer books, relying on libraries, with a deleterious effect for scholarly publishing. He observes that scholarly books have very small and expensive runs because their only buyers are libraries. He concludes "that we are caught in a trap: fewer undergraduates buy books, fewer scholars buy a reasonable number of books, so print-runs go down, the unit cost production rises and so does the retail price, so still fewer books are bought, so the price goes up again, and publishers take the axe to whole sections of their lists" (180). He does have some hope, though: "The light comes from Spain, where students still buy books, scholars build substantial libraries, most publishers of academic books still charge reasonable prices, and several of them work closely with distinguished scholars" (181).

Unfortunately, a report published in *The Times Higher Education Supplement* on November 2005 reports that according to a poll by the Spanish Federation of Publishers, "Spanish university students buy an average of 1.9 books a year and 42 per cent did not buy a single text or reference book last year" (Warden 13). The article indicates that, according to interviews, an academic title would have garnered a printing of 3,500 copies ten years ago, but 1,000 copies would probably be too much today. In the meantime, Microsoft closed its digitalizing project after scanning 750,000 books and indexing 80 million journal articles, while Google's "Book Search" continues to add 3,000 items per day to its index, enticing readers with the suggestion to "search and preview millions of books from libraries and publishers worldwide." The bold "search" in the slogan highlights the possibility of focused searches that will make it unnecessary for students to read a book in its entirety. The enormous expansion of available material has made it necessary to refine the search mechanisms and reduce the time to find what one is looking for. There is no doubt that there is an advantage here, but also the crumbling away of slow reading, of becoming familiar with one book, and of enjoying the thought process of a writer.

In this context the most important new institution in our field to arise in the last decade is the Biblioteca Cervantes Virtual. I am sure we are all extremely grateful for its existence, but I observed this semester that a couple of my students, instead of reading the Cátedra editions which I had recommended, with excellent introduction and notes, were, instead, reading the first, nineteenth-century editions, not for the antiquarian joy, but for economy—and to carry one book less in their backpacks.

There is another reason for the daunting challenge faced today by a Hispanist: what is embraced as a text in the academic institution has expanded considerably. Today the lyrics of contemporary songs, comic books, films, television series, websites, and zines, for example, may appear as respectable topics in graduate courses. This means bringing into consideration numerous other institutions besides the literary publishing industry and its attached consumers and producers of critical commentary: the entertainment industry, the film industry, photography, fashion, publicity, architecture, the law, and so on. Scholars have now a larger tree, with numerous new branches, to explore. The wider opening of the frame is indicated by the designation Cultural Studies, yet there may be more enthusiasm for this appellation in the U.K. and the US than in Spain. It is worth remembering that, in the English-speaking academy, the influence of New Criticism and the attention to close reading created a narrowing of approach that never occurred in either Latin America or Spain, where the concern with politics, power, social class, and history has been constant and deep among students of literature. Classic philologists, medievalists, and students of the Renaissance, for example, have a centuries-old tradition of seeking to become familiar with a society, in all its manifestations, to place adequately the texts they are trying to understand, be they legal documents, epic poems, coins, medical treatises, colonial projects, theological disputes, funeral inscriptions, and so on. As in the previous cases I have described of attempts to narrow the field to make it manageable, we must take a closer look to understand what is actually going on.

If we take as an example the study of popular music, there is a long tradition of efforts to record and study it, not always in a comfortable relationship with what was considered as high literature. When Francisco Rodríguez Marín published in 1882 the five volumes of his *Cantos populares españoles*, he was inspired by the Romantic reverence for the national and the popular. He wanted to celebrate "la fecundísima musa del Pueblo" (I, 10, capitalized in the original), and he dedicated his magnus opus to Victor Hugo. It is instructive to observe how Rodríguez Marín believed that the study of popular songs had evolved:

> En efecto, Fernán Caballero, Lafuente y Alcántara, etc. [whom he saw as his predecessors] dada la relativa antigüedad de sus obras, no habían podido abarcar, en cuanto a las coplas populares, otros puntos de vista que los meramente literarios y estéticos; publicaron sus respectivas colecciones por creerlas curiosas y agradables, y nada más; pero desde entonces esos puntos de vista se han multiplicado, gracias a la rápida propagación de la nueva y amplísima ciencia llamada *Folk-Lore* (Saber popular), y hoy los cantos del Pueblo y las demás producciones del gran autor anónimo son considerados en todos los países como importantísimos elementos para diversidad de estudios que, nacidos ayer, se puede decir, adquieren de día en día notable desarrollo. (I, 11)

(In fact, Fernán Caballero, Lafuente y Alcántara, etc., given that their studies are relatively old, were not able to encompass, as far a popular songs went, other points of view than merely the literary and aesthetic. They published their respective collections because they found them worthy of attention and pleasant, but nothing more. Since then, though, those points of view have become more complex, thanks to the fast expansion of the new and now vast science called *Folk-Lore* (popular Wisdom), and today the songs of the People and all other productions of the anonymous author are considered in all countries as most important documents for many diverse studies that, very recently born, one could say, grow from day to day in importance.)

In several words of this perceptive paragraph we detect a telling difference with today: "meramente literarios" (only literary), "curiosas y agradables" (intriguing and pleasant), and "gran autor anónimo" (great anonymous author). While Rodríguez Marín does not share with previous scholars the same views as to why popular songs matter, he does appear confident about a general agreement as to what the term "literature" entails, connected more to the pleasant and the intriguing—popular literature as an old curiosity shop—than to the understanding of society, reserved to higher levels of literature. Of the two aspects that Horace distinguished in his seminal formulation of his *Ars poetica*, "aut prodesse volent aut delectare poetas" (poets wish either to instruct or to delight), we have come to see, with Rodríguez Marín, instruction in a great variety of texts, reconnecting, in fact, with an old tradition. If anything, in the academic handling of texts the accent has fallen so heavily on what they tell us about society, gender, power, social class, and so on—all valuable insights, without a doubt—that pleasure has been neglected. This is due to the institutionalization of literature—to the fact that it has become a subject matter to test and to select the best students in the gradual sifting of workers and citizens to which the university contributes. Who could ever assign a grade, and how could he, to the pleasure, joy, delight, and passion a student may or may not experience when reading a poem?[3] The accent is on detachment and critical, even ironic and suspicious, reading, as has been superbly well described by Rita Felski in her *Uses of Literature* when she states that "under the pressure of institutional demands" (4), "humanities scholars suffer from a terminal case of irony, driven by the uncontrollable urge to put everything in scare quotes" (2). This leaves little room for confessing to admiration, pleasure, and humble learning.

As for the "gran autor anónimo" (great anonymous author), he or she was, for Rodríguez Marín, what conferred depth and authenticity to the collected texts, which he called "joyas" (I, 10), jewels. Real authors, for the scholar, appear here as the miner for the shopper in an elegant store, who prefers that the miner who extracted the diamond or emerald be anonymous and faceless and not contaminate, with work, sweat, and lack of sophistication, the pure glow of the stone. The emergence of a signature, the threat of intellectual property, and the presence of the author brought an abrupt response from Rodríguez Marín:

[Hay algunas personas] aunque en muy escaso número, que han procurado sorprender mi buena fe, remitiéndome como cantos populares los insulsos productos de sus ingenios, aconsejadas evidentemente por el ridículo afán de ver impresos sus raquíticos engendros literarios. (I, 14)

([There are some people], even if few in number, who have tried to take advantage of my good faith, sending me as if they were popular songs the disgusting products of their talent, prompted evidently by the ridiculous desire to see in print their feeble and monstrous literary creations.)

I wonder how he imagined the gestation and birth of the texts he collected—texts, since he recorded only the lyrics and not the melodies—perhaps as a form of immaculate conception that has echoes and resonances in today's frequent espousal of the death of the author. One less thing to do. The pitiful and scandalous dearth of great biographies of the writers of Spain and Latin America compared with what is available for British, German or French authors, for example, is grounded on many complex reasons, but this efficient disconnect between producer and product, where language ends speaking by itself and about itself, has contributed to this result. I am aware, of course, of the profound reasons to undermine the Romantic illusion of an autarchic ruler over creative work, of a magically powerful signature, and of the spontaneity of inspiration. But I am also aware that there is some wisdom in the interest the general public feels for some writers and for how their craft can be inseparably intertwined with their lives. Many of us are interested not only in writing and reading, but also in the art of living. The institution of publishing exploits the existence of a person who has the aura of having written a popular work, and circulates not only images and interviews, but also the real bodies that are flown to book fairs, symposia, writers' conferences, literary prizes, and any occasion that serves to remind readers of their work. The academy keeps them at a respectful distance, perhaps inviting some to give a lecture, participate in a colloquium in their honor (mostly as spectators), as visiting professors or, exceptionally, as writers in residence. This is at least odd, yet one more way in which the academy handles the abundance of production and reduces it to a manageable universe that can then be evaluated, handled, and passed along to the students.

The divide between popular and high literature (whatever literature may be) proves hard to break down, in spite of the declarations of scholars about its collapse after modernism, especially when we see that the belief in a certain innocence and originality of the people seeps through. There seems to be always a stubborn opposition between the academic and the popular. We can find an example of this in a work that continues Rodríguez Marín's task over a century later, Margit Frenk Alatorre's 1987, *Corpus de la Antigua lírica popular hispánica (siglos XV a XVII)*:

> ¿Hasta qué punto, me pregunto yo ahora, era atinada—por no decir sensata—esa preocupación, esa búsqueda desesperada de la "autenticidad?" Las canciones que durante la Edad Media cantaban los campesinos y pastores, las hilanderas y panaderas, los marineros y pescadores, eran, sí, distintas de la poesía de corte trovadoresco que se practicaba en los palacios señoriales. Distintas y contrastantes, como que respondían por fuerza a una diferente, y aun opuesta, concepción de la vida. Pero entre ambos mundos existían contactos múltiples, que repercutieron en la cultura popular. Ésta no es, ni ha sido nunca, totalmente autónoma, sujeta como está al dominio de los poderosos. (vi)

(How appropriate—not to say wise—I ask myself today, was that concern, that desperate search for "authenticity?" Clearly the songs sung during the Middle Ages by peasants and shepherds, spinsters and bakers, sailors and fishermen were different from the poetry in a troubadour style found in the palaces of the overlords. They were different and a counterpoint, as was fitting necessarily to a different and even opposed conception of life. But between both worlds there were multiple points of contact, which had an effect on popular culture. Popular culture is not, and has never been, completely autonomous, submitted as it is to the authority of those in power.)

Frenk Alatorre places the pure origin in the Middle Ages and is baffled by the difficulty of separating in the centuries he studies, the "real" from its imitations: "Lo único que tenemos entre manos son los productos de la moda popularizante que se inició hacia fines del siglo XV" (vii) (We only have available the products of popularizing fashion which started towards the end of the 15th century). Nevertheless, he confesses that his mission is "la búsqueda de auténticas reliquias del folklore medieval" (vii) (the search for authentic relics of medieval folklore). This religious aura of the popular, its tinge of authenticity—almost like the aroma of a strong coffee waking us away from the overly literary, contrived, and just fashionable—has allowed the incorporation into the canonical of the *romancero*, dignified even more by its connection to the great epic poems.

In other European literatures the Nordic sagas and the songs of the Minnesingers have also found a reputable accommodation. From time to time a popular song manages to sneak into the world of the German classical Lied, which is assured of its respectability, not just by the grand piano, but also for the prevalent use of texts that began as literature and acquired their reputation in their written form before being enveloped in music. But just as very old objects may enter the museum, relatively old ones can acquire the patina of the antique, and just old ones can gain the grace of kitsch, new ones are sold at discount stores and disdained by the cognoscenti; when the lyric of songs is contemporary, the charm is usually gone. The response of an esteemed colleague, when I told him I was teaching a course on rock music and the contemporary Spanish novel, is characteristic: "That can be an excellent way of preparing them to later read some real literature." Given the daily pouring into the market and the airwaves of thousands of new songs, given the international reach of popular music, and taking into account that most of us usually encounter more of our students plugged into their earphones than absorbed into reading a book, the task of attentively listening to the words being sung, to ponder their possible beauty, insightfulness, and creativity is daunting, especially since they may come under the guise of rap, hard rock, rumba, regaetton, cante jondo, and many other varieties. One must grant that often it's the music that does the trick and the text is by itself insignificant, as when one "goodbye" in a Verdi opera can carry more passion than volumes of silent prose, or an invocation to the Virgin heard sung as her image passes by during a Holy Week Procession in Seville can send chills up one's spine. It is true that it could prove dispiriting to *read* the lyrics of some songs that sell over a million copies, such as the very popular "Malabares," included in the 2005 *Voces de ultrarumba* by Estopa, which starts out:

> Hoy me he levantado con un cable cruzado,
> tanto contacto me ha tocado el lado malo.
>
> (Today I got up with a crossed cable,
> So many contacts triggered my bad side.)

Granted that it is not Vallejo, Rimbaud, or Baudelaire, yet sang by David Muñoz, one of the two brothers who constitute the core of Estopa, it is a joyful, whimsical, and thoughtful song, a brisk portrait of waking up young in the great city, both with the deep unrest of a Sartrian character, who needs to be faced by a situation that will reveal his limits and force him out of his rut, and the ambition of Balzac's Rastignac, ready to take over Paris. The jumps from the bedroom to the as yet not described "meollo," to the streets and the bars flooded by anger and beer, force any listener to fill in the gaps with imagination, an ability that young people have in a much greater degree than is usually credited to them in the classroom. For me, at least, the lyrics to "Malabares" are as good as most of the poetry which appears in traditional anthologies, yet I do understand the anxiety of colleagues who already have to deal with other poems about waking up. Here are two examples. The first one is by Antonio Carvajal, a poem called "Maitines," from his book *Del viento en los jazmines*, which starts out with the following exhortation to wake up to the new day and merge with the dawn, which is white and pure ("alba" meaning "dawn" but also "white"):

> Alba, que es alba, amigo.
>
> Mientras el cielo ostenta
> —alba, que es alba, amigo—
> nimbos de alas, serena
> una oración de niños
> escala las secretas
> lindes del viento, sendas del suspiro.
>
> (Dawn, it is dawn, my friend.
>
> While the sky shows off
> —dawn, it is dawn, my friend—
> Nimbus clouds made of wings, a serene

Children's prayer
Climbs over the secret
Borders of the wind, paths of sighs.)

A similar note of awakening to the renewed fusion with a harmonious world, which can in turn become melodic words, can be found in a poem by Francisco Brines, "El regreso del mundo," which begins:

Abrir los ojos, después de que la noche
recluyera los astros en su amplia cueva rasa,
y ver, tras del cristal,
ya visibles los pájaros
en el fanal aún pálido del sol,
moviéndose en las ramas.
Y cantos que hacen mía la bóveda del aire.

(To open my eyes, after night
hid away its stars in her spacious smooth cave,
and to see, behind the windowpane,
already the birds made visible
by the still weak lantern of the sun,
moving among the branches.
And songs that make the air's vault mine.)

My point is not that one text is definitely superior to the others—there can be preferences here—but that they are similar only as far as their topic goes: all three describe waking up in the morning. And yet they are different in the place they occupy today *as poetry* within the institutional framing that creates its subject and therefore decides on what actually *is* poetry. It would be too much to ask from an anthologist of contemporary Spanish poetry to include, within her or his universe, for selection, all the lyrics of popular songs, even if some do make it into anthologies, especially well-known cases of crossover from popular music to literature, as the songs of Joaquín Sabina. Our practice has become to cordon out what originates in loud music and to privilege *suspiros* and *cantos*.

In my opinion, this is understandable, but a great loss. In the case of many relatively contemporary novels, readers who are not familiar with the many allusions to rock music which they contain will miss as much as someone who did not know mythology or had not read the Bible before reading Golden Age literature.[4] The depth of contextual referentiality has shifted, and, therefore, the street is often more astute than the academy in knowing how to read the new forms of literature. It is notable that the poems by Carvajal and Brines from which I quoted above appear in Cervantes Virtual's Portal de Poesía impeccably presented over a peaceful background that shows an empty boat stranded on a beach. The ability to copy the text has been blocked, and no provision has been made for comments. Estopa's "Malabares," instead, can be found at numerous places in the web, not only as a text easily copied, but also in an engaging performance offered in YouTube,[5] where one can read comments such as the following: "qee granDees!," "son la hostia xq aparte de ke son kanela en rama, son los tios la humildad personifikada," and "estopa tremendo, que letras mas buenas!!!!!" I would not mind students, even with this creative orthography, to express a similar enthusiasm when faced with their textbooks' poetry. When I tell them that they already like poetry and listen to it daily, they tend to look at me with the same surprise shown by Moliere's bourgeois gentleman when he was told he had spoken prose all his life, so far removed is to them the academic institution from the popular music industry.

Finally and briefly, since I am sure this matter is extensively treated elsewhere in this collection of essays, another institutional transformation has produced an expansion of offerings and a contraction of the field: the welcome affirmation within the Iberian Peninsula of regional and national literatures. There have always been a few notable writers in Galician and Catalan who have become well known beyond their linguistic region, such as Rosalia de Castro, Salvador Espriu or Mercè Rodoreda, but among the positive developments of the post-Franco years we have seen a notable increase in the protagonism of authors writing in these languages, as well as a wider distribution of their work, both in their original and in Spanish translations. A few examples in Galician are Suso de Toro and Manuel Rivas and, in Catalan, Montserrat Roig, Carme Riera, and the very impressive Imma Monsó. That the relationship with the regional roots are not uncontroversial or a settled matter can be seen in the following examples, presented more as symptomatic than as comprehensive.

In an excellent essay, Kirsty Hooper examines two novels by Galician women, *Memoria para Xoana* (2002) by Marica Campos and *Viajes con mi padre* (2003) by Luisa Castro. The first one is written in Galician and seeks to establish a genealogical continuity with six generations of Galician women. The second novel is written in Spanish and, as Hooper puts it, "is a very public symbol of her desire to avoid the potential pitfalls of being recognized and interpreted as a 'nationalist' or 'minority' writer" (Hooper 53). Hooper quotes Castro as making the following affirmation that expresses pithily the conflicted position in which Galician writers, and Catalan as well, can find themselves:

> I'm not a nationalist, or at least I'm a very moderate and pragmatic one. As an exclusive program it horrifies me. Galicia is a territory where several cultures coexist, the one that's expressed in Galician and the one expressed in Spanish. Any attempt to diminish this reality seems out of place to me. (Hooper 53)

The distinction between territory and culture is fundamental and frequently forgotten. If one is to give an account of the culture at any given time during the last decades in cities such as Santiago de Compostela, it would be irresponsible to neglect mentioning all the creative work taking place in Spanish, next to the one in Galician.

If, on the contrary, one is attempting to write a history of the culture in Galician language, the focus would narrow considerably and reasonably.

A similar phenomenon takes place in Catalonia, where authors, who were born in the region and have written in Spanish extensively and most admirably about it, need to be taken into account if one wishes to describe accurately the cultural life, for example, of Barcelona. Not to mention Marsé or Juan and Luis Goytisolo, all three important chroniclers of the city, would be a case of willful neglect of reality. On the other hand, there is a good case to be made to describe the trajectory of the literature written originally in Catalan. The difficult balancing act is to respect and admire the importance of literatures written in Galician or Catalan—and pay attention to the institutions that nurture it—without identifying it with the whole of the cultural activity taking place in Galicia and Catalonia. This is a task very much in progress, and for Hispanism, it means the new obligation of not making any statement about Spanish literature (as opposed to literature written in Spanish) that does not include a consideration of the important corpus written in Galician and Catalan.

A very similar situation—having to deal with literature written in different languages by citizens of the same country— is now encountered in the United States, where literature written in languages other than English, but by Americans, begins to be incorporated as part of what professors of United States' literature must know and consider. Shelley Fisher Fishkin, in her remarkable presidential address, "Crossroads of Cultures: The Transnational Turn in American Studies," given to the American Studies Association in November 2004, indicates that the concept of the nation as a relatively stable unit, geographically delimited and independent, must be replaced by one that sees "the inside and outside, domestic and foreign, national and international, as interpenetrating" (21), which is to say, to see the "nation as a participant in a global flow of people, ideas, texts, and products" (24). According to the census of 2000, Fishkin reminds us, that in the United States, "nearly one in five inhabitants speaks a language other than English at home" (27). This does not mean that the nation which grants passports and is vigilant of its frontiers has lost the sentimental allegiance of most of its inhabitants, or that they will not cheer for their team during the Olympics.[6] A recent faux pas by the Nobel Prize winner Jose Saramago demonstrates it, since he received an irate reply by the public when he proposed that Portugal become part of Spain. "Não vale a pena armar-me profeta,"Saramago affirmed, but continued, nevertheless, to make a prophetic pronouncement: "Mas acho que acabaremos por integrarnos ... Não deixaríamos de falar português, não deixaríamos de escrever a nossa lengua e certamente com dez milhões de habitantes teríamos tudo a ganhar em desenvolvimento nesse tipo de aproximação e de integração territorial, administrativa e estructural" (qtd. in Céu) (In my opinion we will end up integrating ... We would not stop speaking Portuguese, we would not cease writing in our language, and definitely, with ten million inhabitants, we would have everything to win in development from such approximation and territorial integration, administrative and structural). Spain, he mused, would probably have to change its name to Iberia. Needless to say, his proposal found no supporters and some of the published replies accused him of traitor and madness. And yet it is true that Saramago now lives in Spain, on Lanzarote in the Canary Islands, after a tussle with some of his Portuguese compatriots when the Under Secretary of State attempted to prevent one of his novels, *O evangelho segundo Jesus Christo* (1991) (The Gospel According to Jesus Christ) from participating in the European Union literary prize, Ariosto. European frontiers have become more fluid and movement of citizens has brought greater integration. The highly amusing study by Robert and Isabelle Tombs of the long rivalry between England and France, *That Sweet Enemy*, notices when looking at the most recent period that there has been a real novelty. It is not, they affirm, tourism to each others countries, even if the number of visitors has escalated: "In 2000, 11.9 million Britons—one in five!—spent on average a week in France, and 3 million French a long weekend in Britain" (Tombs 654). What is new is the number of people taking residence abroad, since "by the end of 2000 some 74,000 adult Britons held *cartes de séjour* giving them the right to work in France, an increase of a quarter in ten years" (Tombs 654). Around 600,000 houses were estimated to be owned in France by Britons in recent years. Traffic has hardly been in only one direction: "For the first time ever, there were more French in Britain than British in France. French consulates registered 91,500 French citizens resident—an increase of 250 per cent in ten years. The real number, however, was estimated to be around 300,000" (Tombs 654). The point here is that tourism and foreign residents are not just Spanish issues (or American ones), but part of a much more interconnected world. Among the consequences is that it has become possible, in a more routine way, to conceive of the literature of a country as being multilingual. In the year 2000, Harvard Professors Marc Shell and Werner Sollors published in NYU Press *The Multilingual Anthology of American Literature: A Reader of Original Texts with English Translations*, which includes works, among others, in Arabic, French, German, Lenape (the language spoken by Native Americans living along the Delaware river), Norwegian, Russian, Spanish, and Welsh. Similarly, in 2005, Javier Gómez-Montero published in Madrid *Cuando va a la ciudad, mi Poesía: Das Gedicht und die Stadt*, an anthology with German translations of poems originally published in Basque, Catalan, Galician, and Spanish. In the same vein, one of the notable books of 2007 was a reedition by Almuzara of a book originally published by Plaza & Janés in 2001, but which at that time was given little attention. It was a pseudo-memoir written by a longtime resident of Spain, born in Great Britain but now a Spanish citizen, and a very well-known historian, Ian Gibson: *Viento del sur: Memorias apócrifas de un inglés salvado por España*. In an interview, Gibson attempts to wave away the national issue: "Le diré que, como Lorca, odio los nacionalismos y las fronteras y las banderas y los himnos regionales. No me siento español, es imposible, aunque, claro, tengo la nacionalidad española" (Arriazu) (I'll tell you that, as Lorca, I hate nationalisms and frontiers and flags and regional hymns. I don't feel a Spaniard, that's impossible, even if, of course, I do have the Spanish nationality). In spite of that, he wrote the book in Spanish and is not interested in an English translation. Who should study his work, professors of English or of Spanish? This is far from an idle question and the territorial disputes include the pattern of incorporation and rejection we have found repeated in this study. For example, English departments in the United States wish to teach Latino literature, but then tend to reduce it to the sector written in English. Spanish departments would like to teach it, but focus mostly on the part written in Spanish. So the result is fragmentation and the creation of new units that can concentrate on this field, mostly stressing one or the other language. What place does Catalan, Galician or even Portuguese play in departments of Hispanic Studies (or Spanish, or Romance Languages, or Foreign Languages) in the United States? The situation is murky and the non-Spanish languages of the Iberian Peninsula usually depend on a few people to sustain them.

While the expansion of our subject matter, if it is the literature of Spain, should include works written in Catalan and Galician (the case of Basque is harder to make, given that extremely few academics housed in these departments can read it, but ideally it should also be incorporated), the test of how real this more capacious configuration has become is the utilization in published articles of secondary literature in languages other than Spanish. When we begin to see frequent references in articles about Galician writers to Galician critics, philosophers, historians, and newspapers we will have crossed a threshold that we are far from even approaching today. Similarly, given the extraordinarily rich and sophisticated amount of published works in Catalan we would expect more of them to be quoted in bibliographies and occupy their rightful place in the authoritative realm of footnotes. (There are no references to secondary literature in Galician or Catalan in this essay.)

With the addition of so much material to the national literatures, the academic institution has had to make new choices and, probably, unconsciously and in good spirit, has become enthralled with the synchronic vision of its subject, now an ever expanding archipelago or a frantic, rhizomatic vine more than a gigantic and stable tree. Courses with a diachronic configuration have receded and been replaced by seminars dedicated to a topic or a theory. *Inside Higher Education* reported on December 8 that Harvard was planning to drop its standard English literature survey courses and replace them with a set of four seminars. This is one way to prevent inflation of subject matter, even if not of grades (Redden). (I was told by a Harvard student that the survey courses, since they are large classes, expose many students to a dreaded B, while the new seminars with 25 students and a manageable trimmed-back topic will allow for more predictable A's).

Walter Truett Anderson, the editor of *The Truth about the Truth: De-Confusing and Re-Constructing the Postmodern World*, ends his upbeat introduction with the following statement:

> This time is, for all its jangle, complexity and dissonance, a moment of great beauty and opportunity. We glimpse new ways of thinking about ourselves, new possibilities for coexisting with others—even profoundly different others. We begin to feel a sense of ownership of our worldviews and identities. (11)

I am as grateful as Anderson for living within contemporary changing institutions, but my feeling is much less sanguine about my capacity as a scholarly insect to own my worldviews and identities in this vast process of expansion and subtractions. I feel more like Captain Ahab entangled by his own passion to a magnificent and ultimately unpredictable Moby Dick, which grows larger and more unmanageable by the day.

Notes

1. The neglect of Spain in scholarly journals abroad is not reduced to literature. Adrian Shubert reports that "the historical profession in the English-speaking world, and especially in North America, has a seriously truncated view of what constitutes Europe. Basically, the continent is reduced to Germany and France, with Russia and England, but not the UK, included or not depending on the structure of individual history departments" (358).
2. See Shubert 362 for a brief description of this inbreeding to which he attributes the lack of interest of Spanish historians to go beyond the boundaries of their language and country. There is a disquieting selection of articles about the Spanish university at *www.um.es/gqo/uni3Prensa.htm*.
3. I have written about the loss of the enjoyment of literature when it becomes one more discipline in "El hispanismo dionisíaco." See also on this topic, Luisa Elena Delgado's "El hispanismo ensimismado."
4. For a more extended consideration of the importance of popular music, especially rock, for the contemporary novel, see the book *Generation X Rocks: Contemporary Peninsular Fiction, Film and Rock Culture*, which I edited with Christine Henseler.
5. *www.youtube.com/watch?v=aQxkvrswj_8*.
6. For the very positive view of their nation that most people still hold in Spain, as opposed to the more critical view of the elites, see the well-grounded and convincing essay by Paloma Aguilar and Carsten Humlebaek, "Collective Memory and National Identity in the Spanish Democracy."

Works Cited

Aguilar, Paloma, and Carsten Humlebaek. "Collective Memory and National Identity in the Spanish Democracy." *History and Memory* 14 (2002): 121–64.

Anderson, Walter Truett. *The Truth about the Truth: De-Confusing and Re-Constructing the Postmodern World*. New York: Penguin, 1995.

Arriazu, Ascen. "Entrevista con Ian Gibson." *blogs.nabarreria.com/ascenarriazu/bposts/entrevista-con-ian-gibson*.

Balzac, Honoré de. *Cousin Bette*. Trans. Sylvia Raphael. Oxford: Oxford Classics, 1992.

Brines, Francisco. "El regreso del mundo." *www.cervantesvirtual.com/portal/poesia*

/verfoto.formato?foto=/portal/poesia/brines/elregreso.gif&autor=Francisco+Brines&texto=El+R
egreso+del+Mundo&ref=8711. Accessed October 4, 2009.

Carvajal, Antonio. "Maitines." *www.cervantesvirtual.com/portal/poesia/verfoto.formato?
foto=/portal/poesia/carvajal/maitines.gif&autor=Antonio+Carvajal&texto=Maitines&ref=91
29&enlace=carvajal*. Accessed October 4, 2009.

Céu e Silva, João. "Não sou profeta," *Diário de Notícias* (Lisboa). July 15, 2007. *dn.sapo.pt/
2007/07/15/artes/nao_profeta_portugal_acabara_integra.html*.

Delgado, Luisa Elena. "El hispanismo ensimismado." *Olivar: Revista de Literatura y Cultura
Españolas* 9 (2008): 95–99.

Deyermond, Alan. "The Books of SEMYR: Reflections on Scholarly Publishing in the New
Millennium." *Hispanic Research Journal* 6 (2005): 179–86.

Estopa. *www.estopa.net/letras/letras-cd-la-voces-de-ultrarumba/malabares/*. Accessed October 4,
2009.

Falcones, Ildefonso. *La catedral del mar*. Barcelona: Grijalbo, 2006.

Felski, Rita. *Uses of Literature*. Malden: Blackwell Publishing, 2008.

Fishkin, Shelley Fisher. "Crossroads of Cultures: The Transnational Turn in American
Studies. Presidential Address to the American Studies Association, November 12, 2004."
American Quarterly 57 (2005): 17–57.

Follett, Ken. *Un mundo sin fin*. Trans. Anuvela. Barcelona: Random House Mondadori,
2008.

Frenk Alatorre, Margit. *Corpus de la antigua lírica popular hispánica (siglos XV a XVII)*.
Madrid: Castalia, 1987.

Gibson, Ian. *Viento del sur: Memorias apócrifas de un inglés salvado por España*. 2nd ed.
Cordoba: Almuzara, 2007.

Gómez-Montero, Javier. *Cuando va a la ciudad, mi Poesía: Das Gedicht und die Stadt*.
Madrid: Sial, 2005.

Henseler, Christine, and Randolph D. Pope. *Generation X Rocks: Contemporary Peninsular
Fiction, Film and Rock Culture*. Hispanic Issues Vol. 33. Vanderbilt University Press,
2007.

Hooper, Kirsty. "Alternative Geneaologies?: History and the Dilemma of 'Origin' in Two
Recent Novels by Galician Women." *Arizona Journal of Hispanic Cultural Studies* 10
(2006): 45–58.

Lottman, Herbert R. "Barcelona: The Translation Market in Spain's Trade Capital." *Publishers
Weekly* (December 9, 2002): 28–38.

———. "In Spain, Rights Make Might." *Publishers Weekly* (June 30, 1997): 35–48.

Merino, Ana. *El comic hispánico*. Madrid: Cátedra, 2003.

Ministerio de Cultura de España. *Anuario de Estadísticas Culturales. www.mcu.es/estadisticas/
MC/NAEC/index.html*. Accessed October 4, 2009.

Pope, Randolph D. "El Hispanismo dionisíaco." *Lateral: Revista de Cultura* 106 (2003): 6.

———. "El Hispanismo dionisíaco." *Olivar: Revista de Literatura y Cultura Españolas* 9
(2008): 91–94.

Rodríguez Marín, Francisco. *Cantos populares españoles*. 5 vols. Madrid: Atlas, 1882.

Ruiz Zafón, Carlos. *El juego del ángel*. Barcelona: Planeta, 2008.

Saramago, José. *O evangelho segundo Jesus Christo*. Lisboa: Caminho, 1991.

Savater, Fernando. *La hermandad de la buena suerte*. Barcelona: Planeta, 2008.

Shell, Marc, and Werner Sollors. *The Multilingual Anthology of American Literature: A Reader of Original Texts with English Translations*. New York: New York University Press, 2000.

Shubert, Adrian. "Spanish Historians and English-Speaking Scholarship." *Social History* 29 (2004): 358–63.

Redden, Elizabeth. "English, Redefined at Harvard." *Inside Higher Ed*. Accessed December 8, 2008.

Tombs, Robert, and Isabelle Tombs. *That Sweet Enemy: The French and the British from the Sun King to the Present*. New York: Knopf, 2007.

Warden, Rebecca. "Bookish Scholars on Wane in Spain." *The Times Higher Education Supplement* (November 25, 2005): 13.

7

Political Autonomy and Literary Institutionalization in Galicia

Dolores Vilavedra

The so-called "transition period" to democracy began in Galicia, as in the rest of Spain, after the death of Franco in 1975, although there is little consensus about the chronological order of an intrinsically labile and diffuse phenomenon (Vilavedra, "Unha achega ao discurso narrativo"). Some scholars insist that the beginning of the period goes back as far as 1962 (when Franco's government applied to begin negotiations with the EEC for possible integration in the European Common Market), or to 1968, because of the consequences that the 1968 uprising in France in May of that year had on Spain; others consider that the period began in 1973, with the car bombing assassination of General Carrero Blanco, successor *in pectore* of the dictator. The end of the transition period is considered to have occurred sometime between the failed coup d'état of 1981, and the socialist victory in the 1982 election. However, the timing that I propose (Vilavedra, *Historia da literatura galega*) for the last decades of Galician literary history establishes a cutoff point in 1980, for several reasons.

Firstly, because of the scant involvement of Galicia in the historical-political process (the transition), which was to a certain extent observed from a distance. At the time, Spain was immersed in the task of "inventing" (Fusi) a new national identity that would offer—as an alternative to the disaccredited Francoist Spanishness—a legitimization of political autonomy for regions in terms of ethnicity, to the bewilderment of nationalist sectors in Galicia, Catalonia, and the Basque Country, who once again saw their signs of identity alienated by the central government. Throughout this process, the idea of a certain degree of peripheralization would take hold within Galicia—not only in terms of geographical position but also as regards the marginal position in the public sphere of the new Spanish state, which isolated the region from the dynamics of the transition, which at the time were not perceived to be significant. This explains the survival until the present day of the power structure headed by *caciques* (in some municipalities in Galicia the mayor has held that position for 30 years) and the presence, in the high hierarchies of the autonomous government, of survivors from Franco's regime, notably Manuel Fraga, who was president of the Autonomous Government of Galicia between 1989 and 2005, and had served as a minister in Franco's government for several years. Thus, the idea that the Transition has still not finished (Tusell) is more evident in Galicia than in any other part of Spain.

Secondly, the timeframe I suggest is supported by the fact that the Galician Statute of Autonomy was passed in December 1980, and came into force some months later. The denomination that I propose to refer to the literature of this era as "postautonomy" should now begin to make sense. On one hand, because the repercussions that the actions of the State had on all things related to the self-perception of Galician identity (individual and collective)—and the symbolic codification of this perception—were much wider and deeper than those produced in their day by the death of the dictator, amongst other reasons because the phenomenon was produced from within Galician society itself. Literature, which at that time was a privileged instrument for carrying out this codification, was obliged to assume new responsibilities and, at the same time, to compete and share this task with other media such as TVG (Galician Television). On the other hand, the designation of the literature of this time as "postautonomous" makes sense because the passing, in 1983, of the Law of Linguistic Normalization established the legal framework for the process of institutionalization of the Galician literary system, which was essential for its support and consolidation in a new model of society in which arbitrariness and militancy, until then the foundations on which the precarious structure of Galician literature had been built, were now of little importance. The market took on the function of cultural arbiter and several new rules of play had to be agreed on, among them those which were meant to widen the readership. This was the main challenge that the Galician literary system of the democracy had to meet, and to a large extent it would determine the routes by which its expansion was to be produced in the following decades.

It must be noted that the years between 1975 and 1980 were a period of vacillation, in which Galician society had to assimilate multiple and vertiginous changes. In literature, works which had been written several years earlier were published then, such as *Antón e os inocentes* by Xosé Luís Méndez Ferrín, published in 1976, although written in 1970. Such was also the case with works written by authors who had lived in exile (*O silencio redimido* by Silvio Santiago, written in the 1960s, was published posthumously in 1976), and many classics (by Castelao, Blanco Amor, Fole . . .) were re-published, in accordance with an overall policy of recovering the cultural memory of Galician society. However, in general all of the analysts of this era (González-Millán) agree on the slowness of the process of the quantitative and qualitative dynamization of literary production.

I will look briefly at some of the parameters that define the process of institutionalization of the Galician literary system, which has taken place in parallel with the expansion of Galician-language publishing industry. In the last three decades, Galician literature has ceased to be published and marketed almost exclusively by the historical *Editorial Galaxia*, an unusual publishing house whose main resources are the royalties generated by classic works, and which does not share profits. Today, an increasing number of intermediary agents have become players in this industry. By the end of 2007, there were forty-two companies included in the list of the Galician Association of Publishers (although the Galician Federation of Booksellers deals with almost one hundred and forty editorial enterprises). For a country with fewer than 3,000,000 inhabitants and whose reading population is not exactly the most numerous in Europe, this figure seems to be excessive. The expansion was initially favoured by the demand from schools for both textbooks and literary works of required reading, which made publishing in Galician a tempting business once the Law of Linguistic Normalization (which was aimed at regulating the teaching of, and in, the Galician language) came into force. The hypothetical benefits in terms of literary quality that may be derived from such a competitive scenario have not materialised. Moreover, the excessive number of books that has saturated the market with low-quality products, has frustrated the expectations of many readers and has distanced them from Galician literature. At present, with some 1,200 books published yearly, specialization appears to be the best option, although the norm is an abundance of tiny businesses, often run by one person, whose products are almost invisible and who only survive thanks to the protectionism of the government. As regards literary publishing, the sector is led by four or five businesses[1] that compete with each other to convert their authors into authority figures.

This protectionism has almost always been understood as interventionism, and its most visible consequence has been the proliferation of prizes organized and financed by public institutions (especially councils), which consider such prizes a risk-free investment in cultural legitimacy, profitable in terms of earning symbolic capital from *galleguistas* (supporters of Galician autonomy). Therefore, although in the 1980s and 1990s, the prizes were essential for the public and media-led promotion of Galician literature, they are not always reliable indicators of quality. However, taking these prizes into account is fundamental for understanding the tensions among genres for conquering the hegemony of the literary space. This has been especially noticeable in the rivalry between poetry, which is considered a foundational form, and narrative, which appeared to be an essential instrument in the normalization and modernization of Galician literature. As a result, the *Premio Xerais*, first organized in 1984 by *Editorial Xerais*, and possibly the best known prize offered in Galician narrative, indicates under the slogan "the force of the readers" the new literary agents' interest in dealing with an ever more diverse public.

The attempts to impose a degree of professionalism on the various agents involved in the process of literary production and reception should be interpreted as steps towards institutionalization, which appeared essential to ensure the autonomy of the literary discourse and to liberate it from the resistant and vindicatory role that it had played until 1980. Thus, the Association of Writers in the Galician language was formed in 1980 in order to represent and defend the interests of this group. Interestingly, the Galician Federation of Booksellers had already been functioning since

1976. It was the first of its kind to be formed, and indicated the symbolic value of books in Galicia.

Changes in the image and the social function of the different literary bodies are slow to take place and are not free from tensions and contradictions. Thus, as literature reaches a certain level of institutionalization, the book ceases to be an instrument of cultural and political normalization and becomes a consumer object. However, at the end of the 1980s, several publishers continued to be considered as "cultural activists" and their businesses were deemed to be "cultural, not mercantile" (González-Millán 82–83); as regards the writers group, in their III Congress, celebrated in 1995, they continued defining themselves as "a normalizing group" called on to "avoid all pretension of neutrality."[2] The reformulation of the public image of the writer, limited in his/her responsibilities as the voice of the collective identity—to the extent that the responsibilities were shared with other social agents—was fostered by a certain consciousness of generational rupture, produced at the beginning of the 1980s, after the successive disappearance of those who were the indisputable reference figures in the Galician literary sphere. Ramón Otero Pedrayo, Luís Seoane, Eduardo Blanco Amor, Celso Emilio Ferreiro, Álvaro Cunqueiro, Rafael Dieste, and Ánxel Fole all died between 1976 and 1986, leading to rapid changes in the hierarchy. This explains the vertiginous rise of two authors as different as Carlos Casares and Xosé Luís Méndez Ferrín, who were involuntarily promoted to the category of canonical writers. Both were to undertake this role in a complex and discrete manner, for several reasons: firstly, because of their relative youth (Ferrín was born in 1938, Casares in 1941), in a society as gerontocratic as the Galician one; secondly because of the political commitment maintained by both. Casares worked within the establishment, as an independent member of parliament on the lists of the Spanish Socialist Party in the first Galician government. He also dedicated a large part of his time to publishing and to literary journalism. Unlike Casares, Ferrín was on the margins of the system, as he was committed to the radical nationalism of the left. Yet, because he was always ambiguous as regards his narrative works,[3] he managed to separate himself from the model of a professional writer: he asserted that he was "a teacher who writes" and is presently recognised more as a poet than as a narrator. If to all of this we add that these authors opted to develop very different literary trajectories, outside of fashions and trends, we can better understand the difficulties that the literary system had in placing them in the authoritative positions and their reluctance in occupying such positions. Perhaps this, and the sudden death of Casares in 2002, helps to explain the rapid canonization in the 1990s of two young narrative writers, Suso de Toro and Manuel Rivas (born in 1956 and 1957, respectively), while reserving the role of patriarch of Galician literature for Ferrín. The fact that Ferrín was recently (in 2008) awarded the first *Premio Nacional de Literatura* (National Prize for Literature) instituted by the Galician Government, and the active role that he has played since joining the Galician Royal Academy, have contributed to emphasize this patriarchal image.

As regards the diffusion and analysis of Galician literature, the situation has been, and continues to be, paradoxical. The are numerous specialized platforms in Galicia, related to a greater or lesser degree to academic fields, which arose in order to articulate an autonomous field of meta-literary reflection, but they are few in number (and are unstable and scarcely visible). This obviously makes it difficult to break with the almost endemic elitism of Galician literature, asphyxiated within a highly endogamous and minority cycle of production-reception. The Web helps mitigate this lack of information and divulgation, but the contents available often lack academic rigor. A good example of the importance of these public spaces is the fact that fundamental debates have been developed around the concept of Galician literature, its limits, priorities, and deficiencies, essential in a process such as that which has taken place in Galicia over the last decades, a time which witnessed a radically new concept of the literary phenomenon. We will see how this has developed in each of the different genres.

Poetry

What has happened with this genre provides a good example of the tensions that surrounded the progressive articulation of the Galician literary field. If, as we shall see, a criterion that we can call "functional" was imposed onto narrative (with the aim of reaching new readers), in the 1980s, the criterion of immanency was applied in poetry, apparently on the basis of the literary quality of the texts, although this is not sufficient to explain the rapid canonization of a generation of poets who applied themselves with enthusiasm and relative success to the task of disseminating their works beyond the usual limits imposed on Galician literature by the language, and whose poetry was rapidly translated and anthologized.[4]

The aim of these writers was the construction of an autonomous poetic discourse, with its own internal dialect and that conversed, without intermediaries, with the surrounding cultures. Their literary project, necessarily elitist, put aside the ideological commitments that had burdened Galician poetry. They attempted to apply a kind of shock therapy that consisted of high doses of formal rigour compatible with a concern for developing a cultivated register (let us recall that in the 1980s, the Galician language was undergoing a process of normalization and regulation), assimilation of the European and North American literary tradition, semantic density created from a wide and impenetrable source of cultural references of all types (musical, philosophical, pictorial, etc.), and incorporation of eroticism, until then rarely seen in Galician poetry. What prevailed was an enunciative perspective dominated by the "I," which aimed to impose itself as an alternative to the "we" that characterized social poetry.

The success of the group was received in different ways by critics, whose responses varied from consideration of the period as a marathon that enabled Galician poetry to recover lost time and to reach a certain level of literary normality (if such a thing exists), to those who judged this time often referred to by others as the "golden decade" of the 1980s as a straitjacket that stagnated the genre and prevented it from evolving. If the latter was the case, then it must have lasted a short time. The fact that almost all the members of this generation of poets are included today amongst the great voices of Galician poetry is not a coincidence. Rather, it is an indication that their project of renewal had a solid base and was approached from a position of creative honesty, which has allowed writers such as Miguel Anxo Fernán Vello, Ramiro Fonte, Xavier Seoane, Manuel Forcadela, Xavier Rodríguez Baixeras, and Xosé Mª Álvarez Cáccamo to continue evolving along individual routes.

This generation of the 1990s had to open up a pathway in a space occupied by writers not much older than themselves, but who had been quickly and efficiently canonized. To do this they opted, on one hand for a total rupture with their immediate predecessors, and on the other for the development of a discursive model, with a well differentiated aesthetics, which made them visible as a collective. Santiago de Compostela recovered its position as the nerve centre of poetic activity, which it had lost in the 1980s to Vigo and A. Coruña. Moreover, unusual publishing initiatives proliferated in the Galician capital (cooperatives, amateur publishers . . .) and recitals became the new ideal formula for a younger public, seeking to recover poetry from conventional spaces and take it to popular venues. Thus, pubs, public squares, and festivals of all types admitted an army of enthusiasts, often organized by literary groups with different vocations, from the civil commitment of the *Batallón Literario* on the *Costa da Morte* to the devastating irony of the Ronseltz group.

If the total break to which I referred to earlier can be summarized by "kill the father. Cut him up and bury him in quicklime"[5] as suggested by the poet Rafa Villar, the new socioliterary model was developed from the conception of poetry as communicative art, which immediately translated in a formal departure from baroquization, recovery of the collective enunciation and opening up of the poetic space to the new conflicts of the end of the century and to the possible responses: anti-militarism, environmentalism, and feminism. In accordance with this desire, narrativity and polyphony were imposed as formulae for textual expansion. As regards "kill the father," hermeneutic development would also take place through the subversive re-reading by the new poets of their own traditionally known myths as well as universally known ones; this task of "re-vision" (González Fernández 32) was led by the poets who aimed to reconstruct a genealogy of their own references which abound with Penelopes and Antigones, but also Lolitas. Thus, as Helena González states (in a work that is essential for the study of Galician poetry written by women in recent decades), "the women decided to show themselves as rebels;" (31) hers is "a new retrospective look that searches in history not for model women (who represent equality), but for women who break with convention, who are indomitable and rebellious" (González Fernández 31–32).

Without a doubt, this has been the great contribution of the generation of the 1990s to Galician poetry. Beyond the different postmodern experiments, of the suggestive poetic fictions inspired in the everyday or in the oneiric world, of the minimalist contention, the 1990s involved the definitive re-appropriation on the part of the poets of an imaginary discourse and a personal discourse, characterized furthermore by a surprising variety of repertoires only partially explained by the different ages of the writers who joined in resolutely in the creation of poetry. The veteran Mª Xosé Queizán published in 1991 her first book of poems, *Metáfora da metáfora*, at the age of 52; Chus Pato did the same at 36 (*Uránia*, 1991); then came others: Xela Arias, Ana Romaní, Olga Novo, Yolanda Castaño, Enma Couceiro, Helena de Carlos, and many more, some of whom were very young. Amidst this type of feminine *big-bang*, these writers were capable of cultivating their individuality to develop their particular creative projects at the same time as radically transforming Galician poetry, almost without realising it and within little more than a decade, thus: "The appropriation of language, textualization of the silenced identity and subversion of the legacy comprise the three fundamental axes of the articulation of the new repertoire" (González Fernández 241). After that time it was no longer possible to write like before.

Narrative

At the beginning of the 1980s, narrative appeared to be the only genre capable of achieving the modernization of Galician literature, thus enabling it to survive in the scenario of free competition brought about by the new historical era. Reaching an ever more diverse public appeared to be essential, not only from an economic point of view but also in order to consolidate the legitimacy of the literary discourse itself. Originality, plurality, and quality were the fronts on which to fight, and from this perspective the Galician narrative was launched into a dynamic of diversification of genres that was resolved with variable degrees of success.

The starting point of the process of reversal of the canonical genre can be pinpointed to the call for the first *Premio Blanco Amor*, Blanco Amor Prize, for best novel, in 1980. The inversion was first based on the non-critical (and somewhat ingenuous) imitation of foreign models, particularly that of the detective novel, followed by the awarding, in 1984, of the first Xerais Prize to *Crime en Compostela* by Carlos G. Reigosa, a novel written according to the most conventional models of crime fiction.

The controversy began and was aggravated by the fact that many poets rushed to try their hands as crime fiction writers, encouraged by the high degree of codification in the detective novel, which made it appear particularly appropriate for their initiation as novelists, and also because they were tired, as one admitted, of "always being sublime," following the creative tension generated by the process of poetic renovation developed in the 1980s. Crime fiction, science fiction, even erotic fiction: any subgenre was apparently suitable as long as it attracted new readers.

The response was rapid and voices were very quickly raised, judging these attempts as "exercises in alienating through imitation" and advocating the search for inspiration in traditional popular models. Thus, little by little and as a reaction to the above mentioned rush of voices, a line of indigenous vocation arose, inspired by the dialectical revision of the autochthonous literary tradition and the desire to construct useful symbolic alternatives for the Galician readers of the 21st century.

The fact that this route was not only possible, but that it constituted a creative alternative was demonstrated by the successful sales of *Galván en Saor* by Darío Xohán Cabana,[6] a demystifying but respectful reinterpretation of the Arthurian tradition, with hints of Cunqueiro. The same ethnically-inspired impulse arose through certain well-intentioned attempts to create an autochthonous genre of detective fiction based on subject matters such as drug-trafficking, nationalistic terrorism, and corruption among politicians and property dealers. The recent reappearance in Galician narrative of this style,[7] after several years of absence and apparently having overcome the state of disrepute into which it had fallen, may be interpreted as a symptom of the normalization of the functioning of the literary system.

The historical novel also followed this route in order to re-establish links with the autochthonous tradition, furthermore stimulated by the evident need to rewrite the history of Galicia, since only outsiders' versions of the history were known. The urgency of this task explains the proliferation of these types of texts in the mid-1980s, and the high degree of canonization, which led to numerous prizes. The Middle Ages is the era that has most inspired Galician narrative writers: on the one hand, because it is the golden age crucial to Galician history, when the Galician language and literature were references within the European context and when Galicia lost its last chance to become an independent kingdom; on the other hand, because of the great liberty that the far distant and nebulous medieval world offers to the writer. However, the fundamental change that the historical novel underwent in these years was to abandon the underlying objective of creating an anti-history (sustained by the recovery of myths and autochthonous symbols) that compensated for the disintegration of identity that Galicia had long suffered from, to focus on the selection of a set of relevant facts to which a certain meaning was attached, which enabled them to be incorporated—in a suitably conceptualized form—in the collective memory. Likewise, fantasy, a thematic mode that has enjoyed a long tradition in Galician literature, had been abandoning the objective of (re)creating mythical ideas on which society could construct an imagined identity, to focus on codifying the problematical relation between the real and the fictitious, the empirical and the oneiric, presented as an alternative model to the tyranny of rationality.

Perhaps this need to conceptualize certain historic moments as key to a collective chronology explains the great wave of narrative treatment of the civil war, dealt with in very different ways by the different generations. Those writers, in many cases exiles (now dead) who opted to approach the subject from the viewpoint of protagonists remembering the period, in order to leave some record of their vicissitudes, were replaced by those for whom the 1936–1939 civil war was the subject of family discussions, a taboo subject discussed in hushed tones: these writers (born in the 1930s) took on the role of transmitting the surviving memory of the events. The next generation of writers took a different stance: urged on by a desire to know and intrigued by the silence that surrounded the central occurrence of the history of the country in the 20th century, the younger narrators used snippets of memory to drive their fiction, preventing us from reading their works as documentaries, perhaps because of their wishes not to feel obliged to stick rigidly to the facts, which would possibly imply a series of ethical problems, while at the same time being committed to describing some characters and events that would only exist if talked about.

That Galicia has been for so long (and still is) a gerontocracy explains why Galician culture is based on memories: in Galicia the elderly rule (something explained by economic and demographic factors), which leads to the frequent confusion between historical facts and "remembered facts." Hence, we see the remarkable literary manipulation to which Galician writers have subjected historical matters, and how easily they slip into mythology as a strategy to escape from more or less imposed allegiances. This fascination for memory explains the current success of a certain type of hybrid text, halfway between diary and fiction, a chronicle and a novel, which now interferes with the phenomenon of blogs, a fascination for the present that feeds on the voyeuristic habits of the new generations, educated through television and other visual media in the casual invasion of distant intimacies.

It is within this context that the unquestionable success of Manuel Rivas has been produced, a literary phenomenon that is often explained simplistically, by referring to the strong support and publicity from the group backing the author. In my opinion, the social consensus among publishers, readers, and critics that Rivas's work generates is due to the fact that it represents an axiological synthesis of the many identities that compete within the Galician public sphere. This synthesis provides us with a range of symbolic alternatives with which to prop up a new collective identity that encompasses—in permanent dynamizing tension—traditional and alternative values. Of course the canonization of Rivas was helped by the writer being awarded, in 1996, the *Premio Nacional de Narrativa* (Spain's National Prize for fiction) for *¿Qué me queres, amor?* and by the relative success of two films based on his works: *A lingua das bolboretas* (which combined three stories from within the previously mentioned novel) and *El lápiz del carpintero* (inspired by the novel of the same name). However, in my opinion, these elements have had a greater influence on his exportation than on his central position in the Galician literary system, in which factors such as the author's commitment to the Galician language and to certain environmental causes have undoubtedly played a role, particularly the visible role that he played in denouncing the catastrophe caused by the sinking of the oil tanker *Prestige* off the Galician coast in 2002.

The role of protagonist displayed by the written word in Galician culture, as metonymic evidence of the eternal problem of language, and our secular faith in its salvational, thaumaturgical power, has led to a general "hyper-philogization" of cultural life, which in literary terms explain the persistence of intertextual and metaliterary currents that in other cultures would be the response to the practical need to materialize the postmodern problematization of the act of writing itself. However, the metaliterary system is also a shamanic practice, along the lines of the consecration of the written word to which I just referred, in which the writer invests his/herself with the power of interpreting the literary tradition in which they are involved and invites us to revere that tradition, something that is, moreover, relatively frequent in literary systems that develop in non-normalized linguistic contexts, as in the case of the Galician language.

In contrast to this consecrational impulse, Galician narrative has always maintained a heterodox impulse, ever since the distant 1950s. The exploration of the literary possibilities of the urban and underground worlds, the negation of the conventional limits of genre and the incorporation of new narrative registers (in which the marks of audiovisual and digital languages are evident) followed a principal theme since that time. This impulse led Suso de Toro to try out, in the Galician language, the postmodern discursive code, at a time when no one spoke of this in Galicia—and perhaps without the writer himself being aware of what he was doing. In *Polaroid* (1986) and *Tic-tac* (1993) he gambled with discursive disintegration, polyphony and the demystification of the literary language as strategies to subvert the prevailing canon.

At that time the author recommended, as an exercise in literary hygiene, "making croquettes with the mummy of Castelao and spitting once a day on Otero Pedrayo's portrait" (Toro, *Polaroid* 85).[8] But in the mid-1990s, Suso de Toro made a radical turnabout in his literary work, and moved on from using it to question the sense of existence to using it to try to explain the same. This change was accompanied by a new focus in his relationship with the reader, from demanding a high degree of cooperation in the above-mentioned works, to asking the reader "to submit themselves and let themselves be led by my hand" (Toro, Interview "Vivir como héroes"). Curiously, the change in objectives coincided with the moment when women became the indisputable protagonists of his novels, from *Calzados Lola* (1997) to *Non volvas* (2000) and *Trece badaladas* (2002). The film version of the latter, and the awarding of the *Premio Nacional de Narrativa*, were—as with Rivas—keys to the successful exportation of de Toro's work.

Speaking of women, one of the great achievements of this era must be the consolidation of a noteworthy group of women writers.[9] Traditionally dedicated to poetry, perhaps influenced by the powerful image projected by Rosalía de Castro, the founder of modern Galician literature, the contributions of women writers to the narrative genre have been few and far between. After the exceptional cases of *A orella no buraco* by Mª Xosé Queizán (1965) and *Adiós, María* (1971) by Xohana Torres, some other women writers made appearances in the 1980s, and after publishing one or two works that had scant repercussions, disappeared from the literary panorama. These writers were loosely associated through the feminist movement, but had no other type of connection that would give them a new impulse to develop Galician narrative of female authorship: Marina Mayoral, Úrsula Heinze (the first woman to win, in 1994, a major prize for narrative, with *Culpable de asasinato*) and Mª Xosé Queizán, highly committed to feminism and who returned to narrative to use it as an analytical tool and to bring attention to the questions that preoccupied her.

Until then, the role played by women writers in developing the narrative genre had occupied such a secondary position, that one of the most common questions asked by the critics and scholars of the literature of the period was why there were not more women writers. The year 2000 clearly marked a threshold. The aim of the publication of the collective volume *Narradoras* (which contains texts of varying quality) was to make visible the work of many women authors who were not well known but who decisively opted for the narrative genre, coincided with the moment when many of these writers began to win major prizes. In 2001, Marilar Aleixandre won the *Premio Xerais*, and from then onwards women winners and finalists continued to appear on the lists of this and many other important prizes. The names of Inma López Silva, Rosa Aneiros, Anxos Sumai, Teresa Moure, and Rexina Vega, to mention only a few, began to be recognized by the Galician public.

In my opinion, and unlike what had occurred in the 1980s, when the appearance of what could have been a new generation of women writers was aborted by the lack of interest by the canonizing institutions in backing them, the sudden and absolute consolidation of the works of a series of women writers that we have seen since 2000, is explained precisely by the decisive involvement of certain literary bodies (critics, publishers, prize organizers) in the process.

Within this group the case of Teresa Moure, whose novel *Herba moura*, won the *Premio Xerais* in 2005, is particularly noteworthy as the author was the object of a rapid and almost redundant canonization. Although the novel became the most-awarded piece of Galician literature, both the text and the author (her public image and her ideological discourse) incited among readers heated debates, unconditional loyalties, and ferocious criticism, perhaps because of the explicit commitment of the author and her novel to difference feminism. Nonetheless, and beyond the media's projection, *Herba moura* was an authentic literary shock. Time will reveal the point to which it has (or has not) played a key role in the discursive configuration of Galician narrative of female authorship.

Theatre

Any study of post-Franco dramatic literature in Galicia should take into account a series of peculiarities in the functioning of the system, ignorance about which would distort the object of analysis, to the point of transforming it substantially. These peculiarities are fundamental for understanding the difficulties that the genre has had in being institutionalized, as such, and the fact that dramatic literature has not achieved the same level of canonization observed with narrative and poetry. The status of Galician as a minority language, a language that constitutes the country's most characteristic vehicle of expression and facet of identity, undoubtedly determines many important features in theatre writing, but there is another determining factor in the development of the system: I refer to the extremely low correspondence between the number of published texts and represented texts in the sphere of Galician dramatic literature in recent decades. This means that the body of works in question not only has not been performed, but furthermore, as such, it does not represent an accurate picture of the theatre in Galicia, which is largely produced outside of the field of publications.

Moreover, the delay between the time of writing (and sometime representation) and the publication of many works is notable: it is not uncommon for texts to be published a decade after being written and there are recent cases of gaps of more than thirty years. Such texts are problematical both in terms of placing them in the literary diachrony and in terms of their reception; they also represent a challenge for young actors, who may struggle to maintain an intergenerational dialogue with their forerunners. The question becomes further complicated when we have to place a large number of works considered almost as classics in the literary histography, because although chronologically they belong to prewar generations, most were not published until after 1980, as a result of the efforts made by the literary system to add a range of width and depth to the works available: this is the case with Jenaro Marinhas del Valle (born in 1917), Agustín Magán (born in 1918), Tomás Barros (born in 1922) and Daniel Cortezón (born in 1927).

One of the most unusual characteristics of the publishing of dramatic literature in Galicia is the dependency on the voluntarism of certain agents, something—in contrast to what may appear at first sight—that is not a symptom of the maturity of the system but rather a product of the sharp instinct for survival inspired by many of the decisions made by the sector. Such voluntarism (rife throughout Galician culture), although ethically admirable, is inconsistent with publishing criteria and is moreover the direct cause of the erratic and transitory nature of many publishing initiatives (journals, collections, prizes) and also in the final instance of the difficulties for the potential consumers of dramatic texts to become established as such.

This panorama is beginning to change thanks to the possibilities for diffusion opened up by the digital world. There is some reason for optimism: The Galician Virtual Library has incorporated almost half of the theatre texts published in Galicia in 2002 and 2003. In many cases the rejection of the traditional literary support has been linked to the questioning, explicit or implicit, of other specific instances of the process of literary communication, such as that of the author, leading to a surge of so-called "collective creation," a formula linked to the development of independent Spanish theatre, which developed relatively late in Galicia, in the 1980s and 1990s. This formula was favoured by the precariousness of the professional context, in which specialization appeared little less than a utopia, a context that created a type of group egalitarianism within the companies that was quickly revealed as an illusion created by the hyperdemocratic voluntarism of a society trying to compensate, somewhat ingenuously, for the authoritarian excesses of forty years of dictatorship.

All of the abovementioned may help us to understand why a new generation has not appeared to take over the reins of present day Galician dramatic literature. The young creators prefer to ignore the scarce possibilities offered by the conventional publishers and to opt for alternative spots, ignoring the risk of remaining at the fringe of the canon. Galicia, a gerontocratic society if ever there was one, also reflects—in what it does and does not exhibit in its dramatic literature, the generational gap that in recent decades has marginalized the new generations.

The history of contemporary Galician theatre began in 1973, in the small town of Ribadavia, where a group of young enthusiasts decided to hold a festival of theatre and a competition for theatre texts in an attempt to create new spaces in the monolithic Francoist culture. The group named themselves, significantly, *Abrente* ("daybreak" in Galician), and the success of their initiative, which would continue throughout eight years, was such that Galician theatre as we know it today, is considered to have been born there and then. Firstly, because some amateur groups made the leap to becoming professionals, thus creating a field of employment until then non existent. Secondly, because it was in this competition that it first appeared that some promising young writers would represent the continuity of the Galician dramatic literature, which although always precarious, never lacked illustrious names (Castelao, Cunqueiro . . .).

With the professionalization of the first theatre companies at the end of the 1970s and the beginning of the 1980s, the militant voluntarism of *Abrente*, which had allowed some degree of theatrical activity, almost killed off by censorship, was being replaced by the desire to open up new markets. At the same time the first steps were taken to obtain the support of the different administrations (local, autonomous, state) in the incipient structuring of a space where the thematic and formal renovation required by the new times could be developed, following the populist, allegorical, and hypercritical lines that dominated theatre in the last days of Francoism.

The decade of the 1980s was one of expansion: theatre companies and festivals proliferated, there was a change from self-sufficient companies in which all members took diverse roles, to specialization in exercising the various roles associated with the theatre, the first steps were taken to consolidate performance circuits, publishing platforms specialized in the dramatic genre appeared, and above all there was a spectacular increase in funding for the dramatic arts. The *Centro Dramático Galego* (CDG), the Galician Drama Center, was created in 1984 as a public reference company, although it never achieved the national status that certain sectors of Galician culture yearned for (and still do). The establishment in 1989 of a new administrative body, the *Instituto das Artes Escénicas y Musicais* (IGAEM), the Institute for Scenic and Musical Arts, saw the end of an era in which the foundations for the normalization of theatre activities were laid, and the start of another era in which the need to capture and consolidate new audiences marked not only political strategies, always lacking in imagination and chained to a clearly obsolete model,[10] but also professional and artistic ones. Luckily the decade of the 1990s led to another novelty; the appearance of writers specialized in the dramatic genre, something always lacking in Galician literature, with all that this implied in terms of institutional deficiencies as regards the genre. Thus the names of Roberto Salgueiro, Cándido Pazó, Raúl

Dans, Gustavo Pernas, and the recent (2006) winner of *Premio Nacional de Literatura Dramática*, National Prize for Dramatic Literature, Rubén Ruibal, were added to those of Manuel Lourenzo, Euloxio Ruibal, and Roberto Vidal Bolaño (who died in 2002), enabling Galician dramatic literature to undergo an urgent thematic and formal renovation that finished once and for all with the narcissistic disorientation that had alienated the audiences in the 1980s. The canonization of the latter three authors, survivors of the foundational competition organized by *Abrente*, also implied a kind of reconciliation of Galician theatre with its own eventful history and has allowed the creation of an incipient genealogy that the youngest creators can confront when defining their own proposals. That Galician theater is facing a change is demonstrated by the facts. Firstly, the inauguration in Vigo in 2005 of the *Escola Superior de Arte Dramático* (ESAD), the Higher School of Dramatic Art. Secondly, the imminent official approval, for the first time in 125 years of history of Galician theater (celebrated in 2007), of the *Plan Galego das Artes Escénicas*, Galician Plan for the Scenic Arts, which predicts a tripling in spending on the sector between 2005 (7,000,000 euros) and 2011 (20,000,000 euros), within a new conception of cultural production, now considered a strategic economic sector.

Conclusion

It appears that Galician literature has managed to survive the great social transformations that have accompanied the new millennium, largely because, in recent decades, it has undergone an urgently needed process of institutionalization, which has made the work of its creators visible and has produced the conditions necessary for the articulation of a minimally normalized literary system. This has been facilitated by the fact that the new generations of Galicians are involved in the elaboration of indigenous, but polyvalent, cultural paradigms and are conscious of the possibilities that the alliance with new technologies offers to minority cultures. It has also been hindered by the fact that the reading public has played little part in the institutionalization of our literary system, as it has acted *a posteriori*, accepting or rejecting proposals but demonstrating little ability to generate them. Twenty-five years after *Edicións Xerais* first organized the Prize for Best Novel under the catchphrase "the force of the readers," it would be expected that this would be the determining factor in the configuration of the Galician literary system. However, the slow rate of progress and the difficulties in consolidating the system advised against considering the process as irreversible.

The huge effort on the part of the different parties involved in the development of the Galician literary system would be in vain if it was not directed towards some carefully selected objectives that must be included in a wider project that involves all of Galician society: the construction of a culture able to compete with others in its immediate surroundings because they are capable of offering their creators and consumers valid tools for their individual and collective development. This is the challenge. If it is not met, the vitality of Galician literature will surely be killed off by "museumization," endogamy, and interventionism, no matter the level of institutionalization of the system.

Notes

1. For a well documented analytical synthesis of the present situation regarding publishing in Galicia, see Cabrera-Freixanes 2003.
2. The citation is taken from the report of the congress that appeared in the weekly journal *A Nosa Terra* 693, 28 September 1995.
3. In fact, both passed long periods without publishing anything: Casares published *Ilustrísima* in 1980, *Os mortos daquel verán* in 1987 and *Deus sentado nun sillón azul* in 1996; Ferrín disappeared from the narrative panorama between 1985 (when he published *Bretaña, Esmeraldina* and *Arnoia, Arnoia*) and 1991 (*Arraianos*) and again until 1999 (*No ventre do silencio*).
4. The first anthology of this group appeared as early as 1985: *Dende a palabra, doce voces*, by Luciano Rodríguez, functioned as a reference space for articulation and promotion of the generation of poets writing in the 1980s. In 1990, in the prestigious Visor collection, Basilio Losada presented his selection entitled *Poesía gallega de hoy*; in 1991 César A. Molina and Francisco López Barxas published *Fin de un milenio. Antología de la poesía gallega última*. In the same year Álex Susanna and Xavier Rodríguez launched *Sis poetes gallecs*, in Catalan. I do not know of many similar cases of such rapid and effective exportation of the works of a group.
5. The phrase formed part of a type of generational manifesto read by the authors at the I Congreso de Escritores/as Novos/as (note the self-denomination of the collective . . .) held in Compostela in 1996 (Villar 89).
6. The 17th edition was published at the end of 2007, with almost 50,000 copies sold.
7. With Diego Ameixeiras (*Baixo mínimos*, 2004 and *O cidadán do mes*, 2006), Miguel Anxo Fernández (*Un nicho para Marilyn*, 2003), and his detectives Horacio Dopico and Frank Soutelo, respectively, and with the reappearance (*A procura do falso Grial*, 2005) of Toni Barreiro created by Manuel Forcadela at the beginning of the 1990s.
8. The emblematic figures of Castelao and Otero Pedrayo have traditionally operated as indisputable references in Galician culture, which explains Suso de Toro's subversive "recommendation."
9. For a more detailed discussion of the question, see Vilavedra, "Unha achega."
10. Two data that indicate the abnormal functioning: in 2005 the official registers indicated a large number (84) of professional theatre companies in Galicia, but in the first half of 2006, only 8 companies had presented more than five functions among the 65 points distributed in the 44 councils that form the Galician Network of Theatres and Auditoria (Abuín et al 224).

Works Cited

Abuín, Anxo, et al. *Cento vintecinco anos de teatro en galego.* Ed. Manuel Vieites. Vigo: Xunta de Galicia-Editorial Galaxia, 2007.
Cabrera, Mª Dolores and Víctor F. Freixanes. "Datos para a entrada no novo milenio: Algunhas reflexións arredor do libro galego." *Grial* 160 (2003): 136–43.
Álvarez Cáccamo, Xosé M., X. Rodríguez Baixeras, and Álex Susanna, eds. *Sis poetes gallecs.* Barcelona: Columna, 1990.
Ameixeiras, Diego. *Baixo mínimos.* Vigo: Xerais, 2004.
———. *O cidadán do mes.* Vigo: Xerais, 2005.
Cabana, Darío X. *Galván en Saor.* Vigo: Xerais, 1989.
Fernández, Miguel A. *Un nicho para Marilyn.* Vigo: Galaxia, 2003.
Forcadela, Manuel. *A procura do falso Grial.* Vigo: Galaxia, 2005.
Fusi, Juan Pablo. *La evolución de la identidad nacional.* Madrid: Temas de Hoy, 2000.
Galician Virtual Library. *www.bvg.udc.es.*
González Fernández Helena. *Elas e o paraugas totalizador.* Vigo: Xerais, 2005.
González-Millán, Xoán. *Literatura e sociedade en Galicia (1975–1990).* Vigo: Xerais, 1994.
Heinze, Úrsula. *Culpable de asasinato.* Vigo: Xerais, 1994.
El lápiz del carpintero. Film directed and scripted by Antón Reixa. Based on Manuel Rivas's novel *O lapis do carpinteiro.* 2002.
La lengua de las mariposas. Film directed by José Luis Cuerda and scripted by Rafael Azcona, J. L. Cuerda and Manuel Rivas. Based on short stories of Manuel Rivas's book *¿Que me queres, amor?* 1999.
López Barxas, Francisco; Molina, César A. *Fin de un milenio: Antología de la poesía gallega última.* Madrid: Libertarias, 1991.
Losada, Basilio, ed. *Poesía gallega de hoy.* Madrid: Visor, 1990.
Moure, Teresa. *Herba moura.* Vigo: Xerais, 2005.
Queizán, Mª Xosé. *A orella no buraco.* Vigo: Galaxia, 1965.
Reigosa, Carlos G. *Crime en Compostela.* Vigo: Xerais, 1985.
Rivas, Manuel. *¿Qué me queres, amor?* Vigo: Galaxia, 1995.
Rodríguez, Luciano, ed. *Dende a palabra, doce voces.* Santiago: Sotelo Blanco, 1986.
Toro, Suso de. Interview "Vivir como héroes." *Quimera* 143 (1995): 45–50.
———. *Calzados Lola.* Vigo: Xerais, 1997.
———. *Non volvas.* Vigo: Xerais, 2000.
———. *Polaroid.* Vigo: Xerais, 1986.
———. *Trece badaladas.* Vigo: Xerais, 2002.
Torres, Xohana. *Adiós, María.* Buenos Aires: Castrelos, 1971.
Trece campanadas. Film directed by Xavier Villaverde and scripted by Juan Vicente Pozuelo and Curro Royo. Based on Suso de Toro's novel *Trece badaladas.* 2002.
Tusell, Javier. *Los hijos de la sangre: La España de 1936 desde 1986.* Madrid: Espasa Calpe, 1987.
Vilavedra, Dolores. "Unha achega ao discurso narrativo de autoría feminina." *Madrygal* 10 (2007): 145–51.
———. "De, en, sobre . . . la literatura gallega y la Transición." *Memoria literaria de la*

Transición española. Ed. Javier Gómez-Montero. Madrid-Frankfurt: Iberoamericana-Vervuert Verlag, 2007. 173-83.

———. *Historia da literatura galega.* Vigo: Galaxia, 1999.

———. "La narrativa gallega en el fin del milenio." *Cuadernos de Mangana* 14. Cuenca: Centro de Profesores y Recursos, 2002.

Villar, Rafa. "A poesía: impresións dixitais." *Dorna* 23 (1997): 85–92.

◆ 8

Tensions in Contemporary Basque Literature

Jon Kortazar

(Translated by Stephanie A. Mueller)

It is always difficult to explain in so few pages the complex and ever-changing reality of a minority, or minoritized (depending on who is writing), literature, such as Basque literature.[1] Dealing with a literature that is naturally less stable and more changing than so-called normalized literatures poses an added danger. Minoritized literatures are characterized by conditions of extensive mobility within small temporal spaces due to the social structure in which they lie. Moreover, within these minoritized systems, literary creation tends to be valued for its symbolic capital or appraised based on identitarian or ideological criteria. It is also the case that this same pattern can probably be detected within larger literary systems as well. After all, ideology is the large determinant umbrella within which all literary creation moves about. However, ideology holds even more influence in minoritized systems because their small size results in a higher level of sensitivity within social circles. Like a nervous neuron that jumps more quickly and intensely, a minoritized literary system possesses a greater capacity for immediate responses which can also disappear fleetingly.

Normalized literatures are generally described with more certainty, thanks to a critical body that has already created, detected, and, to a certain extent, determined a recognizable and accepted image for that particular literary system. Therefore, mindful of this essay's function as an exercise in the unstable description of a complex system in constant change, I have limited its scope to an explanation of various tensions or changing historical circumstances that can be observed in Basque literature.

Tensions in Minoritized Literatures

In his analysis of Galician literature, another minority language literary system that in many ways parallels (and in others, notably diverges from) Basque literature, Antón

Figueroa defined the following tensions within the Galician literary system: 1) Spanish can/cannot appear in the text (regardless of a potential lack of verisimilitude). 2) The linguistic norm used must be *x* rather than *y*. 3) What matters is to write in Galician. The use of "good" Galician is of fundamental importance. 4) Thematic norms: the text should have/need not have Galician culture as its referential source. 5) The text should/need not respect linguistic norms. 6) The writer should/need not respect linguistic norms. 7) The writer should/need not uphold a determined political militancy. Public "conduct" is relevant in the evaluation of a text. 8) The writer can/should not write and publish literature in Spanish (Figueroa 107).

For my purposes, I shall substitute Euskara, or Basque, wherever the text says Galician. This schema has been so useful in the study of Galician literature that Helena González Fernández has successfully applied it to the study of women's writing. She has taken the tensions produced upon the creation of a literature written in a diglossic language, grappling with an idea of nation, and has opened them up to a reflection of gender tensions. Just as I have translated and adapted Figueroa's formal schema, I shall also do so with Helena González Fernández's, though in this case I include only the applicable tensions: 1) Thematic norms: the text should have/need not have the feminine as its referential source. 2) The writing should/has no need to be directly related to gender. 3) The writer should/has no need to respect patriarchal grammar. 4) The writer should/has no need to manifest a determined feminist militancy. Public "conduct" is relevant in the evaluation of a text. 5) What matters is that the author be a woman. That what a woman writes is "good" is of fundamental importance (González Fernández 55).

I include González Fernández's schema here to demonstrate how effective Figueroa's is. It should be noted that this double paradigm of reflection has spread throughout the field of Galician literary criticism. By applying Figueroa's schema to the current situation of Basque literature, it is possible to construct a cohesive structure that brings to light certain aesthetic, cultural, social, and identitarian tensions that have developed during the period extending from General Franco's death (1975) to the present moment, when the Basque literary system flourishes.

It may be necessary to modify the order of some of Figueroa's characteristics in order for them to be applicable to the Basque literary system. For example, while Figueroa's first tension ("Spanish can/cannot appear in the text") was a recurring aesthetic and stylistic characteristic of Basque literature, tension eight ("The writer can/should not write and publish literature in Spanish") more deeply and broadly affects the writer's position within the literary system. Therefore, it is from this final tension that I shall begin my reflection on current Basque literature.

"The Writer Can/Should Not Also Write in Spanish"

In late 2007, the writer Mariasun Landa (Rentería, Guipúzcoa, 1949), winner in 2003 of the Premio Nacional de Literatura Infantil y Juvenil (National Prize of

Youth and Children's Literature), published a memoir entitled *La fiesta en la habitación de al lado: París, 1968–1969* (The Party in the Room Next Door: Paris, 1968–1969), which recounts her experience in Paris during those mythical years. What is interesting is that the publishing house simultaneously published the book's translation (and not Landa's own translation) into Basque by Jexux Mari Lasa. Two elements of the process of the book's publication are worth emphasizing here. First, the simultaneity of the publication of the two "versions," the original and its translation, shows that the publishing house had in mind the criterion on which I am now focusing. The publishers foresaw a potential polemic resulting from the publication of a text written in Spanish by a recognized, prestigious writer who had previously established her reputation writing in Basque. And they were correct. But there is a second fact to take into account. When the book appeared, some media reviewed only the Basque version without reporting that it was a translation. This was not due to lack of knowledge or confusion.

Around the same time, Xabier Silveira (Lesaca, Navarra, 1976), a famous *bersolari*, or improviser of rhymed poems, published *A las ocho en el Bule* (Eight O'Clock in the Bule), a novel centered around the effects of street violence. In this case, the author's political ideology was well known; he belongs to the diffuse nationalist left, and his publication of a work in Spanish seemed contradictory.

Sure enough, a debate did arise that lasted from the end of 2007, to the first third of 2008. The two writers argued that they wrote and published in Spanish based on the criterion of "verisimilitude." Lando said that she didn't live "in Basque" in the streets of Paris (and a disinterested observer could say, nor in Spanish). Silveira argued that those who participated in the street violence portrayed in his book spoke Spanish in order to avoid being identified by speaking Basque. Writer Koldo Izagirre (Pasajes, Guipúzcoa, 1953) refuted such arguments, pointing out that verisimilitude did not necessarily have anything to do with the factual truth, and used two other novels as examples. The first, *Egunero hasten delako* (1969) (Because It Begins Each Day) by Ramon Saizarbitoria (San Sebastián, 1944), set in Switzerland and defending abortion, could be said to represent the modernization of the Basque novel. The second, Jokin Muñoz's (Castejón, Navarre, 1963) *Antzararen bidea* (2007) (*The Goose's Path*), is written in Basque, yet deals with the first days of the Civil War of 1936 along the banks of the Ebro, a place where Basque was not spoken.

The debate led to various reflections on the appropriateness or inappropriateness of writing in Spanish, or more broadly, on the ideological bases of creative and discursive practice. Some critics ended up indicating that they preferred, in a clearly ideological choice, Basque writers who defended the Basque Country in Spanish to writers in Basque who did not. One such critic is Lander Garro, whose argument is found on the previously cited web page:

> Ez dut nik españolez (zapaltzailearen hizkuntzan) dihardutenen defentsarik egingo, baina derradan, bidenabar, nahiago dudala españolez españolen kontra aritzen dena,

euskaraz euskaldunon kontra aritzen dena baino, (edo, bestela esanda, euskaraz, españolen alde). (Izagirre)

(I will not defend those who write in Spanish [the language of the oppressor], but I will say that I prefer those who speak in Spanish against the Spanish to those who speak in Euskara against the Basques [or, in other words, those who speak in Euskara in favor of the Spanish].)[2]

Garro then defends his position even more emphatically with this unequivocal phrase: "Nola ez dugu, bada, politikaz hitz egingo, Edorta? Oraindik ez gara literaturaz hitz egiten hasi!" (How are we going to not talk about politics, Edorta [addressing another participant in the debate]? We still have not begun to talk about literature!)

Therefore, linguistic choice in literary creation must be seen in relation to the political and ideological system in which it is inserted. Thus, the systemic tension that Figueroa states as "The writer can/should not write and publish literature in Spanish" is a judgment that goes beyond literary practice. Its contents also relate to the ideological and identitarian configuration of the social practice we call writing. In this way it merges with another tension of Figueroa's schema that will be the next focus of my attention.

"The Writer Should/Need Not Uphold Determined Political Militancy; Public 'Conduct' Is Relevant in the Evaluation of a Text"

Reasons aside, be they comprehensible or not, or weak or solid, this tension is powerful. These questions arise from the first moment: Is Basque literature that which is written in the Basque language? Can a Basque writer use another language in literary creation? I refer here to literary practice in particular. Other types of writing that are considered less symbolic within the system, such as the publication in Spanish of journalistic articles and op-ed pieces do not incite this type of debate and are more easily accepted.

This brings me to literature's relationship with identity and the role of literature's function in the creation of the identitarian conscience of the nation. Itamar Even-Zohar explores this relationship between literature and identity:

"Literature" has been even more indispensable for the creation of the "nations" under these names. In each of these cases, a small group of people, whom I would like to call "socio-semiotic entrepreneurs," popularly known under various titles, such as "writers," "poets," "thinkers," "critics," "philosophers" and the like, produced an enormous body of texts in order to justify, sanction, and substantiate the existence, or the desirability and pertinence of such entities—the German, Bulgarian, Italian and other nations. At the same time, they also had to bring some order into the collection of texts and names which in principle could be rendered instrumental in justifying their cause. (Even-Zohar 52)[3]

Thus the traditional notion that literature reinforces the nation, and consequently that Basque literature must be written in the Basque language in order to be national, is a systemic tension that still lingers in the conscious and in the debate.

Koldo Izagirre, cited above, is one of the figures who has most clearly defined the relationship between language and nation: "Euskara nazioa da berez. Baina nazioa ez da hizkuntzan bakarrik oinarritzen" (qtd. in Odriozola 66) (The Basque language is a nation in itself. But the nation is not based on one language alone).

There also undoubtedly exist more multi-tonal, variable, historical, and profound reflections on this tension. For example, the emblematic writer Bernardo Atxaga (Asteasu, Guipúzcoa, 1951) has reflected on the stamp placed on literature that is written in a minority language and yet looks to establish itself as a universal creative form. It goes without saying that this reflection attempts to reveal interesting new reflections on the role of the writer within society. It should be reiterated that underlying Bernardo Atxaga's words is a preoccupation with the relationship between the writer and her environment, as well as with the relationship between the writer's opinion of herself and her literature and the opinion of the society in which that literature is inscribed. Because of this, and because of his idea of literature, Atxaga rejects the notion that he is a national writer.

His rejection of the label of national writer is a radical one. "It entails the immediate conversion of a living, breathing subject into a papier-mâché subject, which is what national writers are. They perform an abusive reading of your work, with an interest in nullifying you, depriving you of your particularity. I am not a papier-mâché national writer." Atxaga's good humor returns as he explains how he defends himself from the clichés that threaten his identity as a writer. He coined a term for the situation that surrounds the writer who uses a minority language while trying to spread out into the world: the *estereotiposfera* (the stereotypesphere). "You feel like a spaceship that must traverse an extremely dangerous territory, because everything that you are, due to character, family, and education—this little thing that is José Irazu, and that signs with the pen name Bernardo Atxaga—is a space that is immediately occupied by stereotypes. It functions in such a way that it becomes impossible for me to appear as an individual in many parts of the world" (Larrauri).

This negation of the label of national writer is even more apparent in the title of the article: "Los escritores nacionales son sujetos de carton piedra" ("National Writers Are Papier-mâché Subjects"). A few years earlier, Atxaga was straightforward in an interview that he gave to the newspaper *El Mundo*, entitled "Yo no soy el escritor nacional de Euskadi" ("I Am Not the National Writer of the Basque Country") (Rigalt). In this interview he also reflected the minority language writer's itinerary within the creative realm.

Q.—It upsets you when someone asks you why you write in a minority language. I do not want to upset you, and besides, I understand why you write in a minority language. However, I imagine that when a work turns out well for you, you wish for many people to read it. It is the natural aspiration of all writers.

A.—I agree. When my books were not being translated, it saddened me that my friends from Pamplona or Burgos could not read my work, and when I would enter the Shakespeare bookstore in Paris I would dream of seeing one of my books on the shelves. But the itineraries for success are not pre-determined. One does not go along imitating an already prefigured path; all paths are valid if you have some central convictions and some minimum conditions. If I am asked this question in Athens, it is because they have read the work in Greek even though it was written in Basque. What I want to say is that perhaps the idea of beginning in Asteasu in order to end up in Athens is not so crazy after all. It is a longer route, but not an inferior one. I hope for it to always be that way. (Rigalt)

This interview with Carmen Rigalt establishes a two-dimensional reflection of identity and current Basque literature. The question of why a Basque language writer writes in that minority language seems to be a constantly recurring one. This is because the question is situated at the crux of reflections on the ultimate decision to write and publish in a minority language. Therefore, the question formulated by Carmen Rigalt carries special weight.

According to journalistic reviews of the Conference of Basque Writers celebrated in Reno in 2008, the conference attendees have had to answer the question of why they write in Basque on many occasions throughout their careers. This question about the writer's first choice to write in Basque seems to persist through time, and the answer has to do not only with writing in the Basque language, but with writing in a Basque literary system that in its small size offers clear advantages to a writer who uses Basque as opposed to a Spanish.

I must first point out what I have described before as condensation threshold: the instant at which a drop of water emerges from humidity. This phenomenon can be likened to the moment at which a writer's personal and professional expectations are concretized, or in other words, when the writer begins to feel accepted by a literary system that supports, edits, minimally promotes, and provides literary criticism of her work. Continuing with the analogy, I would argue that there is a particularly high concentration of humidity in the Basque literary system. Therefore, it is more likely that the humidity converts into a drop of water, meaning that the inexperienced writer is more likely to be adopted into the system, regardless of the quality and literary value of her work. A second factor to consider is the writer's more than probable presence in the school system. In spite of the reduced presence of Basque literature in educational programs—above all in 11th and 12th grades, or the *bachillerato*—contemporary Basque writers are often included in textbooks and on required or recommended course reading lists. The presence of a contemporary Basque author in the Spanish school system, on the other hand, is almost impossible. Finally, it is helpful to imagine a bundling up of the writer within the system. As I showed at the beginning of this essay, the symbolic capital that moves and mobilizes a Basque language writer is greater than that which moves a Spanish language writer.

When a writer chooses a language of creative expression, she is also choosing, before all else, a literary system, and insertion in the Basque literary system happens far more easily for the Basque language writer than for the Spanish language writer. This has to do with the precarious situation of the literary publishing industry in the Basque Country, as well as with the fact that the Spanish literary system is defined and structured elsewhere. All of this is summed up in the well-known "adage" that it is easier for a Basque writer to publish in Basque than in Spanish (though it is still by no means easy). It is also recognized that the Basque publishing industry, much like any other, needs innovations and fresh writers and trends that draw new intellectuals into the literary system.

It is helpful at this point to return to Bernardo Atxaga, and in particular his talk at the 2008 Reno Conference. Because it is not yet published, I am limited to succinctly commenting on only a summary of his presentation. In Reno, Atxaga revised the position that he had outlined in his 1996 interview with Carment Rigalt. The talk was entitled "The Cork and the Anchor." The cork refers to the aerial possibilities of translation, which would carry a text from Asteasu to Athens. The anchor makes reference to the anchoring of a writer in her literary and identitarian systems. Although Atxaga distances himself from the position of the ideologized writer, he determines that writing in the Basque language entails rooting oneself in a kind of work for "nationism," a word that recalls but is not the same as "nationalism." He also confesses that this new position distances him from an earlier time when he defended autonomous literature. In other words, Atxaga acknowledges (and this interpretation proceeds from what he said) his own movement away from a stance in which he did not view himself as a national writer. This anchoring in "nationism" recalls the function of the "semiotic subjects" defined by Even-Zohar. Certainly once the talk has been published it will be possible to infer more extensive conclusions about the tension Atxaga describes. It is also relevant that in 1977 Bernardo Atxaga gave a little known interview to important Galician writer Xose Luis Méndez Ferrín in which he connected canonical Galician writers with important moments in Galicia's history, or more precisely, with milestones of historical Galician nationalism.

Literature and identity were also the topics of an appeal to Atxaga, unambiguously titled "Bernardo Atxagari" (To Bernardo Atxaga), written by the actor and little known novelist Abelin Linazasoro. There are a few statements from his article that are worth highlighting:

> Baina ez dezagun ahaztu euskara euskaragatik soilik, besterik gabe, ardatz moduan hartzen badugu jai daukagula.[. . .] Euskara kulturarekin, euskaldunon memoria historiarekin eta nazio ideiarekin ez badugu lotzen zer arrazoi egon daiteke euskaraz hitz egiteko? Hizkunta ederra delako? Europako zaharrena delako? Gure amonak egiten

zuen mintzaira zelako? Ez dezagun ahaztu euskara ere Euskal Herriaren kontra erabil daitekeela. (qtd. in Odriozola 136)

(But we must not forget that by relying on the Basque language alone as our base we are asking for trouble.[. . .] If we do not unite the Basque language with the culture, with the historical memory of the Basques, with the idea of nation, what reasons exist to speak Basque? Because it is a beautiful language? Because it is the oldest of Europe? Because it was the language that your grandmother used? We also must not forget that the Basque language can be used against the Basque Country.)

This paragraph summarizes well the arguments made for uniting language and identity in literary practice.

Other Tensions

Antón Figueroa's list contains a number of tensions that are no longer relevant to the current situation of Basque literature, though they did function in past moments. For example, the first four tensions were applicable to the narrative of the 1970s and early 1980s. Again, I substitute "Basque" for "Galician." 1) Spanish can/cannot appear in the text (regardless of a potential lack of verisimilitude). 2) The linguistic norm used must be x rather than y. 3) What matters is to write in Basque. The use of "good" Basque is of fundamental importance. 4) Thematic norms: the text should have/need not have Basque culture as its referential source.

Each of these tensions requires explanation. The first tension has lost its usefulness. It is true that in the name of verisimilitude some social groups (primarily the police and the civil guard) were portrayed in Spanish language expression in 1970s novels, such as Ramon Saizarbitoria's *Ehun metro* (100 Meters) (1976), which was highly criticized for that reason. The question being asked at the time was: If the social sector portrayed in the novel does not speak Basque—and the civil guard was not the only representative of that sector, since bankers, businessmen, and marginalized groups related to the drug world could also pose the same problem—how should the novel fictionalize it without losing verisimilitude? If in the beginning contemporary literature opted for factual representation, as I mentioned at the beginning of this article, verisimilitude is no longer bound to real representation. The source of this change is a combination of readers' acceptance of, and acclimation to, fictional worlds expressed completely in Basque and writers' greater command of narrative techniques.

The tension related to the use of the normative language versus a dialect also produced many debates around 1968, the year that the first norms for Unified Basque were established. It is not surprising that the tension disappeared given that Unified Basque is the principle form used in teaching. Now nearly all writers use Unified Basque, adding dialectical traits not to attack Unified Basque, but rather to strive for verisimilitude in characters' speech, to construct a polyphonic fiction, or to escape stylistic uniformity.

The third tension ("What matters is to write in Basque. The use of 'good' Basque is of fundamental importance") is yet another that has been diminished by social practice. If in a moment of linguistic instability the first option of this tension was acceptable, now a greater aptitude in the use of the language is demanded of the writer. This has happened thanks to new social practices (the reinforcement of Basque in teaching and the strengthening, with everything that this supposes, of academic practice in the Basque language) and literary creations that mark milestones in the dominion of the exactitude of the language. Therefore, it is required that the language used in a literary text be not only correct—experts in the correction of texts are still necessary at publishing houses—but also aesthetic and adjusted to the "spirit of the language system." That is, starting in the late 1990s many critics expressed concern with the language's health and the importance of adjusting oneself to its system by avoiding the use of linguistic imitations and expressions that copy Spanish-language formulas.

The fourth tension of concern here ("Thematic norms: the texts should have/need not have Basque culture as their referential source") also seems to me a minor tension. The Basque reader and writer alike accept that topics can be Basque or can also refer to a place like New York, for example, as does the work of one of the most important young Basque writers, Harkaitz Cano (San Sebastián, 1975). This norm can be interpreted in terms of identity, and can also be considered in light of the Basque writer's insertion in a literary tradition. As is well known, the Basque literary tradition, most notably the narrative tradition, has been scarce. Therefore, contemporary literature and the new narrative, extending from the emblematic year of 1975 and on, are creating the conditions necessary to position themselves within a sustained literary system, but with evident problems. To insert oneself in this literary tradition is not an easy task, not only due to its scarcity and ideological bias, which is generally conservative and nationalist, but also for aesthetic reasons. Although aesthetic norms in decline can be useful in the process of literary renovation, in Basque literature there is a general tendency to completely break from tradition so as to avoid having to adjust one's work according to current epistemic representations.

The tensions surrounding the grammatical or ungrammatical use of the language of literary expression, numbers five and six in the above list ("The writing should/need not respect linguistic norms" and "The writer should/need not respect linguistic norms"), seem to be reactions to avant garde literature and the radical liberties taken by writers that disregarded linguistic and grammatical norms. These tensions have been quelled under the current circumstances of Basque literature, which expectedly follows some of the postulates of postmodernism, including the movement toward reader accessibility, the practice of commercial literature, and the adaptation to the molds of popular literary genres that allow for the fast, comfortable reading practice most favorable to the market as well as to the institutionalization of literature through the school system.

New Tensions in the Literary Field

If Basque literature's historical and social development has eliminated some tensions, then it is also true that new ones have been produced in the changing historical realm of our literary practice.

Iban Zaldua (San Sebastián, 1966) has dedicated two books (2002 and 2005), neither of which lacks irony, to the description of the new spaces of tension that have arisen in the literary field. Some of these relate to the new industrial landscape created upon Basque language and literature studies' insertion in obligatory schooling and the passing of the 1982 Law of the Normalization of the Basque Language. And, without a doubt, the Basque language publishing houses play a key role. Zaldua provides a distinct view of the tensions of current Basque literature that is not academic, but rather creative and ironic.

The first new tension is generational and also affects the canon. Both the title of and range of dates considered in Zaldua's first book, *Obabatiko tranbia: Zenbait gogoeta azken aldiko euskal literaturaz, 1989–2001* (The Train from Obaba: Reflections on Recent Literature in Basque, 1989–2001), make reference to the two Basque novels that were awarded Spanish Narrative Prizes: Bernardo Atxaga's *Obabakoak* (1989) and Unai Elorriaga's *Unai: Sprako tranbia* (A Streetcar to SP) (Getxo, Vizcaya, 1973). Atxaga and Elorriaga have become symbols of the generations born in the 1950s and the 1970s, respectively. In between lies a generation of writers (those born in the 1960s) that has not won the national prize (though some members have received other prizes at the autonomous level, such as Zaldua's 2006 Euskadi award). One can distinguish, then, a group of "frustrated" writers wedged between the two national prizes. Another related topic deals with the canon of writers firmly established around Atxaga (1951) and accompanied by Ramon Saizarbitoria (1944), Anjel Lertxundi (1948), Koldo Izagirre (1953), and Joseba Sarrionandia (1958). According to findings by Idurre Alonso, who performed sociological research on 11th and 12th grade student reading assignments, the canon proposed by the academic world is unstable; although Bernardo Atxaga and Joseba Sarrionandia are the first to be assigned to students, the rest of the canon is substituted for writers who limit themselves to one particular genre (especially Jon Arretxe [Basauri, Vizcaya, 1963] and Fernando Morillo [Azpeitia, Guipúzcoa, 1974]).

A second new tension also relates to genre. It is necessary to recognize a precariousness of narrative forms, as well as three types of substitutions: the substitution of poetry by narrative, the substitution of narrative of prestige by commercial literature or narrative of genre, dubbed "placebo literature" by Zaldua, and the substitution of longer, prestigious novels for lighter works of modest length. I have more than once witnessed students who, after their professors allow them to choose one book to read from a selection, opt for the thinnest one on the list.

There are a few tensions yet to be mentioned, and I find that Zaldua's "Plan estratégico para convertirse en escritor vasco de éxito" ("Strategic Plan for Becoming a Successful Basque Writer") shows with humor and imagination some of the tensions present in current Basque literature. These are the qualities that, according to Zaldua, a Basque writer must possess in order to achieve success: 1) Be young, preferably under thirty-five; 2) it helps to be a woman or a member of a marginalized minority; 3) be able to get along well with all (literary) people; 4) if you feel the need to write an article about a colleague's book, it must always be positive and flattering; 5) can be discretely nationalist; 6) be politically correct; 7) maintain a certain tenderness toward the reader, avoiding irony, which can be misunderstood; 8) be sincere in your writing; 9) maintain an ambiguous stance concerning literary prizes; 10) it is not prudent to be an avid reader; 11) after growing tired of writing novels, publish a children's book; 12) it is also advisable to publish a travel narrative or nonfiction book; 13) use simple, comprehensible language; 14) finally, it is preferable to write novels. This list, besides parodying the "neutral, commonplace" Basque writer, brings to focus some of the problems that the current Basque writer confronts, such as the nationalist identity issue explored above.

What I find most interesting about Zaldua's description is how he aptly points out the tensions produced by the implantation of the market in the literary world. He also addresses the tensions between distinct literary genres. Finally, Zaldua concerns himself with the insertion of the topic of terrorist violence and its social implications, a concern that forms part of his writing's aesthetic. According to Zaldua, the treatment of the topic and the importance granted to its visibility produce a narrative that, instead of searching for definitive truths, generates uncertainties and emotional shocks in response to tragedy.

Basque literary society, and this is a recent debate, lies between a postmodern literary practice and an intensely identitarian political practice. I have already cited such characteristics as the market and packaged literary products. I could also mention other elements present in current literary practice, including the representation of weak subjects, heterotopic spaces and temporal confusion, metafiction, pastiche, parody, the impossibility of accessing and therefore, telling the truth, polyphony, and pop culture. At the same time, there is a strong identity-affirming message present in Basque society.

Along with postmodernity has come globalization, evident in the Basque literary field's effort to reach a larger audience through translation. With the help of the Consejería de la Cultura del Gobierno Vasco (Basque Government Counsel of Culture), there are now a number of publishing houses regularly distributing Basque literature in Spanish, English, German, and Italian. Though invitations to international forums are not abundant among Basque writers, the numbers are increasing. Yet another opportunity for the Basque literary field lies in the July 2008 launching of the Etxepare Institute, an organism similar to the Instituto Cervantes in its functions of teaching and promoting culture.

Zaldua, in his usual ironic fashion, detected this new phenomenon, and this time offered five suggestions to the writer heading overseas to give a presentation: a) display a "been-there-done-that" attitude; b) realize that you are not only promoting yourself, but you are the representative of an entire country whose idyllic beauty you mustn't fail to mention, disregarding its present industrialism; c) do not forget to point out that Basque is the oldest language of Europe; d) do not cite other contemporary Basque literature (the guest is the only recognized Basque writer), but do make copious references to universal writers, paying special attention to writers from the conference's host country; e) morph your political opinions according to the audience's political leanings: if the audience seems democratic, present yourself as a supporter of the Basque government; if the audience seems radical, present yourself as a nationalist; if you are unsure of the audience's political mindset, it would be best to talk about the natural beauty of the land (Zaldua "Bost aholku").

Not missing from all of this, however, is the significant tension experienced by a literature now forced to compete with videogames and with an audiovisual market that draws increasingly larger audiences and dominates the population's leisure time.

Notes

1. This essay forms part of the GIU 06/65 Research Project financed by the University of the Basque Country.
2. All English versions of Basque citations have been translated from Spanish.
3. For a more recent book on this topic, see J. Manuel Barbeito, et al. *National Identities and European Literatures*.

Works Cited

Alonso, Idurre. *Euskal literaturaren didaktika Hego Euskal Herriko Batxilergoan* (The Teaching of Basque Literature in 11th and 12th Grades in the Continental Basque Country). University of the Basque Country, forthcoming.

Atxaga, Bernardo. *Obabakoak*. Donostia: Erein, 1988.

Barbeito, J. Manuel, et al. *National Identities and European Literatures*. Bern: Peter Lang, 2008.

Elorriaga, Unai. *Sprako tranbia*. Donostia: Elkar, 2001.

Even-Zohar, Itamar. "The Role of Literature in the Making of the Nations of Europe: A Socio-Semiotic Study." *Applied Semiotics/Sémiotique appliquée* 1.1 (1996): 39–59.

Figueroa, Antón. "Literatura, sistema e lectura." *Anuario de Estudios Gallegos* (1994): 97–107.

González Fernández, Helena. *Elas e o paraugas totalizador: Escritoras, xénero e nación*. Vigo: Xerais, 2005.

Izagirre, Koldo. "Le train express Durkheim-Castejón." *Bazka: Literaturaren Soziologia Baterako*. December 13, 2007. *www.bazka.info/?p=266*. Accessed September 28, 2009.

Landa, Mariasun. *La fiesta en la habitación de al lado. París 1968–1969*. Donostia: Erein, 2007.

Larrauri, Eva. "Los escritores nacionales son sujetos de cartón piedra." *El País*. March 17, 2007.

Muñoz, Jokin. *Antzararen bidea*. Donostia: Alberdania, 2007.
Odriozola, Joxe Manuel. *Abertzaleak eta euskara*. Donostia: Elkar, 2008.
Rigalt, Carmen. "Bernardo Atxaga: 'Yo no soy el escritor nacional de Euskadi.'" *El Mundo*. July 21, 1996.
Saizarbitoria, Ramon. *Egunero hasten delako*. Donostia: Kriselu, 1969.
———. *Ehun metro*. Donostia: Kriselu, 1976.
Silveira, Xabier. *A las ocho en el Bule*. Tafalla: Txalaparta, 2007.
Zaldua, Iban. *Animalia disekatuak* (Libeloak, panfletoak eta beste zenbait taxidermia-lan) Donostia: Utriusque Vasconicae, 2005.
———. "Bost aholku." *El País*. País Vasco. July 29, 2007.
———. *Obabatiko tranbia. Zenbait gogoeta azken aldiko euskal literaturaz. 1989–2001*. Irun, Alberdania, 2002.

◆ 9

The Persistence of Memory: Antonio Gamoneda and the Literary Institutions of Late Modernity

Jonathan Mayhew

The rise of Antonio Gamoneda to his current position of pre-eminence in contemporary Spanish letters requires some explanation. Although he was born in 1931, and hence ought to belong—chronologically—to the cohort of poets who came of age in the 1950s and 1960s, the famed "Generation of the 1950s," Gamoneda was still a relative unknown when he published his collected poetry, *Edad*, in 1987. Poets like Claudio Rodríguez, Jaime Gil de Biedma, and José Ángel Valente, in contrast, had attained their place in the canon by the end of the 1960s. *Edad*, an edition of Gamoneda's collected poetry published by Cátedra in the prestigious Letras Hispánicas series, won the Premio Nacional de Poesía in 1988, establishing Gamoneda, hitherto a regional poet closely identified with the province of León, as a strong presence on the national scene.[1]

In 2006—nearly twenty years after he emerged from his provincial or regional stage—Gamoneda was awarded both the Premio Reina Sofía de Poesía Iberoamericana and the Premio Cervantes in recognition of his life's work. Throughout the 1990s and the first half of the subsequent decade, he had published major new books (*Libro del frío*, *Libro de los venenos*, *Arden las pérdidas*) along with numerous other editions of his poetry—a process that has continued unabated. The 2004 appearance of a second volume of his collected poetry, *Esta luz*, which, like *Edad*, featured a long critical essay by Miguel Casado, represents the culmination of this phase of his career. The publication of so many books by Gamoneda, many of them largely redundant in their contents, could be seen alternatively as a cause or an effect of his newfound canonical status.[2] The awarding of the Reina Sofía and the Cervantes also made Gamoneda into a public figure—a role that he occupies with a certain ungainly *gravitas*. One senses that he is essentially a modest and private person who is somewhat ill at ease with his own newfound fame.

The secondary bibliography in Casado's edition of *Edad* consisted of only three texts—including one by Casado himself—all of which treated him explicitly in a regional context.[3] Gamoneda's emergence onto the national scene in the period be-

149

tween 1987 and 2006, then, is quite dramatic, given the circumscribed nature of this earlier reception. As I write this essay, in 2008, Gamoneda is considered, by some at least, to be the most significant living Spanish poet, and consequently as one of the most important writers in the Spanish language of the last thirty years. As Casado has pointed out in his 2004 epilogue to *Esta luz*, this canonization is not yet complete: "Incluso hoy perviven ciertos desajustes: el prestigio y la influencia indudables de la voz de Gamoneda no encuentran a veces su justo eco en medios académicos, en manuales de estudio, en las enumeraciones pretendidamente canónicas" (Gamoneda, *Esta luz* 576) (Even today there persist certain imbalances: the undeniable prestige and influence of Gamoneda's voice do not always find their deserved echo in academic environments, in study guides, in purportedly canonical lists). Gamoneda is absent, for example, in Luis García Jambrina's 2000 anthology *La promoción poética de los 50*, which limits itself to eight male poets who were already well known in the 1960s. One obvious factor in the uneven acceptance of Gamoneda into the canon is that his career does not fit neatly into the still widely accepted generational scheme—the basis of García Jambrina's selection. In its classic formulation, the theory of the literary generation predicts that writers will reach their peak between the ages of thirty and forty-five. This model could not have anticipated, then, that the major poets of the last two decades of the twentieth century would be poets in their fifties and sixties, like María Victoria Atencia, José Ángel Valente, and Antonio Gamoneda.

Another factor in the resistance to Gamoneda is the barely contained hostility of a movement that was—supposedly—the "dominant tendency" in Spanish poetry of the current period, the so-called *poetry of experience*. After Gamoneda's Cervantes prize, even poets and critics affiliated with this movement have had to acknowledge his prestige, even as they continue express their resentment in various ways.[4] As we will see below, Gamoneda's centrality in contemporary Spanish poetry represents a fundamental threat to some of the ideas that gave rise to this movement.

Anglo-American Hispanism has also been slow to accept Gamoneda into the canon. The only sustained critical work on his poetry in English, to the best of my knowledge, is a chapter from my own 1994 book, *The Poetics of Self-Consciousness* ("Rhetoric and Truth in Antonio Gamoneda's *Descripción de la mentira*" 80–95). His name is conspicuously absent from the index of Debicki's 1994 *Spanish Poetry of the Twentieth Century*, published in the same year, and from the work of Debicki's numerous students.[5] There is no single explanation for the neglect of Gamoneda among American Hispanists. Among the relatively small group of scholars devoted to this field in the States, there is no clear consensus about the state of contemporary Spanish poetry; the healthy diversity of research programs among individual scholars does not allow for a unified approach to the field in any case. The situation is very different in Spain, where a devoted group of poets and critics have lined up behind Gamoneda, working in concert to actively champion his work.

Gamoneda's first major work, *Descripción de la mentira*, was published more than thirty years ago, in 1977, shortly after the death of Franco. The rise of Gamoneda is, in fact, co-terminous with the entire post-Franco period, which is now almost as long as the thirty-six-year dictatorship itself. My guiding hypothesis in the pages that follow is that Gamoneda's recent institutional canonization stems from his convincing embodiment of the role of the (late) modernist "culture hero" in a way that resonates strongly with the central historical concerns of the transition to democracy, specifically the intense interest in "historical memory" throughout the 1990s and the first decade of the current millennium. This contention, however, raises a question: how can a poet of the contemporary period possibly fill the shoes of the "great moderns," the poets who defined modernity in the first three decades of the twentieth century? In theory, at least, a modernist poet like Gamoneda should not have arisen at the *end* of the twentieth century. As Fredric Jameson has famously argued,

> If the poststructuralist motif of the "death of the subject" means anything socially, it signals the end of the entrepreneurial and inner-directed individualism with its "charisma" and its accompanying categorial panoply of quaint romantic values such as that of the "genius." Seen thus, the extinction of the "great moderns" is not necessarily an occasion for pathos. Our social order is richer and more literate, and, socially at least, more "democratic." . . . It no longer needs prophets and seers of the high modernist and charismatic type, whether among its cultural producers or its politicians. Such figures no longer hold any charm or magic for subjects of a corporate, collectivized, post-individualistic age; in that case, goodbye to them without regrets, as Brecht might have put it: woe to the country that needs geniuses, prophets, Great Writers, or demiurges. (306)

Luis García Montero might very well agree with Jameson here. Concepts like *la poesía de la experiencia* and *la otra sentimentalidad* [the other sentimentality] ostensibly "dominant" in Spanish poetry of the 1980s, were premised on the obsolescence of modernist ambition and charisma in the democratic society of contemporary Spain. A "normalized" postmodern society called for a poetry for the normal, well-adjusted citizen rather than a radicalized literary avant-garde (Mayhew, "The Avant-Garde and its Discontents").

The "great moderns," larger-than-life figures like Rilke, Cavafy, Eliot, Pessoa, or Lorca, rightly belong to the first third of the century, not to the age of postmodernism and late capitalism. The claim that Gamoneda embodies a role in any way comparable to that of the pioneering generation of modernist poets, then, requires a shift in perspective. Isn't it precisely the weakening of "quaint romantic values" in contemporary society that creates a certain nostalgia for culture heroes in the modernist mold? The myth of a heroic age when giants walked the earth is, in fact, the creation of this later age. With a few notable exceptions, the "great moderns" only emerged *as such* in the postmodern age: in many cases they did not enjoy the same level of prestige or recognition during their own lifetimes.

Jameson's contention that the vatic ambition of modernism has nothing to contribute to contemporary literature, then, largely misses the point. In an age dominated by "cultural producers," the emergence of a *poet* is welcome news. This argument does not depend on the claim that Gamoneda is, in fact, a figure of the stature of Lorca, Cavafy, or Pessoa. My own view is that he will be considered to be a major Spanish poet fifty years from now, but that it is too soon to essay a definitive judgment. For my purposes here it is enough that such comparisons occur spontaneously to *other* champions of his work, such as the French poet and translator Jacques Ancet: "Descubrí la poesía de Gamoneda con *Libro del frío*. Todavía me acuerdo de la impresión profunda que me produjera su lectura. La misma que me produjeran antaño Baudelaire o Rimbaud, Lorca o Aleixandre, Ritsos o Faulkner, Beckett o Paz" (Gamoneda, *Libro del frío*) (7) (I discovered the poetry of Gamoneda with *Libro del frío*. I still remember the profound impression that its reading produced in me. The same produced in me formerly by Baudelaire o Rimbaud, Lorca or Aleixandre, Ritsos or Faulkner, Beckett or Paz). This list of names, while presented in the context of Ancet's visceral reaction, neatly assimilates Gamoneda into a not particularly idiosyncratic version of the high modernist canon, one with its roots in French symbolism. The rhetorical gesture of evoking a list of "great moderns" is quite common among those who support the "late modernist" agenda in the contemporary period. The particular names might change from one list to the next, but the technique of summoning up an aura of "greatness" remains the same in every case. If Gamoneda's work provokes comparisons with the poets of modernism, it is because he is, in his aspirations at least, a modernist poet of the same basic type. This does not mean that he will necessarily enter the canon on an equal footing with more established names, but that the terms of any comparison will be those provided by modernist poetry in all its scope and ambition.

One factor in Gamoneda's embodiment of the late modernist poet was his friendship and affiliation, in the waning years of the twentieth century, with José Ángel Valente, another poet who attempted to sustain the heroic mode of modernism consigned to the dustbin of history by Jameson. Although we can surmise that Gamoneda might have been the same poet if Valente had never existed, his institutional reception and canonization might not have taken the same path. Valente, a pioneering literary theorist among contemporary Spanish poets of the "late modernist" camp, provided the intellectual undergirding for Gamoneda's reception.[6] Gamoneda has essentially inherited the group of poets and intellectuals who have also championed the poetry of Valente. Some examples might include the aforementioned Jacques Ancet, who translated Valente and Aleixandre long before discovering *Libro del frío*; the Galician poet César Antonio Molina, who has served as director of the Instituto Cervantes and as the Minister of Culture in the government of Rodríguez Zapatero; Amalia Iglesias, who edits *La Alegría de los Naufragios* with Molina; and Julián Jiménez Heffernan, an influential critic and translator of John Ashbery.

Valente maintained a long association with the Catalan painter Antoni Tàpies. Since the late 1970s, numerous books by Valente have featured images by Tàpies on their cover, who also designed the *logo* for the publications of the Cátedra José Angel Valente at the University of Santiago de Compostela. Gamoneda himself collaborated with Tàpies on *Tú*, later incorporated into the second edition *Libro del frío* with the title "Frío de límites."[7] A design by Tàpies also graces the cover of Gamoneda's *Esta luz*. Since Tàpies's images are easily identifiable—to the point of being formulaic—his *logo* has become almost a brand marker for the Valente/Gamoneda line of late modernism.

The notable aesthetic differences between Valente and Gamoneda are less significant, for my purposes here, than the fact that their *institutional* bases of support are substantially overlapping, though not completely identical. *Esta luz*, like many of Valente's own books, came out with Galaxia Gutenberg/Círculo de Lectores, a prestigious Barcelona publisher firmly committed to late modernist poetics. In 2002, the same publisher brought out the controversial anthology *Las ínsulas extrañas*, edited by Valente along with Eduardo Milán, Blanca Varela, and Andrés Sánchez Robayna, which makes a strong case for the persistence of the high modernist heritage in both Peninsular and Spanish American poetry of second half of the 20th century (Milán). Galaxia Gutenberg, not coincidentally, is also the publisher of Varela's own collected poetry (2001), a volume which features an epilogue by none other than Antonio Gamoneda himself, as well as of the complete works of García Lorca.

In addition to the support Gamoneda has received from intellectuals already closely identified with Valente, he also enjoys the backing of a many poets and novelists from the province of León, and, more generally, from the Autonomous Community of Castilla-León and other Northern regions of Spain. Among writers from León itself, Juan Carlos Mestre, Ildefonso Rodríguez, José María Merino, Julio Llamazares, and Antonio Colinas come to mind. The Spanish press frequently mentions that Gamoneda is the favorite poet of José Luis Rodríguez Zapatero, the current President of the Government, who is also from León and whose father was a friend and associate of Gamoneda. Although there is not really a "School of Gamoneda" in contemporary Spanish poetry, Gamoneda's poetry has influenced a wide range of poets, from Mestre and Rodríguez to Miguel Casado, Olvido García Valdés, Juan Carlos Suñén, Jorge Riechmann, and Vicente Valero.

The secondary literature on Gamoneda, in its initial phases and to some extent today, has been a project carried out by those in Gamoneda's own orbit, beginning with Miguel Casado, a poet and critic originally from Valladolid, and radiating outward in concentric circles. That Gamoneda began as a more or less "provincial" poet has turned out to be a paradoxical advantage, in the more decentralized environment of the transition. There has been a shift in the balance of power, away from Madrid and Barcelona and toward a recognition of the importance of poetry in peripheral zones, like Luis Feria's Tenerife, María Victoria Atencia's Málaga, or Antonio Gamoneda's León. The importance given to Autonomous Communities in the Constitution of 1978, not only favored languages other than Castilian—"las otras lenguas españolas"—but also the cultural autonomy of regions like Castilla-León, which can seem paradoxically central and peripheral at the same time.

Another notable shift in power that has benefited Gamoneda and the poets loosely associated with him is the failure of the so-called "dominant tendency" of the 1980s, the "poetry of experience," to dislodge the modernist paradigm from its position of prestige. In the 1980s this new paradigm seemed to be ascendant, but the claim that the best way to renovate the lyric genre was by "desacralizing" it, ridding it of its traditional aura, could not be sustained in the presence of a poet like Gamoneda, who showed that modernism was still viable.[8] Furthermore, the fact that Gamoneda's poetry is rooted *both* in high modernism and in the leftist tradition of social poetry meant that it could not be relegated to a position of political irrelevance, as though it were a form of evasive "art-for-art's sake." García Montero and his group have also attempted to claim the heritage of social poetry during this same period, but they could not claim exclusivity when committed leftist poets like Jorge Riechmann seemed to be more in the orbit of Gamoneda.

A unique confluence of literary, cultural, and political factors, then, has facilitated the rise of Gamoneda to his current position of prestige. He stepped into a role that was already prepared for him by Valente, while his cause was taken up by a small but influential group of poets and critics who wanted to preserve the literary values that his work exemplifies. The cynical interpretation of these events is that Gamoneda won the Cervantes prize because he enjoyed the political support of the Rodríguez Zapatero government, and that his success is the accidental result of a convergence of political and cultural power. The institutional forces behind his canonization are strong, but without Gamoneda's poetic work itself such a process could not have been successful. A less convincing poet, in other words, could not have stepped into this particular role. Only a poet with a certain degree of aesthetic ambition, a poet who might be credibly compared with any given list of "great moderns," could lay claim to this particular position. In addition, Gamoneda's work carries with it a particular kind of cultural *gravitas* that commands respect.

It is Gamoneda's exploration of the problem of historical memory that sets him apart from other contemporary Spanish poets. He is a modernist poet, but his intellectual seriousness puts him at odds with other modalities of the Spanish cultural avant-garde, in fields like architecture and cuisine, that emphasize gaudy spectacle over critical reflection. The Catalan celebrity chef Ferran Adrià "deconstructs" cuisine in spectacular fashion in foamy, aerated dishes. However brilliant Adrià might be as a chef, it cannot be denied that this is an inherently trivial form of the cultural avant-garde, one that substitutes weightless consumerist spectacle for the philosophical interrogations of Derrida's deconstruction. Gamoneda, a personal witness to the repression of the Civil War and clandestine struggle against Francoism, offers something that Spanish intellectuals like Eduardo Subirats have called for: a serious historical reflection about the problem of historical memory. Gamoneda's *gravitas* stands opposed, implicitly, to the trivialization of the avant-garde, the parodic forms of modernity that is characteristic of certain forms of Spanish postmodernism.

Since Gamoneda is sometimes dismissed as a hermetic modernist poet, it might be worthwhile noting the presence of a more direct, "testimonial" voice in his work, as in this prose poem from *Lápidas*:

Sucedían cuerdas de prisioneros; hombres cargados de silencio y mantas. En aquel lado de Bernegas los contemplaban con amistad y miedo. Una mujer, agotada y hermosa, se acercaba con un serillo de naranjas; cada vez, la última naranja le quemaba las manos: siempre había más presos que naranjas.

Cruzaban bajo mis balcones y yo bajaba hasta los hierros cuyo frío no cesará en mi rostro. En largas cintas eran llevados a los puentes y ellos sentían la humedad del río antes de entrar en la tiniebla de San Marcos, en los tristes depósitos de mi ciudad avergonzada. (*Esta luz* 257)

(Strings of prisoners followed; men burdened with silence and blankets. On that side of Bernegas people saw them with friendship and fear. A woman, exhausted and beautiful, would approach with a basket of oranges; every time, the last orange burnt her hands: there were always more men than oranges.

They crossed under my balconies and I went down to the iron bars whose cold will not leave my face. In long ribbons they were brought to the bridges and they felt the dampness of the river before entering the shadow of San Marcos, the sad reservoirs of my humiliated city.)

According to Gamoneda himself, the texts in this third section of *Lápidas* derive from his own memory of "el miedo secretado por 'los acontecimientos' de julio de 1936" (*Edad* 369) (the fear secreted by "the events" of July, 1936), in other words, the nationalist repression in León at the onset of the Civil War. The speaker of the poem is recreating his childhood experience of seeing caravans of political prisoners pass by his house. It is undeniable that the poet typically transposes biographical information onto a more symbolic plane, substituting a mythic time for the historical specificity of a particular event. Nevertheless, specific, identifiable events continue to underlie even his most abstract or symbolic writing.

A passage like this, from *Descripción de la mentira*, illustrates Gamoneda's transposition of historical memory unto a symbolic plane:

Una mujer, absorta en la blancura, ciega en lienzos inmóviles, habla de mí en un tiempo conmemorado; dice mi nombre en otra edad, bajo las hojas de un gran viento. Es madre de muertos y este poder está en su lengua. (*Esta luz* 210)

(A woman, absorbed in whiteness, blind in motionless canvases, speaks of me in a commemorated time; says my name in another age, beneath the leaves of a great wind. She is the mother of the dead and this power is in her tongue.)

The woman who appears here is not any particular woman, but a stylized, archetypal "madre de muertos." She appears, not in any specified historical moment, but in "un tiempo conmemorado . . . otra edad."

I would contend that movement away from historical time does little to conceal the historical subtext of *Descripción de la mentira*, which was written directly in the wake of Franco's death. A useful shortcut for interpreting Gamoneda is to take him *literally*, temporarily bracketing the symbolic resonance communicated by his tone and treating his statements as more or less referential. In this case, the "madre de muertos" might represent the women who lost their children in the war and the postwar repression. Is it simplistic to read *Descripción de la mentira* as a "descriptive" or literal attempt to come to terms with the lies and repression of the Franco dictatorship? Julio Llamazares notes that this was the way in which he and others understood certain phrases from this work when it was first published:

> Sé que a Antonio Gamoneda, tan poco amigo de las simplificaciones, la lectura que algunos hicimos entonces de su libro no le agradaría mucho, aunque, con su buen estilo, nunca dijo nada en contra. Me refiero a esa lectura que identificaba un tanto simplistamente (era la época y era también nuestra ingenuidad) la mentira del título de su libro con la que este país había vivido durante años. A través de ella, versos como el que abre el texto—"El óxido se posó sobre mi lengua como el sabor de una desaparición / El olvido entró en mi lengua y no tuve otra conducta que el olvido / y no acepté otro valor que la imposibilidad"—cobraban a nuestros ojos un sentido muy directo, tan directo quizá como distinto al que el poeta había querido darles. Y no digamos aquellos otros que expresamente apuntaban: "Los que sabían gemir fueron amordazados por los que resistían la verdad, pero la verdad conducía a la traición / Algunos aprendieron a viajar con su mordaza y éstos fueron más hábiles y adivinaron un país donde la traición no es necesaria: un país sin verdad." Esto, para mí y para mis amigos, en aquel año de 1977, era toda una declaración. (Llamazares, "Descripción de la mentira")

(I know that Antonio Gamoneda, so hostile to simplifications, did not like the reading the some of us made of his book, although, with his good manners, he never said anything against it. I'm referring to the reading that identified a little simplistically [because of the epoch and also because of our naiveté] the lie of the title with the lie that our country had suffered for so many years. In this reading, lines such as those that open the text—"Rust settled on my tongue like the taste of disappearance / Forgetfulness entered my tongue and I had no conduct other than forgetfulness / and I accepted no value other than impossibility"—took on in our eyes a very direct meaning, as direct as it was different from that which the poet had meant to give them. Not to mention those other lines that expressly stated: "Those who could moan were gagged by those who resisted the truth, / but truth led to treason. / Some learned to travel with their gag and these were more skillful and prophesied a country where treason would not be necessary: a country without truth." This, for me and for my friends in that year of 1977, was every bit a declaration.)

While Llamazares is dismissive of his own, earlier interpretation, it is equally true that a reading that simply *ignored* the purportedly "simplistic" connection between the words on the page and the historical reality of post-Franco Spain would be needlessly obtuse. Does the word *país* refer to some country other than Spain itself? Isn't it significant that the work was, in fact, read in these terms when it first appeared, both by Llamazares and his immediate group of friends, and, without a doubt, by many other readers as well?

While Llamazares uses the author's (imputed) intention as a corrective to his own, admittedly naive interpretation, Gamoneda himself has often insisted that his poetry is firmly rooted in referential reality. He does not view poetry as an essentially *fictional* genre, but as a form of truth-telling. It is not unreasonable to view Gamoneda, like his friend Juan Gelman, as a poet of historical memory. Gelman's writing about the *desapariciones* of the Argentine "dirty war," of which his own son, daughter-in-law, and granddaughter were the victims, echoes Gamoneda's evocation of the disappearances of his own comrades during the resistance to the Franco regime.

Even when Gamoneda's poetry is *tonally* metaphorical, then, this literal or referential dimension does not necessarily disappear.[9] The larger-than-life prophetic voice who speaks the first lines of *Descripción de la mentira*, saying: "Durante quinientas semanas he estado ausente de mis designios" (*Esta luz* 174) (For five-hundred weeks I have been absent from my designs), is certainly not identical to the authorial subject "Antonio Gamoneda," who has not written or published any poetry for a period of many years before beginning this work. Yet it is impossible to avoid drawing a parallelism between the biographical author and the prophetic speaker of the poem.

The uncertain boundary between the real and the symbolic planes of expression in Gamoneda's poetry also has implications for the supposed "hermeticism" of his poetry. Works like *Descripción de la mentira* obviously require an intellectually rigorous reading, but Gamoneda's poetry often says exactly what it means, or employs a symbolic code that is not overly difficult to decipher. The capacity for relatively direct, literal language is already evident in *Blues Castellano*, a work written in the 1960s but not published until 1982. Indeed, the language of this work might strike some readers as *excessively* literal. Had this work appeared in its proper moment, it would have represented a significant contribution to the social poetry of postwar period, though its belated publication robbed it of its historical impact. While *Descripción de la mentira* can be read "naively," as Llamazares has suggested, as a direct statement on end of the Franco regime, such a reading does not exhaust the text. In the case of *Blues Castellano*, in contrast, a more literal-minded reading is virtually the only possible one, in the absence of either irony or allegory.

What Gamoneda did find in *Blues Castellano* is a certain *gravitas*. The solemn tone, the repetitions of lines with very small variations (in direct imitation of the blues stanza), and a preference for images of slowness and immobility make Gamoneda's verse weighty and serious, even in poems that are not necessarily brilliant:

> Antes algunos hombres se sentaban a fumar
> y a mirar la tierra despacio.
> Antes algunos hombres se sentaban a fumar

y poco a poco comprendían la tierra.
Ahora no se puede fumar cuando viene la noche.
Ahora ya no queda tabaco ni esperanza.
("Blues para cristianos," *Esta luz* 116)

(Before, some men would sit down and smoke
and look slowly at the earth.
Before, some men would sit down and smoke
and little by little they would understand the earth.
Now you can't smoke when night comes.
Now there is no more tobacco or hope.)

Gamoneda continued to search for convincing and weighty poetic forms in the biblical cadences of *Descripción de la mentira* and the rhythmic "blocks" of prose in *Lápidas* and *Libro del frío*. These formal experiments are never tentative or ironic. They show little of the austere minimalism of Valente's prose poetry either. Instead, they constitute a kind of "rhetoric of authority" wholly at odds with "postmodernism"—however that notoriously slippery term is defined. Gamoneda's poetic modernism might be seen in predominantly *rhythmic* terms, as an adaptation of the rhetorically powerful free-verse style of St. John Perse and similar poets. *Libro del frío* is particularly effective in its rhythmic organization: short, sometimes extremely short, fragments of poetic prose, each occupying a single page, accumulate a kind of density through repeated words, images, and syntactic constructions. The result is a major late modernist long poem that combines lyric intensity with a loose narrative structure. In such works Gamoneda not only establishes himself as a major author, but also restores primacy to poetry itself by breaking out of the decidedly minor mode of the late century lyric vignette. Poetry is not one literary genre among others, in his view, but a mode of signification that can take various generic forms. In this respect, there is no need to privilege the lyric over more ambitious forms of writing, or to confine "poetry" to conventional verse ("Más allá de los géneros literarios," *El cuerpo de los símbolos* 37–50).

At this point in literary history, "modernism" represents a nearly century-old ethos. It not surprising, then, that Gamoneda occupies a different relation to the literary institution than writers of the early part of the twentieth century. It is worth reflecting on why a modernist of the end of the twentieth century has turned out to be an autodidact from the provinces, like Gamoneda, rather than a cosmopolitan intellectual. Fernando R. de la Flor argues convincingly that Gamoneda's cultural role is to remind a more advanced, prosperous society (the Spain of the early twenty-first century), of its not so remote history of poverty, dictatorship, and war:

> Lo que se representa y toma forma en la poesía de Gamoneda es el gran enfrentamiento entre dos momentos mayores de la historia, los dos atravesados por el poeta: la experiencia de la detención y estancamiento temporal que el franquismo impuso

a las vidas bajo su singular régimen y, por otro lado, la precipitación y aceleración de nuestro mismo tiempo de ahora, en el seno del cual el poeta actúa como uno de los agentes más vivaces y comprometidos en su hora de ahora. (10)

(What is represented and takes form in Gamoneda's poetry is the great confrontation between two major moments of history, both of which the poet has traversed: the experience of the the temporal stoppage and stagnation the Francoism imposed on lives under its unusual regime, and, on the other hand, the precipitation and acceleration of our own time of today, in the heart of which the poet acts as one of the most lively and committed agents of the present moment.)

In Spain, the modernist literary tradition has often taken root in provincial backwaters, like Valle-Inclán's Galicia or Lorca's Andalusia. Gamoneda's name is not infrequently linked with that of Lorca, that other great poet of "el subdesarrollo español" (Spanish underdevelopment). Not only is Gamoneda a modernist poet by tradition, but his poetry often acquires a distinctively Lorquian resonance, though he replaces Lorca's Andalusian imagery with the colder northern landscape of León.

In retrospect, Gamoneda's canonization might seem almost inevitable, in light of the convergence of cultural institutions described above, along with the ethical and aesthetic depth of the poetry itself, its capacity to breathe new life into modernist forms. It is all too easy, however, to make predictions about what has already happened, through a sort of prophecy-after-the-event (*vaticinium ex eventu*). To claim that Gamoneda's success was predictable or inevitable is to ignore the inconvenient fact that few if any *did* predict it before the publication of *Edad* in 1987. Spanish poetry of this period, on the contrary, still appeared to be moving in the opposite direction, away from modernist principles.

Gamoneda has attained his current position in the canon through very conventional means: books published by prestigious presses, the support of influential literary critics, the awarding of official prizes and honors. In this respect, too, the road to the canon seems predictable. Fernando R. de la Flor and Amelia Gamoneda have argued, however, that the literary institution needs Gamoneda much more than he needs it:

El "caso Gamoneda," leído en perspectiva literario-sociológica, consiste en que . . . es una demanda estructural al momento posmoderno en que se vive el reinstalar ese discurso poético, de carácter extemporáneo y de aparente inactualidad, en el centro mismo de un sistema desvitalizado, el cual, mediante esta operación, recupera la energía simbólica que se le escapa (a chorros). (Gamoneda, *Sílabas negras* 74)

(The "case of Gamoneda," understood from the perpective of the sociology of literature, consists . . . in a structural pressure on the postmodern moment, in which we experience the reinstallation of this poetic discourse, seemingly anachronistic and passé, in the very center of a decadent system, which, through this operation, recuperates the symbolic energy that is escaping it [in bucketfuls].)

A work's inclusion in the literary canon is, almost tautologically, a measure of its prestige. Nevertheless, there is no reason why a given culture needs to enshrine certain literary texts as especially worthy of esteem in the first place. Even the desire to open up the canon to newer works, or to make it more representative of socially democratic values, depends on the idea of the value of literature as part of the cultural patrimony. What the poet's daughter and Fernando R. de la Flor are arguing, as I understand it, is that Gamoneda injects new value into the canon itself, by producing works of a certain *gravitas* and thus legitimating an institution that was in danger of losing a large part of symbolic capital.

Gamoneda's recent institutional success, then, can be seen as a sign of the continued viability of a certain "high modernist" idea of culture—but in a cultural context in which this particular idea of culture does not enjoy universal acceptance. What is open to debate is whether other poets and writers will have equal success in keeping this older idea of culture alive, or whether Gamoneda is, in effect, the last modernist. I, myself, reject the idea that the literary and ethical values exemplified by Gamoneda's work are irrelevant to contemporary Spanish culture. On the contrary, the response to his work over the past twenty years illustrates a deep hunger for precisely those values that are threatened by the postmodern trivialization of culture.

Notes

1. An earlier book, *Sublevación inmóvil*, was published by Rialp in 1960, placing Gamoneda in the company of Rodríguez, Brines, Sahagún, Valente, all canonical members of the "Generation of the 1950s" whose works appeared in this collection. Rialp published the winners and runners-up to the Premio Adonais, which were among the most significant books of poetry published during the 1950s and 1960s.
2. *Antología poética*, edited by Prieto de Paula, and *Sílabas negras*, edited by the poet's daughter Amelia and Fernando R. de la Flor, are two examples of editions that are basically redundant in their contents. *Reescritura* is a volume that contains only poems and fragments of longer sequences that Gamoneda has revised. In many cases the value of such publications resides in their critical apparatus rather than in their duplication of poems easily available elsewhere. See, for example, Jiménez Heffernan's useful "Glosario" (glossary) in the 2003 edition of *Descripción de la mentira*.
3. The appearance of *Edad* in a series devoted explicitly to the classics of Spanish-language literature was, in effect, a projection, claiming for Gamoneda's work a canonical status that it did not yet possess and, in the process, helping to enact such a status.
4. The death of Ángel González in 2007 provided an occasion for the flare-up of this poetic conflict. Joaquín Sabina and Almudena Grandes, the wife of Luis García Montero, both attacked Gamoneda for having suggested in an interview that González's poetry had

suffered a decline. To be fair, it should be noted that this kind of sniping has occured on both sides of the debate. In my opinion, such phenomena are of negligible critical interest. The only reason to take note of them here is that my subject is the institutional context of Gamoneda's reception.
5. Antonio Candau's article in *Hispanic Review*, written in Spanish, also came out in 1994, but is not often cited in the secondary literature on Gamoneda.
6. Gamoneda himself has not sought to be the kind of literary theorist that Valente was, although the essays of *El cuerpo de los símbolos* are indispensable for understanding his own poetics.
7. I have not been able to consult the original edition of *Tú*. I have in my possession, however, a copy of *Froid des limites*, a translation of this work by Jacques Ancet, which reproduces Tàpies's designs.
8. Needless to say, these debates continue today. My subjective sense, however, is that the "poetry of experience" as a "dominant" or "hegemonic" tendency is on the decline, and that the poetry wars of the 1980s and 1990s are not as relevant to younger Spanish poets. García Montero will continue to be a prominent poet, even if his specific arguments about literary history do not carry the day.
9. Miguel Casado offers an extremely useful discussion of the way in which Gamoneda's poetry exploits "la tensión fundamental entre autonomía del texto y referencia autobiográfica" (*Esta luz* 579) (the fundamental tension between the autonomy of the text and autobiographical reference).

Works Cited

Candau, Antonio. "Antonio Gamoneda: La conciencia y las formas de la ironía." *Hispanic Review* 62 (Winter 1994): 77–91.
Debicki, Andrew. *Spanish Poetry of the Twentieth Century: Modernity and Beyond*. Lexington: University Press of Kentucky, 1994.
Gamoneda, Antonio. *Antología poética*. Ed. Ángel Luis Prieto de Paula. León: Edilesa, 2002.
———. *Blues Castellano*. Gijón: Noega, 1982.
———. *El cuerpo de los símbolos*. Madrid: Huerga & Fierro, 1997.
———. *Descripción de la mentira*. Glosario de Julián Jiménez Heffernan. Madrid: Abada, 2003.
———. *Edad (Poesía reunida 1947–1986)*. Ed. Miguel Casado. Madrid: Cátedra, 1987.
———. *Esta luz*. Epílogo de Miguel Casado. Barcelona: Galaxia Gutenberg/Círculo de Lectores, 2004.
———. *Froid des limites*. Trans. Jacques Ancet. Illustrations by Antoni Tàpies. Paris: Éditions Lettres Vives, 2000.
———. *Lápidas*. Madrid: Trieste, 1987.
———. *Libro del frío*. Prólogo de Jacques Ancet. Madrid: Germanía, 2000.
———. *Reescritura*. Madrid: Abada, 2004.
———. *Sílabas negras*. Ed. Amelia Gamoneda and Fernando R. de la Flor. Salamanca: Ediciones de la Universidad de Salamanca, 2006.

García Jambrina, Luis, ed. *La promoción poética de los 50*. Madrid: Austral, 2000.

Jameson, Fredric. *Postmodernism, or, The Cultural Logic of Late Capitalism*. Durham: Duke University Press, 1991.

Llamazares, Julio. "*Descripción de la mentira*." *farogamoneda.blogsome.com/category/textos-de-julio-llamazares*. Accessed September 28, 2009.

Mayhew, Jonathan. "The Avant-Garde and its Discontents: Aesthetic Conservatism in Recent Spanish Poetry." *Hispanic Review* 67 (Summer 1999): 347–63.

———. *The Poetics of Self-Consciousness: Twentieth Century Spanish Poetry*. Lewisburg, PA: Bucknell University Press, 1994.

Milán, Eduardo, Andrés Sánchez Robayna, José Angel Valente, and Blanca Varela, eds. *Las ínsulas extrañas: Antología de la poesía en lengua española (1950–2000)*. Barcelona: Galaxia Gutenberg/Círcula de Lectores, 2002.

R.[odríguez] de la Flor, Fernando. "Antonio Gamoneda y la poética del subdesarrollo español." *Ínsula* 736 (April 2008): 8–10.

Varela, Blanca. *Donde todo termina abre las alas: Poesía reunida (1949–2000)*. Prólogo de Adolfo Castañón y epílogo de Antonio Gamoneda. Barcelona: Galaxia Gutenberg/Círculo de Lectores, 2001.

Part III
Challenging Identities

◆ 10

The Curse of the Nation: Institutionalized History and Literature in Global Spain

Gonzalo Navajas

Versions of Cultural History

Manuel Azaña, the influential president of the Second Spanish Republic and one of the most significant figures of twentieth-century Spanish history, viewed the history of Spain as an overwhelming and burdensome process whose analysis and critique became the central drive of his intellectual and political program. In his essays and political speeches, Azaña acknowledges that his obsessive fixation with the apparently intractable problems of his nation conditioned entirely his personal as well as his public life. From his autobiographical novel, *El jardín de los frailes*, to his emotionally charged speeches during the final days of the Republic, Azaña devoted his efforts to overcoming the curse of a nation that, alluding to Joaquín Costa, he considered as a "raza atrasada . . . y presuntuosa . . . incapaz para todo lo que signifique evolución, para todo lo que suponga discurso, reflexión. Pueblo de mendigos y de inquisidores, rezagado tres siglos en el camino del progreso" (*Plumas y palabras* 186) (a backward race . . . and a presumptuous one . . . incapable of anything that means evolution, of anything that supposes discourse, reflection. A people of beggars and inquisitors, lagging behind three centuries on the road to progress). Thus the nation constitutes for Azaña the source and the motivation of all his actions while at the same time it is a gigantic barrier that prevents him from achieving his goal of fully integrating himself in a wider supranational context that would surpass the narrow bounds of a frustrating cultural environment. The Second Republic embodied for him his vision of a regenerated nation. The ultimate failure of that vision with the defeat of the republican forces in the Civil War only contributed to magnifying his deterministic view of Spanish history.

Azaña's personal and political profile is emblematic of Spain's cultural and political trajectory that has been characterized by an apparently insurmountable conflict between the need to permanently cast away the traditional parameters of national history and the imperative to critically study that history in order to definitively overcome its limitations. Thus, within this cultural model, the nation is both the most powerful originating agent of cultural and intellectual creativity, albeit in a traumatic and turbulent manner, and a repressive and all-powerful force that prevents those under its influence to realize their personal objectives. The fate of Azaña, who died in exile and was implacably denigrated by the propaganda apparatus of Franco's regime, is a representative illustration of the fearful consequences of the predominant cultural trend that has directly determined both the intellectual history of the country as well as the lives of many Spaniards.

In a divergent manner, the last two decades of the twentieth century and the beginning years of the twenty-first have opened up new opportunities to begin the reversal of the fateful nature of national history. At the same time, they have unleashed heretofore unknown and unpredictable tendencies in the intellectual history of the country. A rigidly institutionalized version of history, within which all the principles and premises for the understanding and interpretation of the past were permanently set, has yielded to a different view in which the past is viewed as a shifting and malleable concept, devoid of immutable and fixed characteristics. That notion of the past is best studied from intellectual positions that challenge ontological views of temporality and foreground the rhetorical and fictional components of time narratives (Vattimo 34; Ricoeur 192). Furthermore, those perspectives contain the key for the emergence of an intellectual reconfiguration of the past and its relevant links with the present that could end the fatalistic view of national history that has hampered Spanish intellectual discourse for the last three centuries.

The new political and cultural reality of the country has brought an end to the view of Spain as a cultural and political "anomaly," a grotesque and absurd version of the conventional paradigm of Western culture. The extreme version of this view is exemplified by Ramón M. del Valle-Inclán in literature, and it was actualized in political terms in the senseless destruction of the Civil War and its aftermath of isolation and intolerance. At the same time, it may bring about a legitimate alternative to the defensive position toward national history incarnated, across a diverse ideological spectrum, by Marcelino Menéndez y Pelayo and Miguel de Unamuno, on the one hand, and the apologists of the Francoist regime, on the other. That position found the country's redemption in the uncompromising reaffirmation of an institutionalized view of history, a view founded on the belief that the country could find the basis for its unique identity only in a primordial and metaphysically defined past.

Following this view of cultural evolution, past national history was *in toto* a source of inspiration for the present, not a feared and despised burden but a model to be ardently praised and closely imitated. Imperial politics and its correlated ideology and art (Quevedo, Calderón, Velázquez, Herrera, Zurbarán) were the apex of a glorious period that signaled the universal projection of the country and could be successfully projected into the present. This view was shared not only by traditionalist figures (like Menéndez y Pelayo, Ramiro de Maeztu or José María Pemán), but also by authors whose ideological position demanded the extensive renovation of the country. Prominent among them are Unamuno and José Ortega y Gasset. In both authors, the great cultural referents of the past are used to mitigate the insufficiencies of the present; Saint John of the Cross, Cervantes, or Velázquez provide the conceptual instruments for a regenerative understanding of the issues faced in the present. In this case, monumental history functions not as a static factor but as a vital political and intellectual force, a structuring and harmonizing agent of culture.

Both the exaltation of institutionalized history as well as its critical rejection share one trait in common: their originating and constitutive premises focus on the unmitigated power of the past to determine and define the development of the present. Ultimately, the affirmation as well as the negation of institutionalized history have proven equally futile because they both lack the capability to evaluate properly the nature of the past in order to incorporate it actively into the present. Both visions were conditioned by a rigid view of cultural events that became invalid when confronted by significant changes in cultural and political circumstances such as the ones experienced by Spain at the end of Franco's era.

The developments of the last three decades have decisively and perhaps definitively altered the pattern of historical determinism that has characterized the modern history of the country. It is in the cultural area where the most significant changes have taken place. Literature and film provide the illustrations for this noninstitutionalized and fluid approach to historical time. Pedro Almodóvar and Arturo Pérez-Reverte are among the leading examples. From different perspectives, both figures ground the epistemological premises of their work on a concept of national history that, through different methods and procedures, calls into question the conventional principles that have determined the Spanish intellectual discourse and have prevented it from becoming integrated in the mainstream of international culture.

Almodóvar exemplifies the position of the undoing of the continuity of history, not because the elements of that history may not be relevant to the present, but because he considers that the fixation of the intellectual and artistic processes in the past prevent new approaches to the country's contemporary reality. Almodóvar does not deny the existence of the many ideological confrontations of modern Spanish history, the repeated eruptions of the almost perpetual civil war that has characterized social and political relations in Spain. He assumes rather the theoretical perspective that his work is circumscribed to the present and is centered on what Ferdinand Braudel calls "la poudre de l'histoire," the apparently less significant data or "dust of history" (Wallerstein 75). He thus favors the anonymous subjects of contemporary life over the monumental figures and great institutions of history and he makes them the bases for its visual narratives. Almodóvar replaces the *Grande Histoire* with the apparently unremarkable developments of everyday life to which he confers aesthetic legitimacy and conceptual power. His films, from *Pepi, Luci, Bom* and *Qué he hecho yo para merecer esto* to *¡Átame!* and *Volver* actualize this reversal of the interpretive premises of the understanding of history.

Pérez-Reverte assumes a more inclusive position toward the past. Instead of the elimination or deliberate omission of a burdensome time, he reconstructs and redefines selected segments of that past temporality infusing in them an aura of ethical exemplarity that should be a *paragon* for a present that he considers devoid of all attributes of greatness. This approach is not intended as an objective rendering of historical events. On the contrary, the narrative feels free to insert in the past the qualities that have been devalued or destroyed in the present. This process of *re-écriture*, or exalted rewriting, already takes place in Pérez-Reverte's first novel, *El maestro de esgrima*. In that novel, Don Jaime Astarloa, a humble private instructor of fencing, is portrayed as an exceptional man that incarnates the attributes of honor and impeccable loyalty to high ethical principles that the narrative finds wanting in the present.

The multi-volume work, *Las aventuras del capitán Alatriste*, expands on that approach. Alatriste, a destitute soldier of the *tercios* in Flanders and other European battlegrounds, displays the integrity and capacity for self-sacrifice and generosity that generals and noblemen lack although, because of their privileged social status, they would be expected to have. Alatriste and Íñigo de Balboa, who is both his military partner and the novel's narrator, appear as the moral consciousness of a narrative that is ambivalent toward the great events of imperial macro-history. On the one hand, the narrator admires that past because it displays the values of heroism and personal dignity that he considers essential for the continued greatness of his country. On the other hand, that same narrator implacably analyzes the political and social structure of an empire in progressive disarray. The attacks against King Philip the Fourth and his all-powerful Prime Minister Count-Duke of Olivares are a counterbalance to the retrospective nostalgic move that envelops the reconstruction of the period.

Thus the narrative engages in a double interpretation of the past. One reading is normative since that past is a model for the present. The other offers a relentless critique of the apparently omnipotent empire as a gigantic structure that has become dysfunctional because of the gross incompetence and intolerance of its leaders. The differences between the positions of Almodóvar and Pérez-Reverte become apparent. Almodóvar counters the deterministic influence of a negative past by erasing its references to it. Pérez-Reverte assumes the burden of history by transforming it through a move that is both nostalgic and critical. In Almodóvar, history is made dispensable and accidental when confronted with the pressures of the present. In Pérez-Reverte, history exists through the filter of the subjective mirrors of the various narrative selves, particularly, Íñigo de Balboa, Alastriste, and Quevedo. In both cases, monumental history and its icons and institutions have a conflictive relation with the present since they can be a hindrance to its understanding.

These two modes of the narrative concept of time illustrate the configuration of the new Spanish culture toward institutionalized history. In fact, the central drive of the changes Spain has experienced in the last thirty years has taken place precisely in relation to the evolution of the cultural and political discourse toward the past. My essay focuses on five determining factors that have shaped the development of Spanish culture vis-à-vis its own history. I will study the nature of each of these factors, analyzing, at the same time, the response that the new cultural Spanish environment has devised to confront them.

The Context of the Local Nation

The modern history of Spain has been overwhelmingly focused on the stifling force of national and local circumstances. After the period of exploration and expansion typical of the imperial enterprise, the country became increasingly self-centered and it retreated into itself identifying with the defense of institutions and values that were disconnected from the more advanced trends of European culture. Isolation and localism have been a continuing trait of the Spanish cultural evolution throughout modernity. Narrowly introverted and limited, instead of pursuing creative objectives, culture became the server of institutions that were interested only in the perpetuation of parochial ideas and issues. In a way that parallels Azaña's position, liberal thinkers, and writers—from Mariano José de Larra to Benito Pérez Galdós, Leopoldo Alas "Clarín," and Pío Baroja, among others—were forced into the exclusive consideration of local issues because the weight of the national circumstances prevented them to become truly integrated into the discourse of modern European culture.

These trends were magnified during Franco's regime because the dictatorship exacerbated the predominant characteristics of the past. Culturally, their more deleterious effects impacted even the thought of the dissident cultural figures that unambiguously opposed the regime. The work of Juan Goytisolo is a good illustration. Although he left the country and he has repeatedly denounced the mediocrity of national cultural life, his work from *La resaca* and *Señas de identidad* to *Juan sin tierra*, was obsessively fixated on the critique of the unmovable national intellectual environment and in particular the intolerance and mediocrity of Spanish culture. That passionate interest in the exposure of the country's vices infuses his works with powerful ideological intensity and testimonial force. Yet it that does not allow him to connect with the most active and innovative issues of international contemporary culture. A similar process can be ascertained in other dissident authors and creators who, like Goytisolo, suffered the consequences of the dictatorship. The representatives of the social realism movement in literature (Antonio Ferres, Gloria Fuertes, and Alfonso Sastre, for instance) and film (Carlos Saura, Luis García Berlanga) were conditioned by an imperative local context that led them to insist on the monotonous repetition of recurrent themes.

The new Spanish cultural situation brought about innovating developments in the repositioning of the author in relation to his/her local milieu. For the first time in modern history, the country has undertaken a successful process of overcoming its perennial international cultural deficit. This process has taken place at various levels and, again, for the first time in modernity, there has been a rapprochement and occasional confluence of the abstract and often visionary projects of the intellectual groups and the political reality. The divide between the two, which Manuel Azaña and other figures like Ortega y Gasset, Eugenio D'Ors, and Julián Besteiro regretted and attempted to remedy, has been diminished and the situation of marginalization of the intellectual has been partially improved.

The narrative actualization that these cultural and political developments take is an illustration of the general cultural change. Literature and film are privileged media that are able to promote, with intuitively persuasive and compelling procedures, the many changes that are needed at the institutional and social levels. The aesthetic medium cannot replace the practical effectiveness of the political forces of society. It can, however, offer visions of change that may help configure collective action.

As Pierre Bourdieu demonstrates, official institutions are, by nature, reluctant to internal change and the cultural realm is the vehicle to energize them and induce them to redefine themselves. Like Bourdieu asserts in relation to Flaubert, the writer may be the "membre pauvre de la famille," a peripheral force of society, but, precisely because of his condition as an outcast, he can propose radical changes that more conventional figures do not dare to entertain (165). Contemporary narratives make apparent the power of the aesthetic medium to broaden and renovate the narrow national culture and integrate it into diversified international currents. Let us consider some examples.

The first example is Javier Marías. His vast work is driven by a critical rejection of the local and conventional Spanish cultural parameters and an expansion into other cultural environments. This development takes place both at the linguistic and semantic levels. Although Marías writes in Spanish, his ties to Spain appear conflictive and tenuous in his work. Like in the cases of Luis Cernuda and Juan Goytisolo, who explicitly limit their connections to the fatherland to the language in which they write and scorn all other links, Marías openly criticizes what he considers the traditional shortcomings of Spanish culture. His comments can be quite explicit, and even devastating, openly denigrating what he perceives as the social ineptitude and cultural obtuseness of many of the citizens of his country. Often those defects are made more glaring when compared to the apparently superior cultural ways of other societies. For instance, one of his narrators says of a typical Spaniard: "tenía esa mezcla de cursilería y zafiedad, ñoñería y ordinariez, edulcuración y brutalidad, que se da tanto entre mis compatriotas, una verdadera plaga y una grave amenaza (sigue ganando adeptos, con los escritores al frente), los extranjeros acabarán tomándola por rasgo predominante del carácter nacional" (*Tu rostro mañana*, I, 74) (he had that mixture of pretentiousness and boorishness, feebleness and vulgarity, sweetness and brutality, which is so common among my compatriots, a real plague and a grave menace [gaining supporters, with writers at the forefront], foreigners will end up taking it as a predominant trait of the national charácter). This is a representative sample of a large repertoire of critical comments found in Marías's work regarding the negative qualities of a national character that he repudiates.

Language remains Marías's strongest link to his national origin, but his Spanish has distinctive and unique qualities because it works to undo the rigidity and conventionalism typical of traditional Spanish that is conditioned by the strictures of the Academy. In a way that replicates the approach followed by Joyce and Nabokov in relation to literary English, Marías recreates literary Spanish—he lets it become penetrated by the lexicon and syntax of other languages, English and Italian in particular. Marías works are inspired by the style of major English-writing authors—Shakespeare, Nabokov, Conrad—as well as lesser literary figures, like John Gawsworth. Through them, his Spanish acquires a new linguistic and aesthetic nature that includes both classical literature, as well as more contemporary modes of expression.

Marías's international linguistic exposure spreads also to the thematic components of his narratives. His novels transcend a narrowly limited national focus. They take place in different urban settings, from London to New York and Havana, that are contrasted favorably with Madrid, a city for which the author does not display much affection or attraction. A primordial and recurrent center of Marías's narratives is Oxford, both the university and the town, whose history and protagonistic figures recur throughout Marías's narrative from the seminal *Todas las almas* to the trilogy *Tu rostro mañana*. Another common trait of Marías's work is that his references to national origin appear filtered through the gaze of foreign eyes, specifically academic figures of Hispanic studies, who are interested in Spain as an object of research and study rather than as a country that directly determines their personal lives. The result is a more detached and objective vision of Spain, typical of an external observer who is free from the emotional involvement of someone whose life has been determined by the specific Spanish political and cultural context.

Likewise, global cultural issues and icons replace the national themes that have prevailed in Spanish literature preventing its true insertion in world history. This is the reason why events related to World War II are essential in several of Marías's books becoming even more prominent and central than those linked to the Spanish Civil War. The world conflagration is the motivating force for the organization of several of his most significant novels. The first volume of *Tu rostro mañana* is an example. By shifting the center of attention from Spain to England and from Madrid to London, Marías effects a fundamental shift from the local and national to the global and supranational thus signaling a true reversal of the traditional orientation of Spanish intellectual history. A fluid and shifting global setting replaces the static and provincial nature of more conventional Spanish literature.

In a parallel manner, Antonio Muñoz Molina has progressively evolved from a strictly local orientation to an international one. His first novel, *Beatus ille*, centered on the traumas of the Spanish Civil War and its effects on Spanish society during Franco's regime. *Beltenebros* elaborates on the same topic but from a more ambiguous moral perspective. In a different vein, later works, like *Sefarad* and *Ventanas de Manhattan*, present a distinct opening to other milieus. Even in works where Spanish history constitutes the originating motif of the narrative, such as *El jinete polaco*, the international ramifications of national history—through the complex network of human relations developed in the exile community—emerge as the centers of the text.

Like in Marías, the references to Spain in Muñoz Molina are filtered through the critical look of an observer—more or less distant vis-à-vis Muñoz Molina, himself—who judges the social and cultural conventions of the country. In *Ventanas de Manhattan*, the observer sees the open windows of Manhattan's skyscrapers as emblems of the accessibility and communication that he sees missing in the closed windows of the country he has left behind and that, to him, symbolize hermetism and fear of innovation and change: "Me sorprenden y me gustan tanto las ventanas grandes de Manhattan, anchas, rectangulares, despejadas, admitiendo espaciosamente el mundo exterior en los apartamentos, revelando en cada edificio, como en capítulos o estampas diversas, las vidas y las tareas de quienes habitan al otro lado de cada una de ellas" (*Ventanas* 55) (I am surprised by and I like so much the large windows of Manhattan, wide rectangular, clear, admitting spaciously the exterior world in the apartments, revealing in each building, as in different chapters or pictures, the lives and the tasks of those who live on the other side of each of them).

New York is presented as the global city par excellence and the language of the jazz musicians and marginal artists of New York is the preferred vehicle to articulate and describe the explosion of local barriers. Likewise, English appears as a language of personal liberation and creativity that reminds the narrator of his childhood when "aprender inglés era una manera de empezar a irse de aquel mundo agobiante y estrecho" (*Ventanas* 342) (learning English was a way of beginning to leave that oppressive and narrow world). For Muñoz Molina the integration—and often dissolution—of the national milieu within the parameters of global cultural represents the most promising orientation of the contemporary cultural discourse.

Even a writer intensely focused on the most directly and intimately local issues, like Bernardo Atxaga, has opened his discourse to a broader international area. In his most ambitious work, *El hijo del acordeonista*, he ventures into a territory far removed from the primordial and mythical land of Obaba that constitutes the nucleus of his first works. California, a land with mythical connotations, is inserted into the domain of the local, thus disrupting the predictable order of the nation. In the case of Atxaga's novel, the journey into the supranational is a brief and ephemeral interlude that concludes with a return to the abandoned original land. This return, however, lacks the epiphanic attributes of Ulysses' return to Ithaca since what is found at the end of the journey is not an essential and ultimate Home—a permanent *Heimat*—but a social and cultural reality torn asunder by violence and self-doubt. The assertion in the local as a way to protect the individual subject from the depersonalization and uniformity of a new mode of civilization cannot truly take place in a pure form in the twenty-first century, as it was still possible in its Romantic version. The assertion of the right of the individual to join in a collective national identity shared equally by all its members appears now as self-delusional and utopian. That assertion has become, today, only a tentative and often equivocal manifestation of the complex interaction between the various forms of an immediately recognizable identity and the contrasting different cultural Others.

In film, the interconnections between the most immediate reality and the supranational become also apparent in visual narratives that explore venues for the overcoming of the burden of the local environment in Spanish intellectual history. Almodóvar can provide an illustration in an idiosyncratically contradictory and ambiguous way. His works are, on the one hand, quintessentially Spanish since they deal with the most blatantly stereotypical aspects of the Spanish cultural image in the world: bullfights, flamenco, and passionate emotions. From this perspective, Almodóvar not only confirms the most conventional tendencies of Spanish art, but he takes them to their ultimate realization. Bullfighters, flamenco singers, and impulsive women and men, as they are found in *Carmen* and other similar icons of the most romantic profile of Spain, constitute the first defining nature of his films. However, this is only an initial position of his work that is undone by an ironic countermove, one that explodes the traditional nature of the local by subverting it through interrogations and doubts.

The examples of this paradoxical orientation are many. For instance, in *Talk to Her*, the image of extreme masculinity typically associated with the figure of the bullfighter is put into question by a woman bullfighter who surpasses her male counterparts in her qualities of absolute valor and bravery. Likewise, the customarily degraded and scorned figure of the homosexual, a *bête noire* of Spanish culture, is foregrounded in *Talk to Her* and other Almodóvar films, to the point of providing the central perspective of the narrative. In many of Almodóvar's films, transvestites and sexual-social misfits portray the most defining attributes of cultural realization.

Volver is an another example of the reversal of national stereotypes, since the female characters take entirely over the film, towering over the few minor masculine figures, who devoid of emotional and psychological depth quickly dissipate in between the twists of a narrative controlled by feminine voices. The displacement of the traditional agents of Spanish history, unmistakably linked to masculinity and ideological purity and normativity, toward the figures that have been ostracized and have been treated with suspicion and contempt, is a clear indication that the conventional hierarchy of national values and principles has been fundamentally altered. Through the parodic and often light-hearted cultural critique of his films, Almodóvar brings about a radical change in the foundations of the cultural make-up of the nation and the intellectual and social expectations that sustain it.

In Almodóvar, the most prominent and traditional signs of the nation are reconfigured in an extreme and hyperbolic manner to undermine precisely the principles that those signs represent. The national, although constantly and ubiquitously present, emerges in him as a chaotic amalgamation of the broken pieces of a common mirror in which Spaniards have ceased to recognize themselves.

Another filmmaker, Isabel Coixet, takes the reconsideration of the national identity mark to a new dimension. In her works, the signs of the national have diminished to the point of becoming merely inconsequential and ethereal leftovers of the previously immutable essence of the Spanish nation: fragments of the lyrics of a song, accented expressions, sporadic, and vaguely nostalgic allusions to a remote national culture. Unlike in Marías or Muñoz Molina, in Coixet, not even the language, Spanish, has a role since a good number of her films are filmed in English and they feature well-known English-speaking actors and actresses, like Tim Robbins, Sarah Polley, and Ben Kingsley.

In addition to the biographies and the language of her films' characters, the space of Coixet's cinema has also been disassociated from specific national origins. *My Life Without Me,* for instance, was filmed in Vancouver, Canada, but the city is not identified by name and, in fact, it could be interchangeable with many other urban settings in the Western world. *The Secret Life of Words* takes place in a forlorn oil rig platform in the middle of the ocean. Furthermore, the rig workers are rootless figures who seem to belong nowhere, having lost all apparent need for a national origin that they would rather forget. In Almodóvar, the values of the nation are delegitimized through rhetorical figures such as sarcasm and parody. In Coixet, in a way that adopts and rewrites Michelangelo Antonioni's existential perspective, identifiable space and time are seen as a Kierkegaardian distraction from the consideration of the radical isolation of the human condition. In fact, for both Antonioni and Coixet, the national reference is seen as an obstacle in the consideration of the only significant goal for art: the search for the creation of powerful links among human beings separated precisely by the traditional communal bounds of the fatherland, family, and language.

As the leading character of *The Secret Life of Words* demonstrates, violence and suffering are universal, they transcend geographical borders, and they are independent from their national origin whether that is Sarajevo, Darfur, or any of the politically torn societies in the world. Human destiny, rather than the national milieu in which this destiny is contextualized, is the drive of Coixet's cinema. Isabel Coixet, a woman director, filming and producing outside Spain on topics that surpass the national and the local, is an excellent illustration of the new orientation of the Spanish intellectual discourse in its quest of a full reinsertion in modernity. Coixet's films bypass the institutional cultural network that has restrained the cultural history of the country.

The Weight of the Central Nation

The concept of the nation in Spain has been articulated throughout history around a unifying center that has been traditionally associated with the administrative, institutional, and cultural power of Madrid. Even the figures of the Generation of '98 that came from the periphery of the country, like Unamuno, Azorín, and Antonio Machado, maintained that the essence of the national entity was intrinsically linked to Castile and the cultural emblems that were attached to that region of Spain. Unamuno, for instance, adopts as the icons that illustrate his personal redefinition of Western intellectual history authors and texts directly linked to Castilian culture; Don Quixote and Cervantes, Saint Teresa, and Calderón are among them. Furthermore, he bases his intellectual project as a whole on the language, values, and ideas that derive from Castile and a centrally oriented view of the nation.

Ortega y Gasset identifies the alienation of the various parts of the country away from the Castilian center as the cause for the progressively dysfunctional nature of the Spanish political condition. As a solution, he advocates a return to a hierarchical organization of Spanish society that would have Castile as its main amalgamating component. For him, the regeneration of the country must follow the guidance of the center. The Franco regime took that goal to an extreme realization and made it one of the cornerstones of its program of cultural repression. However, even during that culturally monolithic period, the disjunction between the official institutions and the cultural and social developments in the daily life of the country became increasingly apparent, especially in the last decade of the regime that led to its ultimate demise.

The new political situation has brought about a reversal of the relations between the center and the periphery. The center continues to have a predominant role, but the other national and cultural entities have become openly legitimate by themselves, overcoming many of the vulnerabilities that burdened them in the past. The process of change is ongoing and it will probably never reach a definitive closure since the relations between the various administrative, political, and linguistic areas of the country will always be subject to dialectical exchanges potentially leading to friction and conflict. What is distinctive in this development is that it is happening at all, after a long history of having had only a muted and repressed existence.

The removal or reduction of the overpowering influence of the center is conceptually linked to the notion of the *soft* nation and the *"pensiero debole"* or soft thought that thinkers like Gilles Lipovetsky and Gianni Vattimo have underscored as a defining component of the postmetaphysical and hypermodern condition (Vattimo 182). According to Lipovetsky, the "hypermodernité" is founded on a general devaluation of overcomprehensive and solidly ontological notions that have lost their hermeneutic power to explain the phenomena of the current global condition (104). The soft nation is thus not tantamount to social and political disintegration and chaos, but it is rather a sign of political maturity leading to more equitable relations between different cultural communities.[1] The emergence of peripheral voices in contemporary written and visual narratives, such as those of Bernardo Atxaga, Imanol Uribe, Suso de Toro, and Sánchez Piñol, is an illustration of the assertion of the "other" peninsular cultures on a par with the culture in Castilian. The model of disintegration that Ortega y Gasset ascribed to the weakening of the center as well as the current apocalyptic predictions that see in this weakening an unmistakable path to national doom is gradually being replaced by a different model of cultural interchange that, avoiding the imbalances and abuses of the past, attempts to create an interconnective network of differentiated political and cultural options.

The Canonical Norm

The Nation and its Center are the conceptual categories upon which cultural normativity is founded, as the canon that organizes and evaluates cultural production according to values that function as the universal criteria that determine national culture. The academic system actualizes and puts into practice the specific components of that canonical normativity. Texts and authors that consolidate and confirm the accepted view of the nation and its constitutive principles are favored over those that question that view.

This is not exclusively a Spanish phenomenon. As Harold Bloom shows in *The Western Canon*, canonical principles and values have functioned as instruments of the preservation of the stability of the American and Western structures of cultural identity and power: "without Shakespeare, no recognizable selves in us, whoever we are . . . without the canon we cease to think" (40). What has been more specific of the Spanish case is that the canon has been decisively—and often exclusively—oriented toward the promotion of a centralized and ideologically orthodox view of the nation. Dissidence and deviation from the status quo have not had a significant place in the development of the Spanish cultural canon, which has favored the traditional, the normative, and the central. The margins, be they geographical and cultural (the literature and arts of the periphery) or ideological (the nonconforming voices of intellectual difference) have been relegated to a secondary role, and frequently they have been completely ignored.

What Bourdieu asserts about the resistance to change typical of official institutions in general is particularly applicable to the academic system which is intent on the continuity of the structural equilibrium that unifies its components and members. In the Spanish case, that balance has been traditionally linked to the defense of the nation and its center, especially during the Franco regime that drastically expurgated difference from the conventional curriculum of Spanish intellectual history. The new cultural situation has opened up inroads in the academic system, but universities have proven remarkably reticent to substantial change, although, in principle, they would need to be at the forefront of new cognitive venues.

The Spanish university system lags behind the significant changes that have taken place in the country as a whole, particularly in the area of new social and cultural developments. The Spanish academic discourse has not broken the paradigm of the traditional view of the humanities and it remains closed to the analysis of authors and texts according to contemporary criteria defined by methodological diversity and complexity, thematic hybridity, and post-national perspectives. The multiple voices of difference in gender, ethnicity, and language will need to be given a more significant space in institutional culture for that culture to gain broader representativity and legitimacy.

The ideological and methodological rigidity that has hindered the development of institutional Spanish culture from Menéndez y Pelayo to the prolonged phase of hermetism and narrowness of the university of the Franco period is still partially active today. Yet, it is destined to end. A society that is increasingly constituted and driven by difference and diversity cannot continue to adhere to a version of culture based on uniformity and the preponderance of a centralized and monolingual repertoire of texts and cultural ideas.

The Burden of the Transcendental

The guiding ideas of the Nation, the Center, and the Canonical Norm produce the establishment of a predominant cultural discourse that is fixated on ideology and the on repetitious concepts that reaffirm the status quo. From the texts and works of the masters of the Golden Age (Calderón, Saint Theresa of Jesus, Zurbarán, El Greco) to the works of social realism in the post-Civil War period, Spanish literature and culture have been associated with heavily transcendental and metaphysical notions linked to religious and moral issues. Even in the voices of intellectual and ideological dissidence, such as those of Galdós, Unamuno, and Juan Goytisolo, literature has been the instrument for the advocacy of programs and ideas (religious and political; conservative and liberal) conceived and promoted to save the nation and, in some cases, even the world. Unamuno, for instance, envisions a quixotization of European culture to redeem it from its morass of confusion and decadence.

The stakes for this type of moralistic and ideological literature have always been very high in favor of the programmatic and social rather than the personal and introspective. This orientation tends to produce works that focus on the absolute and abstract rather than the subjective. In them, the individual is sidelined and it is often overwhelmed for the sake of the defense of a particular program or ideology. This reality applies especially to the literature of a traditionalist bent—from Calderón to Pereda and Pemán—but also to the texts that typify the liberal discourse. The works of Galdós, Clarín, and Blasco Ibáñez are good examples, but also those of Blas de Otero, Alfonso Sastre and Juan Goytisolo to name just a few of the cases of a literature subordinated to a program or ideology that hampers the autonomy of the text to explore challenging concepts in innovative ways.

The new cultural situation is the first time that the country has had the opportunity to try a path that is not burdened with the overwhelming responsibilities that the past imposes. It is not that the new literature and culture have been diminished in their significance and objectives. It is rather that the artist has been freed to create works of art that are independent and self-sufficient regardless of any particular program.

Almodóvar has achieved the liberation from the burden of the transcendental and the eternal in favor of the contingent and the ephemeral through narratives that explore the *hic et nunc* of individual situations rather than immutable realities. Even when he deals with issues of moral responsibility and guilt, as in *La mala educación*, he shows that that reality that can be subjected to parody and ridicule rather than absolute condemnation. Almodóvar has validated the everyday experience, the non-transcendental, the minimal and forgettable events of contemporary societies.

Other texts share this tendency toward the foregrounding of the non-transcendental. Carlos Ruiz Zafón's *La sombra del viento*, for example, treats the tragic period of the repression of the post-Franco period from the perspective of the entertainment novel, mixing the denunciation of the dark aspects of a painful and violent period of Spanish history with the twists of the mystery novel reconfigured according to the aesthetic category of the gothic. Javier Cercas's *Soldados de Salamina* provides a more intellectually ambitious approach to the dramatic history of the Civil War. Yet the framework of the mystery novel and the political intrigue around the figure of Rafael Sánchez Mazas, an anti-hero with dubious political credentials, are determining in the conception and organization of the book.

I will conclude this section asserting that, by putting aside their previous programmatic and unidimensionally moral positions, Spanish literature and culture have entered the post-metaphysical era of contemporary culture, a time in which the overly ambitious and absolutist utopian proposals of the nineteenth and twentieth centuries have become unmasked and disqualified (Navajas 35).

The Diseased Nation

The last and most detrimental burden of Spanish intellectual history has been the self-perception of the country as a severely diseased body destined to progressive degradation and decline. The image of disease has been a powerful and pervasive metaphor that has shaped modern European thought, in particular with the advent of the various forms of materialism and realist aesthetics in the second half of the 19th century. From Nietzsche and Zola to Kafka, Thomas Mann, and Camus, national societies have been viewed through the analogy of a sick body that needs to be cured by drastic and urgent means in order to prevent its impeding demise and death.

Nietzsche, himself a diseased man, spoke repeatedly of a German nation on the verge of self-destruction due to its multiple collective illnesses that, according to him, had contaminated the European continent (198). His concept of the *Übermensch* corresponds to the hallucinations of a feverish mind haunted by a frantic desire to recover from a devastating illness and, by association, extend its recovery to that of the German nation. Spanish thought on the subject of social disease is, thus, not unique and it should be viewed within the wider European paradigm. What is distinctive of the Spanish discourse on the subject of national disease, however, is its pervasive extent and depth. Disease is not just the occasional view of an isolated or marginal author. From Quevedo to Valle-Inclán and Luis Martín-Santos, Spanish history unfolds as a deepening process of deterioration and death. Appropriately, the victorious side in that conflict presented itself as possessing the right therapy for the country's illnesses and it frequently compared its task to that of a surgeon capable of extirpating the mortal cancer fast spreading through the national body.

In fact, the Civil War was the ultimate manifestation of the inability of the political class to find the appropriate prognosis and treatment for the national problems. The entire country succumbed to the perception of Spanish society and culture as too frail to achieve a path toward recovery. Therefore, Spain was apparently doomed to be the permanently sick nation of Europe, unable even to share in the grandiose and futile figurations of Nietzsche leading to the *Aufhebung* of a potential future Overman. The only project with a horizon of self-affirmation and recovery was the path of total political revolution—particularly in its anarchist and fascist versions—that was intent on the complete extinction of all contrary notions and thus it could never become a socially and culturally inclusive program.

There is no doubt that Spain has had a difficult relation with modernity and that its incapacity to effectively insert itself in the dynamics of the modern project has had a deleterious influence in the cultural evolution of the country. Spain has shown many of the symptoms associated with a sick and dysfunctional society, but it is not, however, the only country displaying those disturbing characteristics within the turbulent history of modern Europe. Other countries and areas of Europe (Germany, Italy, Poland, the Balkans, etc.), have also had a history of internal turmoil and destruction, often more extensive and intense than those of Spain. Beyond the undeniable problems of the country, the perception of the intellectual class and in particular that of its literary figures that the country was terminally ill has conditioned the national cultural history. Intellectual fatalism and institutional inaction and powerlessness have been decisive factors in the configuration of the country as doomed to failure.

The new cultural situation has brought a significant change in national self-perception. Instead of the metaphor of disease and decline linked to a regressive concept of time fixated in an ecstatic past and devoid of an open horizon of expectations, there now exists a cultural framework that, without obviating the difficulties presented by Spain's new diversified configuration, allows to view the country as fully integrated in the global discourse through the double path of a consolidated Europe and the vast and increasingly influential Hispanic world.

Conclusion: The Micro-projects

Spanish political and cultural history have traditionally moved within mutually exclusive parameters of self-delusion and false expectations that have prevented the realization of the full potential for the country. The forces oriented toward the past favored the reconnection with the glories of an era that was never as illustrious and superb as they pretended it to be and that, furthermore, contained within itself the seeds of its ulterior failure. On the other hand, the groups that viewed the ideology that shaped the past as the obstacle for evolution and progress, oscillated between ominous appraisals and destructively sarcastic analyses (Larra and Valle-Inclán are prototypical cases) and unabashedly apocalyptic predictions for the country. The voices of the many exiles of national history are examples. Luis Cernuda and Juan Goytisolo provide some powerful testimonies of this position that is anchored in the absolute denial of the values of the national culture. This extreme polarity as well as the collective incapacity for a less absolute and more precise national self-assessment contributed to the creation of a context of intractability and hopelessness in the approach to the many conflicts of the modern history of the country.

The new situation can hopefully contribute to the emergence of a diminished and modest but also more credible and functional collective conscience. Having started the critical reconsideration of a painful past—in particular the historically representative Civil War period—and having sidelined the previous uncompromising and totalizing ideological aims that had such negative consequences, the country is now poised for a reappraised perception of itself. After the abandonment of the mirages and delirious promises of the *Grande Histoire*, the time has now come for the country's engagement in the smaller but also more feasible and specific projects of a more inclusive and internationally open history.

Note

1. The analogy of this concept with the process of transformation in gender relations is relevant since the all-powerful and imperial vision of the nation relied upon a dominating masculine self that excluded other generic configurations.

Works Cited

Atxaga, Bernardo. *El hijo del acordeonista*. Madrid: Alfaguara, 2004.
Azaña, Manuel. *El jardín de los frailes*. Madrid: Alianza Editorial, 1988.
———. *Plumas y palabras*. Barcelona: Crítica, 2002.
Bloom, Harold. *The Western Canon*. New York: Harcourt Brace, 1994.
Bourdieu, Pierre. *The Field of Cultural Production*. New York: Columbia University Press, 1993.
Cercas, Javier. *Soldados de Salamina*. Barcelona: Tusquets, 2001.
Goytisolo, Juan. *Juan sin tierra*. Barcelona: Seix Barral, 1975.
———. *La resaca*. París: Club del libro español, 1958.
———. *Señas de identidad*. Mexico: Joaquín Mortiz, 1969.
Lipovetsky, Gilles. *Les temps hypermodernes*. Paris: Bernard Grasset, 2004.

Marías, Javier. *Todas las almas*. Barcelona: Anagrama, 1990.
———. *Tu rostro mañana, I: Fiebre y lanza*. Madrid: Alfaguara, 2002.
Muñoz Molina, Antonio. *Beatus Ille*. Barcelona: Seix Barral, 1986.
———. *Beltenebros*. Barcelona: Seix Barral, 1989.
———. *El jinete polaco*. Barcelona: Planeta, 1991.
———. *Sefarad*. Madrid: Santillana, 2002.
———. *Ventanas de Manhattan*. Barcelona: Seix Barral, 2004.
Navajas, Gonzalo. *La utopía en las narrativas contemporáneas: Novela/Arquitectura/Cine*. Zaragoza: Prensas de la Universidad de Zaragoza, 2008.
Nietzsche, Friedrich. *Twilight of the Idols/The Anti-Christ*. London: Penguin, 1990.
Pérez-Reverte, Arturo. *El capitán Alatriste*. Madrid: Alfaguara, 1996.
———. *El maestro de esgrima*. Madrid: Alfaguara, 1992.
Ricoeur, Paul. *Time and Narrative*. Vol. 3. Chicago: Chicago University Press, 1998.
Ruiz Zafón, Carlos. *La sombra del viento*. Barcelona: Planeta, 2001.
Vattimo, Gianni. *The Adventure of Difference*. Baltimore: The Johns Hopkins University Press, 1993.
Wallerstein, Immanuel. *The Uncertainties of Knowledge*. Philadelphia: Temple University Press, 2004.

11

Postmodernism and Spanish Literature

María del Pilar Lozano Mijares

To understand what has happened in Spanish literature from the time of the Transition to the present, the only truly comprehensive way to proceed is by accepting postmodernity as the episteme (in the Foucaultian sense of the word) of democratic Spain; that is, by assuming that the structure of knowledge in that country changed—as it did in all the other Western nations some ten years earlier—and that this change affected all artistic and cultural forms of expression. My aim in this essay is not to examine the controversy surrounding the reception of postmodern literature in Spain, as if it were something coming from outside, something external, but rather to analyze literature in Spain (particularly fiction) from the perspective of postmodernity—in other words, from a new way of looking at the world, a new epistemological structure that has permeated life there since the mid-seventies and has rapidly brought Spain up to date with other Western societies, which had found themselves in this new episteme since, symbolically speaking, 1968.

I will first address the emergence of the controversy regarding postmodernity in Spain within its socio-cultural context. Then, I will review what can be considered postmodern Spanish literature, with an emphasis on fiction. Finally, I will illustrate the two stages of postmodern Spanish narrative (from the 1980s' dark novels of disenchantment to the fiction of partial assertion of the nineties) through an analysis of two paradigmatic texts: *La verdad sobre el caso Savolta* (The Truth about the Savolta Case) by Eduardo Mendoza, published in 1975; and *La música del mundo o El efecto Montoliu* (The Music of the World or the Montoliu Effect) by Andrés Ibáñez, published in 1995. I consider those to be the greatest exponents of early and late Spanish postmodernism, respectively.

Postmodernity in Spain

Unlike other Western countries, in Spain postmodernism had in the beginning the status of a superficial fashion, something frivolous and imported, a perception it has yet to shake off. Just as Spanish painting resorted, in the early 1980s, to an abstract Informalist aesthetic, inherited from Tapiès, Saura, and Oteiza, while the other Western countries were already experiencing the return of figurative art characteristic of postmodernism, in Spain the advent of postmodernity was belated, a fact which came to underline its apparent ephemeral and trivial character.

As Bessière points out (49–68), the period from 1984 to 1988, was the key time frame for the publication of articles concerning postmodernity and, as a result, the beginning of the controversy in Spain. The newspaper *El País* had been playing a leading role since 1982, but there were other fundamental contributions, including the ones made by the denominational magazine *Razón y Fe*; by the colloquium "Pensar el presente" which took place in Madrid's Círculo de Bellas Artes in the spring of 1989 (attended by Jean-François Lyotard and Eugenio Trías, among others); by *Los Cuadernos del Norte* (issue number 43, July–August 1987); by the magazine *La Luna*; and by Francisco Umbral's book *Guía de la posmodernidad: Crónicas, personajes e itinerarios madrileños* (1987).

Two events marked the beginning of the debate in Spain, both linked to *El País*. The first was a colloquium on postmodern fiction that took place in Madrid and was reviewed in *El País* on March 15, 1984, under the headline "Nuevos narradores intentan definir la posmodernidad" (New Authors Try to Define Postmodernity). Manifestos were presented at this colloquium about a new kind of aesthetics, whose main core of supporters rallied around the neo-avant-garde magazine *La Luna*, published in Madrid. This publication served as an outlet for a new urban movement in which different theories of aesthetics coexisted, and was driven by an eagerness to create new art forms. Its initial success came mostly from the absence of a renovating project or a teleology, which were substituted by an acceptance of eclecticism. The novel *Larva*, by Julián Ríos, was declared the paradigm of postmodern Spanish literature.

The second event consisted in the polemic which, throughout 1984, went back and forth in the pages of the same newspaper between representatives of what Jesús Ibáñez (27) calls the Historical Left—Alfonso Sastre, Carlos Castilla del Pino—and representatives of a new left that defended postmodernity without incurring in an ideological right-wing position: José Luis Brea and Javier Sádaba. José Tono Martínez has since put together an anthology with articles from both sides.

In the beginning, Spanish postmodernism was, thus, concentrated in Madrid. Symptoms such as the cybernetic culture, the apotheosis of rock music and video, political apathy (*pasotismo*), the separation of technology from any aesthetic or moral consideration, eclectic and playful hedonism, the acceptance of show business as a way of life, etc., are all signs of the social sensitization towards postmodernity as episteme.

Regarding Spanish art, postmodernity gave rise to many different approaches. Painting soon aligned with the international trends: Miquel Barceló's neo-expressionism; the eclectic neo-figurativism of Ferrán García Sevilla, Luis Gordillo, Guillermo Pérez Villalta, Chema Cobo, Carlos Alcolea, and Manuel Quejido; the Informalist technological abstraction of José Manuel Broto and José María Sicilia; and Joan-Pere Viladecans's fluctuation between the abstract and the figurative. New artists emerged, but they no longer had approaches that were as well-defined as in the past: postmodern art is syncretic, even regressive. The central figure of "new figurativism" was Luis Gordillo, who had an enormous influence on the younger generations in the 1980s. Pictorial postmodernism featured the same characteristics in Spain as it did internationally: the recycling of traditional materials, which then bestow a new meaning on the reference or make an ironic parody of it; the heterogeneity of the hybrid; the negation of modern dogmas; chaotic sensibility; historic revitalization.

The first appearances of irony and contextualism in Spanish architecture took place between 1972 and 1975. They are landmarks along Madrid's Castellana Avenue: the *Bankunión* building by José Antonio Corrales and Ramón Vázquez Molezún; the *Bankinter* building by Rafael Moneo and Ramón Bescós; and the *Banco de Bilbao* by Sáenz de Oíza.

This type of architecture is a reaction against the dogmas of the International Movement. It rejects functionalism and proposes a free interpretation of tradition and history, like Rafael Moneo's exposed Roman brick wall of the National Museum of Roman Art (Mérida), or the recreation of the 1950s in the building on Doña María Coronel Street (Seville) by Antonio Cruz and Antonio Ortiz. Classicism, neo-traditionalism, regionalism—especially in the Basque Country, Andalusia, and Murcia—and eclectic rationalism or neo-rationalism are combined in the architectural projects by Bofill, Moneo, Navarro Baldeweg, and Linazasoro.

Barcelona, Madrid, and Seville are the three paradigmatic cities that symbolize the definitive acceptance of postmodern architectural principles in monument restoration and historical reinterpretation, as can be seen in the work undertaken as result of 1992: Moneo's Atocha train station; Antonio Vázquez de Castro and José Luis Iñíguez de Onzaño's elevators in the Reina Sofía Museum; the San Pablo airport in Seville, by Rafael Moneo; the *Moll de la Fusta*, by Manuel Solá-Morales and, generally speaking, the huge city blocks that make up Barcelona's Olympic Village.

Madrid's *Movida* (*the scene*) which, according to García Rodrigo, ended in 1988 (the same year the magazine *La Luna* came to an end), was the symbolic epicenter of this new, postmodern Spain. More specifically, it consisted of a cosmopolitan urban culture located around the Madrid neighborhood of Chueca and its bars (Ras, Casi Casi, Gris, No Se Lo Digas A Nadie), of personalities such as Almodóvar, of comics (*Cimoc, Cairo, Comix Internacional, Zona 84, El Víbora*) and magazines: *Madriz*, published by the Youth Department of the Madrid City Council (therefore, a government-supported magazine), edited by Carlos Otero and Felipe Hernández Cava; *Madrid Me Mata*, edited by Óscar Mariné Grandi; and, especially, *La Luna*, a cohesive element of the *Movida* from its first issue in 1983, published with neither official subsidies, nor financial support by Permanyiare, and whose first editor, Borja Casani, set an editorial line defined by the breaking of rules. It was in *La Luna* where Almodóvar published the first episode of the story of Patty Diphusa, and many authors collaborated, including Aranguren, Molina Foix, Lourdes Ortiz, Jesús del Pozo,

Ramoncín, Kiko Veneno, Javier Sádaba, Fernando Savater, and José Mª Caballero Bonald.

It should also be noted that in the early 1980s, the culture of consumerism fully entered Spain, which was by then immersed in a brand-new atmosphere of freedom and intellectual cosmopolitanism. Art became just another product on the market, something that had already happened in other Western countries. These, and other developments, made Spanish society postmodern and post-industrial. The *Movida* was, therefore, an expression of the postmodern episteme in democratic Spain, a sign that reveals its transformation into an advanced capitalistic society: its cultural logic, to use Jameson's words.

However, Spanish society did not only suffer from the disillusionment linked to the demise of the 1968 utopia and the loss of faith in social revolution, which marked the beginning of postmodernity in the West in general. Many left-wing artists and intellectuals were also disappointed in the Transition and the slow, tolerant tread towards Democracy, all of which was happening within the framework of growing international distrust in the ideals of progress and the technological improvement of humankind. Spain, then, became postmodern through a double disillusionment (national and international), and began to take on the cultural and social features characteristic of the new episteme: economic prosperity, uncontrolled consumerism, the search for pleasure, and the rise in values such as success, the ostentation of wealth, and youth. Madrid's *Movida* reflected a time of political and moral disarmament and of cultural apathy. In conclusion, the historical, social, and cultural events taking place from the seventies on, changed the worldview of the Spanish reality, throwing it into the postmodern episteme. Since the time of the Transition, Spanish literature has been, broadly speaking, postmodern, because the society within which it is produced also is, de facto, postmodern.

Key Issues in Postmodern Spanish Literature

Just as we cannot refer to postmodernity as something unique or encapsulated, we will not find one single stream of postmodern art, but, rather, different ways in which the new episteme affected art; in other words, what could be called the cognitive strategies of postmodernism. When applied to literature, these strategies could be summarized as follows:

> 1. **The portrayal of the world as an ontological problem,** or what I shall refer to as the "impossibility of realism," understood in its traditional, mimetic sense. In postmodern literature, reality vanishes to become an image, a simulation, and the self is satisfied, ironically and playfully, with this loss. In McHale's words, the postmodern novel deals with ontological issues related to questions about what the world is, who we are, and what the relationship is between the real, the possible, the impossible, etc. Therefore, the two basic genres for postmodern novels are fantasy and historical

fiction (in its variant known as historiographic metafiction), since they are suitable vehicles for the portrayal of unstable ontological worlds. These two genres express the non-distinction between reality and the image of reality, the impossibility of distinguishing truth from lies, the ontological abyss.

2. **The deconstruction of the subject, of space, and time.** The subject (as embodied in the author, the reader, the narrator, or the character) is no longer considered a coherent entity that generates meaning Its perception of reality and fiction is not formulated by total binary oppositions, but rather by an unstable play of coexistence that ends with the superposition of both—it is Jameson's schizophrenic subject. This fragmented, schizophrenic subject gives the novels' characters a keenness for deconstruction, not only of their own identity and psychology, but also of their relationship—or rather their inability to relate—with others. That is why the recurring themes in postmodern novels are the lack of communication, the fragmentation of emotions, the world's loss of meaning, spatial/temporal paranoia, and the absence of a relationship between mind and body. The character has become an itinerant being, and he drags the reader along with him to share in the process of creating the novel. The weak, postmodern subject affects time and space. In realist or modernist texts, the perception of the subject—the narrator or character—organizes narrative time and space. What happens when the subject vanishes? The result is a non-time that is shut away in a flat present without any signs of identity of its own, dominated by historical amnesia, and a non-place, multiple and heterogeneous, that is constructed and deconstructed at the same time—a space identified with the Foucaultian heterotopia, with McHale's "Zone," or with Augé's non-places.

3. **The immersion in metafiction,** by means such as recursivity, parody, appropriationism, and pastiche. The postmodern novel shows the very process of codifying strategies of meaning, which betray its fictional character. The reader's attention is thus drawn from the projected world towards the linguistic medium, making him think that there is no difference between reality and fiction. The construction of the world is reduced, in the end, to the result of a word game, since, as Lyotard has taught us, reality is a flexible web of language games.

4. **The skepticism towards the great discourses about reason and the search for other cognitive channels,** symbolic or mythic, to find meaning. The disillusionment that followed the last revolution against Reason, that of 1968, reaffirms the impossibility of utopia. Radicalism of any kind must be rejected and substituted by a tolerance that, for many, is nothing more than indifference and neo-conservatism, but that, for others, is the only way out (though, granted, a weak one). This ludic, ironic tolerance is conceived of as the only way to acknowledge the growing loss of meaning in the world and to keep on living in spite of it: to endorse chaos and adopt an ethic that may survive the fragmentation process of the great certainties. The omnipresent, ludic element works as a necessary distancing, as a relativization of the tragedies,

great or small, that postmodern characters suffer and, as readers, we identify with; it teaches us not to take life too seriously, to play with (in the sense of enjoying) the present, which is all we have, and to retrieve a mythic, symbolic childlike mentality, that physical/mathematical reason, taken by modernity to its extreme application, has snatched away from us.

If we follow these four cognitive strategies of literary postmodernism, can we speak of the existence of a "Spanish postmodern novel?" This is not a simple question, since there are many authors who even deny the existence of postmodernity in Spain. I do believe that we can speak of the postmodern Spanish novel in the same way that we have already spoken of postmodern painting or architecture in Spain. The difference, compared to other Western cultures, is basically a question of timeframe. We can find the first expressions of postmodernism in Spanish literature in the poetry of the *Novísimos* in the 1970s, and the publication of *La verdad sobre el caso Savolta* by Eduardo Mendoza (1975), marked the symbolic beginning of the postmodern Spanish novel.

The Earliest Spanish Postmodern Fiction: Eduardo Mendoza

Chronologically speaking, I must point out that 1975 does not mark a radical change in the evolution of fiction in Spain. The first novels which we can identify as postmodern had already emerged at the beginning of the 1970s; they came from the death throes of experimental fiction, from the deconstruction of experimental procedures, and they signaled the initial return to conventional narrative techniques. Most prominent among those were the novels of Gonzalo Torrente Ballester, a writer with ties to the end of the experimental novel, the end of the reign of metafiction, and to the return of seemingly more traditional ways of narrating, but only seemingly so, as parody was always a part of his approach (see *La saga/fuga de J. B*). The precedents of the Spanish postmodern novel lie, therefore, in the last experimental novels. I agree with Benson that *Tiempo de silencio* by Luis Martín-Santos marked the beginning of the end of modern assumptions: the break with the traditional concept of mimesis and the end of the hopes of overcoming the chaos of the real through a representation of the world dominated by the author's almighty self. But experimental novels are not necessarily postmodern, as is demonstrated by the two basic elements which make most novels from the eighties postmodern: the return to narrativity and the reprivatization of the novel, both of which will be discussed further down.

Nonetheless, we must recognize 1975 as a key date for the Spanish postmodern novel, from a symbolic point of view, in the same way that 1968 may be said to signal the beginning of postmodernity in the Western world. The year 1975 marks not only the beginning of the Transition—and, with it, the change of episteme in Spanish society—but also the publication of the first Spanish novel which is fully postmodern and completely removed from the experimental novel: *La verdad sobre el caso*

Savolta. In my view, as a result of the social and cultural atmosphere pervading after 1975, which would span the 1980s, this first postmodern novel is closely associated with the so-called "fiction of disenchantment" (see Martínez Cachero, Spitzmesser). However, this novel not only reflects the disappointment and broken illusions surrounding the Spanish democratic reality, but also, and especially, the lucid bitterness of the postmodern episteme.

Therefore, the first point that we should consider when describing Spanish postmodern fiction is disenchantment, a disappointment that provoked, on one hand, the return to narrativity, and on the other, the reprivatization of the novel. Both consequences came as a response to the changes introduced in Spain by the postmodern episteme. In thematic terms, this disenchantment is conveyed by themes such as: the disappointment in the political reality of democracy in Spain; historical amnesia concerning the Civil War; unfulfilled lives; difficult or failed human relationships; disconnected, illogical individual desires; nostalgia for former security; anguish regarding the responsibility of democracy; self-pity, self-indulgence, and a lack of solidarity; escapism. In structural terms we encounter the following procedures: multiple levels of diegesis ("Russian doll" texts); parodic hybridization of canonic and marginal writing forms; plot structures involving mystery or intrigue; unfulfilled derealization of space; pastiche.

This is the kind of disenchantment that informs *La verdad sobre el caso Savolta*, whose content and formal features have just been summarized in the paragraph above. Mendoza's novel, regardless of the fact that it is set in the troubled 1920s, speaks of a crisis of trust that extends to all of Spain's administrative, organizational, and social structures. The witness who, theoretically, knows the truth, Nemesio Cabra Gómez, is a quasi-Homeric madman, to whom no one listens; the policeman, Captain Vázquez, who in the beginning makes an effort to uphold justice, is exiled, and finally decides to give up his goal due to existential exhaustion. Truth and justice are unattainable and everything dissolves into conspiracy theories, which not even the ending (left neither open nor closed) manages to clear up. Uncertainties are not only left unsolved, but they are amplified to infinity, including the final melodramatic detail pointing to the possibility that Lepprince may be the son of the lawyer, Cortabanyes, which reduces him to just another puppet, a very postmodern antihero at heart, like the main character, Javier Miranda, who describes himself in the following terms:

> En cuanto a mí, ¿qué puedo decir? Todo aquello me traía sin cuidado, indiferente a cuanto no fuera mi propio caso. Creo que habría recibido como una resurrección la revolución más caótica, viniera de donde viniese, con tal de que aportara una leve mutación a mi vida gris, a mis horizontes cerrados, a mi soledad agónica y a mi hastío de plomo. El aburrimiento corroía como un óxido mis horas de trabajo y de ocio, la vida se me escapaba de las manos como una sucia gotera. (Mendoza 196)

(As for me, what can I say? I didn't care about any of that, I felt indifferent to anything that didn't concern me directly. I think I would have welcomed the most chaotic revolution—wherever it may have come from—like a resurrection, if it had only brought a slight mutation to my gray life, to my closed horizons, my anguished solitude and my leaden tedium. Boredom corroded my hours of work and leisure like rust, life was running through my hands like a dirty leak.)

Miranda perfectly embodies one of the cognitive strategies of postmodernism pointed out above: the deconstruction of the subject. A being without will, absurd, ridiculous in his amorous experiences (his ironically licit ones—María Coral—as well as his explicitly illicit ones—Teresa) and in his frustrated attempts at heroism, Miranda does not control his own life and is subject to powers which he either does not know, or does not want to face. And when he is able to make a decision, fear and apathy triumph over him, allowing him to continue in a senseless, aimless status quo. In the end, disillusionment leads to the reprivatization of the novel—that is, the impossibility of objectively representing a world and the constant ontological destabilization—and to the return of narrativity, to the very need of telling stories as the only escape from the metastories which constituted the previous modern episteme.

The return to narrativity involves the return to a (supposedly) traditional kind of fiction, whose basic function is to tell stories, to narrate. The new narrators publish novels that seem to return to realism, but are enriched by a formal, psychological treatment, a false mimesis in the traditional sense—false because the recovery of the literary past and the return to traditional narrative forms refer to the inscription/subversion process of postmodernism, to ironic and intertextual parody. This is why we can speak of an apparent realism, the same kind which gives *La verdad sobre el caso Savolta* its structure.

In short, it could be said that the novel of the 1980s reflects the end of social realism and of experimentalism. The return to postmodern narrativity, therefore, consists in the recovery of the need for a plot, something that experimental narrators, in their destructive effort against modernity, had forgotten, which made them drift away from the readers, and led to the absolute impossibility of describing identity or the world. The plot, thus, again, became the main driving force of the story, in an attempt to reclaim reader through intrigue and entertainment, through the mere pleasure of telling a story. This is what caused the boom of historiographic metafiction, texts which present adventures set in times past, whose events and characters are, at the same time, true and false, historical and invented: the difference no longer matters; it was deconstructed when History died as a metastory of modernity. The only crucial element is verisimilitude; the appearance of truth lends reality to the character or anecdote, making the unreal real and the real unreal, while identifying essence with appearance in a hyperreal environment. From this point of view, *La verdad sobre el caso Savolta* is the first Spanish novel of postmodern historiographic metafiction. It is set in the realm of what "seems," what "might be," and what "depends," where truth is embedded in postmodernity; or on the limits of parody, of mockery, as we see in a letter Captain Vázquez writes his helper, Sergeant Totorno, during the first days of his exile in Tetuán:

> Querido amigo:
> No pierda la moral. Si se siente desfallecer, piense que la lucha a favor de la verdad es la más noble misión a que un hombre puede aspirar sobre la tierra. Y ésa es, precisamente, la misión del policía. (Mendoza 168)

> (Dear friend:
> Don't let things get you down. If you feel your spirits flagging, remember that the struggle for truth is the noblest mission a man can have on this earth. And that is, precisely, the mission of the police.)

The return to narrativity goes hand in hand with the recovery of paraliterature, with the genre pastiche, which also reflects the democratization of art characteristic of postmodernity: urban, crime, detective, erotic, romantic, autobiographical fiction, etc. There are no clear demarcations: the postmodern hybridization of genres and typologies is widespread, leading to the breakdown of the boundary between highbrow and popular novels, making pastiche the quintessential technique—the mix, almost always playful or ironic, of elements that come from mass media cultural products, with references traditionally considered highbrow. But the recovery of paraliterary genres and a supposedly traditional narrativity will never be the result of a realist mimetic effort. There will always be an ironic distance, a transgressive or even destructive purpose. The best example of this transgression in *La verdad sobre el caso Savolta* is the parody of the melodrama genre (which is completely ridiculed) and of the police and court drama genres (their procedures are subverted when their fundamental objective—to unveil the truth—is not carried out).

This demise of traditional realist mimesis, already deeply wounded by experimental fiction, is also apparent in the reprivatization of the Spanish novel. The superposition of the self, of the intimate and the subjective, on the former ambition of portraying the world objectively, is not only a desire, a conscious decision of the new narrators, it is also the acknowledgment that it is no longer possible to describe reality in terms of oneness and totality, and that this loss of referents has caused the end of the modern, Cartesian subject, the fading of the postmodern self.

Faced with this essential loss of its own identity and with the world surrounding it, the Spanish postmodern novel of the 1980s claims feelings and memory as tools to make an investigation into the self, to rebuild it. That is why it has been called a narcissistic, self-absorbed, private, or neo-existentialist novel, though with one basic nuance; such rebuilding will be impossible, the attempt will be frustrated, and the only possible option is the exaltation of a multiple, scattered reality, resulting in a fall into nihilistic hedonism, or an escape in time or space. The consequences in narrative terms are clear, especially in *La verdad sobre el caso Savolta*: a breakdown of space/time barriers, the indissoluble mix of fantasy and reality, a relativizing polyphony and a subjective narrator—a narrator, who always self-constructs within the text, with the resulting dose of contradiction, doubt, and perplexity—and, finally, social uprooting and depolitization.

The message the new novel sends out is the skepticism, implied by the negation of any set of values other than a personal one, and even these values are in a state of continual fluctuation. However, this skepticism is related to the postmodern vision of the world, and, from that point of view, these writers are profoundly realistic. In a world in which the reproduction of reality is entrusted to audiovisual media—and these reproduce the hyperreal, since the Real as a single, true entity has ceased to exist.

La verdad sobre el caso Savolta sums up, step by step, the traits mentioned as key components of the postmodern Spanish novel of the 1980s. By using a fragmented and polyphonic narrative structure, that combines the alleged reproduction of formal, reliable judicial texts, with journalistic articles, omniscient narration, and the first-person account by the main character, Javier Miranda, the novel expresses the problematization of the representation of the story and, therefore, the acceptance of the past as a metastory and the resulting ontological destabilization of the represented world. As we said earlier, this is the first text of Spanish postmodern historiographic metafiction, and it opened the doors to other paradigmatic novels that came later, such as *La parábola de Carmen la Reina* by Manuel Talens and *Fabulosas narraciones por historias* by Antonio Orejudo. In *La verdad sobre el caso Savolta*, reality is diluted into fragments, and truth depends on how these fragments are put together, on the subjectivity of the narrator and the reader, who is forced to reconstruct the pieces and, therefore, to include his/her own interpretation into the facts, re-creating them together with the author. And time has become a schizophrenic flat space, since the thread that united it in an organized fashion of past-present-future is broken. Javier Miranda says:

> Los recuerdos de aquella época, por acción del tiempo, se han uniformado y convertido en detalles de un solo cuadro. Desaparecida la impresión que me produjeron en su momento, limadas sus asperezas por la lija de nuevos sufrimientos, las imágenes se mezclan, felices o luctuosas, en un plano único y sin relieve. (Mendoza 122)

> (Due to the effect of time, my memories from that period have become uniform, like the details of a single painting. The impression they made on me at the time has vanished, their roughness filed down by the sandpaper of new suffering, and so the images, happy or painful, are now mixed together into one single, flat surface.)

La verdad sobre el caso Savolta is also a perfect example of the return to narrativity and of the new pact made with the reader, though keeping in mind the lessons learned from experimentation, as many of the experimental resources run through the novel. Mendoza's basic aim is to tell, to narrate, and in the process, he appropriates the narrative macro and micro structures of paraliterature in an unprecedented hybridization or genres pastiche: crime, court drama, espionage, romance, melodrama, picaresque, social tableau. As a kind of experiment, we can read side by side any fragment from the inflammatory article by Domingo Pajarito de Soto in the newspaper *La Voz de la Justicia* or from his conversations with Javier Miranda about anarchy; another fragment from the impassioned romantic narration of the impossible love between Miranda and Teresa or María Coral; another from the comical, ironic transcript of Judge Davidson's interrogation of Miranda; another of the crazed picaresque scene at the cabaret where Lepprince and Miranda meet to hire María Coral's pair of thugs; another of Captain Vázquez's depositions; and we could see how the concept of the modern novel explodes, destroyed by Mendoza's playful, postmodern rather cinematic pastiche.

The final message of Mendoza's text could not be more postmodern. He speaks of a radical disenchantment, an extreme distrust towards the revolutionary utopia, personified by the senseless anarchists we see in the novel, who are absurd in their heroism and pathetic in their impossible victory; of the acceptance of history as just another metastory, of the ontological destabilization of a world in which there is no distinction between reality and fiction; of the impossibility to find truth even in the sacrosanct realms of objectivity and reason, here personified by the transcript of the trial held in the United States, by those dialogues filled with irony where Mendoza mocks the claims of objectivity of court trials which try to narrow life to yes/no questions, a claim that is substituted, by the means of parody, by the "it depends" of postmodernity.

1990s Postmodernism: Andrés Ibáñez

Up to this point, I have reviewed the main traits of post-1975, dark novels of disenchantment, as exemplified by Eduardo Mendoza's inaugural text. But, what happened in the 1990s? Do the same parameters continue to apply? Some of the critics actually seem to think that postmodernity, that belligerent and destructive postmodernity of the 1980s, became itself a metanarrative, and then disappeared.

From a sociological point of view, the fiction of the 1990s seems to have changed very little in comparison with that of the 1980s. Yet, the novel was to take a new turn around 1995. What changed in Spain was the social and cultural landscape, which became fully integrated with the European and, by extension, the larger Western context. In 1989, the Berlin wall came down and, with it, the possibility of communism as an alternative to capitalism; we learned the meaning of the terms *globalization, neo-liberalism,* and *illegal immigration*; we became disillusioned with the utopian welfare society, especially with state companies being constantly privatized and the increasing cuts in the protection offered by the State; we suffered the outbursts of a more and more radical Right, and a Left which rejected the classical models to take refuge either in a Center very similar to the Right, or in anti-globalization groups.

The turn taken by Spanish literature around 1995, must be viewed within the context of widespread changes in Western society. The Spanish novel was to enter what Navajas calls the "new aesthetics of partial assertion" or "neomodernism" as it tried to go beyond the emptiness of the postmodern impulses of the 1980s, in order to present a new set of proposals. The fiction of the 1990s tended to reconstruct the self, space, and time through the filter of the narrator's subjectivity. This does not mean that modern considerations regained currency; rather, once the impossibility of objective historicism had been assumed, attempts were made to account for it through the lenses of a self which was aware of its own instability.

The fiction of the 1990s was, therefore, essentially nostalgic. It responded to the disappearance of the totalizing expectations that earlier postmodernism destroyed, by acknowledging the extinction of all the great causes. But, again, this did not mean a return to the modern episteme: the self was questioned, not summarily rejected. This is how the fiction of that decade responded to the solipsistic, hermetic totalitarianism of initial postmodernism.

The latest postmodern writers do not go back to mimetic, totalizing constructions of reality, nor do they reaffirm the possibility of a direct correspondence between the sign and the referent. Rather, they are overcoming the skepticism and the nihilistic emptiness of the first postmodern authors through the creation of imaginary and subjective (but metaphorically real) worlds, in a hopeful attempt to give an account of their own reality and their own selves, if only a partial one, through words. Andrés Ibáñez's work can be placed within this framework.

Ibáñez's novels propose a new way of perceiving reality that accepts and exceeds the logical/rational approaches of modernity: space, time, identity, the relationship of cause and effect, and so on. Those principles altered in order to enter another dimension which, after all, is rather old, since it looks back towards thousand-year-old cultures, or at our own origins, which were swept away by the force of reason. This new creative gaze has its most direct theoretical equivalent in Jameson's proposals: postmodernity implies a change in the perception of time, space and identity, and this change imposes on art the need to propose a new way of looking. Jameson calls this "radical difference," that is, to perceive reality not like something fragmented which, in the end, refers back to a notion of oneness, to an ultimate rational truth and to the measure of man—the specialty of the modern episteme. Rather, it is a matter of perceiving the fragments as such, as chaos within a new order, while also overcoming the nihilist emptiness of dwelling on chaos and fragments (the position represented by Mendoza's novel).

Andrés Ibáñez's first novel, *La música del mundo o El efecto Montoliu* (1995), sets the framework for his fiction in terms of postmodernity. The novel is approached from the start as a fable, as a story that knows it is a narrative: "la historia comienza con un muchacho que coge el tren al anochecer, con un viejo escritor" (Ibáñez 11) (the story begins with a boy who takes the train at nightfall, with an old writer). It is not a coincidence that this first sentence does not follow the punctuation rule of capitalization: it is a false beginning. In reality, there is no beginning to Ibáñez's novel, for if there were one, it would put us in a lineal, causal timeframe. In *La música del mundo* time is a motif, a musical phrase that is repeated in many variations. The events narrated are "episodios entrecortados que terminan en sí mismos y que no consiguen salir de la inmovilidad anónima de la naturaleza" (12) (jagged episodes that end in themselves, incapable of getting away from the anonymous immobility of nature). They do not head towards an end, nor do they recover a past; they are self-sufficient and, therefore, immobile. Such is, for Ibáñez, the time of the story: "parece que la música del bosque conoce ya toda la historia, desde mucho antes de que suceda" (13) (it seems that the music of the forest already knows the entire story, long before it may even take place). Everything we are going to read is already there, in nature, in reality, as if it were a musical recording. Like a guide, Ibáñez shows us how to listen; the staffs are the key to the structure of the novel, the mode we must adopt in order to read it. From time to time, we are reminded that the book becomes something physical, that it never ceases to be paper and ink.

"Todo tenía su melodía en la música del mundo, la vida tenía su melodía y también era una melodía la muerte" (16) (everything had its melody in the music of the world, life had its melody and there was also a melody for death): in the novel's system of representation, reality is not made of words, of a logical and ordered system; it is made of temporal undulations, in other words, music. In this world, the conversation between a dog and a cat in a remote street of Vienna is completely real, as real as Block (one of the main characters, together with Jaime and Estrella), strolling down this same street. A different question is if we are able to understand that conversation, because our capacity for thinking does not enable us to listen to it. With this Cervantine wink, "El sol de Viena" (Vienna's Sun), the first chapter, constitutes the first movement of a symphony: what is left behind is the motif of the escape, which is completed as a kind of a circle with Países's escape at the end of the novel.

The narrator constantly meddles in the story; like an orchestra conductor, he sets the tempos and conducts the reader. He shows her the path and explains the steps she has to take. He does not allow us to enter the mimetic system of representation, even though he is telling us a story. It is as if we heard two voices at the same time: one that narrates the events; the other telling us "don't forget that this is fiction." This way, the reader and the text gradually position themselves on the same level of diegesis. Ibáñez wants us to be aware of the fact that we are reading. The book is not fiction, just as Andrés Ibáñez is not fiction when he addresses us, the readers, from the pages of his novel. If Ibáñez does not give us freedom, it is because he wants us to realize that, even when we are reading, we are not free.

This impossibility of fiction is combined with the impossibility of placing the narrative within time or space. What is theoretically real is confused with the imaginary; the past (or what, in a hyperreal way, we identify as past: a nineteenth century, post-romantic, or even a medieval atmosphere) is mixed in our perception with the present time of television or a student party filled with drugs, alcohol and sensuality. We seem to lose the time/space anchors even before we have even read thirty pages. "Años de peregrinaje" (Years of Pilgrimage) tells us about Block's past, about his flight from Tristenia with his mother, his life in Paris and, afterwards, in Vienna.

It is a regressive movement, but it already includes some prolepses, the future: it mentions the Residencia, Jaime, and Países. Indeed, we cannot forget the assumption made since we started reading: "parece que la música del bosque conoce ya toda la historia, desde mucho antes de que suceda" (13) (it seems that the music of the forest already knows the whole story, long before it may even take place).

"Block en Países" (Block in Países), a section within the novel, completely submerges us in the ontological destabilization. We were unable to recognize the space and time in which the story was set in the first two chapters but, here, we are told of a more concrete, though foreign land, making the time uncertainty much easier to come to terms with. Problems begin when we encounter Block, strolling around a city called Países (countries), where, surprisingly, there is a Biblioteca Nacional (National Library), a Círculo de Bellas Artes, streets called Serrano and López de Hoyos (and even a gas station on the corner of López de Hoyos and María de Molina), as well as an "Atocha beach." Atocha, a train station located on the south side of Madrid, is real, like the rest of the aforementioned places in Madrid. But Madrid, at least up until now, is not on the coast; and it has a river, although it is not called Obrantes. Ibáñez constructs a space that is real and imaginary at the same time: it is Madrid and it is not Madrid, or at least not the Madrid we see, in the same way that the novel's Servadac Park is the Retiro Park and, yet again, it isn't. Or could it be that we have just never seen it well? The ontological doubt Ibáñez causes is such that we go so far as to ask ourselves if Madrid could be on the sea, even if we had never noticed. Little by little, the geography of Países/Madrid identifies itself as the Biblioteca Nacional, the Servadac/Retiro Park, and the mythical space of the Región Confabulada, and we get to know it under the guidance of a peculiar, eighteenth century character, Halifax y Farfán. In the Biblioteca Nacional, Jaime discovers a book, signed by this enlightened erudite, in which he describes a "Jardín de Flores" (Flower Garden). We sense that the Jardín de Flores is the Retiro Park, and we witnesses how Jaime, Block, and Estrella experience the power of this invention at the Almadrea ruins inside the park. Halifax y Farfán's dream, a Botanical Garden in the image of the world, containing all the world's knowledge, is the Servadac Park, the Retiro, which, in turn, represents the real.

In this non-context (since we don't know very well where we are, or when) Ibáñez gives us the aid of a theory: the Montoliu effect, Montoliu being Jaime and Block's professor. Thus we find the essential postmodernism of *La música del mundo*:

> transformamos la casualidad en la historia de nuestra vida, convertimos la realidad multiforme en una obra de arte, y eso es el efecto; de un torrente de impresiones y percepciones inventamos un 'yo', del cúmulo de actos en los que participa o se ve envuelto ese 'yo,'inventamos una 'vida,' con increíble talento, arreglando aquí y allá, quitando y añadiendo, componemos unos recuerdos y los dotamos de una belleza y una felicidad que jamás tuvieron, ése es el efecto. (Ibáñez 309)

(we transform chance into our life story, we turn multiform reality into a work of art, and this is the effect; from an outpouring of impressions and perceptions we invent a "self," from the host of acts this "self" participates in or gets wrapped up in, we invent a 'life,' using great talent, fixing it up here and there, adding and taking away, we put together memories and bestow on them a beauty and happiness they never had, that is the effect.)

The effect, in the language of postmodern theorists, is the metanarrative or the metastory, an intellectual structure learned *a priori*, which contains our capacity to perceive reality. It is, therefore, the Foucaultian episteme, and Ibáñez, as if he were one of Borges's characters, proposes escaping from the parameters in which the West has shut away reality: the idea of time, the idea of causality, the idea of identity, and what combines all of them, language. Imagination is the means to escape this effect. The freedom of human beings lies, then, in their capacity to rid themselves of the chains of thought.

We perceive reality within a given set of *a priori* parameters and, therefore, we distort it at the same time we perceive it. What this novel tries to do is to perceive without understanding, to feel without thinking, because this is the only way to get away from the effect and to really live. The metatextual processes of ontological destabilization, the lack of any grounding on space/time, the author's continual appearances, the self-quotes, and the philosophical digressions, are all intended to make us aware of the process of perception, as if the novel was life. Ibáñez wants us to escape from the effect, and the first step must be reading in a different way, without understanding, just following our intuition and moving ahead.

The novel works, then, on two levels: that of pure theory, in which Ibáñez tries to make us understand the problem, so that we may process it intellectually; and that of pure experience, where the theory may be lived out. Jaime, Block, and Estrella's experiences are found on this second level: their walk through Servadac Park, the *praderabruckner*, everything that is experience without logical/rational thought. In the *praderabruckner* ceremony, we begin hearing a phrase that will be often repeated: "el final de una época del mundo" (Ibáñez 153) (the end of a world era). It is the relative end: the end of a certain kind of thinking, that of modern Western culture; the end of the separation of people from nature; the end of dualistic thought, dissolved into a holistic interpretation of reality that is much older than our own rational models.

Through Block, who experiences the moment of initiation with the prediction of a journey of knowledge in the Servadac Park, Ibáñez warns us: watch out, reader, wake up, open your mind, put aside your need for understanding, and just feel. In order to feel, the narrative has to become three-dimensional, it has to reach all of the senses: the many drawings Ibáñez places within the pages make us see *La música del mundo* like a coded map. It is not only a hybridization of genres or artistic systems as a textual process, like we saw with Mendoza, as a provocation against the rules that govern literary theory. Rather, it is the understanding of the novel as a genre that includes all the genres, thus canceling the very concept of genre.

In the same way that we can find poems, musical staffs, or drawings in a novel, the Servadac Park appears as the realm of the Possible, the space where anything can happen. In this space of the Possible, Block has an illumination, the magic moment when he discovers, by intuition, his place in the world, who he is, and he realizes that this illumination must be our aim in life. The question is not forgetting it, remembering it against the effect. And the only way to achieve this, the path for obtaining this knowledge about reality, is through hearing, through music, rather than sight, which brings us to the object, and from object to concept, and from the concept to thought. Hearing the music of the world, then, is nothing more than getting away from the effect. It is the path for acquiring knowledge of a true reality, since we only understand fragments of reality. And the same thing happens with Ibáñez's novel: there comes a time when we no longer want to understand. But we keep reading, and the words penetrate us without looking for a logical, cognitive meaning. They simply are; they are there and, in some respects, this is the only way they can be understood. The opposite consists in being inside the effect, which characterizes of our Western world. Ibáñez's postmodernist approach lies in this attempt to overcome the fragment (the chaos where we have seen Mendoza take refuge), through means that do not imply a return to the assumptions of modernity. He exceeds these assumptions and proposes a new vision of the world.

The stroll through Servadac Park is the climax of the novel. After that, all we can do is make our way down to the final conclusion. Ibáñez begins closing circles; Montoliu's theoretical talk (the effect) is juxtaposed with the experience of the *praderabruckner* (music), and both take us to Servadac Park (the exit from the effect is associated to the experience of music), in order to finally go back to Montoliu. But this time it is a very different Montoliu. "Montoliu en su camping" (Montoliu in his Campsite) is a prose poem, an epic of the everyday. After reading entire pages of poetic prose, it seems peculiar that Ibáñez chooses verse to convey a narrative, throwing us into the reality of the effect, and into the reality of metafiction: Ibáñez, as the real author, intervenes abruptly to discuss his own text.

The novel's descending movement begins with this poem: Montoliu surrenders, he stops fighting against the effect and allows himself to go along with it, accepting his insertion in the academic and professional world of literature. This exhaustion is necessary for Block and Jaime's evolution: after learning all they could learn from Montoliu, the latter must disappear for the two main characters to follow their own path. Here Estrella's role begins to take on real importance. We gradually identify her as a key player in the necessary escape from the effect, as she seems to be able to observe the world from an angle that is different from that of Jaime and Block's: she is much closer to nature, much further away from the great intellectual constructs Jaime creates. Estrella sees everything in a simpler way because her close contact with pleasure, with the natural world of the senses, makes her purer. This is why she is more capable than the male characters of withdrawing from rational thought, a kind of reasoning which fights against itself and ends up shattered.

The end of summer leads to the end of the lessons. Time in "Invierno de zarzamora" (Blackberry Winter) goes far beyond the theoretical approach of the beginning of the novel. We could say that the word (the theory) becomes flesh: time really becomes what Estrella calls "trans-time," a time that can no longer be conceived in the old way (circular), that is not broken or fragmented (as in Mendoza's case), but which is simultaneous—it stretches and goes back on itself. Things happen and, at the same time, they don't happen; events are narrated and denied. The ontological universe has been completely destroyed, or perhaps it has entered another dimension, an Einsteinian dimension, in which time has actually become a flat space. The main characters of this new dimension are Block and Estrella, whose love frames the new events and the new perception.

Block and Estrella's training moves away from the purely intellectual/speculative form and towards the sensual/intuitive. We gradually sense that the Región Confabulada is reality, that it is inside what we understand as reality. It does not designate a different space, but rather a different perception of the same space. The narration, then, becomes simultaneous, and Ibáñez leads us through paths of a time that is multilinear, spatial. Block, from the folds of his bedspread, is the one who observes and, at the same time, experiences all the paths of time. Events take place and they don't. Block is under his comforter and, at the same time, strolling through the streets of Países or eating in a restaurant on Christmas day. He does not imagine it or dream it, nor is it a metaphor to be interpreted. That is how it happens.

The end of the experience with trans-time leads us to the second most important metafictional moment in the novel, together with Montoliu's prose poem. This time, it includes a further ontological twist, since it is not only Ibáñez who speaks to us from the pages of his novel, but now it is the characters themselves who discuss it. The ontological destabilization is complete. The breakup of trans-time and the beginning of the love between Block and Estrella take us back to the beginning of the novel through an intra-textual quote. The opening sentence of the novel is repeated again, like a persistent memory. The beginning leads to the end, and the end to the beginning. The symphony is letting us know that it is about to end. And it seems as if this prelude to the end needs explaining: Estrella's rational and metafictional explanation of the mystery of the novel—Block is an agent for the Región Confabulada—and also the absurd explanation, the non-explanation, of "El monzón de mayo explicado a los niños" (The May Monsoon Explained to Children), an ironic quote from Lyotard's book on postmodernism and the only place in the entire book when punctuation marks are used. Ibáñez seems to be telling us that the pretension of rationality—an explanation—can only pertain to metafiction or philosophical theory, which is useless, judging by the author's mockery.

After the theoretical and metatextual interlude, events follow quickly. The May monsoon causes Block to drift away from Jaime and Estrella, as well as a series of chain reactions, a kind of banalization or normalization of the characters' lives: the calm which, like with a monsoon, precedes the storm. They are preparing for "the end of a world era" (Ibáñez 408). Jaime's desire to cross over to the other side, to investigate into the Región Confabulada, dies out, and he completes his insertion into the effect. In contrast, the Región opens up for Block and Estrella, as it is the space for love: Franz and Diotima's androgynous union between the intellectual and the sensual, which annuls time.

When we finish the last page of the book, we are left with a feeling that, from the beginning, the Región Confabulada *is* Países, that Países *is* Madrid, and that what we confront *is* reality. The characters are not aware of it—neither are we, the readers—because they are inside the effect and they cannot see it. Block sees it from the height provided by love and magic, either because he has been an agent since the beginning (as it is said in the novel), or because he has been turned into an agent.

La música del mundo is, in reality, a *Bildungsroman*, a novel of learning about happiness which, in short, consists in living outside of time, outside of the effect. Ibáñez allows himself, like any nineteenth century narrator, to conclude with a wish predicting the arrival of happiness in the world after we have freed ourselves from the effect, from thought, and everything is music without meaning, pure being-in-grace:

> llegará un mundo en que reinará la felicidad, los más sabios serán más felices . . . será un mundo no interpretado, un 'universo oído . . .' las cosas significarán menos, o apenas significarán, y esto nos permitirá vivir . . . entro por entre los árboles, en el jardín del mundo, y entonces comprendo . . . nuestro *yo* no será tan fuerte, no importará mucho la intención . . . si quieres saber algo del mundo del mañana, escucha, porque así será . . . las mujeres se pondrán trajes de lujo para ir al campo, los cristianos practicantes tendrán imágenes de Siva copulando con Kali . . . habrá entre las cosas nuevas relaciones, los significados se relacionarán de una manera diferente, o apenas se relacionarán . . . se debilitará el sentido, el efecto ya no tendrá apenas efecto . . . no se trata del mundo al revés, o el caos, sino de la libertad, de la pureza . . . cada acción será pura, sin intención, sin significado, y entre unas acciones y otras podremos curvarnos como melodías . . . libres del yo, nos libraremos de los grupos, de las consignas, ya no tendremos tanto miedo. (Ibáñez 472)

> (a world will come in which happiness will reign, the wisest will be the happiest . . . it will be an uninterpreted world, a 'heard universe . . . ' things will mean less, or will barely mean anything at all, and this will allow us to live . . . I enter amidst the trees, in the garden of the world, and then I understand . . . our *self* will not be so strong, the intention will not mean much . . . if you want to know something about the world of tomorrow, listen, because that's how it will be . . . women will wear luxury dresses to go to the countryside, practicing Christians will have images of Shiva copulating with Kali . . . new relationships will form between things, meanings will relate in a different way, or will barely relate . . . meaning will weaken, the effect will barely have any effect . . . it is not a question of the world upside down, or chaos,

but freedom, purity . . . each action will be pure, without intention, without meaning, and between some actions and others we will be able to bend ourselves like melodies . . . freed from the self, we will be free from groups, from slogans, we will no longer be so afraid.)

But this wish is projected into the future. Like Ibáñez himself indicates, *La música del mundo* is a book from "the Montoliu effect's last generation": its characters, its author, its readers . . . we are all inside the effect, not outside. Perhaps, in some cases we may be more or less aware of the effect (postmodernism as an episteme is nothing more than the awareness of the effect and the desire to get away from it). But, regarding this novel, we are placed on the edge. That is why we are searchers. We have yet to hear the music of the world, although we have sensed it. A new generation will have to come before we can announce the death of the effect, a world that, while still being ours, will also be new, and it is announced at the end of *La música del mundo*: this generation is the protagonist of Andrés Ibáñez's following novel, *El mundo en la era de Varick* (The World in the Times of Varick).

As I have attempted to show, Spain has been a postmodern society since roughly the time of its transition to democracy. Much of its literature shares the postmodern features of a large portion of Western literature from the last two decades. The experimental novel represents the end of the modern episteme. And, even while this kind of novel may be said to negate it, it is still part of a modern worldview.

There is not a specific type of Spanish postmodern fiction, but rather a series of *narrative strategies* that are the consequence of the postmodern episteme in Spanish literature: the portrayal of the world as an ontological problem; the deconstruction of the subject, of space and time; the immersion in metafiction; the skepticism towards the great discourses about reason and the search for other cognitive channels. Needless to say, not all Spanish novels after 1975 are postmodern. Many of them belong to the modern episteme, in terms of their acceptance, continuity, and even exaltation of its principles (and this statement does not imply any judgment value of these novels). Similarly, not all the writers who published their fiction after the transition are postmodernist, although none of them can avoid to be termed "postmodern" as individuals, whether they are in favor or against the phenomenon of postmodernity.

Works Cited

Augé, Marc. *Fictions fin de siècle suivi de Que se passe-t-il? 29 février, 31 mars, 30 avril 2000*. Paris: Librairie Arthème Fayard, 2000.

Benson, Ken. "Transformación del horizonte de expectativas en la narrativa posmoderna española: de *Señas de identidad* a *El jinete polaco*." *Revista canadiense de estudios hispánicos* XIX, 1 (1994): 1–20.

Bessière, Bernard. "Du serpent de mer au tigre de papier: Le post-modernisme à l'espagnole."

Post-modernité et écriture narrative dans l'Espagne contemporaine. Ed. Georges Tyras. Grenoble: Université Stendhal (CERHIUS), 1996. 49–68.

Foucault, Michel. *The Order of Things: An Archaeology of the Human Sciences.* New York: Pantheon Books, 1971.

García Rodrigo, María Luisa. "Consideraciones para un estudio de la década prodigiosa." *La cultura spagnola degli anni ottanta.* Ed. Carla Prestigiacomo and M. Caterina Ruta. Palermo: Flaccovio Editore, 1995. 21–25.

Ibáñez, Andrés. *El mundo en la era de Varick.* Madrid: Siruela, 1999.

———. *La música del mundo o El efecto Montoliu.* Barcelona: Seix Barral, 1995.

Ibáñez, Jesús. "Tiempo de post-modernidad." *La polémica de la posmodernidad.* Ed. José Tono Martínez. Madrid: Ediciones Libertarias, 1986. 27–66.

Jameson, Fredric. *The Cultural Turn: Selected Writings on the Postmodern.* London; New York: Verso, 1998.

———. *Postmodernism, or the Cultural Logic of Late Capitalism.* Durham: Duke University Press, 1991.

———. *The Seeds of Time.* New York: Columbia University Press, 1994.

Lozano Mijares, Mª del Pilar. *La novela española posmoderna.* Madrid: Arco/Libros, 2007.

Lyotard, Jean-François. *The Postmodern Condition: A Report on Knowledge.* Minneapolis: University of Minnesota Press, 1984.

———. *Postmodern Explained for Children: Correspondence, 1982–85.* London: Turnaround, 1992.

Martín-Santos, Luis. *Tiempo de silencio.* Barcelona: Seix Barral, 1962.

Martínez, José Tono, ed. *La polémica de la posmodernidad.* Madrid: Ediciones Libertarias, 1986.

Martínez Cachero, José María. *La novela española entre 1936 y el fin de siglo: Historia de una aventura.* Madrid: Castalia, 1997.

McHale, Brian. *Postmodernist Fiction.* London: Methuen, 1987.

Mendoza, Eduardo. *La verdad sobre el caso Savolta.* Barcelona: Seix Barral, 2006.

Navajas, Gonzalo. *Más allá de la posmodernidad: Estética de la nueva novela y cine españoles.* Barcelona: EUB, 1996.

Orejudo, Antonio. *Fabulosas narraciones por historias.* Madrid: Lengua de Trapo, 1996.

Ríos, Julián. *Larva.* Sant Boi de Llobregat: Edicions del Mall, 1983.

Spitzmesser, Ana Mª. *Narrativa posmoderna española: Crónica de un desengaño.* New York: Peter Lang, 1999.

Talens, Manuel. *La parábola de Carmen la Reina (Epístola a Teófilo).* Madrid: Cátedra, 1992.

Umbral, Francisco. *Guía de la posmodernidad: Crónicas, personajes e itinerarios madrileños.* Madrid: Temas de Hoy, 1987.

◆   12

African Voices in Contemporary Spain

Cristián H. Ricci

Introduction

The two former Spanish colonies in Africa, Morocco and Equatorial Guinea, provide ambivalent literary responses towards autonomous, indigenous, and national identities. The fact that Spain had been in those countries for quite a long time, and that nowadays, the presence of the Spanish government has been replaced by private corporations, Spanish Satellite TV, Spanish NGOs, and official institutions such as Cervantes Institutes and Spanish Cultural Cooperation Centers, forces us to deconstruct irremediable "processes of hybridization" (García Canclini, "Noticias recientes" 5–6) of identity markers between the autochthonous and the Spanish/European in the field of cultural production of both countries. As an example of the continued presence of Spain and of Spanish, one could mention the fact that there are six Cervantes Institutes in Morocco, the second largest number in any one country in the world (Brazil has eight). In Equatorial Guinea, a country that "does not have a single newspaper stand nor a bookstore" (Eloisa Vaello Marco), the work of the Spanish Cultural Centers of Malabo and Bata is key, not only to help local writers to publish their books but also for the promotion and distribution in Guinea and Spain of the same authors that Spanish presses publish in the Peninsula.

In this essay I will briefly analyze the works of authors that reject the idea of monolithic identities and those of African intellectuals who, in Moroccan philosopher Mohamed Abd al-Jabri's words, "break away with certain kind of fundamentalist relation with tradition [. . .] in order to artistically approach an ampler personality, liberating, contemporaneous, dialogical, political, and religiously independent" (1, 129). At the same time, my purpose is to build my analytical discourse following reflections by Guinean writer Donato Ndongo. He has argued that the language of African writers makes it possible to impose the texture, sound, rhythm, idiom, and vocabulary of his/her culture as signifiers of a cultural experience constructed as "difference" ("Literatura guineana" 3, 6). In this vein, I advocate for a critical dialogue among texts and authors that creates an intracultural exchange with other "southern-subaltern" cultures: "[Nuestra literatura] también debe ser útil, para que sirva a nuestras necesidades sociales, puesto que luchamos al mismo tiempo por la construcción cultural de nuestras sociedades, contra todas las formas de manipulación, contra las tiranías que nos sojuzgan y condicionan nuestras vidas, contra el racismo, contra todas las formas de mixtificación de la realidad" (Ndongo, "Literatura guineana" 6) (a literature that aims to reconcile ethic and aesthetic towards the ultimate goal of representing the social needs of Africans; a literature that fights against all kind of manipulations, against the tyrannies that oppress African nations, against racism, against all forms of mystification of reality).[1] The essay will be divided into three sections: 1) Moroccan literature in Spanish; 2) Amazigh (Berber) literature in Catalan; and 3) Equatorial Guinean Literature in Spanish.

Spanish Language in Morocco: From the Protectorate to the "Return of the Moors"

Moroccan intellectuals have been writing in Spanish since the times of the Protectorate (1912–1956). Most published journalistic chronicles and/or political columns (Abdul Latif Jatib, Mohammad Tensamani, and Mohamed Ibn Azzuz Hakim were the most active writers since the late 30s to the 50s). The latter, a pro-Franco historian, became a referent for short story Moroccan writers in Spanish with his books *Rihla por Andalucía* (1942) and *Cuentos populares marroquíes* (1955). Also, during the Protectorate, there were Moroccan literati who published short stories and poems in Spanish in newspapers such as *España*, *Marruecos*, *Unidad Marroquí*, *Diario Marroquí*, *Diario de África*, *El Lukus*, among others. Later, on the verge of Independence, during the late fifties, sixties, and seventies, literary journals such as *Al-Motamid* (in Larache), *Ketama* (in Tétouan), *Mauritania* (in Tangier) and *Cuadernos de la Biblioteca de Tetuán* published Moroccan writers of Spanish expression. Besides the daily news section in Spanish of the Moroccan Television Network (RTM), that started in 1970, and that have been anchored by two journalist and fiction writers such as Mohamed Chakor (eight books of narrative and poetry published and self-published in Spain) and Said Jdidi (four novels published in Morocco), it is also important to mention that in 1980 the French newspaper *L'Opinion* started publishing a weekly section called "La página en español." In the latter there were contributions from the mentioned Chakor and Jdidi, along with the renowned Hispanist Mohamed Larbi Messari, who was also an ambassador, Minister of Culture, prolific essayist, and chief editor of one of the two most important Moroccan newspapers, *Al-Alam*. In 1990, the first and only modern Moroccan newspaper entirely written in Spanish by Moroccan journalists, school teachers and university professors was established in Casablanca. The newspaper was called *La mañana* (1990–2006) and its first editor-in-chief was Mohamed Lahchiri.

The first literary works addressing modern migration of African citizens to Europe during the seventies were written in Arabic: Abdallah Laroui (*al-Gurba*, 1971, translated in English as *The Exile* or *The Loneliness*) and Mohamed Zafzaf (*al-Mar'a wa-l-warda*, 1970, in English *The Woman and the Rose*, in Spanish *La mujer y la rosa*). With the second largest arrival of Maghribi-Arabs to Spain that occurred on February 7, 1992, new Moroccan authors have opted to use Spanish to address the migration surge in Moroccan and Spanish newspapers and literary journals. Goncourt Prize winner Tahar Ben Jelloun was the first Moroccan writer to publish a literary essay on North African migration to Spain in *El País* ("¿Cómo se dice 'boat people' en árabe?"). Ben Jelloun's piece motivated a group of Moroccan Hispanists to denounce the flagellum of migrants who cross the Strait of Gibraltar in search of the European *El Dorado*. As the result of the awakening of Moroccan literature in Spanish (which remained somewhat dormant between 1956 and 1990, with the exception of the above mentioned literary publications in *L'Opinion* and *La mañana*), Abdelkader Uariachi published the first Moroccan novel written entirely in Spanish, *El despertar de los leones* (1990), published first in *L'Opinion* between 1986 and 1987. Mohamed Sibari—who is now one of the most prolific writers of this group, with thirteen books of narrative and poetry—published the second Moroccan novel written entirely in Spanish, *El caballo* (1993). *El caballo* is the story of a migrant from Larache, whose trip to Spain is frustrated by the Tangier mafia. After Sibari's *El Caballo*, other short stories have appeared (by Sibari, Mohamed Bouissef Rekab, and the Sephardic writer from Larache, León Cohen Mesonero, among the most noteworthy) and a novel (the first one published in Spain), *El Diablo de Yudis* (1994) by Ahmed Daoudi, all of which address the subject of migration. In all these texts, the desire of migration, moral degradation, and a moralizing rhetoric become recurrent topics.

As a response to the harsh Spanish media reports of the modern migration phenomenon in terms of a revival of the Berbers' invasions of the seventeenth-century, a new kind of fiction of resistance arose in Morocco between 1995 and 2000. This literature employed irony, neo-symbolism, and a stirring of the historical annals to allow the tracking of the North African presence in Spain as a form of validation for the new migrant experience. During this period, fifteen novels and short story books were published in Spanish in Morocco and Spain. In the latter we can see a conscious depuration of style, an effort to build more complex characters as well as well crafted narrative structures. Also, towards the turn of the century, Spanish presses became increasingly interested in translating works of Moroccan literati of Arabic and French expression: among others, Zafzaf's *La mujer y la rosa* (1997), Mahi Binebine's *Cannibales* (1999, translated in Spanish as *La patera* in 2000), Rachid Nini's *Yawmiyyat muhayir sirri* (1999, translated to Spanish as *Diario de un ilegal*, 2002) and a compilation of short stories by José Monleón, *Cuentos de las dos orillas* (2001). Among the stories included in this anthology it is imperative to highlight Miloudi Chaghmoum's "La quema de los barcos" and Mustafa al-Misnawi's "Tariq, aquel que no conquistó Al-Andalus," because they combine the socio-economical and cultural condition of the migrants as well as a tendency to purer forms of fiction by incorporating myths, legends, fantastic, and/or supernatural episodes that, without appealing to magical realistic formulas, help to connect Moroccan literature with Spanish readers (Ricci, "Literatura marroquí" 93–94).

There is also a fourth group that proliferated in the last eight years that, in my view, will place Moroccan literature written in Spanish within the framework of a literature without borders. This literature, written in Morocco by Moroccans, with Moroccan topics and characters, is developing a series of questions about the use of the language of the Other, the aesthetic practices of Western literature, and a deeply critical observation on the influence of the Western media in Morocco. These authors also address the prolegomena of the March 11, 2004, bombings in Madrid while, at the same time, recreate the shadows of intolerance represented by a return to the darkest days of the fifteenth-century Inquisition and of Franco's dictatorship. The "threat" of terrorism is answered in literary texts that, while writing Maghribi immigrants' lives and arrival to Spain, are inundated by the "ghosts" of Spain's own Muslim past (Flesler 55).

Moroccan Borderland Literature in Spanish

In previous essays, I have analyzed the paradigms of the Moroccan literature about the diaspora of Maghrebis in Spain.[2] I believe that it is time to insert Moroccan literature written in Spanish and Catalan within the wider context of borderland literature studies. In this sense, there is a group of Moroccan authors who affirms and develops what Enrique Dussel, Mohamed Abd al-Jabri, and Mohamed Mesbahi call the "cultural alterity from the post-colonization," subsuming the best of Spanish and European modernity, not to develop a cultural style that tends to a globalized unit, undifferentiated or empty, but to a *trans-modern pluriverse* (one with many universalities: European, African, Islamic, Christian, and Latin American).

A sort of "historical sensuality" towards Spain or the Spanish has been present in Morocco. A great number of Moroccan intellectuals kept in their memory stories of the "tiempo de perlas" (Al-Sabbag 91) (times of pearls) of Al-Andalus, when the kingdom of Castile and the Muslim Caliphate had comparable power around the thirteenth-century. It could be argued, using Gramsci's terminology about voluntary associations, that some Moroccan intellectuals have concurred with the representatives of the West on the idea of European superiority, in its political, social and, even, cultural version. Taking into account this phenomenon of *Occidentalism* in Moroccan society, it is possible to observe how, in variable degrees, the assented practice of the valuation of Spanish or Spanishness presents at least three perfectly identifiable variants in Morocco's borderland literature written in Spanish.

On the one hand, there is a *costumbrista* literature that approaches topics of Northern Moroccan folklore (Tétouan, Larache, and Tangier, essentially). Some of these texts, written in Spanish about the customs and people of Morocco, contribute to demystify a series of ethnocentric clichés that many travelers, historians, and European literati held about Morocco and the rest of the non-Western world. However, if one takes into account that most of these authors—particularly Mohamed Sibari who published eleven of his thirteen books in Morocco—do not manage to sell their books in Spain (nor in the rest of the Spanish-speaking world), it cannot be measured to what extent their native version on Morocco and its customs could convince anybody. Thus, it is rarely taken seriously by researchers. Some of them, of Moroccan origin, think that it is embarrassing that this kind of literature, "huera [. . .], simplista, localizada a pie de calle" (El Gamoun, "La literatura marroquí" 159) (empty [. . .], silly, and clearly denotative) is burying and cheapening the national literature. On the other hand, the reader should not confuse this localist literature with authors and artists who, trying to preserve the *Legado Andalusí* (Andalusian common patrimony), approach the literary and artistic manifestations of both sides of the Mediterranean through an intercultural perspective. An example of the latter is Oumama Aouad Lahrech, a renowned researcher and occasional writer, who in her refined literary essays—such as "La Biblioteca del Ryad Andalusí"—finds commonalities between "North and South," "East and West," and "across the Atlantic, the other *Mare Nostrum*" (252–53, my translation).

There is also Moroccan literature written in Spanish that narrates the crossing of the Gibraltar Strait. At this point it is necessary to clarify that the realist aesthetic and the didactic-moralizing content of these writings (chronicles, diaries, memories) are common to the sprouting of other borderland literatures that try to show the socioeconomic and cultural problems of migrants. At the same time, this kind of literature responds to a tradition in Moroccan literature (of Arab expression, particularly in the short narratives of the 1970s) of social intention (Amrani 14). In this sense, it seems that these texts on the crossing of the Gibraltar Strait have not managed to overcome the immediacy of a testimonial urgency, without greater historical depth. One of the representative authors of this narrative genre is Mohamed Bouissef Rekab, who has several short stories posted on his personal web page[3] as well as a couple of novels about migration, *El motín del silencio* (2006) and *La señora* (2006). It is also fair to say that Bouissef's later novels (particularly *Aixa, el cielo de Pandora*, 2007) are increasingly leaning to a more connotative stage, proposing new approaches to the experience of female characters that disentangle from the orthodox Muslim socio-cultural tutelage of men, and, at the same time, destroy the ethnocentric clichés that many Westerners have about Muslim women (often depicted as "submissive" and "battered"). Another narrator of migration testimonies, whose narrative technique is a mix of *costumbrismo* and sensationalism, is Abdelkader Benabdellatif. He has authored a novel entitled *El reto del Estrecho* (2005) and a drama, *Las columnas de Hércules* (2005) (both titles were published in one volume), and struggles to sell his books both in Morocco and Spain.

An unusual case is Abderrahman El Fathi, who has published six books: *Triana, imágenes y palabras* (1998), *Abordaje* (2000), *África en versos mojados* (2002), *Primavera en Ramallah y Bagdad* (2003), *El cielo herido* (2003, in Spain), *Desde la otra orilla* (2004, in Spain), and a short play, *Fantasías literarias* (2000). El Fathi unifies the subaltern voice of the "pateristas" (boat people), "harragas" (illegal immigrants), and refined lyricism, while denouncing the double standard of European politicians that falsely inculcates democratic processes of "convivencia" (living together) and the free market while, at the same time, validates new displacements (cultural and economic), and massive infringements of human rights. The colonial legacy has produced in the imaginary of borderland poets and narrators a dichotomist feeling of fraternity and rejection: the longing of Al-Andalus and the modern interpellation towards elements that, sheltered in economic-cultural-religious parameters, reject any attempt of "Averroist" approximations between both sides of the Mediterranean Sea. The poetic space "in-between" that trespasses the official border between Spain and Morocco becomes the interstice where the poetic voice feels at home. El Fathi's "Patria Poética" is an alienating place that also turns out to be his locus of inspiration, doubt and confusion: "Lloré tanto aquella noche / Navegué, hacia un Sur yendo al norte" (*Abordaje* 34) "mi mente atraca / desde una roca / para arribar a un puerto del Sur. / Siempre el Sur, / pero es el Norte" (*Abordaje* 28) (I cried so much that night / I sailed towards a South going North / my mind tied up / at a rock / to arrive at a seaport in the South. / Always the South, / but it is the North).[4]

In the same vein, in order to avoid a "literary submission" to the West, some of the twenty-first-century Moroccan writers of Spanish expression began a new critical vision of its peripheral culture with respect to Europe. These borderland writers reconstruct their alterative position within European modernity from an outer perspective; that is to say, from a world-wide standpoint (as counterpart of the "provincial perspective of the European" [Bhabha 18]). Consequently, in a world where the "literary canon" has been aggressively questioned, I endorse the thesis that transnational histories of migrants, of colonized (or neocolonized), or of political refugees would be the fertile lands where a world-wide literature could settle, surpassing the subdivisions based on political frontiers and unattainable cultural essentialisms. Moroccan writers such as Ahmed Ararou, Ahmed El Gamoun, Larbi El Harti, Mohamed Lahchiri, and Abderrahman El Fathi are very conscious of the ontological and epistemological differences between both cultures, and can cross from one side to the other (from West to East), and criticize both cultures, with no need to request a "visa" from any academic guard. Without apostatizing their Arab-African-Muslim culture, in many cases, they know better "la casa del vecino [España], más que la propia" (El Harti, "La alienada" 40) (the house of their neighbor [Spain], more than their own). In Ararou's, El Gamoun's and El Harti's narratives there is a "selective rejection" to westernization, typical of postcolonial literature, as well as a strong bet on the philosophy of liberation. In this sense, they are not revolutionaries who fight for the beginning of history in the future; they do not represent the typical liberal discourse that mystifies national emancipation against Spain; nor are they Indigenists who deny the developments after the French and Spanish invasions. Rather, they propose to reconstruct history in its integrity. From an Eastern and Western historical frame, they recover the historical identity of Morocco, a history that has similar characteristics to other post-colonialist literatures and that is conscious of the neo-colonial relations that the new world order imposes.

Ahmed Ararou's fiction is paradigmatic of this type of (still) marginal literature, which tries to lay its way. He considers himself a "writer without a portfolio." He is also marginal because of the nature and substance of his statements that are, paradoxically, reaffirmations of a modern Western literary canon. He talks about comparative linguistics, applied psychology, and literary criticism; he uses stylistic resources of Western and Eastern "canonical" writers, and he also incorporates stories or anecdotes of Moroccan folklore. With that amalgam of literary resources, Ararou constructs an oeuvre that is irreducible to any attempt of categorization. Ararou manages to surpass the artistic flexibility of postmodernism through the recognition of difference and the coexistence with tradition. In this sense, his literary project exceeds, in form and content, the mere tracking of roots and the romanticizing of the Arab presence in Al-Andalus. If, with Moroccan writers of the 1980s, such as Miloudi Chaghmoum and Mustafa Al-Misnawi, the stories of exploitation, submission, and the evolution of resistance strategies are authenticated from the periphery, Ararou situates the reader on what Homi Bhabha and García Canclini denominate the cultural hybridization of the borderland condition (Bhabha 6). This hybridization allows Ararou to translate, and therefore to re-inscribe, the social imaginary of the Metropolis and the modernity imposed or consented in Morocco, by Moroccans.

Ararou, but also El Gamoun, El Harti, and Mohamed Lahchiri, are aware that the pact of civilization consists of recognizing that Morocco is a policultural area with an enormous variety of traditions from which they can choose the elements for a new model of literary development. At the same time, this type of literature accompanies the modernization of Morocco, always supervising analytically the Western offer of products and beliefs, especially those that arrive through the signals of satellite television. The work of stirring in the annals of mythology is fundamental in the narratives of El Gamoun and Ararou so that the Spanish reader, regardless if she or he is familiarized with Moroccan and Arab myths such as Gilgamesh or the Hercules' caves, can relate the narration to other utopia territories like Aztlán, Atlán, Tollán, Atlas, Atarant, Auru, Aalu, and others in the traditions of the natives of North and South America. In this regard, I see that a peripheral dialogue "South-South" exists between these Moroccan writers and thinkers of Asia, Latin America, indigenous North American, and Chicanos who face imperialistic cultures.

El Gamoun's and Ararou's literary projects materialize what Enrique Dussel and the Moroccan philosopher Mohamed Mesbahi call "the popular post-capitalist culture." They surpass the reductive limits of a fallacious monolithic culture, reconstructing the cultural history of Morocco within the frame of world-wide history: from Asia, through the Asian-Afro-European proto-history, until the Hispanic Christianity; from the Spanish Protectorate to the postcolonial and the neocolonized Moroccan culture. At the same time, by incorporating the fantastic and the mythological, as well as Arabic metaphors and the use of multichronic spaces, the texts of Ararou, El Gamoun, and El Harti promote a semantically and structural transgression that makes possible the trans-modern project (endorsed by al-Jabri) of establishing a strategy of creativity towards a renovated culture, not only appealing to decolonization, but also to originality.

In the short story "Trabanxi," Ararou plays with the interpolation of Occidental and Oriental myths to locate the reader in the imaginary land of literature, where there are no real borders, but rather interminable and continuous territories through the narrative act. The narrator shows the importance of the creative process, as well as the capacity a story teller has to illustrate or fool his countrymen regarding the Babylonian or Biblical origins of their humble town, called Arcilla (clay). Trabanxi, the main character and storyteller, is accused of heresy and collaborationism with the Spanish Protectorate by another man, "cegado por su nacionalismo transárabe" (68) (blinded by his Trans-Arab nationalism). His story is plagiarized by the same nationalist prosecutor, and is translated (or rather it is written) (in) Arabic; and the Biblical or Babylonian origins of Arcilla happen to comprise the history and foundation of the city of Tangier. All the natives of the dispossessed town become infuriated with the news of the substitution and begin to venture in "pateras de carcomida madera por las aguas fronterizas del Estrecho" (70) (boats of decayed wood through border waters of the Straits). The neighbors of the North (Spain) "viven hoy [. . .] por segunda vez, el terrible episodio histórico del 'No pasarán' " (70) (live [today] for the second time, the terrible Civil War episode of 'No pasarán' [They shall not pass]). As time goes by, those who manage to cross the Strait have produced a radical change in the humble town that now has an annual festival, a soccer stadium, and three-star hotels, all of it because of the "Western Union's money transfers" (70), on which ninety percent of the shanty town inhabitants live. The children of the city dream about being professional soccer players for Real Madrid or FC Barcelona, marriageable girls dream to marry their cousins who live on the other side of border, and everybody in Arcilla, "hipnotizados por el silbo digital de las parabólicas sirenas del nuevo Dorado" (70) (hypnotized by the irresistible digital whistles of parabolic sirens of the new El Dorado), fantasize with "mundos, personajes, productos, sabores y colores del más allá" (74) (worlds, characters, products, flavors, and colors of the other world). This story shows a diachronic representation of the various stages of Moroccan history, its long history of corruption, and the importance of the incipient Muslim fundamentalism. At the same time, this type of literature accompanies the modernization of Morocco, but always supervising analytically, and in literary form, the imposition of Western products and beliefs, especially those that arrive through the signals of satellite television. The (des)informative interference of the First World becomes an obsession for some Moroccan intellectuals. The narrator of "La Atlántida," Amhed El Gamoun's short story, narrated in cinematographic style, fears "la catástrofe de una colisión" (160) (the catastrophe of a collision), that, although it is described in ironic and figurative terms, alludes to the devaluation of the North African cultural essence in favor of the Westernization of Morocco.

Larbi El Harti and Mohamed Lahchiri also proclaim a "selective insubordination" towards the West, writing within the Occidental's literary codes and incorporating Moroccan traditions. El Harti in his short story book, *Después de Tánger*

(2003) and in "La alienada," makes his characters of middle-class students or professionals travel to Europe, return to Morocco, and draw conclusions from their experiences. Lahchiri, in his three short story books (*Pedacitos entrañables, Cuentos ceutíes* and *Una tumbita en Sidi Embarek*) narrates the transformations of territories and people of the former Protectorate into unequal and antagonistic spaces of post-independence modernity. The trips of El Harti's characters serve to literally complete the "going beyond" proposed by Bhabha and Franz Fanon: to go beyond the historical and instrumental hypotheses. In this regard, the trip not only provides the knowledge of the characters' own personalities and their culture, but also the discovery of the temporary barrier of a present in cultural collision. It is in the narrative of El Harti where it is more feasible to verify that the border commitments of the cultural difference can be as much consented as conflicting. In "La alienada," the main character confuses the definitions of tradition and modernity. He begins to feel surprised and disoriented by the relocation of his native country and the world (the feeling of surprise or *unhomeliness* of Bhabha, 13), something characteristic of the condition of contemporary extraterritorial and intercultural literary initiatives.

For his part, Lahchiri takes the reader to analyze a complex group of literary techniques that also responds the interstitial position of a borderland writer, leading to intertextual correspondences with texts and writers of Morocco and the rest of the Arabic world (particularly Egypt's Naguib Mahfouz) in order to represent the "discomfort in culture" and the vacuum in Moroccan narrative after its Independence. In this regard, Lahchiri takes after Abdallah Laroui's *al-Gurba*, surpassing the proto-novel and nationalist stages of Moroccan literature (mainly known for its social realism) in order to embrace modern elements of fiction such as the disembodiment of the individual, the recovery of childhood, the enjoyment of literature for literature's sake (evident in "Recordar un cuento"), the representation and interpretation of social injustice ("Las moras pisoteadas"), the employment of irony to counteract racist stereotypes, and the comparison between a past of belonging, of progress, and the crumbling of Post-independence major projects ("El morito de Arcila"). It is also worth noting that not only Lahchiri's short stories, but also El Harti's "La alienada," "Me llamo Rosa" and "Mi amiga Ghanu," El Gamoun's "La Atlántida" and Ararou's "Trabanxi," "AMÉ ... RICK" and "La Resaca" present similar reactions to broken illusions due to geographical and economical displacements.

El Harti offers his readers a complex network of experiences that surpasses the Morocco-Spain/Arab-Spanish binarism, where diverse and conflicting perspectives are interrelated in continuous forms. "La alienada" is a short story that takes place Spain, France, England, Jordan, Syria, and some humble town of Morocco, not specified. In El Harti's "La alienada" the cultural conflict becomes obsessive, human, philosophical, and existential. The main character adventures to investigate his historical identity, to finally become aware of his individuality with respect to the social contour that, as much in Europe as in his own country, makes him understand that he is also an unprivileged guest in an "orgía de la fractura" (49) (orgy of [humankind] fracture). In this sense, El Harti follows the line of Mohamed Abed al-Jabri, who thinks that modern critical intellectuals are those who control the election of hegemonic modern instruments (European) and traditional Arabic-Islamic. The combination of approaches will be as useful for the critical reconstruction of their own tradition as for the evaluation of neocolonized cultures (226). At the same time, he gives sufficient weight to contradictions, in order to not fall in the error of sweetening what continues being foreign to a certain culture. El Harti's, Lahchiri's, El Gamoun's and Ararou's short stories "interpellate" cultural Eurocentrism and, at the same time, point to the necessity to continue questioning peripheral cultures in their double function of victims and perpetrators of the oppression.

In Spain there is some curiosity about Moroccans writing in Spanish. The University of Cádiz-Aula del Estrecho has organized four conferences on Moroccan Literature of Hispanic expression. Its organizer, the Arabist Juan José Sánchez Sandoval, is also the editor in chief of the collection Algarabía of Ediciones Quorum-U of Cádiz. Quorum published several translations of renowned Moroccan authors as well as Abderrahman El Fathi's compilation of poetry, *Desde la otra orilla*, and Mohamed Bouissef Rekab's *Aixa, el cielo de Pandora*. In Madrid, Ediciones Sial has also published Moroccan authors who write in Spanish, such as El Harti (*Después de Tánger*, 2003), Mohamed Akalay (*De Larache a Tánger*, 2006) and Bouissef Rekab (*La señora*, 2006), among others, as well as the most recent anthology, *Calle del agua: Antología contemporánea de literatura hispano-magrebí* (2008). It is imperative to mention that as early as 1985, Mohamed Chakor and Sergio Macías published *Antología de relatos marroquíes en lengua española*, the first anthology of Moroccan literature in Spanish that, together with the creation of the Moroccan Association of Writers in Spanish (AEMLE) in Tangier in 1997, promoted the latest literary works of many writers who live in Tangier, Larache, and Tétouan. The Junta de Andalucía, as well as the University of Granada, has recently published anthologies of Moroccan authors of Spanish expression (*EntreRíos* and *Entre las dos orillas*). Along with Ignacio López-Calvo, I published *Caminos para la paz: Antología de escritores judíos y árabes en castellano* in 2008. Above all, so far the best and more comprehensive anthology of Moroccan literature in Spanish was published by Destino in 2004, *La puerta de los vientos: Narradores marroquíes contemporáneos*, edited by Lorenzo Silva, Marta Cerezales and Miguel A. Moreta.

Imazighen (Berber)-Catalan Women and the Forging of an Afro-Iberian Identity

Spanish is no longer the only language of the Peninsula used by Moroccans; nor is it any longer the case that the literary field is dominated by men. In the last four years, Catalan presses have been publishing female Moroccan-Amazigh voices, who write in Catalan and who have lived in Catalonia since their childhoods.[5] The significance of these narratives adds controversy to the ongoing political and language rivalry between Spanish and the different nationalisms of the Iberian Peninsula (particularly Catalan). Laila Karrouch published her autobiography in 2004, *De Nador a Vic* (*Premi Columna Jove*, published by Planeta/Oxford in Spanish in 2005 under the title *Laila*). During the same year (2004) the Catalan press Columna, published Najat El Hachmi's autobiography, *Jo també sóc catalana*. Moreover, in 2008, El Hachmi was awarded the *Premi de les Lletres Catalanes Ramon Llull* for her novel *L'últim patriarca* (Planeta, 2008; in Spanish, *El último patriarca*, October 2008), a novel that could be defined as an "autobiographical fiction." These narratives of cultural and economic survival bind together several discourses. One can find the immigration experiences of Laila Karrouch and Najat El Hachmi mixed with the founding texts on the exile experience of the already mentioned Muhammad Zafzaf, Abdellah Laroui, and Rachid Nini; the sociological narrative (in Spanish) of Pasqual Torregrosa and Mohamed El Gheryb, *Dormir al raso* (1994); and those of Sami Naïr and Juan Goytisolo, *El peaje de la vida* (2000) and *España y sus ejidos* (2003).

Karrouch and El Hachmi refer to their writing as a therapeutic process which assists the characters towards the closure of their life-learning cycles. In this respect, Morocco (The Rif) lies in the past and Catalonia in the future. Linguistically, both authors confirm that their "Catalanness" does not define itself through the antithesis of their "Moroccanness" or "Amazighness," but rather, their identities multiply themselves according to their class status, the male or female version of their testimony, and their place in the generational and immigration lines. Thus, my goal here is to analyze how the subaltern voices of immigrants may disrupt (or antagonize) the modern canon of the literatures of the Peninsula, as well as, following Anjali Prabhu's reminder, understand how hybrid discourses are able "to dismantle power structures" (xiv).

Given the implicit pedagogical and moral intention of the author to promote "tolerance" and "convivencia," Karrouch's autobiography tends to lessen the identity crisis she suffers upon arrival to Catalonia. However, it does bring forth the economic hardships that her family must overcome to live in Spain, and the "contradictory" role of Muslim women living in the West that "must" submit to the will of their husbands and fathers. In addition to overcoming the sporadic racist comments of her classmates when they call her "mora," the author marks 1992 as the year "the integration environment is disrupted" by the massive flow of immigrants: "L'aprenentatge del català i el castellà i la integració en general es van fer més difícils, i la mescladissa de gent va començar a disminuir, i a l'escola es formaven, sovint, grupets d'estrangers i grupets de catalans i castellans" (109) (The learning of the language and the integration in general became more difficult, and people started blending in less. At school, often small groups of foreigners were formed, and small groups of people speaking Catalan or Spanish).[6]

El Hachmi combines the contradictory feelings arising from the contact between languages with a certain degree of alienation that will "regnar en la meva vida" (*Jo també* 47) (reign over [her] life). In *L'últim patriarca*, the narrator's (and main character's) intention is to "negotiate" (279)[7] her beliefs with God, as well as the ritual practices of Islam, and, above all, mark her situation as a "retournée" in order to emphasize her condition of *mestiza*, crossbreed, of foreigner both in her North African culture as well as in Europe.

Thus, it is not coincidental that Najat El Hachmi assumes a traumatic-anomalous-deviated discourse in writing *L'últim patriarca*. She accounts for the complex, controversial, and contradictory literary and hybridizing processes of marginal and borderland literatures. El Hachmi is aware that the colonial difference of the "borderland enunciating subject" (Mignolo, *Local Histories* 28) is not only uttered through a resisting and dissenting discourse, but is also materialized in the literary representation of the pain and anger of her "fractured" stories, of her memories, of her subjectivities. Overall, the novel highlights the *misovire* (neologism coined by Cameroon writer Warewere Liking) nature of the narrator, that is, of a woman who doesn't seem to find a man worthy of admiration, as well as the clear intention to apply what Abdelkebir Khatibi defines as "the double criticism of the paradigm-Other" (72). The narrator questions and "disengages" (73) the values imposed by the Muslim society (in our case Muslim-Amazigh), "so theological, so charismatic, so patriarchal" (72), and the hegemonic structure of Western societies, be it Catalan, Spanish, or European.

L'últim patriarca is divided in two parts. In the first part, we learn about the birth, childhood, and adult life of the man who will be the last patriarch of an Amazigh family of Northern of Morocco (Nador). In the second section of the novel, we follow the narration of the life of Mimoun Driuch (the patriarch) already established in the capital of a Catalan district (Vic, main destination of the Amazigh community in Catalonia) in the eighties. The novel is completely told by the third—and only—daughter of Mimoun, a girl who announces at the story's onset the "abrupt ending of any forthcoming lines of the patriarch" and of his "discriminatory and dictatorial procedures" (7). Although in the beginning of the second part the narrator adopts the role of main character in the story, the role of the patriarch is omnipresent. In this second part, the teenage years and adulthood of the narrator is presented (she does not reveal her name). In the first part of the novel the author recreates the Amazigh-Riffian microcosm of Northern Morocco, adding all the ingredients that would fit in the recipe for another Orientalist text—written by a European, indeed. Once the eldest son in the family is born, the text highlights the excesses of paternal authority, the physical abuse, and the anal vexation Mimoun suffers from his uncle. From that moment on, the fictional autobiography that El Hachmi provides is told from the point of view of a grown woman, a textual move that subverts and perverts the status imposed by religious practices and traditions of a society, as many others—including the European—that encourage the phallogocentric supremacy.

As the novel moves forward, the narrator becomes a mirror of the patriarchal structure she goes against; she speaks in the language of the patriarch and inscribes her discourse into the patriarchal set of values. Simultaneously, the judgement El Hachmi makes towards new and old colonial habits is of vital importance in her eagerness to approach the impossibility of defining her literature and identity, distancing herself from binary thinking. Therefore, in *L'últim patriarca* the taxonomical categories are torn apart one by one; to evidence that the point is not merely to fictionalize the differences between Africa and Europe, man and woman, sensuality and eroticism, or heterosexuality and homosexuality. Instead, the author attempts to challenge Afro-European identities, to delve into the role of male-like women that use and impersonate roles traditionally assigned to men, to bluntly represent pornographic sensuality and to reflect the hermaphroditism in the sexual awakening of young women. As a consequence, the written, plural, and transgressing insubordination of El Hachmi becomes a fight, a negotiation of the difference, an encounter/de-encounter between the obsession of North African markers and "the anxiety of influence" of the European. The coexistence with the Catalan/Spanish, the Muslim-Amazigh nature, and the voluntary adoption of Catalan as an artistic expression, results in four perfectly defined cultures, with their sum acting as the basic foundation for a fifth: hybrid, interstitial, and interpellating in equal amounts of the Amazigh culture, as well as the Catalan.

In the writings of Karrouch and El Hachmi there is evidence of a continuous conflict between exoticism and the universal scope of North African literature, reinforced in this case when dealing with female writers. Najat El Hachmi wrote a "Carta d'un immigrant" ("A Letter of an immigrant") in 2004, a message to an anonymous immigrant whose ending can be seen as very appropriate for an understanding of the concept of borderland: "Aprendràs a viure, finalment, a la frontera d'aquests dos móns, un lloc que pot ser divisió, però que també és encontre, punt de trobada. Un bon dia et creuràs afortunat de gaudir d'aquesta frontera, et descobriràs a tu mateix més complet, més híbrid, més immens que qualsevol altra persona" (You will learn to live, finally, in the interstice of these two worlds, a place that could mean division but that also represents an encounter. One day you will think yourself lucky to *enjoy this interstice* and you will discover yourself more complete, more *hybrid*, more immense than any other person) (my emphasis). As Walter Mignolo points out, in this mutation process, language is not merely a neutral tool that represents the honest wish to tell the truth, but also—and here lies the literary fact in itself in the narratives of Ararou, El Gamoun, El Harti, Lahchiri and, of course, El Hachmi—a tool for the construction of a history and the invention of realities ("Colonial and Postcolonial" 122). It is even closer, I think, following Prahbu, to the creolization that possesses the potential to elucidate cultural creation, as well as the judgment of power relations (inequality, prestige, and resources) that promote innovations, and cultural and linguistic exchanges (Prahbu 4, 5). In the same vein, I concur with Anjeli Prabhu that a distinction between diasporic and creolization narratives is possible. While the former is based on a past trauma that constitutes and links the members of a group towards a discourse of victimhood, the latter may be seen to display an overweening pride in hybrid agency, and is forward-looking and concerned with interaction (13, 14). Najat El Hachmi combines both impulses, which are crucial to the forging of a discourse, adequate to the multiple tactics, required for a successful postcolonial praxis. The literary project of Najat El Hachmi is significant in the sense that it goes beyond the merely feminist view as the only criteria of analysis of the social situation, to render what could be the origin of an Afro-Iberian identity, free of political considerations, as well as critically engaged in feelings of *unhomeliness* and exclusion.

Judging the marketing strategy of Editorial Planeta (including book cover designs and spending more than 300,000 Euros in "Orientalist advertisements" in *El País*), some people might argue that El Hachmi is a doubly-colonized subject (by gender and race). Definitely, Planeta is more interested in selling postcolonial women's writing—and, at the same time, fulfilling the European's desire for exoticism—than in giving voice to those traditionally kept in the shadows. The fact that Spanish publishing houses care about publishing subaltern voices of immigration should be a good sign (and, in fact, there are positive examples as the presses mentioned above). However, one wonders what exactly the authors are willing to "negotiate" for their books to appear in display windows of bookstores.[8] In regards to the use of Catalan as the language of expression, we must say that Karrouch's *De Nador a Vic* was translated into Spanish without any reference to the place of reception (Vic, Catalonia), nor to the particular problems that imply being Moroccan or just a foreigner in Catalonia. The translation into Spanish brings about the implication of making the message universal and not restricting it to a purely regional circle, even if the deliberate elision of any Catalan topographic marker would mean "accommodating" the message of the book to discourage any political issues between Catalans and Spaniards. On the other hand, unmarking the text of any Catalan vestige was another "marketing strategy" of Editorial Planeta/Oxford University Press, as the author confessed ("Interview with Laila" 2007). The autobiography of Karrouch "ha esdevingut una referència literària per al professorat (especialment de secundària) en la selecció de lectures per a la multiculturalitat" ("Itineraris" 6) (has become a literary reference for teachers [especially in high school] in the division of readings assigned to multiculturalism). Her autobiography has sold more than ten thousand copies (six thousand in Catalan and four thousand in Spanish). *Jo també sóc catalana* of Najat El Hachmi had no such luck. Nowadays it can only be read in Catalan. The author recently acknowledged that Columna did not want to translate the book into Spanish for being "too Catalanist" ("Interview El Hachmi").

We shall end this section with a note from El Hachmi in regards to what kind of reader *Jo també sóc catalana* was aiming for: "A los que se llenan la boca con la inmigración y solo han visto al inmigrante de lejos. Pero también a los que están preocupados por el tema de la identidad catalana" (Navarro, "Entrevista") (To those carrying on about immigration, and have only seen it from afar. But also to those who are worried about the issue of Catalan identity). Regardless of the Orientalist marketing strategies of Planeta, *L'últim patriarca*, by showing critical perspectives in relation to the double postcolonial oppression of women, and not leaving up the task of unmasking the differences in race, class, and gender in the immigration communities, finally achieves the objective El Hachmi has previously delineated in her autobiography: that was to "desferme del meu propi enclaustrament, un enclaustrament fet de denominacions d'origen, de pors, d'esperances sovint estroncades, de dubtes continus, d'abismes de pioners que explorin nous mons" (*Jo també* 14) (get rid of one's own isolation produced by the designation of origin, by fears, by frustrated hopes, by constant doubts, by the abysses to which the pioneers are exposed to in the exploration of their new worlds).

The Outset of Colonial Literature in Equatorial Guinea

Equatorial Guinea's first written manifestations came out in a pro-colonial journal entitled *La Guinea Española*, published for the first time in 1903 by the Claretian missionaries of Banapa (now Bioko).[9] The journal published news on everyday aspects of the Spanish colony as well as cultural sections ("Página literaria," "De nuestra biblioteca africanista"), and some basic anthropological notes ("Estudios Etnográficos," "Estudios Coloniales"). Priests-ethnographers working with the indigenous population wrote those articles. In 1944, there was a call for creative writing pieces through a contest entitled "Concurso de la Guinea Española" aimed at "colonial pens" (García Ramírez 62), where there was no trace of participation from the Guinean population. However, three years later, in 1947, the section "Historias y Cuentos," that claimed to be "the best representative of the mind of our natives, collected traditionally in stories, tales, proverbs, and songs, so that we can contribute to immortalize and promote them" (*La Guinea Española*, January 10, 1947), offered the natives the possibility to submit their own literary works. This new section, aimed to a very specific indigenous profile, granted a controlled platform of expression to the native population embedded in the official colonial framework (Guinean pupils of the seminar, native members of the Escuela Superior Indígena and catechists). Gradually, these orally-structured narrative forms were revisited and developed by the first Guinean authors in a mixture of what M'bare N'gom has called the intermediation agent that synthesized the figure of the traditional *griot* or *djéli* and the canonical (Western) written forms of literature ("La literatura africana" 412).

The progressive transformation of a collective patrimony into a more personal imprint culminates in 1953 with the appearance of the first African novel in Spanish, *Cuando los Combes luchaban (Novela de costumbres de la Guinea Española)*[10] by Leoncio Evita. The novel is about the life of a white protestant missionary in pre-colonial, continental Guinea, who acts as an asymmetric literary symbol of contrast, against the native characters. There is an ethnographic approach to the autochthonous culture in the plot, but in turn, there is a departure from this traditional lifestyle, which is measured up with the superior civilization. The phenomenon is striking, particularly because the other relevant novel of the colonial period, *Una lanza por el boabí* (1962),[11] by Daniel Jones Mathama—even though its main character is not white—still admits that the *boabí* becomes a better man by the contact with the superior civilization, and considers it to be "un deber ineludible proclamar por todo lo alto la gran labor que España está realizando en aquella isla" (309) (an inescapable duty to proclaim all the way the great work Spain is making in the island). Although this narrative of "un-resistance"—that defends and even justifies the colonial enterprise—is regarded by Ndongo-Bidyogo as a positive sign of serenity and respect for the folklore and tradition of Guineans (*Antología* 30), there is a clear point of divergence from other African literatures such as those written in French and English, mastered under the discourse of anticolonialism and a quest for black identity. This unique Guinean trait of "tolerance" towards domination shows a clear alienation, as well as the impossibility of self-recognition, the *aliénation intellectuelle* described by Frantz Fanon.

After Equatorial Guinea's independence in 1968, and later *coup d'etat* (1969), all creative processes came to a sudden halt. Francisco Macías Nguema's dictatorship not only suspended the previous constitution (Decree no.115, May 7, 1971), but also jailed or murdered nearly half of the population, expelled all foreigners (Lipski 70), and "silenced" the voices of dissidents and any sort of intellectual expression. His tyranny resulted in a massive Guinean exile during the mid-seventies. During those years "of silence" (1969–1979) all creative work was written outside Guinea (N'gom, "La literatura africana" 414). The literature of writers in exile was fragmented from within as there was little or no contact between the exiles: their presence in Spain was not only clandestine, but also geographically scattered. Had those writers met and gathered in literary/intellectual circles in cities such as Madrid or Barcelona, I believe that the creative production and collective artistic and literary vindications of Guineans could have followed a similar pattern to that of the Latin American *boom* in Barcelona, or the earlier *négritude* movement in Paris.

While language proved to be a source of conflict for other postcolonial literatures, the use of Spanish was only a secondary issue for these writers.[12] In fact, since Macías prohibited the use of Spanish both in public and in private, using it became a weapon against the regime for Guinean authors in exile. Moreover, as Marcelo Ensema Nsang, Juan Balboa Boneke and Antimo Esono Ndongo point out, Spanish became "una altavoz de amplias resonancias. Con ello se extiende más el mensaje que un escritor colonizado lanza al mundo. Eso favorece la integración de lo negro-africano en el concierto de las letras y cultura universales" (qtd. in Lipski 86) (a loud-speaker of ample resonance. [With it] the message of the oppressed writer is extended to the world. This fact also favors the integration of the Black-African in the concert of cultures and letters of the world). The relevant handicap this group suffered was the "Generational Dislocation" (García Ramírez 63); in other words, that "Lost Generation" could not look back for literary references due to the pro-colonial nature of the first Guinean novels (Evita, Jones Mathama).

The group of Guinean exiles includes writers such as Juan Balboa Boneke and Cristino Bueriberi Bokesa. Their diasporic discourse is set clearly against the dictatorial regime and emphasizes the historical and cultural trauma experienced by Guinea. The poetry of the time introduces the configuration of an alternative form of fixated nostalgia that embodied itself in the rhetoric of orphanhood[13]: "¡Oh! Guinea Patria mía, / hoy gimes y lloras de dolor, / a voz en grito clamas / y lloras tu esclavitud; / en tus hijos buscas tu Libertad, / pero ... éstos ¿dónde están?" (Balboa Boneke 51) (Oh! Guinea my Land / today you moan and cry in pain / your voice cries out in clamour / and you shed tears in front of slavery / you search for Freedom in your offsprings / but ... where are they?). Cristino Bueriberi Bokesa's "Nostalgia de mi tierra" continues in this manner: "Me dirás, tú, mar inmenso. / ¿Dónde está mi bella tierra, / que desde esta lejanía / divisar quiero con afán marinero?" (55) (You will tell me, immense sea / Where is my beautiful land, / that from afar I wish / to discern with sailor's yearning). Benita Sampedro also notes that this melancholic longing for the lost land is completed by two other motifs: the exaltation of Nature, and the return to tradition as a rejection to the oppressive regime, a case "in which the poet desperately attempts to recover his tribal autonomous manhood, and his capacity to resist" (Sampedro 211).

This diasporic poetry coexists with the emergence of the narrative of writers such as Donato Ndongo-Bidyogo and Francisco Zamora Loboch. These authors, again, revaluate the evocative loss of their Motherland in opposition to the un-homely European city. However, according to N'gom, after the end of the Macías's regime and with Teodoro Obiang's "Golpe de Libertad" (in fact another *coup d'etat*), a renaissance of these dislocated writers was possible, both through the already democratic Madrid of the late 1970s, and the Centro Hipano-Guineano of Malabo's Press under the direction of Donato Ndongo-Bidyogo (416).[14] The latter published *Las Tinieblas de tu memoria negra* (1987) (trans. into English by Michael Ugarte, *Shadows of Your Black Memory*), a point of inflection for the modern *postcolonial* Afro-Hispanic novel, and the first volume of his diachronic trilogy *Los hijos de la tribu*, completed by *Los Poderes de la Tempestad* (1997) and *El Metro* (2007). The title of Ndongo's first novel, *Las tinieblas*, is a reflection (and translation) of a poem by Léopold Sédar Senghor, and an homage to the cultural *négritude* movement (Fra Molinero 163). The child protagonist in Ndongo's novel is torn apart between two excluding paradigms. On the one side, his uncle (Tío Abeso), appears as the symbol of the traditional culture that resists the colonial ideological oppression, while reassessing the indisputable value of the native culture; and on the other, his own father impersonates "the white mask," mimicry of the civilization agent. The boy acts as a dislocated translational link between his uncle and Padre Ortiz, the Catholic priest of the colonial *mission civilisatrice*. As Baltasar Fra Molinero points out, "[c]omo intérprete lingüístico, este niño tiene que adoptar alternativamente la voz de dos adultos, sin poder dar rienda suelta a sus propias opiniones" (167) (as a linguistic interpreter, this boy has to alternatively adopt the voice of the two adults without being able to speak out his own opinions). Also, during this highly productive period for Guinean literature and the subsequent Spanish discovery of these outlying emerging signs, another relevant and versatile author, Francisco Zamora Loboch, publishes an ironic essay of black resistance against racism in Spain, *Cómo ser negro y no morir en Aravaca* (1994) and a poetry book entitled *Memoria de Laberinto* (1999).

The women writers of this period left Equatorial Guinea when they were young. The first Guinean female writer is Raquel Ilonbé, who in 1978 published *Ceiba*, a poetry book, and in 1987, a book of children's literature entitled *Leyendas guineanas*. Her poetry does not reflect the diasporic experience present in the poetic corpus of her contemporaries; she delves into a fascinating search for a traditional culture and its influence in the Western world (N'Gom, *Diálogos* 60). On the other hand, María Nsué Angüe, author of the novel *Ekomo* (UNED 1985) explores the cultural attitudes towards African women through the voice of a male character, and more interestingly, addresses new questions that arise from the growing conflict between the patriarchal Fang tradition on the verge of extinction and the realization of a changing modern present. According to Adam Lifshey, this is the first post-independence novel of Equatorial Guinea whose "collective cultural memory at hand is being lost at a tribal and continental level, not being gained within a new national context" (173). Among the few females voices present in the literature of Equatorial Guinea, there is also a playwright, Trinidad Morgades Besari, and a writer of short fiction, María Caridad Riloha.

In 2005, Guillermina Mekuy made her debut with a novel entitled *El llanto de la Perra* (Plaza y Janés 2005). Mekuy's first novel was a success and soon she became a mass media phenomenon. In 2008, Mekuy published *Las tres vírgenes de Santo Tomás*, which narrates the story of three mulatto sisters under the strong influence of a black African father who believes he is the reincarnation of St. Thomas Aquinas, and a white Spanish mother, an animist sorcerer initiated in Africa. This parental crossing-over of cultures ("tenían las almas cambiadas" [39] [their souls had been exchanged]) enables an extreme metaphysical dialogue between African traditional beliefs and a mystic, radical version of Christianity. This *bakhtinian* inversion of rigid religious identities associated to race is overcome through the complete abolition of the black animist/white Catholic stereotype: "Mi padre era, en realidad, pese a ser negro, más blanco que mi madre, y ella, a pesar del color claro de su piel, más negra que Tomás" (39) (My father was, really, in spite of being black, whiter than my mother, and she was, in spite of her fair skin, blacker than Thomas).

In order to preserve their virginity and achieve sainthood, the three sisters are subjected to religious African cleansing sessions and are confined to a convent, from which, later, they escape. At this point, the main character (María Fátima) begins a journey of emotional education by trespassing all sexual and social taboos and engaging in a non-prototypical sexual behaviour. The text recreates an "Africanist" scenario of magic, ritual dances, and Spiritism practices that curiously never quite clashes with the convent's Catholic female erotic-mysticism. Both religious manifestations, Catholic and Animist, are staged in such an extreme manner that they finally complement each other, finding common ground and mutual approval. However, this levelling strategy states a non-excluding Afro-Iberian religious *convivencia* that does not solve the gender distinction present in the novel. As it happens in El Hachmi's *L'ultim patriarca*, there is a strong willingness to escape the shadow of patriarchal domination, bringing forth the role of the male-like woman, in order to resist the phallocentric discourse: "A partir de ese instante trataría de pensar y ser como un hombre. Ese ser que era más perfecto que la mujer, ese ser que podía disponer de sí mismo de los que engendraba" (93) (From that moment on, she would try to think and act as a man. A being far more perfect than women, a being that could do whatever he pleased with himself and with those he engendered). Clearly, the discourse of the young protagonist assumes a process of self-creation that aims at both gender as well as cultural hermaphrodism: "Ahora soy dueña, en mi interior, de dos culturas, me pertenecen dos países y tengo la enorme riqueza de dos lenguas, la española y la *fang*, que forman mi presente y mi pasado (192) (Now, I own two cultures, two countries belong to me, and I have the enormous wealth of two tongues, Spanish and Fang, both conform my present and my past). At the same time, liberation comes through pleasure (sex) and culture (education), both hegemonic symbols of freedom in the paradigm of gender inequity. Therefore, the hybridizing process is personified in the main character, who is never torn between both worlds, but rather restores a new reality through the integration of both of her cultures: "Yo veo las imágenes de un mundo en constante fusión, un mundo que se recrea constantemente" (192) (I see the images of a world in constant *fusion*, a world that is *reinvented* constantly) (my emphasis).

Liminal Designation in the Twenty-First Century

The first group of authors who have been writing from the 1990s into the twenty-first-century compound the "Nuevo costumbrismo nacional" or "Nueva narrativa nacional" (N'Gom, "Literatura africana de expresión española"). Within this group, I want to highlight the following writers and titles: Maximiliano Nkogo Esono (*Adjá-Adjá y otros relatos*, 1994 and *Nambula* 2000), José Fernando Siale Djangany (*Cenizas de Kalabó y Termes*, 2000, *La revuelta de los disfraces*, 2003, and *Autorretrato con un infiel*, 2007) and Juan Tomás Ávila Laurel's latest novel, *Avión de ricos, ladrón de cerdos* (2008).

Autorretrato con un infiel (2007) of José Fernando Siale Djangany presents the reality of Equatorial Guinea from an African "mythical realism," where not only designation becomes the container for a new symbolic cartography of historical trauma (*Poór Donanfer*, Fernando Poo; *Franck Nkó* for Franco; *Isco de Coor*, Isla de Corisco), but where the author builds a plot of underlying criticism aimed at both the old colonizing empires (*Puerto Galo* for Portugal and *Cabo Norte* for Spain) and at the new African state. This novel depicts a polyphonic representation of the transition from the colonial to the postcolonial era as a much needed mechanism to avoid the loss of history. The literary figures of historians, anthropologists, sociologists, and missionaries all act out to adulterate and conspire to destroy material records of African history. The painting by Father Delatorre "Self-portrait with an Infidel," from which the title of the novel is taken, is an ironic statement asserting that the subaltern cannot yet "sketch himself." In other words, the African character is still being drawn by the dominating powers in their own aesthetic terms. The other revealing element is the figure of the traditional storyteller who is asked about the underlying meaning of folk tales, and is not able to answer at all. While in the novel, reading is also censored, the native characters are trapped in a space where they are not able to speak out their own culture (the traditional rites and customs have lost their original contents and act as empty containers, pure forms), nor have access to the typographical culture. In Siale's novel there is an absolute nullification of the postcolonial subject dispossessed both of the oral and the written. "Do you exist?" asks Roberto Fernández Retamar (23) in regards to the colonized being a distant echo, an attempted cultural and historical void.

In the same manner, reference to the past in Siale's novel (as well as in other African authors such as Ben Okri and Nuruddin Farah) is constructed through common mechanisms for interpreting the chaotic present. Such narrative strategy is not only aimed to represent a re-visitation of the past, but also to question whether the old colonial framework has really concluded or if it is maintained under different signs and practices. *Nambula* (2006),[15] a short novel by Maximiliano Nkogo Esono, also follows the narration of the process of formation of a new African republic. There we read: "El vendaval de la democracia y su irresistible corriente multipartidista procedente del Norte levanta auténticos torbellinos de ambiciones fratricidas y sacude con portentosa fuerza los sagrados pilares sobre los que hasta ahora se había asentado cómodamente el tradicional modo de ser del Sur" (5) (The heavy winds of democracy and its irresistible multi-party currents arriving from the North raise authentic whirlwinds of fratricidal ambitions and shake with colossal strength the sacred pillars on which, until now, the traditional ways of being in the South had rested comfortably). This making and unmaking of the African reality through corruption, incompetence, unemployment, mercenarism, bureaucracy, and paramilitary violence, brings forth the depiction of an "afro-occidental" political parody, in which there is a clear questioning of the authenticity of the African transition process into a modern nation-state, shaped after "democratic-civilized" Western models.

In the novels of the authors mentioned above, the characters see themselves as involuntary protagonists of a situation they disapprove of, and which they criticize through an absurd exaggeration of charismatic power demonstrations and humorous misinterpretations of Western political formulae. There is still a manifest depiction of traditional African elements that find themselves unnaturally placed in a fossilization process that clashes deeply with what seems to be a rehearsal of modern, foreign ways. Issues that are common in this "Nueva narrativa nacional" are the coexistence of tradition (amulets, fetishes, witchcraft, initiation rites, *griots*), Western political methods and theatrical diplomatic equations that are narrated as clumsily embedded in the African society. Such hypercritical, yet comic passages, are absorbed in the text in a satirical manner, ridiculing not only the new African politics, but its original Western forms, expressing the disillusionment of the post-colonial era and overcoming, simultaneously, the "rhetoric of blame" against the West (Said 19). This group of writers shares two major topics with other African literatures: the clash between the modern way of life and tradition, and the need to reconcile past and present. They use literature as an agent of social transformation, and consider that, while it is true that the idea of European modernity cannot be validated, neither can the newly installed African republic, which is as deceitful as the previous one.

This century marks a period of dynamic coexistence between this last generation that produced the Guinean literature of the last two decades of the twentieth-century, and what I consider the breakthrough work of César Mba Abogo, who in 2007 opened up a new path for Guinean literature with his eclectic *El porteador de Marlow: Canción negra sin color*. The structure of the book combines short stories, poetic prose, poetry, and a short descriptive catalogue of European and African cities. In *El porteador de Marlow* there is an explicit intertextuality with Italo Calvino's *The Invisible Cities*, a literary game which also interconnects the gazes of Marco Polo's West and Genghis Khan's Far East. At the same time, Mba's book introduces a new literary object that cannot be properly defined, it has its own decoding system. The configuration of the book is polyhedral, subverting the rigid form of European narrative by introducing a flexible and pragmatic aesthetic sense, more akin to African oral traditions. Mba's text does not share the coordinates in content and style of his contemporaries, but rather occupies a contingent "in-between" space that innovates and interrupts the discourse of the past: "Estoy condenado a vivir en una frontera / En la desidia ambigua y en la tormenta del exilio" (100) (I am sentenced to live in a frontier / In an ambiguous indolence in the storm of exile), a "liminal space, in-between designations of identity" (Bhabha 5). This interstitial location, caught in between monolithic and directly opposing identities, offers the chance of a hybridizing outlook that not only negotiates the difference without the presence of identitary hierarchies, but also searches for a new definition: a definition that aims to the colonized subject as well as the old colonizing Metropolis. Europe is not taken anymore as the absolute symbolic ego of post-colonial rejection, as an ontological trap for the Others' creative expression, but rather as an ambivalent scenario of "newness":

> No paro de avergonzarme de mi cotidianeidad en esa Europa en la que soy a la vez hijo y forastero [. . .]. Pero, por mi parte, cuanto más intento vaciarme de las nomenclaturas de la historia para ser transparente como la conjunción de varios neo-mundos que forman un todo-mundo inédito que ignora las nociones de centro y periferia y del que ninguna sociedad es metrópolis de otra, el lamento de Wallcot en su *A Far Cry From Africa*, ya sea en forma de mosquitos o libélulas, siempre acaba llegando hasta mí y aplastándome bajo su peso. (123)

(I cannot stop feeling shame for my day to day life in this Europe in which I am her son as well as a foreigner [. . .]. However, as much as I try to resist the nomenclatures of history in order to be as transparent as the conjunction of several neo-worlds conforming a new, inedited total-world which ignores the notions of center and periphery, and in which no society is the metropolis of another, Wallcot's lament in his *A Far Cry From Africa*—be it in forms of mosquitoes or dragonflies—always ends up getting me and squashing my soul under its weight).

This subversive dialogism that attempts to level the outdated North-South discourse through literature, endures simultaneously a social and ideological fragmentation within a single estranged language of Europe-as-Self and Europe-as-Other. "He vivido en Europa / He vivido en el paraíso / He vivido en el infierno / Cuando me reúna con mi gente / Hablaré de los hombres y las mujeres de Europa / Hombres y mujeres como nosotros" (98) (I have lived in Europe / I have lived in Paradise / I have lived in Hell / When I come together with my people / I will speak of the men and women of Europe / men and women like us). This challenging division in the locus of enunciation is perfectly defined in a dreamlike episode of one of the characters: "He had an undecipherable conversation with a very strange man. He had two mouths: "Mantuvo una conversación indescifrable con un hombre muy extraño. Tenía dos bocas, una estaba donde están las bocas habitualmente y la otra estaba en la nuca. Hablaron como si fueran miembros de una familia desunida y extensa" (51) (one was placed where mouths generally are, and the other one was at the nape of the neck. They spoke as if they were members of a separate and vast family). As I suggested above, following Bhabha and García Canclini, the borderline engagements of cultural difference may as often be consensual as conflictual and indeed, as Mba points out, the postcolonial subject has now two mouths from where s/he can speak, one "where it should be" and the other hidden, yet not silent.

In *El porteador de Marlow*, the city of Madrid becomes a declaration of contradiction (hospitality/hostility), both these signs coexisting separately. The city offers a place of cultural intersection producing a heterotopic environment: "Velos islámicos. Turbantes sijs. Gente paseando abrazada. Balcones adornados con macetas y sábanas que gritaban su repulsa a la guerra de Irak. Ka se sentía como en un decorado de una película independiente" (65) (Muslim veils. Sikh turbans. People strolling, holding each other. Balconies decorated with flowerpots and sheets that yelled out their rejection to the Iraq War. At that moment, Ka [the main character of "Hora de Partir"] felt that he was in the set of an *independent* film) (my emphasis). In spite of the episodes in which the old metropolis still acts as a setting for old racial and cultural prejudices, the city is also seen from an opposing perspective of renewal, and the text proposes the possibility of reconciliation through a potential "total-world." However, the author also insists on telling the stories of hardship and immigration, acting as a "translational agent" of a vital experience which does not belong to him. He is now, too, a foreigner in this sense, and speaks from a de-automatized position, impersonating the tragedy of other African immigrants ("En algún lugar bajo el Atlántico" 59). Still, Madrid and Barcelona are no longer the cold unwelcoming cities that reluctantly received and excluded the characters in the narratives of the "Lost Generation." In César Mba's texts Malabo is Puerto Fraga; España is Soladia; Madrid is Amilcarna, showing the emergence of a "literary frontier-city" (García Canclini, *Culturas híbridas* 298) that must necessarily acquire new names to designate a recent reality of transculturation in a process of amplification of discursive and cultural diversity. In such contrapuntistical environment, both the reality of origin as much as the country of reception are evaluated in an uncomfortable position through a specific liminal perception: "Puedo vivir sin las columnas los templos o los palacios de Europa / Puedo vivir sin Florencia, son los Beatles, sin Calvino . . . / Pero cada vez que tengo listas las maletas / La sombra del miedo se abalanza sobre mí" ("Las soledades del Poeta" 131) (I can live without the columns, the temples or the palaces of Europe / I can live without Florence, without The Beatles, without Calvino . . . / But every time my bags are ready / The shadow of fear throws itself against me). Therefore, the writer-character is no longer completely African, yet not entirely European. He is transformed instead by the complex construction of an identity of the "In-between" in a neo-identitary, post-essentialist era.

Regarding the lack of national and international projection of these contemporary authors, it seems that Spain is particularly affected by the invisibility of Guinean postcolonial literature. At least from the fifties, and in many cases, prior to this date, French and English presses opened the market to many authors from the former colonies. Simultaneously, literary and academic circles paid critical attention to their works. The latter allowed the Francophone and Anglophone African literatures to become a solid phenomenon worth of study not only in Europe, but also in the United States. Unfortunately, this has not been the case with Equatorial Guinea in Spain (with the exception of scholars Gustau Nerín, Jacint Creus, Gloria Nistal Rosique, and Guillermo Pié Jahn, who, except Creus, do not teach at Spanish universities). Maya García de Vinuesa points out that this literature has been only studied seriously outside Spain, particularly in the United States by the pioneer work of scholars such as M'bare N'gom, Benita Sampedro, John Lipski, Baltasar Fra Molinero, Jorge Salvo or Susan Martin-Márquez. The emergent literary presence of an "African Spain" is a clear statement of defiance against the pure "Spanish" or "European" identity propaganda, particularly when authors such as Agnès Agboton (Benin), Michael Ohan (Nigeria), Guy Merlin Nana Tadoun or Inongo Vi Makomé (Cameroon) have chosen Spanish as their language of creative expression. They subvert the "language-as-border" concept that endangers the possibility of a multicultural process of exchange, as well as an enriching African language-shaping process of Spanish.

To end this section and the essay, I would like to quote César Mba Abogo: "Es preciso sembrar algo en este continente que arrastra tantos monólogos y diálogos inconclusos" ("Pero es preciso sembrar algo" 120) (It is necessary to grow something in this continent dragging so many unfinished monologues and dialogues). Here the reader is not sure exactly which continent he is referring to, or whether the message is aimed at both Europe and Africa in a timid statement of a transmodern project of Afro-Europeanization, one that is present in what I believe to be a seminal work for "Afro-Hispanic" literatures in the twenty-first century.

Notes

1. All translations are the author's. It should be noted that there is also very prolific and active group of Saharawi authors who write in Spanish (poetry, narrative, and theater). Due to the limited space of this essay, and because most (if not all) Saharawi literature in Spanish does not reflect hybridizing processes, I will not analyze them here. Adolfo Campoy, a PhD student at the University of Chicago, is writing his dissertation on Moroccan and Saharawi authors. For a list of authors as well as their works, I recommend the web pages of *Literatura saharaui, literaturasaharaui.blogspot.com/, Generación de la Amistad Saharaui, generaciondelaamistad.blogspot.com/, Poemario por un Sáhara libre, poemariosahara.blogspot.com,* and *Tiris Novia de Poetas, tirisnoviadepoetas. blogspot.com/.*
2. Cristián H. Ricci, "El regreso de los moros a España: Fronteras, inmigración, racismo y transculturación en la literatura marroquí contemporánea," "La literatura marroquí de expresión castellana en el marco de la *transmodernidad* y la hibridación poscolonialista," "Najat El Hachmi y Laila Karrouch: Escritoras marroquíes-imazighen catalanas en el marco del fenómeno migratorio moderno," and "*L'ultim patriarca* de Najat El Hachmi y el forjamiento de la identidad amazigh-catalana."
3. Mohamed Bouissef Rekab, *Cuentos,* see *www.usuarios.lycos.es/mohbouissefrek.*
4. Moreover, not only does El Fathi sell his books in Andalusia, a region that has traditionally produced high quality poetry, but it is also very innovative how his verses "cross the Strait" through the music of songwriter, Ramón Tarrío. This kind of artistic and genre reconversion has not only helped the promotion of El Fathi's literature (Tarrío's latest CD is also called *África en versos mojados*) but also, of course, promulgated new kinds of hybrid forms. Ramón Tarrío is now interpreting Mohamed Chakor's sufist poems from the book *La llave y Latidos del Sur* and has toured through Morocco and Andalusia with with his new musical project, *ADUATAIN (Dos orillas),* in which he incorparates verses of Fathi, Chakor, Lamiae El Amrani, and the Spanish writers Juan José Téllez and Paloma Fernández Gomá.
5. Mohamed Toufali published in 2007 an anthology of contemporary Riffian authors (*Escritores rifeños contemporaneos: Una antología de Narraciones y Relatos del Rif*). Some of the writers in the anthology, like him, Karima Toufali, Karima Aomar, Driss Deiback, Rachid Raja, and Mohamed Lemrini write in Spanish. Mohamed Toufali also claims that there is a Riffian literature in Spanish in the Eastern Yabha region: Alhucemas, Midar, Nador, and Berkan (275). Riffian author Saïd El Kadaoui published a novel entitled *Límites y fronteras.* El Kadaoui moved to Catalonia when he was seven. He is now a psychologist. The novel is about a Moroccan'Amazigh character, Ismaïl, who suffers a psychological breakdown due to an identity crisis. After being hospitalized, Ismaïl will discover that the psychotic crisis was an opportunity to assemble his dreams and multiple identities into one.
6. I am translating from Catalan edition as I consider the text to be more faithful to the original intention of the author: it narrates her autobiographical experience as an immigrant from Nador to Vic/Catalonia and not, as the edition in Spanish gathers, from Nador to an unidentified place in "Spain."

7. I am translating from the Catalan edition of *L'ultim patriarca*.
8. The "commercial success" of *L'últim patriarca* would have to be analyzed more deeply in further studies. As for now, suffice it to say that addictions and (supposed) perversions depicted by the characters, Muslim as well as "Christian" (alcohol, drugs, lesbian episodes, and prostitution) are recurrent topics in other "rebellious writers" from Africa. Authors such as Ken Bugul (*El baobab que enloqueció*, 1982), Calixte Beyala (*Assèse l'africaine*, 1994) or Halima Ben Haddou, the first Moroccan woman to write a novel (*Aïcha la rebelle*, 1982), express in critical ways "the degradation of the moral values of the West as a staring point for a search of another Africa" (Miampika, "Narrativa subsahariana" 25). Ricci, in *"L'ultim patriarca de Najat El Hachmi,"* analyzes the existing correspondence between El Hachmi's novel and the writings of the Algerian-Amazigh Assia Djebar, *Femmes d'Alger dans leur appartement* (1980) and *Lejos de la Medina* (1991); Taos Amrouche (*L'amant imaginaire*, 1975), Yamina Mechakra (*La grotte éclatée*, 1979); the Moroccans Fatema Mernissi in her autobiography *Sueños en el umbral* (1995) and Badia Hadj Nasser (*El velo al desnudo*, 2007); and the Catalans Mercè Rodoreda (*Mirall trencat* 1974) and Víctor Catalá in *Solitud* (1904). El Hachmi in *L'ultim patriarca* makes explicit correspondences with Chicana writer Sandra Cisneros's *The House on Mango Street* and English Zadie Smith's *White Teeth* and *On Beauty*.
9. Ducinea Tomás has suggested the names of most of the authors and their literary works analyzed in this section. She also wrote a first rough draft of this section, to which I added theoretical and literary criticism quotations. Both Dulcinea Tomás and I edited and re-wrote the entire section.
10. The Combé or Ndôwé tribe is an ethnic group of Equatorial Guinea.
11. A *boabí* is a minor monarch in African political systems.
12. For further reading on this issue, see Gloria Nistal Rosique and Guillermo Pié-Jahn, *La situación actual del español en África*.
13. All of the poems cited above can be found in Ndongo-Bidyogo's *Antología de la literatura guineana*.
14. The Centro Cultural Hispano-Guineano's Press published at the time *Africa 2000*, a quarterly journal established in 1985 that was transferred to Madrid in 1987. *El Patio* was a monthly journal established in 1990 under the direction of Juan Tomás Ávila Laurel. *El Patio* changed its name to *El árbol*. Both journals were key in the promotion of Guinean literature.
15. The fictional African country *Nambula* is taken from *Cause Celeb*, a novel by Helen Fielding that portrays the decision of the bored European bourgeois to work in the Third World through the organization of a contest in Africa for the rich and famous, in order to raise money for food.

Works Cited

Al-Jabri, Mohammed Abd. *Crítica de la razón árabe*. Barcelona: Icaria, 2001.
Al-Sabbag, Muhammad. "Al-Andalus, manuscrito raro árabe." *Miradas desde la otra orilla: Una visión de España. (Antología de textos marroquíes actuales)*. Madrid: AECI, 1992.

Amrani, Muhammad. "Introducción." *Antología de relatos marroquíes*. Mohamed Chakor and Sergio Macías. Murcia: Universidad de Murcia, 1990. 13–26.

Amrouche, Taos. *L'amant imaginaire*. 1975. Paris: Éditions Joële Losfeld, 1997.

Ararou, Ahmed. "Tabanxi." *La puerta de los vientos: Narradores marroquíes contemporáneos*. Barcelona: Destino, 2004. 65–75.

Ávila Laurel, José Tomás. *Avión de ricos, ladrón de cerdos*. Barcelona: El Cobre, 2008.

Azzuz Hakim, Mohamed Ibn. *Cuentos populares marroquíes*. Madrid: Instituto de Estudios Africanos, 1954.

———. *Rihla por Andalucía*. Tetouan: s/n, 1949.

Benabdellatif, Abdelkader. *El reto del Estrecho*. Tetouan: Université Abdelmalek Essaâdi, 2005.

Ben Haddou, Halima. *Aïcha la rebelle*. Paris: Jeune Afrique, 1982.

Beyala, Calixte. *Assèze l'africane*. Paris: J'ai lu, 1994.

Bhabha, Homi K. *The Location of Culture*. New York: Routledge, 1995.

Bouissef Rekab, Mohamed. *Aixa, el cielo de Pandora*. Cádiz: Quórum, 2007.

———. *El motín del silencio*. Tangier: AEMLE, 2006.

———. *La señora*. Madrid: Sial, 2006

Bugul, Ken. *Le baobab fou*. 1983. *El baobab que enloqueció*. Madrid: Zanzíbar, 2002.

Català, Víctor. *Solitud*. 1905. 15th. ed. Barcelona: Selecta, 1976.

Cerezales, Marta, Moreta, Miguel A. and Lorenzo Silva. *La puerta de los vientos: Narradores marroquíes contemporáneos*. Barcelona: Destino, 2004.

Chakor, Mohamed. *La llave y Latidos del Sur*. Madrid: Cálamo, 1997.

Chakor, Mohamed, and Jacinto López Gorgé. *Antología de relatos marroquíes en lengua española*. Granada: Editorial A. Ubago, 1985.

Chakor, Mohammad, and Sergio Macías. *La literatura marroquí en lengua castellana*. Madrid: Magalia, 1996.

Cisneros, Sandra. *The House on Mango Street*. Houston: Arte Público, 1984

Daoudi, Ahmed. *El diablo de Yudis*. Madrid: VOSA, 1996.

Djebar, Assia. *Femmes d'Alger dans leur appartement*. Paris: Édition de femmes, 1980.

———. *Loin de Medine*. 1991. *Lejos de la Medina: hijas de Ismael*. Madrid: Alianza, 1993.

Dussel, Enrique. "Transmodernidad e interculturalidad (Interpretación desde la filosofía de la liberación)." México City: UAM-Iz, 2005. *Web de la Asociación de Filosofía y Liberación*. June 24, 2006. www.afyl.org.

El Fathi, Abderrahman. *Abordaje*. Tetuán: Université Abdelmalek Essaadi, 1998.

———. *África en versos mojados*. Tetouan: Université Abdelmalek Essaâdi, 2002.

———. *El cielo herido*. Cádiz: Aula Literaria José Cadalso-S. Roque, 2003.

———. *Desde la otra orilla*. Cádiz: Quórum, 2004.

———. *Fantasías literarias*. Tetouan: Université Abdelmalek Essaâdi, 2000.

———. *Primavera en Ramallah y Bagdad*. Tetouan: Université Abdelmalek Essaâdi, 2003.

———. *Triana, imágenes y palabras*. Tetouan: Université Abdelmalek Essaâdi, 1998.

El Gamoun, Ahmed. "La Atlántida." *La puerta de los vientos: Narradores marroquíes contemporáneos*. Barcelona: Destino, 2004. 151–64.

———. "La literatura marroquí de expresión española: Un imaginario en ciernes." *Escritura marroquí en lengua española II (1975–2000)*. Fez: U Sidi Mohamed Ben Abdellah, 2004.

El Hachmi, Najat. "Carta d'un immigrant." *Inauguració del Congrés Mundial dels Moviments.*

———. *Humans i Immigració,* organitzat per *l'Institut Europeu de la Mediterrània.* 2004.
———. *Jo també sóc catalana.* Barcelona: Columna, 2004.
———. *L'ultim patriarca.* Barcelona: Planeta, 2008.
El Harti, Larbi. *Después de Tánger.* Madrid: Sial, 2003.
El Kadaoui, Saïd. *Límites y fronteras.* Barcelona: Milenio, 2008.
Evita, Leoncio. *Cuando los combes luchaban.* Madrid: Sial, 2000.
Fernández Retamar, Roberto. *Calibán: Contra la Leyenda Negra.* Lleida: Universidad de Lleida, 1995.
Flesler, Daniela. *The Return of the Moor: Spanish Responses to Contemporary Moroccan Immigration.* West Lafayette: Purdue University Press, 2008.
Fra-Molinero, Baltasar. "La educación sentimental de un exilado africano: *Las tinieblas de tu memoria negra* de Donato Ndongo-Bidyogo." *Afro-Hispanic Review* 21.1–2 (2002): 161–170.
García Canclini, Néstor. *Culturas híbridas: Estrategias para entrar y salir de la modernidad.* Barcelona: Paidós, 2001.
———. "Noticias recientes sobre la hibridación." *Revista Transcultural de música* 7 (2003). December 18, 2007. www.sibetrans.com/trans/trans7/canclini.htm.
García Ramírez, Paula. *Introducción al estudio de la literatura africana en lengua inglesa.* Jaén: Universidad de Jaén, 1999.
Goytisolo, Juan. *España y sus ejidos.* Madrid: Muley-Rubio, 2003.
Hadj Nasser, Badia. *El velo al desnudo.* Jaén: Alcalá, 2007.
Ilonbé, Raquel. *Ceiba.* Madrid: Editorial Madrid, 1978.
Jones Mathama, Daniel. *Una lanza por el Boabí.* Barcelona: Tipografía Casals, 1962.
Karrouch, Laila. *De Nador a Vic.* Barcelona: Columna, 2004.
Khatibi, Abdelkibir. "Maghreb plural." Capitalismo y geopolítica del conocimiento: El eurocentrismo y la filosofía de la liberación en le debate intelectual contemporáneo. Comp. and Intro. Walter Mignolo. Buenos Aires: Ediciones del Signo, 2001.
Lahchiri, Mohamed. *Cuentos ceutíes.* Casablanca: AEMLE, 2004.
———. *Pedacitos entrañables.* Casablanca: SERAR, 1994.
———. *Una tumbita en Sidi Embarek y otros cuentos ceutíes.* Casablanca: Dar Al Karaouine, 2006.
Lahrech, Ouama A. "La biblioteca del Ryad andalusí." *La puerta de los vientos: Narradores marroquíes contemporáneos.* Barcelona: Destino, 2004. 235–53.
Lifshey, Adam. "Ideations of Collective Memory in Hispanophone Africa: The case of María Nsué Angüe's *Ekomo.*" *Hispanic Journal* 24.1.2 (2003): 173–85.
Lipski, John. "The Spanish of Equatorial Guinea: Research on 'La Hispanidad's Best-Kept Secret.'" *Afro-Hispanic Review* 21.1–2 (2002): 70–97.
Mba Abogo, César. *El porteador de Marlow: Canción negra sin color.* Madrid: Sial, 2007.
Mechakra, Yamina. *La grotte éclatée.* Argel: SNED, 1979.
Mekuy, Guillermina. *El llanto de la perra.* Madrid: Plaza y Janés, 2005.
———. *Las tres vírgenes de Santo Tomás.* Madrid: Suma, 2008.
Mernissi, Fatema. *Sueños en el umbral: Memorias de una niña del harén.* Barcelona: El Aleph, 1995.

Mesbahi, Mohamed. "La otra cara de la modernidad de Averroes." *Hesperia. Culturas del Mediterráneo* 3 (2006): 183–97.
Miampika, Landry Wilfrid. "Narrativa subsahariana en lengua francesa: Tendencias actuales." *Otras mujeres, otras literaturas.* Ed. Inmaculada Díaz Narbona and Asunción Aragón Varo. Madrid: Zanzíbar, 2005. 35–62.
Mignolo, Walter. "Colonial and Postcolonial Discourse: Cultural Critique or Academic Colonialism?" *Latin American Research Review* 28.3 (1993): 120–34.
———. *Local Histories/Global Designs: Coloniality, Subaltern Knowledges, and Border Thinking.* Princeton: Princeton University Press, 2000.
Monleón, José, ed. *Cuentos de las dos orillas.* Granada: Junta de Andalucía, 2001.
Moreno Torregrosa, Pasqual y Mohamed El Gheryb. *Dormir al raso.* Madrid: Vosa, 1994.
Naïr, Sami, and Juan Goytisolo. *El peaje de la vida.* Madrid: Aguilar, 2000.
Navarro, Nuria. "Entrevista: Najat El Hachmi: La 'pornografía étnica' también nos hace daño." August 8, 2007. *www.gencat.net/salut/portal/cat/_notes/trans/nachat.pdf.*
Ndongo-Bidyogo, Donato. *Antología de la literatura guineana.* Madrid: Editora Nacional, 1984.
———. "Literatura guineana: Una realidad emergente." Conference in Hofstra University, April 3, 2006. 1–6. November 26, 2006. *www.hosfra.edu/Academics/HCLAS/LACS/LACSevent040306.cfm.*
———. *El metro.* Barcelona: El Cobre, 2007.
———. *Los poderes de la tempestad.* Madrid: Morandi, 1997.
———. *Shadows of Your Black Memory.* Trans. Michael Ugarte. Chicago: Swan Isle Press, 2007.
———. *Las tinieblas de tu memoria negra.* Madrid: Editorial Fundamentos, 1987.
Nkogo Esono, Maximiliano. *Adjá-Adjá y otros relatos.* Malabo: CCHG, 1984.
———. *Nambula.* Malabo: Morandi, 2006.
N'gom, M'bare. *Diálogos con Guinea: Panorama de la literatura guineoecuatoriana de expresión castellana a través de sus protagonistas.* Madrid: AECI, 1996.
———. "La literatura africana de expresión castellana: La creación literaria de Guinea Ecuatorial." *Hispania* 76 (1993) 410–18.
———. "Literatura africana de expresión española." *Cuadernos Centro de Estudios Africanos* 3 (2003): n/p.
Nini, Rachid. *Diario de un ilegal.* Guadarrama (Madrid): Ediciones del Oriente y del Mediterráneo, 2002.
Nistal Rosique, Gloria, and Pié-Jahn, Guillermo. *La Situación actual del español en África.* Madrid: Sial/Casa de África, 2007.
Nkogo Esono, Maximiliano. *Nambula.* Malabo: Morandi, 2006.
Pérez Beltrán, Carmelo. *Entre las dos orillas: Literatura marroquí en lengua española.* Granada: University of Granada, 2008.
Prabhu, Anjali. *Hybridity: Limits, Transformations, Prospects.* Albany: SUNY Press, 2007.
Nsué Angüe, María. *Ekomo.* Madrid: UNED, 1995.
Ricci, Cristián H. "Interview with Laila Karrouch." 2007. August 10, 2007.
———. "Interview with Najat El Hachmi." 2008. May 18, 2008.

———. "La literatura marroquí de expresión castellana en el marco de la *transmodernidad* y la hibridación poscolonialista." *Afro-Hispanic Review* 25.2 (2006): 89–107.

———. "Najat El Hachmi y Laila Karrouch: Escritoras marroquíes-imazighen catalanas en el marco del fenómeno migratorio moderno." *Revista EntreRíos* 6 (2007): 92–97.

———. "*L'ultim patriarca* de Najat El Hachmi y el forjamiento de la identidad amazigh-catalana." *Journal of Spanish Cultural Studies*. Forthcoming.

Ricci, Cristián H., and Ignacio López-Calvo. *Caminos para la paz: Literatura israelí y árabe en castellano*. Buenos Aires: Ediciones Corregidor, 2008.

Rodoreda, Mercè. *Mirall Trencat*. 1974. 3rd ed. Barcelona: Club Editor, 1978.

Said, Edward. *Culture and Imperialism*. London: Vintage, 1994.

Sampedro, Benita. "African Poetry in Spanish Exile: Seeking Refuge in the Metropolis." *Bulletin of Hispanic Studies*, 81.2 (2004): 201–14.

Siale Djangany, José Fernando. *Autorretrato con un infiel*. Barcelona: El Cobre, 2007.

———. *Cenizas de Kalabó y Termes*. Ávila: Malamba, 2000.

———. *La revuelta de los disfraces*. Ávila: Malamba, 2004.

Smith, Zadie. *On Beauty*. New York: Penguin, 2005.

———. *White Teeth*. New York: Random House, 2000.

Toufali, Mohamed. "¿Existe una literatura rifeña en castellano?" *La puerta de los vientos Narradores marroquíes contemporáneos*. Barcelona: Destino, 2004. 273–78.

Uariachi, Abdelkader. *El despertar de los leones*. Tetouan: s/n, 1990.

Vaello Marco, Eloisa. "África-España: Lengua española, imaginario cultural y representaciones Interculturales." *De Guinea Ecuatorial a las literaturas hispanoafricanas*. I Congreso Internacional. Estudios Literarios Hispanoafricanos. Instituto Cervantes, Madrid. November 24, 2008.

Zafzaf, Mohamed. *La mujer y la rosa*. Trans. Beatriz Molina Rueda and Zouhir Louassini. Madrid: AECI, 1997.

Zamora Loboch, Francisco. *Cómo ser negro y no morir en Aravaca*. Barcelona: Ediciones B, 1994.

———. *Memoria de laberintos*. Madrid: Sial, 1999.

◆ 13

From Literature to Letters:
Rethinking Catalan Literary History

Stewart King

The 2007 Frankfurt Book Fair was perhaps the most important event in the history of modern Catalan literature.[1] When two years earlier Catalan culture was formally invited to what is, arguably, the world's most important book fair, Catalan politicians, writers, and cultural commentators alike greeted this honor as a unique opportunity to present their culture to the world. To this end, very little expense was spared. The Institut Ramon Llull (IRL)—the organization charged with promoting Catalan language and culture internationally—reported spending €12 million, although several journalists have noted that the real figure was much more ("Bastant" 46). This sum, which was the most expensive in the history of the Fair (Knapp), was used to invite approximately 120 Catalan-language authors to Frankfurt to participate in over 140 acts, as well as subsidising over fifty translations of Catalan works in German. In addition, the IRL supported fifteen exhibitions and sixty-three performances, including a two-hour spectacular of spoken word, dance, and music by seventy-five Catalan artists.[2]

While the Frankfurt Book Fair helped to gain international recognition for Catalan literature, it was not without controversy. The IRL's decision to support only those authors who write in Catalan and the subsequent absence of Castilian-language writers, such as the internationally renowned Juan Marsé, Eduardo Mendoza, Enrique Vila-Matas, Nuria Amat, and Carlos Ruiz Zafón, again raised the issue of how Catalan literature is defined. Using as a starting point the debates which the 2007 Frankfurt Book Fair has provoked, in this article I explore the construction of Catalan literary studies, paying particular attention to the marginalization or silencing of those elements which do not conform to the national model. I argue that the traditional understanding of Catalan literature as literature written in Catalan—while perhaps once relevant and even necessary—is an outmoded approach which can no longer adequately explain the diversity and complexity of literary production in those areas where Catalan is spoken today. In its place, and again drawing on debates from the Catalan experience at the Fair, in conclusion, I propose an alternative approach to Catalan literary history that is sensitive to multicultural and multilingual difference.

"Singular and Universal": Catalan Literature at the Fair

Frankfurt was undoubtedly a success for the promotion of Catalan culture to an international audience. Never before had the Catalans had such a willing and receptive audience to which to spruik the quality and quantity of Catalan writing from the Middle Ages until the present day. And it worked. The *Frankfurter Allgemeine Zeitung* echoed Cervantes's hyperbolic praise for Joanot Martorell's fifteenth century chivalry novel, *Tirant lo Blanc*, describing it as "*Das beste Buch der Welt*" ("Das beste" L8) (The best book in the world). Quim Monzó and Jaume Cabré were invited onto *Das Blaue Sofa* (The Blue Sofa), a prestigious television program which only interviews those considered to be the Fair's major writers. Catalan writers and their works were prominently displayed at individual publisher's stands, such as Albert Sánchez Piñol, who shared equal billing with international publishing sensation Naomi Klein at the Fischer Verlag stand. Moreover, due to a clever marketing campaign devised by the Catalan ministries of tourism and culture, Catalan literature was promoted throughout Germany, as 450 bookshops entered a competition to produce the best window display of Catalan titles ("450 llibreries" 47).

The visibility of Catalan literature in the build up to, and during, the Fair facilitated sales of works in translation. Carles Porta sold 8,000 copies of *Tor. Tretze cases i tres morts* (Tor: Thirteen Houses and Three Deaths) in less than a month, while translations of novels by Maria Barbal and Jaume Cabré made the German bestseller lists. Barbal's *Pedra de Tartera* (Stone of Debris) sold 40,000 copies and Cabré's *Les veus del Pamano* (The Pamano Voices), translated into German as *Die Stimmen des Flusses* (The River's Voice) and published by Suhrkamp, sold 25,000 copies in 15 days. Cabré's success was due in part to the former German Minister of Foreign Affairs, Joschka Fischer, who hailed *Les veus del Pamano* as the book of the Fair ("Alemanya" 52).[3] In addition to the 50-odd books translated specifically for the Fair, the IRL reported that contracts for the translation of a further 46 Catalan titles had been signed during the five days of the Fair, and more were under negotiation (Castells 46).

The slogan "Cultura Catalana—Singular i Universal" proved inspired, as Catalonia, it seemed, had shaken off its provincial image to claim a rightful place as a significant European culture. The classics of Catalan literature were recognised as important works in the European literary tradition while contemporary writers also received very positive reviews in the German press. The lasting legacy of the Book Fair according to publisher Cristina Mora was the greater international awareness of Catalan culture and literature. In the future, Mora believed, foreign publishing houses would not be so wary of agents promoting Catalan authors (Gelí 49).

Despite the successful promotion of Catalan literature, the criticism which appeared in the press in Spain and abroad about the exclusion or absence of Catalan authors who write in Castilian cast a shadow over the success of the Fair for the Catalan Guests of Honor.[4] In response to this criticism, some Catalan cultural commentators began to question openly the role ascribed to Catalan literature in the nationalist project. Such questioning goes to the very heart of how Catalan literature has been conceived. To understand this, it is first necessary to examine the construction of Catalan literary history from its origins in the nineteenth century until the present day.

Once Upon a Time: A History of Catalan Literary History

Literary history is an exercise in storytelling (Hutcheon and Valdés xi). As Benedict Anderson reminds us, stories are central to the construction of national identities, for it was through the development of mass print culture associated with capitalist modernity—specifically realist literature and newspapers—that enabled nations to be "imagined" in the eighteenth and nineteenth centuries. For Anderson, nations are imagined when readers began to identify the fictional world of the novel with the "real" world in which they lived. In this analysis, citizens or members of a cultural group identify with a specific social space through the constant repetition of images and ideas which are easily recognisable to them. These images help to develop "deep, horizontal comradeship with others," which, in turn, distinguishes the members of one nation or group from those of another (Anderson 7).

Literary history, like literature itself, became intricately and intimately bound to the nation-building enterprise during the nineteenth century (Ríos-Font 15). Just as literature created spaces in which the nation could be imagined, David Perkins argues that "the function of literary history is to produce useful fictions about the past," particularly the national past (Perkins 182). For Perkins, literary history parallels national history in its use of "metaphors of origins, emergence from obscurity, neglect and recognition, conflict, hegemony, secession, displacement, decline, and so forth" (Perkins 33).

The development of Catalan literary history since its beginnings in the nineteenth century follows the pattern described by Perkins, as Catalan literature has traditionally been divided largely into three distinct eras, each of which closely mirror Catalonia's political fortunes (Molas 257, 263). The first era encompasses the Middle Ages from the earliest fragments in Catalan in the eleventh century and first preserved text in Catalan—the late twelfth century *Homilies d'Organyà*—until the mid- to late-fifteenth century. This period is seen as the crowning moment of Catalan literature during which writers, such as Bernat Metge, Ramon Muntaner, Joanot Martorell, Ramon Llull, San Vicenç Ferrer, Jordi de Sant Jordi, and Ausiàs March produced the classics of Catalan literature. Importantly, this era also corresponds to the period when the Catalan linguistic area was politically independent: the Counts of Barcelona ruled over a vast Mediterranean empire which included the Crown of

Aragon, the Kingdom of Naples (corresponding to approximately half of modern-day Italy), Sardinia, and the Duchy of Athens.

The second period, known as the *Decadència*, is assumed to be framed by two dates: 1459 and 1833. The first date marks the death of the great Valencian poet Ausiàs March. It is from this moment on that the quality and quantity of literature produced in Catalan, as the name given to this period suggests, began to decline. During this period, following the marriage of Isabella of Castile and Ferdinand of Aragon in 1478, Castilian became the language of the royal court, and as a consequence Catalans increasingly abandoned Catalan and adopted—without much success—Castilian as a language of literature (Rubió y Balaguer 3, 890; 4, 534; 5, 223).

The impoverishment of Catalan literary culture, the increasing adoption of Castilian, and the waning of Catalonia's political influence in the Iberian Peninsula had profound implications for the development of a Catalan national culture (Resina 286). When other European states were consolidating their national cultural-building processes during the Renaissance, the formation of a Catalan national culture was hindered by the fact that Catalan was not a language of prestige (Resina 286–87). As a consequence, Castilian-language civilization largely came to occupy the space of Catalan national culture, resulting in the marginalization of the Catalan-language patrimony.

The next period—the *Renaixença*, or rebirth—begins symbolically with the publication in 1833 of Bonaventura-Carles Aribau's poem "Oda a la pàtria" (Ode to the Fatherland). This romantic poem of exile and cultural and historical continuity made possible by the Catalan language sparked a revival of interest in the Catalan language as well as Catalan history and literature. The terms *Decadència* and *Renaixença* are intricately linked, given that the *renaixentistes* interpreted the period prior to their movement as a break in Catalan cultural continuity and with the abandonment or even the loss of the national patrimony. Although the extent of the loss was perhaps exaggerated, as Catalan was still a language widely used in Catalonia (Prats 40), many middle- and upper-class Catalans believed that they were losing their language and cultural identity and their principle aim was to assure their survival. Influenced by the ideas of Herder, Schiller and the works of Walter Scott, the *renaixentistes* sought to revive Catalan as the language of culture in Catalonia and to restore it to the central position it had occupied prior to the so-called *Decadència*.

The *Renaixença*, however, was much more than the simple reconstruction of Catalan culture. It was also an ideological movement that, primarily through literature, created a series of myths that defined what it was to be Catalan. In what is considered the first conscious *renaixentista* manifesto—Joaquim Rubió i Ors's prologue to his collection of poems, *Lo gaytè de Llobregat. Poesies* (1841)—Rubió laments the deplorable state of the once glorious Catalan language and he argues that it is the duty of all Catalans, particularly writers like him, to save it. This was not just an exercise in linguistic revival; it was central to how the *renaixentistes* saw Catalan identity. If they did not rescue the language, then not only would their cultural heritage be lost; so too, they believed, would their "true essence" as Catalans disappear forever, a loss which, it can be assumed, would turn them into uniformed Spaniards. To avoid this cultural assimilation, Rubió maintains that to achieve Catalan cultural independence it is necessary to create "una lliteratura propia y á part de la castellana" (Rubió i Ors ix) (our own literature separate from Castilian).

Rubió's prologue cum manifesto had a profound effect on the formation of a national Catalan literary canon. Whereas five years earlier in 1836, Felix Torres Amat had published his *Memorias para ayudar a formar un diccionario crítico de escritores catalanes* in which he studied all writers from Catalonia regardless of their language of literary expression, including writers like Abraham Ben R. Chija who wrote in Hebrew, Rubió's call for literary independence marks the beginning of the linguistic divide that would largely define Catalan literature until the present day. From Rubió onwards, the Catalan philological tradition would define Catalans who write in Castilian as Spanish, while those who write in Catalan are Catalan. Thus, to write in Castilian means to belong to a different literary and national cultural tradition.

As a result of the strict link between language and identity, Castilian came to be considered incapable of expressing Catalan culture. In fact, for many *renaixentistes*, speaking and writing in Catalan were crucial to consider yourself Catalan.[5] Josep Torras i Bages, the ultra-conservative Bishop of Vic, argued in his *La tradició catalana* (1892) that to lose one's language also means the loss of one's identity, it signifies being an "estranger a Catalunya" (Torras i Bages 56) (foreigner in Catalonia).

Strikingly, the use of language as an exclusive marker of Catalan literature is still in operation today.[6] In the first of the eleven-volume *Història de la literatura catalana* the distinguished scholar Martí de Riquer draws on aesthetic and linguistic criteria to define what Catalan literature is meant to be. The first—aesthetic—criterion limits literature to the traditional notion of *les Belles Lettres*: poetry, theatre, and narrative, although he also includes memoirs, chronicles, speeches, and religious sermons. The second criterion is linguistic: Catalan literature is defined exclusively as literary texts written in Catalan. De Riquer recognises that Catalans have written in languages other than Catalan, but he argues that when authors do so they belong to the literary tradition of that language and he cites the example of the Valencian author, Vicente Blasco Ibáñez, who wrote exclusively in Castilian (de Riquer 11). This also applies to authors who have produced literary works in both Catalan and Castilian, such as the late Terenci Moix. This has led to some artificial cultural and literary dismembering, such as when the Valencian intellectual, Joan Fuster, studied the Catalan-language works of Sebastià Juan Arbó, but ignored his Castilian-language novels on the grounds that his focus is the study of contemporary Catalan literature (Fuster 374).

More recently, the *Nou diccionari 62 de la literatura catalana* edited by Enric Bou in 2000 in some ways provides an exception to the traditional approach to Catalan literary historiography. Maintaining the linguistic equation, Bou defines the subject of the dictionary as "autors, obres i elements del sistema literari [. . .] en el domini lingüístic català" (Bou vi) (authors, works, and elements of the literary system in the Catalan linguistic domain). Bou is, however, more inclusive than either de Riquer or Fuster, as the dictionary contains entries on writers who, prior to the *Renaixença*, use other languages (Bou vii). Although there is a long entry dedicated to literature in Castilian (Bou 382–88), from the *Renaixença* onwards this multilingual approach is largely reduced to the study of authors who write in Catalan (Bou vii). Bou does not explain the decision to study works by Catalans in other languages during the period prior to the *Renaixença*, but not afterwards. Nevertheless, given that it was during the *Renaixença* that the link between language and national literary identity was firmly established, the assumption which seems to underlie Bou's classification is that post-*Renaixença* writers make an active choice to belong to a specific linguistic and literary community. Many Catalan critics share this assumption. For example, the Mallorcan poet and critic Josep Maria Llompart argues that choosing to write in Catalan is an act of national, cultural and linguistic loyalty (Llompart 109). This was particularly true during the Castilian-centric Franco regime when writing in Catalan was seen as a means of protecting and maintaining Catalan identity. The symbolic role ascribed to Catalan literature in the defence of Catalan identity has led literature to be considered the "fonament on reposa l'edifici sencer del catalanisme" (the base on which the entire Catalan nationalist structure rests), in the words of Xavier Bru de Sala, a noted writer, journalist, and one time senior public servant in the Catalan Department of Culture (Bru de Sala, "Literatura" 97).

This nationalist imperative does not mean, however, that Catalan literature is closed to outside influences. Rather, the linguistic definition has allowed—without much fuss or resistance—for the incorporation into the Catalan canon of works by recent immigrants to Catalonia, such as the English born and bred, Matthew Tree, or Najat El Hachmi, an immigrant from Morocco, who was awarded the 2008 Premi Ramon Llull for her novel *L'últim patriarca*. This novel of the recent migrant experience is just one of a growing number of texts which have opened up Catalan literature to new voices and new ways of imagining what it means to be Catalan in a globalized world. According to Xavier Pla, the creative director of the Catalan stand at the Frankfurt Fair, the effect of immigration from the 1950s onwards has meant that the very idea of Catalanness is understood in the plural, Catalan identities rather than Catalan identity (Alós 62).

There is a limit, nevertheless, to multiculturalism in Catalonia. While Catalan society and culture have long been recognised as multilingual and multicultural, acknowledging this reality in the literary realm has been problematic, as the concept of multiculturalism in literature does not extend to multilingualism when it comes to literature written by Catalans in other languages, as we have seen in the different histories of Catalan literature by de Riquer, Fuster and—to a lesser extent—Bou. It is this paradoxical approach to Catalan literature—multicultural, but not multilingual—that permitted the controversial accusations of Catalan literary and cultural chauvinism to be levelled during the Frankfurt Book Fair.

Taking stock of the Catalan experience at the Fair, newspaper editors and cultural commentators, such as Sergio Vila-Sanjuán writing in *La Vanguardia*, argued that the failure to deal adequately with the question of Catalans who write in Castilian was seen as harmful to Catalonia's international reputation (Vila-Sanjuán 55).[7] In a response to the negative image that nationalism brought to Catalan literature, Xavier Bru de Sala proposes that writers and critics should distance Catalan literature from what he refers to as the so-called nation-building project (Bru de Sala, "Después" 21). Bru de Sala's statement is doubly surprising. First, as a committed Catalanist, it is a complete reversal of his stance 20 years earlier and, second, as we have seen, Catalan literary history has been specifically conceived as a nationalist project. Given that Bru de Sala does not explain the form that a de-nationalised Catalan literature would take, his call for the decoupling of literature and nationalism begs the question: how can a non-nationalist Catalan literary canon be conceived?

Toward a New Literary History: From Literature to Letters

To detach literature from nationalism in the Catalan context—as suggested by Bru de Sala—requires a complete revision of the central tenets of what might constitute Catalan literature. Such an undertaking should necessarily take as its starting point the question of language. Linda Hutcheon argues that the validity of a single national literature "premised on ethnic and often linguistic singularity, not to say purity must be rethought in the context of the globalised multinational world of today" (Hutcheon 3). Homi Bhabha makes a similar point, arguing that "[t]he (relative) sovereignty of the nation-state and the assumed unity of national cultures, upon which such a perspective is based, are both fundamentally disturbed when the core areas turn into multivalent and ambivalent networks that project the periphery internally. Global migration acquires a new historical and theoretical importance in the post- or transnational context" (Bhabha 436).

To some degree, Catalan literature has been open to the cultural challenges of globalization and multiculturalism. As Quim Monzó noted in his opening address at the Frankfurt Book Fair, Catalan literature is, by its very nature, a destructured and deterritorialised literature (Monzó 80), spread across four nation states—Spain, France, Andorra, and Italy—and the four Spanish autonomous communities—Catalonia, Valencia, the Balearic Islands, and Aragon—where Catalan is spoken. This territorial diversity without a nation state to support it—with the exception of the tiny principality of Andorra—has meant that language has been considered the only legitimate defining feature of Catalan literature.

Given the symbolic importance of language to literature in the Catalan context, Xavier Vidal-Folch, author and assistant editor of Spain's major daily newspaper, *El País*, suggests that recognising the cultural and linguistic diversity of literary production by authors in the Catalan-speaking areas may only be possible by abandoning the concept of literature altogether. Given that literature, he argues, is invested with too much nationalist meaning in the Catalan context, Vidal-Folch recommends replacing it with the notion of Catalan "letters" (Vidal-Folch 50). Such a move would change the focus from literature as the expression of a specific language, as defined in the *DRAE*, to a multicultural understanding in which attention is placed on the literary production of any given society or culture, irrespective of the language in which it is written.[8] As Mario Santana notes in a different context, "we should strongly object [. . .] to the validity claims of presenting the study of literary production in only one language as a way of gaining knowledge of the totality of a culture" (117). The move from "literature" to "letters," proposed by Vidal-Folch, goes some way towards recognising this, given that it marks a shift away from language as the defining feature of a culture's literary production to recognise the literary production of a given society in its entirety.

In a multicultural approach to literary studies, any attempt to divide a particular community by literary systems based on language of expression can only be achieved by distorting reality. For example, a multicultural approach to literary studies would not exclude the Castilian-language works of Sebastià Juan-Arbó because they were not written in Catalan, as Joan Fuster does in his *Literatura catalana contemporània*. Instead, it would situate them within not just Juan-Arbó's oeuvre, but would also examine the broader cultural and political factors which led him to switch languages. Furthermore, a multicultural approach would seek to explore the often rich dialogue that occurs between authors irrespective of the language in which they write. For example, Montserrat Roig expressed a direct debt to Juan Marsé, as it was through reading Marsé's *Si te dicen que caí* that Roig realised the extent to which immigrants were marginalised from Catalan culture (90). Without this dialogue, Roig may never have written her brilliant novel of Catalan nationalism and Castilian immigration, *L'òpera quotidiana*.

The model for a new Catalan literary history may, in fact, be found within traditional Catalan literary studies itself. The distinguished twentieth century literary critic and historian, Jordi Rubió i Balaguer, proposed the need for a multilingual literary history in his study of Catalan literature during the so-called *Decadència*, when some Catalans had abandoned Catalan as a language of literature. For Rubió i Balaguer, the loss of language does not necessarily result in an inability to communicate and he argues that cultural historians have an obligation to study the literary production of a given society regardless of whether writers use the "native" or a "borrowed" language. Such a project would lead to "la història literària d'un poble, en diverses llengües" (159) (the literary history of a society in several languages). Rubió i Balaguer's approach allows for a broader understanding of the literary production of a given community and the circumstances in which it is produced.

If Catalan literary studies are to avoid being a closed autonomous literary system then definitions of just what constitutes Catalan literature need to be opened up to appreciate how Catalan literature engages with not only its internal multicultural diversity, but also with its position in a post-national, globalised world. The Frankfurt Book Fair did mark a shift in both these areas. Catalan literature, it seemed, had shaken off its isolation, and now belonged fully and proudly—and was recognised as such in the German press (Serra 38)—to the European literary tradition (Mesquida 8; "La lección" 30).

While the lack of a single nation-state which can provide the support and recognition for a national literature is often seen as problematic for Catalan literature, it can also be argued that the different social, economic, historical, linguistic, and cultural contexts in which Catalan-language literature is produced means that it is well situated within the hybrid and heterogeneous globalised world. The study of all literary production from those areas where Catalan is spoken would undoubtedly be a complex undertaking, but it is one which offers more possibilities as it allows for innovative and exciting connections to be made between places, peoples, and languages.

The calls for Catalan literary studies to adapt to the changing realities of the societies in which Catalan is spoken should not be seen in isolation. Indeed, a literary history sensitive to internal difference should not just be limited to the Catalan context. Histories of so-called Spanish literature should include works by writers in Basque, Catalan, and Galician. Such a Spanish literary history should also be attuned to cultural difference within Castilian. It should never be taken for granted that Catalans or Basques or Galicians who write in Castilian are simply Spanish writers. Rather, their works should be situated in the literary, historical, social, and cultural contexts in which they were and are being produced. Thus, it should be impossible to discuss the works of Ignacio Agustí and José María Gironella without referring to their decision to switch from Catalan to Castilian following the Spanish Civil War and the Franco regime's policies of cultural and linguistic eradication in Catalonia. Likewise, any discussion of Eduardo Mendoza's oeuvre should engage with the motivations which led him to write plays in Catalan while his novels are in Castilian. Furthermore, the works of Castilian-language Catalan writers should be analysed for the way in which they engage with, complement or disrupt Castilian-language literature from the rest of Spain.[9]

Conclusion

The Frankfurt Book Fair has been a watershed moment for Catalan culture. On the one hand, it has underscored that, although the nationalist role ascribed to literature in Catalan had been useful as a means of resisting Castilian cultural assimilation, the continued exclusion of Catalans who write in Castilian is seen as outmoded and out of place in the so-called New Europe. The lesson from Frankfurt is that the perennial, often bitter disputes about who can be considered a Catalan author and what is deemed a work of Catalan literature will not disappear unless Catalan literary studies can engage constructively with the writings produced by the residents of Catalonia, Valencia, and so forth who use other languages. On the other hand, the international recognition of the diversity and quality of Catalan-language literature which the Fair facilitated has had a profound effect on the way in which this literature is viewed within the Catalan-speaking areas. For the first time, leading Catalan cultural figures, such as Bru de Sala, questioned openly the validity of the nation-building function of Catalan literature. I would argue that this international recognition for Catalan-language literature has made it possible to loosen the moorings which have tied literature in Catalan to the nation-building project and this has the potential to open up Catalan literature to new imaginings and paradigms.

Notes

1. I would like to thank Caragh Wells, Ramón López Castellano, Susanna Scarparo, and the members of the Research Reading Group for their comments and suggestions. Any shortcomings are, of course, my own.
2. In total, 705 actors, musicians, and dancers, among other artists, participated in the Fair's cultural program.
3. A recent article in *La Vanguardia* reports that approximately 226,000 copies of Catalan books in German translation were sold as a result of the 2007 Frankfurt Book Fair (Piñol 42).
4. Another event also threatened the success of the Fair for the Catalan organisers. This was the public burning in Catalonia of photos of the King of Spain, Juan Carlos de Borbón, and other members of the Spanish royal family, by young Catalan nationalists. The absence of Catalans who write in Castilian and the burning of photos were seen—particularly in the German media—to be characteristic of a supposed Catalan nationalistic intolerance and exclusion. The burning of photos, however, was a separate, unrelated issue, and Catalan commentators were quick to criticise the Madrid-based German foreign correspondents for provoking a controversy by linking the two issues. Although the photos were clearly burnt by radical Catalan republicans, this act was a protest against the recent discovery that it was illegal to besmirch publicly the honour of the Spanish royal family, following the banning of an issue of the satirical magazine, *El Jueves*, which had portrayed the Prince of Asturias and his wife having sex. The editor and the cartoonist were later fined €3000 each for their part in insulting the Spanish royal family.
5. There were exceptions. Historian, poet, and novelist Víctor Balaguer criticised the exclusion of Castilian in a letter from 1893 in which he reflected on the Catalan *Renaixença* (cited in King *Escribir* 28).
6. Defining a literature by language is not limited to Catalan scholars, according to Mario Santana. In his analysis of several histories of Spanish literature from the nineteenth century until the present day Santana notes that Spanish literature is largely taken to mean literature written in Castilian (Santana 112–14).
7. See, for example, the editorials in *El País* ("Catalanes en Francfort") and *El Periódico de Catalunya* ("Un Frankfurt agredolç"). In contrast, *La Vanguardia* painted a more positive picture of the Catalan experience at the Fair ("La lección de Frankfurt").
8. Although studies of Catalan literature assume that language is the defining feature of a national literature, somewhat surprisingly, Catalan dictionaries do not attribute a linguistic definition to literature. For example, the *Gran diccionari de la llengua catalana*

(*GDLC*) describes literature as the "[c]onjunt d'obres literàries d'un poble (*literatura catalana*)." So too do Pompeu Fabra's *Diccionari general de la llengua catalana* and the Institut d'Estudis Catalans' *Diccionari de la llengua catalana*, which defines literature as the "conjunt de produccions literàries d'un poble, d'un període, [o] destinades a un públic determinat" (group of literary production of one people, of one period, or destined to a certain readership).

9. See, for example, King ("Un acento propio").

Works Cited

"450 llibreries de tot Alemanya han fet aparadors catalans." *Avui*. October 14, 2007. 47.

"Alemanya com a trampolí a altres mercats." *El Periódico de Catalunya*. October 13, 2007. 52.

Alós, Ernest. "La gran exposició de Frankfurt mostra una Catalunya mestissa." *El Periódico de Catalunya*. October 9, 2007. 62.

Anderson, Benedict. *Imagined Communities: Reflections on the Origin and Spread of Nationalism*. London: Verso, 1991.

"Bastant més de 12 milions." *El Periódico de Cataluny*. October 15, 2007. 46.

Bhabha, Homi K. "Editor's Introduction: Minority Maneuvers and Unsettled Negotiations." *Critical Inquiry* 23 (1997): 431–59.

Bou, Enric, ed. *Nou diccionari 62 de la literatura catalana*. Barcelona: Edicions 62, 2000.

Bru de Sala, Xavier. "Después de Frankfurt '07." *La Vanguardia*. October 12, 2007. 21.

———. "Literatura i literatures." *Segones reflexions crítiques sobre la cultura catalana*. Ed. Josep Gifreu, et al. Barcelona: Departament de Cultura de la Generalitat de Catalunya, 1987. 95-116.

Castells, Ada. "Missió acomplerta." *Avui*. October 14, 2007. 46.

"Catalanes en Francfort." *El País*. October 14, 2007. 14.

"Das beste Buch der Welt." *Frankfurter Allgemeine Zeitung*. October 10, 2007. L8.

"Un Frankfurt agredolç." *El Periódico de Catalunya*. October 14, 2007. 6.

Fuster, Joan. *Literatura catalana contemporània*. Barcelona: Curial, 1980.

Gelí, Carles. "La literatura catalana se coloca en el mapamundi." *El País*. October 14, 2007. 49.

Hutcheon, Linda. "Rethinking the National Model." *Rethinking Literary History*. Ed. Linda Hutcheon and Mario J. Valdés. Oxford: Oxford University Press, 2002. 3–49.

Hutcheon, Linda, and Mario J. Valdés. "Preface: Theorizing Literary History in Dialogue." *Rethinking Literary History*. Ed. Linda Hutcheon and Mario J. Valdés. Oxford: Oxford University Press, 2002. ix–xiii.

King, Stewart. *Escribir la catalanidad: Lengua e identidades culturales en la narrativa contemporánea de Cataluña*. London: Tamesis, 2005.

———. "¿Un acento propio? Cultural Difference in Castilian-Language Literature from Catalonia." *Letras Peninsulares* 15.2 (2002): 278–86.

Knapp, Margit. "Commerce Replaces Politics at the Frankfurt Book Fair." *Spiegel Online*

October 9, 2007. Trans. Christopher Sultan. *www.spiegel.de/international/germany/ 0,518,510291,00.html*. Accessed October 11, 2007.

"La lección de Frankfurt." *La Vanguardi*. October 14, 2007. 30.

Llompart, Josep M. "Literatura i societat." *De la literatura com a signe*. S. Serrano, et al. Valencia: Eliseu Climent, 1980. 85–110.

Mesquida, Biel. "Frankfurt subvertion." *El País Quadern*. October 18, 2007. 8.

Molas, Joaquim. "Sobre la periodització en les històries generals de la literatura catalana." *Symposium in honorem prof. M. de Riquer*. Barcelona: Universitat de Barcelona/Quaderns Crema, 1986. 257–76.

Monzó, Quim. "Discurs de presentació de la literatura catalana a la cerimònia inaugural de la Fira del Llibre de Frankfort." *Onze de Frankfort a Alemanya, en català*. Barcelona: Institut Ramon Llull, 2007. 75–85.

Perkins, David. *Is Literary History Possible?* Baltimore: Johns Hopkins University Press, 1992.

Piñol, Rosa María. "Frankfurt: La cosecha catalana." *La Vanguardia*. October 12, 2008. 42.

Prats, Llorenç. *El mite de la tradició popular: Els orígens de l'interès per la cultura tradicional a la Catalunya del segle XIX*. Barcelona: Edicions 62, 1988.

Resina, Joan Ramon. "The Role of Discontinuity in the Formation of National Culture." *Cultural Authority in Golden Age Spain*. Ed. Marina S. Brownlee and Hans Ulrich Gumbrecht. Baltimore: Johns Hopkins University Press, 1995. 284–303.

Ríos-Font, Wadda C. "Literary History and Canon Formation." *The Cambridge History of Spanish Literature*. Cambridge: Cambridge University Press, 2004.15–35.

Riquer, Martí de. *Història de la literatura catalana*. Vol.1. Barcelona: Ariel, 1984.

Roig, Montserrat. *Los hechiceros de la palabra*. Barcelona: Martínez Roca, 1975.

Rubió i Balaguer, Jordi. *Humanisme i Renaixement*. Barcelona: Departament de Cultura de la Generalitat de Catalunya/Publicacions de l'Abadia de Montserrat, 2000.

Rubió y Balaguer, Jorge. "Literatura catalana." *Historia general de las literaturas hispánicas*. Ed. Guillermo Díaz-Plaja. Barcelona: Vergara, 1968. Vol.3: 730–930; Vol.4: 495–597, Vol.5: 216–337.

Rubió i Ors, Joaquim. *Lo gayté del Llobregat: Poesias de don Joaquim Rubió y Ors*. Barcelona: Estampa de Joseph Rubio, 1841.

Santana, Mario. "Mapping National Literatures: Some Observations on Contemporary Hispanism." *Spain Beyond Spain: Modernity, Literary History, and National Identity*. Ed. Brad Epps and Luis Fernández Cifuentes. Lewisburg: Bucknell University Press, 2005. 109-24.

Serra, G.C. "Redescubriendo a los clásicos." *La Vanguardia*. October 11, 2007. 38.

Torras i Bages, Josep. *La tradició catalana*. Barcelona: Edicions 62, 1981.

Torres Amat, Felix. *Memorias para ayudar a formar un diccionario crítico de los escritores catalanes, y dar alguna idea de la antigua y moderna literatura de Cataluña*. Barcelona: Imprenta de J. Verdaguer, 1836.

Vidal-Folch, Xavier. "Taxonomistas de las mariposas." *El País*. October 14, 2007. 50.

Vila-Sanjuán, Sergio. "Catalunya en Frankfurt: Una impresión." *La Vanguardia*. October 14, 2007. 55.

14

The Space of Politics: Nation, Gender, Language, and Class in Esther Tusquets' Narrative

Laura Lonsdale

Esther Tusquets' writing has consistently been studied in relation to questions of gender, with a particular emphasis on gender identity. While a number of critics have acknowledged, more or less in passing, that social class is also a determining factor in the lives and identities of Tusquets' protagonists, it is arguably the case that gender has remained, in much criticism of this author, a somewhat isolated concern. Separating gender from such questions as nationality and class, particularly in relation to questions of form and language, critics have consequently given little consideration to the ways in which such factors in turn influence the constitution or depiction of subjectivity in Tusquets' writing. Central to feminist thought in the last decade or more is the view that gender is *not* the single most significant constitutive feature of identity, and that theories of gender cannot be isolated from such questions as nationality, ethnicity, and class. Not only has the consistent and isolated emphasis on gender generated a limited idiom of interpretation in relation to Tusquets' writing, but it has also cut her off from the socio-historical context which frames and informs her writing both contextually and formally. In this essay, then, I want to both explore the ways in which Tusquets' writing negotiates the politics of the cultural field in Catalonia, in order to consider some of the political and cultural pressures exerted on her as a writer, and to look at the ways in which the author's consistent focus on spatial experience might be seen to formally connect gender, nationality, and class in her fiction.

Esther Tusquets, now in her seventies, is known for her lyrical, baroque, traumatically repetitive texts, many of which explore amorous and sexual relationships between women. Her female protagonists are routinely unsuccessful in extricating themselves from dissatisfactory and damaging relationships with men, and almost entirely incapable of effecting lasting emotional change in their lives, leading to a sense of stasis and repetitious inevitability in the author's work. The recurring lack of fulfillment and return to the heterosexual norm is interpreted by Ortiz-Ceberio as a "falta de atrevimiento" (67), or cowardice, on the part of a conservative author who will not allow her characters to bring their lesbian relationships to fruition. Ortiz-Ceberio is one of a number of critics, as Miguélez observes, to have expressed a growing frustration with Tusquets, increasingly leading to the view that she is not a feminist writer, and that her work in fact reveals an entrenched masculinism. As Miguélez and I have both argued, the interpretation of Tusquets' work as either paradigmatically feminist or as fundamentally masculinist has largely been supported by readings of the formal attributes of her texts—their style and use of imagery, for example—in terms of dubiously "feminine" or "masculine" qualities (Nichols, "Minding Her P's and Q's"; Ichiishi). This conflation of a thematic concern with female sexuality and formal concerns has been unproductive in a number of ways (Miguélez; Lonsdale), not least because it imposes gender politics as a single frame of reference for readings of Tusquets' narrative, and regards gendered subjectivity therefore as singular cause and effect of the psychological trauma which the author expresses in terms of stasis and repetition. Not only does this not allow for alternative readings of the ways in which *other* cultural and political forces might be said to influence both the form and content of the author's work, but it also ignores the position that Tusquets takes up within the cultural field (the field of production and reception within which every author must operate).

Given the prominence of Tusquets' thematic concern with class in her novels, it is significant to ask why there has been a marked reticence among critics of her work to explore this issue in greater depth. In my view, there is a need to critically address the ways in which the politics of gender and class intersect, not always explicitly, within a certain literary critical frame, the one that portrays high-cultured "literariness" as both sexually exclusive and socially conservative, and the anti-canonical or avant-garde as evidence of a disruptive, marginalised, feminine "otherness." The reticence to explore the question of class in relation to Tusquets' work is, therefore, perhaps associated with a critical uncertainty, even unease, regarding the "literariness" of the author's writing. For Rosalía Cornejo-Parriego, the author's innovative use of language and intertextual allusion represents a feminist and postmodernist challenge to canonical texts and the political conservatism she associates with them (50–51), a reading which claims Tusquets as subversive and marginal, but which, ultimately, only confirms, by default, the view that "high culture" is associated with a negative politics of both gender and class. As for those critics disillusioned with the writer's political stance, they have chosen to hone in on the very question of literariness and the "prism of art" which frames Tusquets' novelistic world as evidence of her profound social and sexual conservatism (Glenn, Nichols, "Minding Her P's and Q's"). For Geraldine Cleary Nichols, formal innovation is not the guarantor of subversive tendencies: indeed, Tusquets' stylistic virtuosity is held as evidence that the author in fact *subscribes* to all that is "masculine" about literature, reminding the feminist literary critic that a "supple and affecting" ("Minding her P's and Q's" 160) prose may conceal an unsavoury and harmful politics. This range of interpretations of Tusquets' gender politics is, in my view, inflected with an implicit class politics drawn from leftist theoretical positions which, however valuable, cannot take into account the particular permutations of the relationship between gender and class in the work of individual authors, a relationship which deserves closer and more open examination in the context of Tusquets' writing.

As Miguélez persuasively argues, and as I have argued elsewhere (Lonsdale), the debate regarding whether Tusquets subscribes to a conservative or subversive politics is debilitating to literary criticism when it rests on dubious interpretations of the "feminine" or "masculine" as identifiable stylistic properties, particularly where these are associated by extension, by implication and usually in abstraction with other types of social conformity or rebellion. It is my view, instead, that gender can and should be read in combination with other concrete cultural and political factors and experiences, all of which are mutable and individual in their formulation and expression. Different authors and texts will, of course, lend themselves to vastly differing interpretations of the ways in which such factors and experiences intersect and gain expression. It is my view that, in Tusquets' writing, it is her emphasis on spatial experience that forms the axis of this intersection and frames the formal expression of a range of themes and concerns in her writing. I, therefore, want to offer a reading of Tusquets which focuses on spatial experience as both a formal and contextual expression of the political and cultural forces which have shaped her life as an author, and the lives of her fictional protagonists. This reading goes hand in hand with a consideration of some of the cultural and political issues which I consider most pertinent to an understanding of the field within which she constitutes herself as an author.

A series of autobiographical texts published in recent years, particularly her latest work, *Habíamos ganado la guerra* (2007) (*We Had Won the War*) provide proof—if proof were needed—of the extent to which Tusquets' writing draws on her personal experience of life in Barcelona since she was born at the beginning of the civil war (1936). While such an awareness of this biographical connection has no necessary bearing on our critical interpretation of her texts, it is interesting, in the context of my concerns in this essay, to note the extent to which Tusquets' most recent autobiographical work explicitly foregrounds the political and cultural forces which shaped her childhood and adolescence. Born to a family of the Francoist bourgeoisie that won the civil war, Tusquets seeks, in her latest autobiographical work, to redress a certain imbalance in memorialist writing about the postwar period:

> Sobre esta etapa ... se ha escrito mucho desde el punto de vista de quienes ... perdieron (la guerra), en libros de memorias y en literatura de ficción, pero me pareció que disponíamos de menos material procedente de los vencedores. ... Creí que mi experiencia personal podía aportar algo. (8)

> (A great deal has been written about this period from the perspective of those who lost the war, in memoirs and in fiction, but it seemed to me that less had been written about it by the victors. ... I believed my personal experience might contribute something.)

Locating herself firmly by the coordinates of her time, city, class, and gender, in *Habíamos ganado* the author recapitulates on many of the most prominent themes, characters, places, and even motifs of her fictional works, concretizing and in some sense actualizing the people and places which permeate her fiction in ways which, in her novels and short stories, are often implicit, mythical, ludic, and oneiric.

This process of concretization and actualization is, for me, particularly evident in regard to the spaces and places which are so central, yet often so abstracted, in Tusquets' fiction. Space in Tusquets' fictional narratives is the source of consciousness; the narrator knows herself by the spaces she has occupied (such as her first childhood home), and knows her society by the places it values (such as the *Liceo* theatre, bastion, and temple of Barcelona's bourgeoisie). Spaces in Tusquets' fiction are recreated imaginatively and figuratively; they are darkness or light, submerged or at sea-level; they are like ships, underground caverns or labyrinths. In *El mismo mar de todos los veranos* (1978) (*The Same Sea As Every Summer*), all space is vital[1]; in *El Amor es un juego solitario* (1979) (*Love Is a Solitary Game*), all space is erotic; in *Varada tras el último naufragio* (1980) (*Stranded After the Last Shipwreck*), the protagonist begins to face exterior space; by *Para no volver* (1985) (*Never to Return*), a struggle with spatial perspective accompanies a painfully developing self-understanding through psychoanalysis. Space in Tusquets' narrative is, therefore, key to the question of subjectivity, and its consistently metaphorical function lends it a prime aesthetic importance. The metaphorised sea, the personified home, the sexualised street, evidently yet not explicitly part of the landscape of Barcelona in her fiction, become, in her autobiography, not only the real backdrop to her personal experience, but also landmarks, not within a psychological landscape this time, but within a determinate socio-historical and geographical setting. This locates both the author and her writing so firmly in the context of her city—the Barcelona that has changed so enormously in her lifetime—that it brings us to question how they fit into yet another landscape, cultural and literary this time, determined, or perhaps overdetermined, by the politics of nationhood and language.

The politics of nation and of language are significant to Tusquets, and to the cultural field within which she is initially received, because she is a Catalan writer who, like many other writers of her generation from Catalonia, chooses to write in Castilian. This has become a contentious political issue in an autonomous and democratic Catalonia seeking to build a national and linguistic identity both in the wake of Franco's repressive linguistic and cultural policies, and in the face of mass immigration from the South of Spain. Jordi Pujol, president of the *Generalitat de Catalunya*, or Catalan government, between 1980 and 2003, "consistently stated in speeches that Catalunya is defined not by race but by language[. . . .] It is language and culture that form the 'personality' of Catalunya" (Smith 94). Arthur Terry observes the "close interpenetration of literature and society which is evident in most phases of Catalan culture" (xv), while Kathryn Crameri notes that "[i]t is the act of choosing to write in Catalan or in Castilian which normally classifies a writer as "belonging to" the literature of [Catalonia] or [Spain]" (52). She describes the important association between *Catalanisme,* or Catalan nationalism, and culture, particularly literature written in Catalan:

> Catalan culture has been essentially politicized during its modern history, so that cultural products have political resonances. The use of literature as a means of nation-building in the nineteenth century and until 1939 set up the seemingly unbreakable link between literature and Catalanism and provided a tried-and-tested tool for rebuilding the nation after 1939. (8)

Crameri observes that Catalonia, emerging from under the dictatorship of Franco during the 1970s, was a region in which "political activity was accompanied by equally frenetic cultural activity, responding to the freedoms which the relaxation of the regime now offered" (1). The "nation-building" function of literature as conceived before 1939 was one which Catalanist intellectuals extended to the literature of the Transition, as the 1970s and 1980s came to be regarded as a key period of cultural and linguistic regeneration. As such, a novelist's choice of language—between Catalan and Castilian—has been regarded as a highly political one: "The implications for the novelist of his/her choice of language obviously extend far beyond the personal choice between writing in Catalan or in Castilian. The Catalan novelist of the post-Franco era lives in an environment in which language choice is a political issue and has consequences which might affect perceptions of individual and group identity" (6).

Emilie Bergmann, drawing on interviews held between Geraldine Cleary Nichols and a number of Catalan women writers in *Escribir, espacio propio,* illustrates the influence of such a political demarcation between languages on authors' linguistic choices:

> [Montserrat] Roig explained her decision to write in Catalan. For her, Castilian represented power and domination, while Catalan was the language of love and affection.... Ana María Moix presents a telling critique of other writers' choice of Catalan as a literary language. She dismisses contemporary prose fiction in Catalan for failing to distance itself from the claustrophobic world of the Catalan petite bourgeoisie. The distance necessary for literary creation is achieved only by embracing a language not connected with everyday experience, and she claims that there is no such tradition of fiction writing in Catalan. (99)

For his part, the novelist Juan Marsé has adopted a sceptical attitude to the politics of linguistic normalization. The Catalan government launched a campaign in the 1980s to encourage the more widespread and correct use of the Catalan language and he ruthlessly satirises the campaign in his novel, *El amante bilingüe* (1990) (*The Bilingual Lover*). Educated exclusively in Castilian during the 1940s, though bilingual of speech (Crameri 159), Crameri writes that Marsé "has been disowned by the Catalan literary establishment but is often referred to in Spain as a whole as a

Catalan. His affinity with the people, culture, and situation of Barcelona make him an excellent point of comparison with those who were also born and brought up in Catalonia but, unlike him, chose to write in Catalan" (11). In spite of heavy criticism from Catalan intellectuals, Marsé remains committed to writing in Castilian, and in fact "delights in his dual position of insider and outside to both camps: 'Mi situación personal es la ideal, porque me encanta mi posición casi de francotirador, es decir, no corresponde exactamente ni a la literatura castellana ni a la catalana. Es perfecto'" (Marsé quoted in Crameri 159) (My personal situation is ideal, because I love being something of a free agent/sniper, in other words, to be in a position where I don't quite fit into either Castilian or Catalan literature. It's perfect).

The author Mercedes Salisachs has also fallen out of favour with the Catalan literary establishment for writing in Castilian: "También nacida en Barcelona, no merece ninguna apostilla por parte de los analistas de la literatura catalana, tal vez porque escribe en castellano y se considera catalana y española a la vez, actitud herética para muchos" (García Gómez, n.p.) (Also born in Barcelona, she doesn't even make it into the footnotes of Catalan literary criticism, perhaps because she writes in Castilian and considers herself to be both Catalan and Spanish at the same time, a heretical attitude for many).

The tense political atmosphere surrounding linguistic choices has led some writers, educated in Castilian during the Franco years, to overcome their "falta de escolarización en su lengua maternal" (lack of schooling in their mother tongue) for explicitly nationalist reasons: "El barcelonés Carles Duarte... ha reconocido haber sufrido al escribir en catalán, acostumbrado como estaba a hacerlo en español. Tanto él como otros han atribuido su etapa castellana a la opresión del régimen de Franco" (García Gómez, n.p.) (The Barcelonan Carles Duarte... has admitted finding it difficult to write in Catalan, accustomed as he was to writing in Spanish. He, like other writers, has attributed his Castilian period to the oppression of Franco's regime). If language appears to be the cornerstone of "Catalan" literature, however, García observes that there is nonetheless some confusion regarding who or what counts in the Catalan literary establishment: "Aún no he llegado a ver con claridad si el referente 'Literatura catalana' es la literatura que se ha escrito y se sigue haciendo en catalán tanto en Cataluña como en Valencia, o sólo en Cataluña, tanto en catalán como en castellano" (I'm still not sure whether "Catalan Literature" refers to the literature which has been and continues to be written in Catalonia and Valencia, or only to that written in Catalonia, in both Catalan and Castilian). His perhaps idealistic conclusion is that "las obras de arte son, o deberían ser, como las aves migratorias, que cruzan las fronteras políticas sin pasaporte" (works of art are, or should be, like migrating birds, which cross political frontiers without a passport). For the Catalan critic Alex Broch, however, "for a writer to be considered part of the corpus of Catalan literature there must be no suggestion that his/her views contradict the implicit assumption of nationalism in his/her choice to write in Catalan" (Crameri 53). As Crameri observes, "this sort of expectation leads to a problematic balancing act for the novelist" (53), as s/he attempts to reconcile creative freedom with political responsibility.

Tusquets herself has contended that, for her, writing in Castilian is a spontaneous, politically unmotivated choice: she claims that "escribir en castellano, en la gente de mi generación, era lo espontáneo, lo que se nos daba ya hecho" (Bergmann 99–100) (writing in Castilian, for people of my generation, was spontaneous, something we took for granted); it would be "a great effort" to write in Catalan, "and it would only be motivated by nationalism." The author has contentiously stated, "no me mueve nada lo catalán, como tampoco lo español. Cataluña es bilingüe, de momento. Si desaparece una de las dos lenguas, y creo que sería muy difícil que lo hiciera el español, no voy a intervenir" (*El amor es un juego solitario* n.p.) (I am unmoved by [the question of whether we should speak] either Catalan or Spanish. Catalonia is bilingual, for now. If one of the languages disappears, and I think it unlikely that Spanish will, I won't intervene).

In a more recent interview with the same newspaper she stated, "no soy nacionalista. Y en Cataluña me indigna lo mal que se enseña el castellano en las escuelas. Éste es un país bilingüe" ("Interview with Agustí Fancelli" n.p.) (I am not a nationalist. And in Catalonia I am offended by how badly Castilian is taught in schools. This is a bilingual country). Though she claims she is proud to be a Catalan, "por lo poco que nos entienden fuera" ("Interview with Agustí Fancelli" n.p.) (because outsiders don't really understand us), it is nevertheless evident from these remarks that Tusquets does not seek to constitute herself as an author within a literary landscape dominated by the politics of language and a nationalist drive towards the revitalization of Catalan language and culture.

It is not my intention here to enter into an ongoing debate regarding the place of Castilian-language writers in Catalan literature and culture, but to explore the ways in which questions of language, space, and power, prominent in feminist criticism of this author to date, might be reformulated within a broader cultural, political, and theoretical context, one which includes the territorial, cultural, and linguistic politics of Catalonia. I will argue that the negotiation of space in Tusquets' writing expresses a particularly fraught notion of "belonging," specifically associated with class as well as gender, which is suggestive when read in the context of the cultural and political history of Catalonia.

If neither national politics nor the Catalan-nationalist question of language raise their heads with any consistency in Tusquets' fictional writing, it would be untrue to say that regional politics are thematically invisible, given the prominence of class as a political concern in her fiction. As Josep-Anton Fernàndez explains, the nationalist politics of Catalonia are intricately interwoven with questions of social class: they inhere in notions of Catalan nationality and identity in the same way as do language and geography (13). Indeed, class has become a key issue, since the advent of democracy in Spain and regional autonomy in Catalonia, in the writing of Catalan history. Fernàndez describes the "often acrimonious debate that has been developing since the early 1980s around the different positions present in Catalan historiography" (13):

> Roughly speaking, the two opposing positions in the debate are, on the one hand, that of those historians who favour a history written from a national(ist) perspective as a narrative of the national construction of Catalonia, and who consider historical teaching and research as a tool in the process of 'cultural normalization' of the Catalan nation; and, on the other hand, the position of Marxist historians who view Catalan history as a landscape dominated by class struggle, and nationalism as an ideological formation used by the Catalan, bourgeois dominant class in order to retain its power and privileges. (13)

This view of a bourgeoisie only concerned with its own "power and privileges," content to exploit the political ideology of the day to its own ends, is strongly present in Tusquets' portrayal of Barcelona's upper-middle class, to which her protagonists belong. If the bourgeoisie is considered, in the above analysis to have exploited Catalan nationalism for the preservation of its own interests, it is also a group associated with an earlier, treacherous political allegiance to Francoism, with all that entailed for the suppression of Catalan language and culture. Though it may be argued that the complexity of the map of political allegiances in Catalonia is not fully represented here, it is undoubtedly the case that the bourgeoisie of Tusquets' fiction is portrayed as entirely self-serving, cowardly and conservative, frivolous and exclusive. In the following passage from *Para no volver*, which describes a "coming-out" ball for young socialites in Barcelona, the narrator recreates the performance of Juliette Gréco, singer and postwar icon of the Parisian left-wing and left-bank:

> Estaban las canciones de la Greco ligadas a los personajes de Sartre, aniquilados por la náusea o exultantes ante el descubrimiento liberador de que Dios había muerto o no había existido jamás, o los de Camus, dando vueltas más o menos atormentadas en torno a la condición humana y los humanos desatinos (54)

> (Gréco's songs were linked to the characters of Sartre, annihilated by nausea or exultant before the liberating discovery that God had died or had never lived, or those of Camus, torturing themselves about the human condition and the foolishness of humanity.)

Gréco sings on this occasion for the members of a class with its roots in a political opportunism, a spiritually impoverished class that cynically "digests" and then "defecates" the revolutionary discourses of Sartre and Camus:

> La Greco ... había cantado con pasión y con agresividad unas canciones cuya letra no había sido seguramente el público capaz de comprender—muy distinto el francés de la Greco al que utilizaban en sus viajes periódicos a París, el de las tiendas de

los Champs Elysées, el barrio de la Opera, los restaurantes caros, los espectáculos nocturnos para turistas adinerados: un idioma distinto en un París distinto—, pero, caso de que sí las hubiera entendido, habrían aplaudido con idéntico entusiasmo, impenetrable la burguesía de esta ciudad, más tal vez que la de otros países, *ya que no en balde habían ganado una guerra civil de tres años y multiplicado a partir de ahí por mil su fuerza y sus privilegios*, que engullían y digerían sin molestias, ya que con idéntica facilidad luego las defecaban, sin haber asimilado ni aprendido nada. (53–4, my emphasis)

(Gréco had sung, with passion and aggression, songs whose lyrics the audience had surely been unable to understand—very different Gréco's French to the language they used during their occasional trips to Paris, in the shops on the Champs Elysées, in the Opera district, the expensive restaurants, the evening shows for moneyed tourists: a different language in a different Paris—, but even if they had understood them, they would have applauded with the same enthusiasm; impenetrable the bourgeoisie of this city, perhaps more so than in other countries, *because it was not for nothing that they had won a three-year civil war and so multiplied by a thousand their power and privileges*, devouring and digesting [the lyrics] without difficulty, since they defecated them with equal ease, assimilating and learning nothing.) (my emphasis)

These passages portray the Catalan *haute bourgeoisie* as profoundly and pragmatically hypocritical, an attitude which is reflected also in their use of language.

Language, in the Catalan experience, is key to both the creation of group identity and to the imposition of political power: Crameri writes that "the way in which the bourgeoisie willingly abandoned their language and nationalist claims under first Primo de Rivera and then Franco, in return for the freedom to continue their business, attracted much criticism from other Catalans" (42). The following passage from *Para no volver* is significant in this context:

Al afirmar un compañero que no era el catalán una lengua sino un dialecto (creencia que compartía la propia Elena, por más prudente que se callara), (el profesor) había replicado que quien dijera algo así era un necio y un ignorante, y no había pestañeado siquiera, se había encogido sólo levemente de hombros, cuando precisó el alumno que el presunto necio e ignorante no era otro que su padre—y los padres de la mayoría de nosotros, había pensado Elena sin despegar tampoco ahora los labios. (51)

(When a classmate said that Catalan was not a language but a dialect [a belief which Elena shared, though she wisely kept it to herself], [the teacher] had retorted that whoever said such a thing was a fool and an ignoramus, and he had barely blinked, had only lightly shrugged his shoulders, when the pupil explained that the supposed fool and ignoramus was none other than his father—and most of our fathers, had thought Elena, still keeping quiet.)

This awareness of the politics of linguistic choices gives a particular resonance to the narrator's description, in *El mismo mar*, of the "castellano adulterado y terrible de las mujeres bien de mi ciudad" (36) (the adulterated and terrible Castilian of the well-to-do women of my city), as well as to Tusquets' description in *Habíamos ganado* of the "denostado y degradado catalán de los barceloneses" (21) (insulted and degraded Catalan of the people of Barcelona). Castilian—which for Roig is the language of "power and domination" (Bergmann 99)—is in Tusquets' novel a language inadequately spoken by the women of the bourgeoisie, their everyday speech inflected with an affected foreignness; Catalan, on the other hand—and Tusquets' choice of adjectives here is remarkable—is a language both "insulted" and "degraded" by those in collusion with the sources of power. Language as a strong marker of national and cultural identity—rooted, located, historicized—is replaced in this context with language as the marker of a group identity founded on the shifting sands of economic privilege and political acquiescence. The adulterated use of both Catalan and Castilian seems to express deep social divisions. The narrator's refusal or inability to adopt the mannerisms of speech associated with both her gender and her class places her in an "incómoda tierra de nadie" (37) (uncomfortable no-man's land); by identifying herself with a more correct use of Castilian, she marginalises herself from the "tribu" (tribe), only to consistently evoke an ironic association between her own use of language and that of the women of her class[2] The sense of oscillation and entrapment identifiable in *El mismo mar* as a feature of the narrator's expression of the world is present here, too, in the regional politics of linguistic choices, where every utterance is filled with unavoidable political resonances.

Tusquets' relentless undermining of Barcelona's *haute bourgeoisie*, with its implicit (and, occasionally, explicit) connections to linguistic, cultural, and political hegemony, should not be read in terms of a covert nationalism (an interpretation without obvious foundation), but as a means of expressing the individual's uneasy negotiation of "complexes of power" (Armstrong 225). As Molinaro observes, power in Tusquets' novels is not predicated on a vertical relationship of oppressor to oppressed, but is diffused through networks which both construct and deconstruct hierarchies (18). Class, gender, and, arguably, nationality, intersect to render the protagonist a subject who is never entirely of the dominant or dominated group, a character continually caught up in a debilitating dynamic of collaboration and refusal. This point can be illustrated with reference to "Los primos" ("The Cousins"), the second in Tusquets' collection of short stories, *Siete miradas en un mismo paisaje* (1981) (*Seven Views Of The Same Landscape*). In this story, the wealthy child protagonist, Sara, describes an occasion when her parents' car strays into unknown and as yet unimagined parts of the city: the "barrios" of the poor. For Sara, frightened, threatened, but ashamed, this marks the dawning of class guilt:

> Algo o acaso todo andaba muy mal en el mundo.... Y por debajo de todo esto ... [sentía] un ambiguo, turbio, mareante, avasallador sentimiento de culpabili-

dad, que había de ir creciendo y creciendo con el transcurso de los años, hasta romper los diques y desbordarla y arrollarlo todo a su paso, y precipitarla en lo más revuelto y proceloso de la corriente, definitivamente perdidas y para siempre inalcanzables cualquiera de las dos orillas. (50)

(Something or perhaps everything was very wrong with the world. . . . And beneath all of this . . . [she felt] an ambiguous, unsettling, dizzying, obliterating sense of guilt, which was to go on growing and growing with the passing of the years, until the dam broke and the feeling overcame her, sweeping away everything in its path, precipitating her into the current at its most turbulent and tempestuous, both banks of the river now definitively lost to her and forever unreachable.)

Sara's awareness of the "odio ajeno" (50) (foreign loathing) of a class of people—the poor—whom she perceives as "remotos como marcianos" (49) (remote as Martians), coupled with her recognition of the brutal exclusivity of her own class, creates an unproductive guilt, distancing her from "cualquiera de las dos orillas" (50) (both banks of the river). Sara's sense of alienation from her own class and, in this story, the explicitly Nazi ideology which underwrites it[3], is heightened by the girl's awareness of her darkening complexion: "¿Cómo podría una andar por el mundo con unos ojos simplemente castaños?" (73) (How could one go through life with eyes that were just plain brown?). The nine-year-old Sara is perhaps the narrator of *Mar* in formation: her developing sense of self is defined by her growing awareness that all the positions she occupies are inadequate and undesirable, productive of guilt but not of alternative choices, and that her very existence is mediated by political circumstances she has not chosen and cannot control.

The sense of stasis that emerges in so much of Tusquets' fictional writing is arguably a product of this dynamic of collaboration and resistance, associated in turn with her characters' inability to generate or fulfil fresh possibilities in their lives and experience. The author's famously digressive and protracted style conveys a sense of tortuous progress through both space and time, challenging the notion of narrative as a journey and suggesting instead a dynamic of constant projection and constant return.

It is interesting to note, in this context, a development in Tusquets' use of interior monologue at the beginning and end of her trilogy of novels (*El mismo mar; El amor; Varada*). Having abandoned the first-person narrative mode after *El mismo mar*—opting instead for a third person mode and shifting point of view—Tusquets returns to the first-person interior monologue at the very end of the last novel, *Varada* (otherwise narrated in the third-person). But the stream-of-consciousness here is qualitatively different from that of *El mismo mar*: all punctuation is removed from Elia's monologue in *Varada*; it is a constant flow forwards, uninhibited by the disorientating parentheses, digressions and re-doublings of the first novel, a fittingly progressive thought process both for the physical journey towards her son, Daniel, and her metaphorical journey towards new beginnings even as she follows "la línea del mismo mar azul de todos mis veranos" [*Varada* 271] (the line of the same blue sea of all my Summers):

> Estoy viva y corro en la carrera y seguiré adelante sola o acompañada... no sé nada de nada pero corro hacia ti voy a buscarte siguiendo la línea del mismo mar azul de todos mis veranos y sabes Daniel estoy contenta de verdad contenta. (271)

> (I'm alive and I'm running in the race and I will keep on going either accompanied or alone... I know nothing about anything but I'm running towards you I'm going to come and find you following the line of the same blue sea of all my Summers and do you know Daniel I'm happy I'm really happy.)

This "spatializing" of the narrative process is also evident at a structural level in *Siete miradas*. The book jacket announces that Tusquets' stories are "tan estrechamente relacionados que constituyen casi una novela" (so closely related that they almost constitute a novel), and this generic uncertainty is, to retain the spatial metaphor that the book's title introduces, disorientating to the reader. The stories (or chapters) are unified by Sara, the central character: she is in each case a young girl of Barcelona's *haute bourgeoisie* in the Spain of the 1950s, but her age and personal characteristics do not remain consistent. The stories are structurally independent from one another, each readable as an independent unit, but they are linked through thematic concerns with puberty and adolescence, the developing awareness of social class, and the first experience of love. Despite this thematic unity and the presence of a central protagonist, it is, for me, the structural independence of each story and the alterations in Sara's character that render this a collection of short stories rather than a novel. The spatial metaphor engaged by Tusquets (the "paisaje" [landscape]) and the evocation of the "mirada" (look/view) suggest that these stories operate as alternative, but very closely associated, artistic renderings of a single panorama of experience. It is a hermetic technique which creates a sense of stifling repetitiveness, congruent with the atmosphere of Spain in the 1950s as evoked by the narrator, and expressive of the consistently unfulfilled nature of desire in each of the stories. The lack of either chronological progress or a sense of forward progression towards narrative conclusion, and the lack of mutuality or interdependence between the stories, in spite of their repetitiveness, creates a sense of stasis arguably much greater even than in *El mismo mar*. Yet, as in all Tusquets' writing (with the possible exception of *El amor*, the darkest and most cynical of her narratives), there remains a small glimmer of hope: the last two stories do offer the possibility of progress, however bitterly conceived. In "La Casa Oscura" ("The Dark House"), the young, and socially disadvantaged, Ricardo discovers that the "recuerdo perenne de la humillación y la injusticia y el dolor" (*Siete* 234) (perennial memory of humiliation and injustice and pain) have the capacity to "impulsarle desde la Casa Oscura hasta donde quisiera, a cualquier parte" (*Siete* 234) (to propel him from the Dark House to wherever he wanted to go, anywhere at all), an affirmation of impulse and movement which is rare in Tusquets' narratives. In the final story, "Orquesta de Verano" ("Summer Orchestra"), Sara finally rejects her class—the class which here as in other stories has been a source of guilt and anxiety—with the decision,

> que nunca se pondría un hermoso vestido largo y escotado y un abrigo de pieles y unas joyas y dejaría que unos tipos en esmoquin le llenaran la copa y le hablaran de amor, que nunca—pensó con asombro—sería como ellos. (250)
>
> (that she would never put on a beautiful, long, low-cut dress and a fur coat and jewels and allow men in dinner jackets to fill her glass and talk to her of love, that she would never—she thought with surprise—be like them.)

This marks an affirmation of alternative possibilities which is also unusual, except in aspirational form, in Tusquets' writing. Nevertheless, it is arguably the case that these stories achieve on a structural level what *El mismo mar* achieves on a syntactic level: a sense of deferred endings, traumatic recapitulation, and stifling overabundance (thematic, imagistic, metaphorical, and lexical).

Tusquets' emphasis on spatial experience in her novels and short stories suggests both a fraught notion of belonging and a sense of stasis, which can be linked thematically to her concerns with both gender and class. Such concerns can be regarded, in turn, as inextricably linked with questions of language and nationality, questions which exert pressure on the text both from within (more noticeably in later works such as *Volver* and *Siete miradas*) and from the cultural field without. It is my view that Tusquets' consistent focus on her characters' inability to resolve the conflictive terms of collaboration and resistance, or (except in the rare cases noted above) to advance temporally and spatially towards new beginnings, is significant not only in the context of gender, but also in the context of the tensions present in the relationship of her characters to their class, language, and nationality, a relationship fraught with both the guilt of the oppressor and the shattered self-confidence of the oppressed.

I have suggested in this essay that Tusquets' writing can be read in the light of a number of political and cultural contexts and influences, framing these in the sociocultural context of Catalonia (particularly the city of Barcelona), which forms the backdrop to almost all the author's fictional and autobiographical work. By looking at some of the academic and political questions which are, in my view, most pertinent to an understanding of the ways in which this author enters the cultural field, and by reading her expression of spatial experience in terms of the political and cultural forces which shape Tusquets as an author and her protagonists as fictional characters, I have sought to offer new perspectives on the ways in which gender can be said to intersect with such questions as nationality and class. In this way, I have shown that the traumatized subjectivity permeating Tusquets' narratives is associated with a range of cultural and political concerns, within a specific geographical, historical, linguistic, and literary context.

Notes

1. The idea of vital space is drawn from Bachelard's *Poetics of Space*: he describes it in terms of our first experience of the house, "our first universe, a real cosmos in every sense of the word" (4). In Bachelard's view, "inhabited space transcends geometric space" (47); as such, "all really inhabited space bears the essence of the notion of home" (5). In the subject's psychological construction of vital space, "memory and imagination remain associated, each one working for their mutual deepening" (5).
2. The narrator describes "las frases . . . casi siempre mal construidas, casi nunca completas o acabadas, plagado así el discurso de sobreentendidos y puntos suspensivos" (36) (the often poorly constructed sentences, rarely whole or complete, that filled their speech with implied meanings and ellipses) which characterize the women's speech. Her own style, with its interminable sentences and multiple digressions, though essentially correct, nevertheless (in my view) evokes these very mannerisms of speech.
3. The association of Tusquets' family with Nazi ideology before the end of the Second World War is highlighted in *Habíamos ganado la guerra*, though it rarely comes through in her fiction. This story is, in that sense, exceptional.

Works Cited

Armstrong, Isobel. *The Radical Aesthetic*. Oxford: Wiley Blackwell, 2000.

Bachelard, Gaston. *The Poetics of Space*. 1958. Trans. Maria Jolas. Forewd. John R. Stilgoe. Boston: Beacon, 1994.

Bergmann, Emilie. "Mothers, Daughters, and the Mother Tongue: Martín Gaite's *El cuarto de atrás* and Roig's *El temps de les cireres*." *Multicultural Iberia: Language, Literature, and Music*. Ed. Dru Dougherty and Milton M. Azevedo. Berkeley: International and Area Studies, U.C. Berkeley, Research Series No. 103, 1999. 93–108.

Cornejo-Parriego, Rosalía V. "Mitología, representación e identidad en *El mismo mar de todos los veranos* de Esther Tusquets." *ALEC* 20 (1995): 47–63.

Crameri, Kathryn. *Language, the Novelist and National Identity in Post-Franco Catalonia*. Oxford: Legenda, 2000.

Fernàndez, Josep-Anton. *Another Country: Sexuality and National Identity in Catalan Gay Fiction*. Leeds: Maney for the MHRA, 2000.

García Gómez, Emilio. "La cuestión literaria." *Etnógrafo*, 2005. www.etnografo.com/cuestion_literaria.htm. Accessed March 25, 2007.

Glenn, Kathleen. "*El mismo mar de todos los veranos* and the Prism of Art." *The Sea of Becoming: Approaches to the Fiction of Esther Tusquets*. Ed. Mary S. Vásquez. New York: Greenwood Press, 1991. 29–43.

Hart, Stephen M. "Esther Tusquets: Sex, Excess, and the Dangerous Supplement of Language." *Antípodas: Journal of Hispanic Studies of the University of Auckland and La Trobe* 3 (1991): 85–98.

Ichiishi, Barbara F. *The Apple of Earthly Love: Female Development in Esther Tusquets' Fiction.* New York: Peter Lang, 1994.

Lonsdale, Laura. "Feminism and Form: Reading for ambiguity in Esther Tusquets' *El mismo mar de todos los veranos.*" *Reading Iberia: Theory/History/Identity.* Ed. Helena Buffery, Stuart Davis, and Kirsty Hooper. Oxford: Peter Lang, 2007: 159–76.

Marsé, Juan. *El amante bilingüe.* Barcelona: Planeta, 1990.

Miguélez-Carballeira, Helena. "Renewing Old Acquaintances: The Conflation of Critical and Translational Paths in the Anglo-American Reception of Mercè Rodoreda, Esther Tusquets and Rosa Montero." Diss. University of Edinburgh, 2005.

Molinaro, Nina L. *Foucault, Feminism and Power.* Lewisburg: Bucknell University Press, 1991.

Nichols, Geraldine Cleary. *Escribir, espacio propio: Laforet, Matute, Tusquets, Moix, Riera y Roig por sí mismas.* Minneapolis: Institute for the Study of Ideologies & Literature, 1989.

———. "Minding Her P's and Q's: The Fiction of Esther Tusquets." *Indiana Journal of Hispanic Literatures* 2.1 (Fall 1993): 159–79.

Ortiz-Ceberio, Cristina. "Dos miradas en un mismo paisaje: el tratamiento del lesbianismo en *El mismo mar de todos los veranos* y *Con la miel en los labios* de Esther Tusquets." *Convergencias Hispánicas: Selected Proceedings and Other Essays on Spanish and Latin American Literature, Film and Linguistics.* Ed. Elizabeth Scarlett and Howard Wescott. Newark: Juan de la Cuesta, 2001. 57–68.

Smith, Paul Julian. *The Moderns: Time, Space and Subjectivity in Contemporary Spanish Culture.* Oxford: Oxford University Press, 2000.

Terry, Arthur. *Catalan Literature: A Literary History of Spain.* London: Benn, 1972.

Tsuchiya, Akiko. "Theorizing the Feminine: Esther Tusquets's *El mismo mar de todos los veranos* and Hélène Cixous's *écriture féminine.*" *REH* 26.2 (1992): 183–99.

Tusquets, Esther. *El amor es un juego solitario.* 1979. Barcelona: Anagrama, 2001.

———. *Correspondencia privada.* Barcelona: Anagrama, 2001.

———. *Habíamos ganado la guerra.* 2007. Barcelona: Zeta Bolsillo, 2008.

———. "Interview with Agustí Fancelli." *El País,* 6 Dec 2007. *www.elpais.com/articulo/ ultima/indigna/mal/ensena/castellano/elpepucul/20071206elpepiult_2/Tes.* Accessed January 10, 2008.

———. "Interview with Isabel Obiols." *El País,* 15 May 2001. *www.joanducros.net/corpus/ Esther%20Tusquets.html.* Accessed March 25, 2007.

———. *El mismo mar de todos los veranos.* 1978. Barcelona: Anagrama, 2002.

———. *Para no volver.* Barcelona: Lumen, 1985.

———. *Siete miradas en un mismo paisaje.* 1981. Barcelona: Lumen, 1993.

———. *Varada tras el último naufragio.* 1980. Barcelona: Anagrama, 1998.

◆ Afterword

Regarding the Spain of Others: Sociopolitical Framing of New Literatures / Cultures in Democratic Spain

Germán Labrador Méndez

(Translated by Jeff Lawrence)

An artifact sums up perfectly the intersection of forces established in the first years of Spanish democratic culture: *El imperio contraataca* (1985), a video clip by the musical group Los Nikis in which Philip the Second appears in the garden of the Retiro de Madrid, accompanied by three electric guitarists, all in the dress of the Golden Age. The monarch's moves are compulsive, frenetic. He spins on the floor like a child; he shouts, applauds, laughs. Between shots, the image of a man in a straitjacket appears. The *maniacal* return of the empire: "Hace mucho tiempo que se acabó, / pero es que hay cosas que nunca se olvidan, / por mucho tiempo que pase. / 1582, / el sol no se ponía en nuestro Imperio, / me gusta mucho esa frase" (Nikis, 1985) (It ended long ago, / but there are things that are never forgotten, / no matter how much time passes. / 1582, / the sun did not set on our Empire, / I love that phrase a lot).[1]

This document says much about the configuration of contemporary Spanish culture, not only because it belongs to the national prehistory of a genre—the video clip—which expresses aesthetic relations traditionally associated with the poetic space, nor because it indicates the emergence of youth culture, nor even because it is an object that calls on us to reconsider the significance of the misunderstood culture of the *Movida*. The imperial counter-text announced by this "pop" monarch parodies, of course, the historical meta-narrative of *franquismo*, but not of *franquismo* alone. If the Transition to democracy saw the opposition between the slogan "con Franco vivíamos mejor" (we were better off with Franco) and "contra Franco vivíamos mejor" (we were better off against Franco), thus embodying a type of progressive culture on the brink of losing its progressiveness, in 1985, Los Nikis, following a tradition inherited from the libertarian culture of the 1970s, opposed both slogans with a third: "we were better off with Philip the Second" (Sempere 155), making of the anachronism a political strategy. Because *El Imperio contraataca* no longer takes the Spanish Transition as a referent, despite having inherited its activist political culture. Its counter-text is, in 1985, projected against the cultural regime of a socialist Spain and its narrative of a reformulated national identity, that of a "euphoric country, European, socialdemocrat-happy, where irony and comedy seemed the only possible literary option" (Chirbes).

Reductio ad Imperium. This satirical counter-text aspired to the status of an anomaly in the cultural field of the 1980s, resistant to certain cultural logics. It is true that its theme is the repetition of history, but only in order to problematize the national configuration in the process of its *normalization*, the key term in the vocabulary of the identity politics of the time. Normalization is, pace Gonzalo Navajas (in this volume), that place of discourse where an entire tradition (or two) of national political (and literary) thought come together in order to confront the 1980s as the decisive moment in which to resolve a structural anomaly linked to an incomplete process of modernization. The anti-*franquista* cultural world had already designated its present a time of deficit, and now, in the years of the construction of democratic institutions, these same cultural forces had assumed the task of financing its mortgage—a task they claimed to have completed from 1988–92, thus accomplishing the first shift in the history of Spanish democratic culture.

The desire to be an empire again. In the varied repetitions of its discourse of *grandeur*, this video clip poses the proximity of the national narrative of *franquismo* with the celebratory discourse of a democratic Spain, signaling the specific site of this global return of the "Spanish": in fashion, in gastronomy, and in the world of sports. These decisive sectors in the marketing of Spain as a world power are convoked according to the most reductive aesthetic marks of Spanish identity; its material culture of underdevelopment reappears in the "Spanish omelette," its institutional folklore in the "red and yellow," and its refurbished basketball team—its *tall* basketball team—works as a metonym for the demographic "overcoming" of a nutritional deficit. And on top of this essential abnormality is set Spain's future condition as the country of arrival for global migration waves and its structural taste for gaming, where the casino functions as a metaphor of the market.

One finds in this three-minute clip all of the preconditions necessary to navigate contemporary Spanish culture. It argues for the need to attend to new forms of cultural production that are the only ones able to give the aesthetic definition of their times, to the existence of a type of popular culture and of new forms of political agency at the heart of a recently-inaugurated mass culture, to the inheritance of the cultural practices of the Transition in the configuration of this political agency, to the decisive link between cultural languages and modernizing projects sealed by an identitarian language whose central category is the idea of normalization, and to the continuous reconfiguration of the contents of this notion through the projection of Spain's (multi-)national pasts.

Afterword

To write an "afterword" to this volume means only to highlight the powerful hypotheses and interpretations of what constitutes an essential cartography of new Spanish cultures. It is an attempt to establish, if briefly, an auxiliary mechanism for relating these cultures with social and political phenomena, using both explicit and implicit categories within which these authors have brilliantly called into question the multi-lingual production of a democratic Spain. The very nature of this collective enterprise determines its necessary fallibility: we are forced to deal speculatively with matters that are still unresolved. This situates us in an analytic tension within which I will construct my argument, for if this volume nominates a New Spain as a discursive and cultural space generated during three decades of democracy, the double allusion to the "new" that this title appeals to in its title obliges us to consider the here-and-now, that of a New Spain emerging from the interior of another New Spain.

I want to make my interpretive strategy clear: inevitably, in their questions, in the cultural objects they analyze, and in the deficits they denounce, these authors are asking themselves about the Spain of the future as well as celebrating the cultural health of the country as an index of its social vitality. They are writing at a point in time defined by the appearance of unprecedented phenomena, whose existence does not respond directly to the politico-cultural logic of democracy, but rather to a juncture of historical manifestations that the postmodern historicity of the wasted landscape of the 1990s can no longer explain. If the Spanish culture of the last thirty years contains an internal historicity in which events no longer take place with the sole reference point of the inaugural moment of the Transition, historiographical cuts must be made. I will therefore propose a periodization of democratic culture that corresponds to the arguments of these authors. I will not be particularly original; I hope only to delimit a series of common reading spaces since, in the end, to write an afterword is to write *regarding* the Spain of others.

It is important to distinguish three cultural moments in democratic Spain, which roughly correspond to its three decades of existence. The first spans the 1980s, and is articulated by a cultural field covering incipient democratic institutions and the cultural hegemony of the Socialist Party (PSOE); I have already traced the major lines of its discourse. The second period spans the 1990s, is characterized by the postmodern regime of representation, and confronts culturally and politically the crisis in the language of the left and the crisis due to the rampant corruption of the socialist government. This second period coexists with the political culture of the Aznar government (or the *Aznaridad*, in Vázquez Montalbán terms) which was not able to produce a hegemonic culture as much as it tried. Finally, the third cultural time begins at the turn of the millennium, and its momentum carries over until 2004, when a change of frame occurs (Lakoff). Obviously, this historiographical model maps onto a societal scene of continuous phenomenon.

The Autonomous Phase of the Literary Field

I might be accused on account of the structural link that I posit between contemporary Spanish culture and the political sphere. Nevertheless, this link may be found in the political, literary, and sentimental capital of anti-*franquista* culture as well as the more direct congruence with the political sphere's aims and interests. One need not carry out an archeology of the *liasions dangereuses* between political parties, institutions, media, and cultural producers. A quick glance at the list of participants in the *Plataforma de Apoyo a Zapatero* (PAZ) shows just how many of the relevant cultural agents studied in this volume appear there. As a case study, it is worth mentioning the work of Miquel Barceló at the UN Headquarters in Geneva, *la Cúpula de la Sala XX de los Derechos Humanos y de la Alianza de Civilizaciones* (2008), where an alternate history of international relations tied to the foreign policy of Zapatero's government is monumentalized.

The question remains: how was the Spanish cultural scene not going to be modified by the tumult of the political scene when this same tumult affected the economic viability of its own products? This is certainly the case with the public financing of Spanish cinema, theater, and expos and funding for new book editions and contemporary art, all of which were much more important than institutionalized literary awards. Even if the market plays a critical role in the production of novels, is it possible to ignore the fact that many creators of opinion are also writers of note, or the intimate connections among publishing houses, communications media, and political interests? Put in a different way: the cultural producers of contemporary Spain possess a marked sensibility with respect to the fluctuations in the political sphere, like changing tides in a marine ecosystem. Finally, when it *is* possible to separate *habitus* from ideology (Bourdieu), it is important to recognize an ethical and political program that has shaped the role of Spanish cultural agents from anti-*franquismo* to the present day and that has determined their mode of representing the world. One cannot separate, for example, the LGTB theme of Almodóvar's films with his participation in PAZ and the sociocultural redefinition of the language of gender in Spain. To periodize is to begin to interpret, and it is for this reason that I posit that in contemporary Spain the *aesthetic climates arise historically around the processes of formation of cultural hegemonies* and that, considered from a long-term perspective, this is a crucial connection to make.

This thesis might seem farfetched, precisely because the common theoretical approaches to the foundational culture of Spanish democracy posit a departure of the literary scene from the political environment, either in terms of disenchantment or trauma (e.g., Buckley, Vilarós, Moreiras) or of a definitive cultural normalization, mature and ultimately inevitable (e.g., Gracia). In fact, the argument that the only thing that occurs in the culture of democracy is a rearticulation of political relations between institutions and cultural production is not particularly novel (Vazquez Montalbán, *La literatura*). What changes, undoubtedly, is the model of the relations that hold during the final phase of *franquismo* and the Transition, where the intervention of cultural agents in the public sphere produces the conditions of possibility for the development of political transformations. Suddenly, these relations normalize, inverting their terms: inspired by the language of political consensus, the cultural agents try to effect a cultural consensus, *pax letrada*, whose results are experienced variously among the cultural agents (Cardín) and which, in practice, ends up erasing from the cultural spectrum a very significant part of the Transitional archive (Labrador, *Letras arrebatadas*).

The irony is that the ritual proclamation of the autonomy of the literary field (Bourdieu) through a debate about postmodernity coincides, as Lozano Mijares has documented in this volume, with the construction of the cultural institutions of democracy and with a clear will to subsidize those objects of culture with which to baptize a new identity for a new Spain—a coincidence that inaugurates a structural pattern for democracy. This institutionalization of culture becomes even more evident in the cases of Catalonia, Galicia or Euskadi, where the institutional necessity of resisting the centrifugal forces of unstable or destabilized linguistic systems is more clearly felt and where the notion of a literary market depends on public or private institutions, since a reading public is never guaranteed. The essays by Olaziregi, Vilavedra, and Kortazar in this volume have been able to bring these problems into focus in a realistic and nuanced way.

More Bad Years Came

The majority of the essays included here implicitly identify the cultural landscape of the 1990s as the representative moment of a democratic specificity that produces an effective shift in the archive of the Transition. It has been assumed, based on this shift, that the Spanish cultural scene has cut the ties with its past, and once consolidated, this past must be thematized as a different cultural time. The 1980s emerge from this focus in a negative light, frequently restricted to the status of a quarry for the Spanish writers of the 1990s.

Although on this point I must remain speculative, since a more detailed study is needed, I will venture that it is impossible to conceive of this democratic representability of the 1990s (with its many faces both hostile and abrupt) without focusing on a politico-cultural phenomenon: the crisis of public languages produced by the corruption of the socialist elite at the beginning of the decade. The rupture with a moral language inherited from the anti-*franquista* struggle and, derivatively, with a series of legitimizing narratives of democracy, enormously restricts the sites from which the social can be narrated. Faced with the breakdown of the cultural hegemony of socialism, the late-capitalist effects on daily life, often attributed only to the middle class, emerge in these narratives: the social dissolves into the individual, individuals become isolated and lose their collective ties, and tales of survival, desolation, and disconcert abound.

Not only the so-called Spanish "Generation X," but also the need for this Generation X, emerges from this intersection. This gives relief (and historical dialectic) to a cultural panorama that, despite its continuous definition in terms of heterogeneity, variability, and peaceful coexistence of styles, was unable to produce a coherent cultural imaginary or a hegemonic language, a state that is often interpreted —the ultimate irony— precisely as a consequence of this desired cultural normalization. Because realistic phenomena such as the Generation X cast shadows over the cultural practices of a cultured middle class that still awaits the story of its social aging, even if it is through the lives of its children. For the writers inscribed in the cultural world of progressivism, the moral crisis at the beginning of the 1990s is disturbing because it dearticulates the pact established among institutions at the beginning of the previous decade ("let's be professionals: for you politics, for us culture") and in the process questions their social identity as cultural agents.

There is no need to appeal to Unamuno for the epistemological dearticulation of the writers of the 1990s (Gracia 145), and the frequent appeals to Jameson or Lyotard are also not very helpful in understanding the type of contradictions that are being posited and resolved in the various positionings in the social field and the praxis of writing. And yet one must recognize in the postmodern critique the capacity to recognize the *stylemes* of a certain literature of the times. At the same time, there is an irony in the fact that the fragmentation of postmodern representations of these literary enunciators is accompanied by an ontological confidence in the material realities of the market and its naturalization in the new economic order. There has been a lot of good work on postmodernism in Spain, but the connections with late capitalism have been neglected or left unexplored.

One must also situate on this map the work of those widely-read long-distance runners who did not participate in the same way in the cultural regime of socialism, and who have been the privileged object of study of Peninsularists *in partibus infidelium*. I am referring to those writers who have systematically been questioned regarding the configuration of a contemporary Spain and who obviously come from a world prior to the Transition to democracy. These "modern classics," as Steenmeijer (in this volume) calls them, present long trajectories of development in which the hardware of contemporary Spanish history is housed. The list of these writers, who have known how to problematize the configuration of the specific type of democratic specificity, that is, the process of normalization, is long: Carmen Martín Gaite, Rafael Sánchez Ferlosio, Juan Marsé, Juan Goytisolo, and even Esther Tusquets (Lonsdale [in this volume] situates her precisely among the conflicts of this *longue dureé*). These generations of historical figures begin to disappear in the 1990s, which makes the crisis of the languages of the socialist world even more complex.

The generation immediately following the *sesentayochistas* must, therefore, seek ethical reinforcements wherever and whenever they can find them. Thus, their poetics is defined in the contradictions between social languages and agencies, in a world of subalterns where, although they can speak, they have trouble doing so. I call attention to the life-affirming character of the culture of the 1990s in the form of a rearticulation of the social from a biopolitical perspective. Almudena Grandes's novels of this period are crucial in this regard, in that they enter into dialogue with a community of readers caught up in analogous types of bioliterary survival. And not just by leaving the family. For others, leaving the town or the neighborhood, and never returning, is a way of representing the safeguarding of their historical destinies as autodidacts, children of the working classes who accede to a moral and economic emancipation in a world without languages of solidarity. These narratives, not out to save the world, but rather the author's own skin, contain all kinds of subtleties and ironic distances. In some cases, they have rearticulated literary quality as a supplement and they have managed to give cultural density to the disturbing landscape of the decade. They are saved by Literature.

Similar phenomena can be traced in film (a terrain in which the peripheral languages only arise at the end of the decade). At the same time, while Spanish comedy triumphs with the return of all sorts of *costumbrista* tendencies, a desire is created for a new opening of a reconstituted social realm, illegible, unlocalizable, but necessary: *Bwana* by Uribe (1996) could be a good bad example of the intersection between both tensions. We must also call attention to the brilliant way in which the *esperpento* of the turn-of-century (Alex de la Iglesia, Santiago Segura, Javier Fesser) was able to express that world.

It is necessary to bring into focus, following Steenmeijer, the disjuncture between the realities of consumer readership and academic criticism, in order to understand something about the readers of turn-of-the-millennium Spain in any of their languages. We spend very little time thinking about how this production circulates in readership communities prior to academic communities. The realization by cultural producers of this fact is one of the most significant developments of the culture of the 1990s. That this is the case for the Hispanists as well means we must ask ourselves how it can be that José Luis Sampedro (or Antonio Gala!) tells us as much as or more than Juan Goytisolo or Javier Marías about the configuration of contemporary Spanish culture.

This reading sees the centralization of the logic of the publishing market as a specific component no longer of the cultural production but of the cultural diffusion of the time, in the words of Steenmiejer. The Spanish book progressively enters into a multi-national design, which implies a connection between media groups and the global trading of information. We are in need of more studies like Steenmeijer's that explain the political and aesthetic space of the Spanish writer on these global maps. It must be pointed out that the integration of Spain in the European Union is not paralleled by a similar circulation in Europe of Spanish symbolic capital, perhaps because the force of the national parameters present a complex limit for ambitious comparativist projects such as that of Enric Bou (in this volume). The potential marketing strategies to combat these symbolic frontiers have been illuminated by King (in this volume) regarding the Frankfurt Book Fair. It might be possible to see a Brumairian repetition of this effect in La Habana Book Fair, where the Xunta bipartite (the left-nationalist and social-democrat government coalition) staged the international arrival of Galician letters.

I have cited José Luis Sampedro, one of the true lost links in Spanish culture, because the Generation X has its luminous reverse in the birth of a type of decisive associationism in the culture of the following decade, without which it is difficult to understand the cultural fabric of the peripheral systems. The 1990s admit responses of solidarity to the dismembering tendency of late capitalism, centralized in the *movimiento del 0.7*, of which Sampedro, who is an economist as well as a novelist, was the *factotum*. And if Sampedro represents a type of narrative production built around the determinations stamped by globalization—taking up the dialectic between postmodernism and postmodernization inspired by Berman—Manu Chao must be considered as the proponent of a similar agenda in music. By unifying his biography with an alternative discourse and a multi-lingual and experimental poetic language, he derived an equation that became the paradigm of a poetics for countless cultural initiatives that appeared in that moment and that saw in the internet new technologies for civic action, from the inside of the new conditions of cultural production.

It is possible for us to affirm, in this case, that the civic sphere and its cultures are ahead of cultural institutions and of Hispanists, both of which will require a certain lag-time to understand the new plane of global action and the circulation within it of identitarian elements. The fact that the websites of the Spanish public institutions are terrible is only a symptom. There are more successful examples: the work of the *Instituto Cervantes*, as Pope notes (in this volume), or the relevance of Biblioteca Virtual Cervantes. Finally, one must mention the globalization process of one of the cultural institutions most marked by its connection to a narrow project of Spanish cultural identity: the Real Academia Española, whose production of cultural meaning at the end of the millennium requires a more specific study.

In the 1990s there are definitive changes in cultural forms, and, with them, in our theoretical categories, as Pope proposes. This view contrasts a Hispanism *in sede petri*, very accustomed to continue thinking in terms of high national culture, and reticent to the poststructural theoretical tides, a resistance that is bolstered by the very model and practice of the university institution (Loureiro) for which other national languages belong to other national traditions, in the ideological scheme proposed by King, which also works in the opposite direction.

In an analysis of the Spanish culture of democracy one must integrate, for example, the role of television and its products, which would distinguish between the cultural times of the 1980s and 1990s. If the first emerged as another pillar of a project of democratization where the necessities of a tele-politics (Muraro) were added to those of a tele-ilustration, in the 1990s, the liberalization of television breaks what was until that moment a necessary identification of television with the public good. The television programs of the 1990s centralize the concept of entertainment: it is not possible to understand a certain aesthetic configuration of the decade without revisiting *Esta noche cruzamos el Mississipi*. But beyond the circulation of certain contents that are suddenly immediately accessible, the terrain of television undergoes, in the cultural sphere, a tectonic fault, which capitalizes on the difficult political, juridical, and journalistic clashes which were called "the football wars" (the media-hype connection with this sport is also decisive in the last years of the century). Finally, I should also mention the attempts to produce a type of television series like *Made in Spain: Cuéntame cómo pasó*, which, connected to the debates about historical memory, is a good example—although not the only one—of the national possibilities of the genre.

This sequence operates within and modifies the social configuration of *Belles-Lettres*, although formalized collectives like poets often act as this has nothing to do with them. If cinema channels the representations of modern culture and the novel has found its fit in the market (and the category "nonfiction" exists for other genres), the question of where to put theater and the once-dominant poetic disciplines is still to be determined. Regarding the dramaturgy of a written theater, which, as Duprey demonstrates (in this volume), continues to be alive, new practices, outside of the scope of this book, embody a new scene: performances, theaters in non-conventional spaces, storytellers. . . . Along these lines, one could mention the corporal theater of Angelica Liddell, the monologues of Quico Cadaval or the iconoclastic dramaturgy of Leo Bassi.

The reevaluation of today's poetry must be connected to urban music, as Pope has argued, or to rituality, which is an integral part of the figure of the poet and decisive in the foundation of democracy, the time of the great social poets and singer-songwriters. This is poetry which, in the contemporary scene, takes place as *religio civitatis*, a religion of the civil, which designates secular moral orders and community transcendences and finds its lay ceremony in the institutional recital. In this sense, building on Mayhew's brilliant analysis (in this volume), it is necessary to add a new argument, since, in the Gamoneda case, the timing is decisive in relation to the sociopolitical logic of the end of the decade. It coincides with the frame change that I have postulated, in the exact moment of the moral recentering of democratic institutions. This is not a capricious declaration: it is enough to compare the ascent of Gamoneda with that of his predecessor, José Hierro, who rose to a similar centrality. Their trajectories are comparable: Hierro came from the world of the Republic, was retaliated against, and anticipated from the point-of-view of existentialism and social realism the aesthetic revolution with *El libro de las alucinaciones* (1964). He produced great books during the democracy as a memory of the formation of Spanish society and a dialogue with his literary past, and, finally, was hospitalized in the 1990s, recited while tied to an oxygen tank, and became a poetic body which corporalized the artificial respiration of a nation bursting with history. Only a *decalage* with the sociopolitical temporalities can help to explain why Hierro did not become Gamoneda and to enter into the coordinates of the last of these cultural interregnums.

The Framing of a New Spain

If the political project of *Aznarismo*—with its neoliberal version of Spanish Catholicism and its bellicose Atlanticism—was not capable of producing a cultural hegemony on a certain level, this is because, despite its cultural penetration through the media, its language did not create the necessary consensus in its social bases or in the entire national territory. Through a lack of human capital, its model of cultural production does not permit this consensus, since there is an identitarian mistrust shared by the Spanish right-wing and the world of culture. It took the cultural professionals a long time to realize the possibilities of effecting institutional culture within the Partido Popular's administration, where a charged environment broke into open war in the second legislature (2000–2004). It is logical, therefore, that *Aznarismo* directed its efforts towards tele-politics, attempting to produce consensus through the media, whose polemical production of reality is, ironically, at the base of the massive mobilizations of the end of the century. This cultural model enters into crisis around the year 2002 through a number of different factors that produce a change in the cultural hegemony, characterizing the cultural field of the last decade at the same time as it initiates an intercultural determination in the configuration of national identities.

On the cultural level, *Aznarismo* was the attempt to propose a compact national identity by resuscitating pre-democratic eschatologies through a constitutional language that produces a heterosexual and phalocentric rewriting of the nation (of its vigor) which, at the same time as it excludes peripheral nationalities, phantasmatically articulates a new world order and a discourse of national security that equates public order, immigration, and ethnic homogeneity. Here I will make a Foucaultian argument: the very definition of a Spain of others is that which produces, incentivizes, and animates the construction of its alterities. In this way, simultaneous to the *aznarist* project one finds the multiplication of nationalist demands, which are expressed institutionally in tensions in the Basque Country and Catalonia, as well as in Galicia, where these demands center around popular outrage at the sinking of the *Prestige*. All of these movements were characterized by a degree of social mobilization that went beyond the institutional. The search for a strong national identity to confront the threat of the economic development at the hands of migrant workers in the second half of the 1990s produces the diffusion of a series of intercultural narratives and infuses the work of NGOs, immigrant associations, and planning committees. The alliance with the Bush and Blair administrations induced an explosion of pacifism and alternative movements. The masculine writing of the nation incentivized feminist associations and the organization of a strong LGBT movement, all of this without forgetting the more classical modes of social conflict found in the young and the working classes, temporarily repoliticized at the end of the decade. The appearance of all of these signals of a *Spain of others* are frequently brought together in the various cultural productions of the end of the century. Their systematic representation not only accompanies and forms the process by which these identities appear; one must also take into account the paradigm shift that is produced and that houses these movements of the New Spain that emerges from the Spain of democracy. Let us concentrate on two concrete examples.

The catastrophe of the Prestige coincided with and contributed to the national circulation of representations of a multi-national otherness. In this context, a generation of Galician women writers (among them Lupe Gómez, Olga Novo and María do Cebreiro) who unite ideas of femininity, Galician identity, and youth, appeal to the dynamism of a literary space that redefines itself under the auspice of "plurality" (the key term for this new paradigm). A new poetic time arises, articulated in the image of a female republic of poets capable of infecting new representations of biopolitics and in the crystallization of an experience that is worthy of giving meaning to the moral and the aesthetic of a modernizing political utopia that clamored for an alternate paradigm for national governance. The celebration of mixing, democratic values, roots, and difference, along with the defense of intimacy, daily life, the "I," traced the lines of a psychic map of what could have been, and even, of what *would* have been great if they could have been subjects of a new superstructural space, of a frame that demanded a poetics. A curious dialectic arose in the national narrative where the peripheral moved in to give a new foundation to the center, a center which found itself devastated by the exercise of a monolithic, phalocentric, and antimodern power (Labrador and Serra). This discourse had a prior history in Galicia and sought a change in the regime of representation by means of the fragmentation of the national poetic voice, something like the many heteronyms of a post-Rosalía, which would intertwine with that proposed by Hooper (in this volume).

Another example of the active emergence of a flood of discourses in conjunction with the attempt to define a new multi-national narrative through civic activism is Alejando Amenábar's film *Mar adentro* (2004). If in *Tesis* Amenábar's investigation of the labyrinth of images of fragmented reality is thematized by snuff films, the white elephant of the 1990s, and defined him as a postmodern filmmaker, in *Mar adentro* Amenábar incorporated an ethical turn. He speculates on the video that filmed the real death of Ramón Sampedro, which would become evidence in the later trial—a video that was in real life removed from the public space and which, in the fictional rendering of the movie, can be seen by the viewer.

Mar adentro is an activist film that attempts a social and juridical intervention through the creation of a new consensus about euthanasia, a demand that, as with all matters of civil rights, had been displaced from the institutional agenda of the left. At the end of the decade, it was once again posed in the Catalan arena, inspired by experiences in other countries. The way in which culture acts as a diffuser and producer of social change requires a more detailed study in the global context in which Spanish cultural producers are not only best sellers but also win Oscars and participate in the global debate on euthanasia. Here I simply want to analyze the type of representation of the nation that is in play in *Mar adentro*, which coincides in an exemplary way with the profile of a pluralistic, civil, and modern Spain, no longer the Spain of 1992. If the figure of the poet and free-thinker Ramón Sampedro is republicanist, the attention to the workplace and the situation of women is remarkable. Even more notable is the multi-lingual representation of the nation: the use of language is faithful to the sociological reality: within Ramón's family Galician is spoken, and Javier Bardem *tamén fala galego*. And the world of the lawyers and of the *pro muerte digna* activists comes from Catalonia and is expressed in Catalan. This type of multi-lingual representation is realist, it is true, but nevertheless becomes a political statement since it is unprecedented in Spanish film.

The entirety of this frame shift is decisive in the set of discursive practices (literary, legal, forensic, and political) that comprise the complex and multi-faceted movement referred to as the "recuperation of historical memory," a category that determines many of the texts in this volume. Spurred on by the exhumation of the common graves from the civil war, historical memory as a narratological category proposes a connection between contemporary Spain and its past, rewriting its foundation *ex nihilo* through links and continuities. To narrate the past in terms of historical memory implies an assumption of the collective inheritance of prior moments in the fight for liberties, in a meta-narrative that links the Second Republic, the civil war, anti-*franquismo* and the Spanish Transition as the patrimony of a collective citizenry systematically opposed to the exercise of oligarchic powers. It implies the assumption of a historical dialectic in which the democratic citizenry (narratively prefigured) is the subject of twentieth-century Spanish history, which, in terms of identity, offers democratic institutions and their representative potential a lineage of experiences different from the one that had been proposed at the time of its foundation (Labrador, "Popular Filmic Narratives").

The primary effect of this movement has been the multiplication of the narratives of historical memory that have imposed a specific literary modulation according to which the beginning of the century must be historicized. Not only in the novel, but also in documentaries and testimonials, in film and even in academic works, historical memory has functioned as a supplement for all kinds of cultural productions. Additionally, the narratives of historical memory have allowed for access to the cultural archive of the Spanish twentieth century, in which, in the fictional space, knowledge that serves the imagination of a collective identity has been disseminated. In the debates about institutional action with regard to historical memory, novelists and other agents have played a decisive role as creators of opinion. The interesting aspect of this conjunction is the active role that literature and film have played in the production of cultural consensus that has produced legislation in the past few years.

In addition to its civic character, in the terms of this New Spain, these phenomena demand our attention because they transform the symbolic representation of the nation at various levels. In the first place, these are simultaneous phenomena in all of the cultural systems of Spain and all of its languages, meaning that we must treat them jointly. Additionally, they are interrelated, and it is not an overstatement to say that they often arise in the periphery: the story *A lingua das bolboretas* by Manuel Rivas, and its subsequent translation and adaptation to film, can clearly be seen as a starter pistol for these narratives. Besides Rivas's novels, it is legitimate to read Javier Cercas's *Soldados de Salamina* (2001) as Catalan literature, although for this categorization we must look to the interesting dialectic proposed by King. In any case, the circulation of all of these narratives produces the fiction of a historical multicultural collective that brings to earth the transcendentalism of certain peripheral historical narratives, forcing them to negotiate their meaning with a shared historical memory.

Don't Think of a Seagull

The electoral victory of the socialist party in March 2004 is the parliamentary indicator of a change in the hegemonic culture, a process in which, following Lakoff, changes in the collective language precede institutional political change. The base of this movement is the historical conjunction of multiple cultural forces in synchrony with various mobilized sectors of civil society. This is not to forget the accumulation of history that is produced at this moment in the temporal break implied by the attacks of March 11, which still await their narrative and mourning. The optimistic but critical view on the health of peripheral systems that can be seen in this volume is the fruit of the legibility of this change of political and symbolic representation. The shift in parliamentary majority in 2004 also signals the partition of the votes of the pluralities represented. The subsequent politics of parliamentary alliances expresses the symbolic renovation of the national center, which becomes permeated by the periphery and, if the reading of the testament of the republican grandfather of the president of the government at his inauguration symbolically recognizes the changes effected by the narratives of historical memory in the national syntax, the acceptance (ephemeral and provisional) of the use of autonomous languages in parliament represents symbolically the changes effected in the expression of its multiculturalism.

The fiesta of civil society and the changes in mentality that it produces are multiple. The participation of cultural agents is decisive, even if they can be seen only in their capacity to create consensus in the public sphere and translate them politically into legislative changes and institutional action. In this sense, although Amenábar's efforts in *Mar adentro* did not result in new legislation about euthanasia, Almodóvar's films are crucial to an understanding of the profound changes in the public and legal recognition of homosexuality, just as an understanding of the rejection of the structural violence of gender in Spanish legislative as well as emotional contexts cannot be understood without the films of Icíar Bollaín (as a metonymy for a series of films and novels), which helped to produce a biopolitical redefinition of feminine identity concurrent with the emergence of women as primary consumers of culture and decisive political agents.

In this environment new arenas of resistance open up in the narrative of this New Spain. Even more broadly, this period must be seen from the perspective of the disjuncture between an economic sphere operating in late-capitalist terms and a reformist political action and a modernizing cultural logic. This dissymmetry is at the core of the tensions in the Spanish culture of the start of the millennium and will dominate its future narratives. These were the years of the economic bonanza that saw the unequal but undeniable socialization of the surplus values that were labeled an "economic boom" according to the cultural myth of Spain as the "eighth world power."

The culture of this New Spain will undoubtedly have to reconcile the appearance of a civil society with the consequences of the end of an economic cycle that, despite having produced the myth of an endless flow of capital, projects an unemployment rate of 20% for the period of 2009–2010. Thus this culture will have to decide whether its civil rights agenda will be articulated in terms of social or individual rights. This will be the time to do away with the measures that have led to massive debt among families, a precarious system of production based on the service industry and residential construction, an atrocious urbanism that transformed the landscape and destroyed the patrimony, an economy that speculated on an emerging housing market and that, ironically, has not guaranteed access to housing, a society that excludes the same immigrant population that caused its prosperity and does not know what to do with its classless youth. If Isaac Rosa in *El país del miedo* (2008) was able to narrate the way in which the middle class in Madrid lived through this process, it has been Rafael Chirbes who, after anticipating in novels like *La larga marcha* (1996) how these ruptures would be expressed with regard to the national past, has focused in *Crematorio* (2007) on the disasters of this time, explaining how the socialization of the surplus values also signaled the socialization of moral corruption.

I mentioned Spain's youth and its immigrants as the critical determinants of this redescription, because they constitute two differentiated and emergent historical subjects. The first (the generation of *mileurismo*) has been scantly problematized, but it is necessary to ask why in a volume titled *New Spain, New Literatures* the median age of the authors analyzed is around fifty-five. Nevertheless, the rising generation (born after 1975), the first generation that has lived only under democratic governments, is the most directly responsible for the narration of the history of this New Spain. The authors who are brought together in the essay by Ricci (in this volume) take as their theme the experience of migration, which is without a doubt the most important phenomenon of the last few decades, a phenomenon that has radically transformed the dialectic between culture and identity in contemporary Spain. Thanks to this text it is possible to formulate questions about immigration from the ex-colonies in Africa (the presence of an always-active Saharaui culture) and the Latin American immigration. Peninsularism must train itself to recognize the cultural production registered by their emergence, still in the process of coalescing into something like the phenomenon of Chicano literature. There is a post-autonomous multiculturalism and, when we used the theoretical bibliography of the last decade to explain the identities and cultural conflicts of Spanish culture, perhaps we were not aware of the fact that these were so well suited to the sociological reality of globalization, and even less so of the fact that Spain would soon be the ideal site for their application.

If we combine the Spanish youth population with the immigrant population we can see the emergence of urban cultures. Today an underground cultural scene exists that is constructed around the idea of the precarious. Some of its manifestations: associationism, fanzines, documentalism, short-films, graffiti, and situationism. Even beyond the rock scene (Pope) there are movements that are capable of defining the tensions mentioned earlier: hybrid music, urban rock (or *rumba catalana*, or techno-pop . . .), *reggaeton*, as well as powerful reliefs in the hip-hop scene, which has created an important community on the very border of industry with a strong sense of formal demands, an enormous cultural capital, a humanist program, and a great capacity for sociological analysis. Seville and Zaragoza are some of its pioneer outposts. *Barrio* culture, immigrant culture, and gypsy culture coincide in this space, which is characterized by the emergence of subaltern identities. An album like *Vivir para contarlo* (2006) by Violadores del Verso gives an idea of the maturity of the genre in Spain: its massive circulation in these collectives has made it a necessary but not sufficient interlocutor to interpret new literatures and the New Spain to come.

Note

1. The complete video can be viewed at *www.youtube.com/watch?v=rS-_EZgRb0w*.

Works Cited

Amenábar, Alejandro, dir. *Mar adentro*. Sogepac, 2004.
———. *Tesis*. Las Producciones del Escorpión S.L., 1996.
Berman, Marshall. *Todo lo sólido se desvanece en el aire. La experiencia de la modernidad*. Madrid: Siglo XXI, 1989.
Buckley, Ramón. *La doble transición: Política y literatura en la España de los años setenta*. Madrid: Siglo XXI, 1996.
Bourdieu, Pierre. *Les regles de l'art: Genese et structure du champ littéraire*. Paris: Seuil, 1998.
Cardín, Alberto. *Como si nada*. Valencia: Pre-Textos, 1981.
Cercas, Javier. *Soldados de Salamina*. Barcelona: Tusquets, 2001.
Chirbes, Rafael. *Crematorio*. Barcelona: Editorial Anagrama, 2007.
———. "Entrevista a Rafael Chirbes: Los libros siempre saben más que su autor." Biblioteca Babab. January 2002. Interview with Santiago Fernández. *www.babab.com/no11/rafael_chirbes.htm*. 1 November 2009.
———. *La larga marcha*. Barcelona: Editorial Anagrama, 1996.
Cuéntame cómo pasó. Exec. Producer Miguel Ángel Bernardeau. Grupo Ganga Producciones S.L., 2001–2009.
Esta noche cruzamos el Mississipi. Exec. Producer Teresa Calo. CEDIPE, 1995–1997.
Gracia, Jordi. *Hijos de la razón: Contraluces de la libertad en las letras españolas de la democracia*. Barcelona: Edhasa, 2001.
Hierro, José. *El libro de las alucinaciones*. Madrid: Bolaños y Aguilar, 1964.
Labrador, Germán, and Pedro Serra. "*Red Shoes*: Nuevas poetas gallegas (identidad y biopolítica)." *Revista de Erudición y Crítica* (REC-Castalia) 5 (Spring 2008): 104–13.
Labrador, Germán. *Letras arrebatadas. Poesía y química en la transición española*. Madrid: Devenir, 2009.

———. "Popular Filmic Narratives and the Spanish Transition." *Post-Authoritarian Cultures: Spain and Latin America's Southern Cone*. Ed. Luis Martín-Estudillo and Roberto Ampuero. *Hispanic Issues* 35. Nashville: Vanderbilt University Press, 2008. 144–74.

Lakoff, George. *Don't Think of an Elephant: Know Your Values, Frame the Debate*. Vermont: Chelsea Green Publishing, 2004.

Loureiro, Ángel. "Desolación y miseria del hispanismo." *Quimera* 139 (September 1995): 31–36.

Moreiras, Cristina. *Cultura herida: Literatura y cine en la España democrática*. Madrid: Ediciones Libertarias, 2002.

Muraro, Heriberto. *Políticos, periodistas y ciudadanos: De la videopolítica al periodismo de investigación*. Mexico City: FCE, 1997.

Los Nikis. *El Imperio contraataca*. Madrid: Dro/Tres Cipreses, 1985.

Rosa Camacho, Issac. *El país del miedo*. Barcelona: Seix Barral, 2008.

Sempere, Pedro. *Los muros del posfranquismo*. Madrid: Castellote Editor, 1977.

Uribe, Imanol, dir. *Bwana*. Aurum, 1996.

Vázquez Montalbán, Manuel. *La aznaridad: Por el imperio hacia Dios o por Dios hacia el imperio*. Barcelona: Mondadori, 2003.

———. *La literatura en la construcción de la ciudad democrática*. Barcelona: Crítica, 1998.

Vilarós, Teresa. *El mono del desencanto: Una crítica cultural de la Transición Española (1973–1993)*. Madrid: Siglo XXI, 1998.

Violadores del Verso. *Vivir para contarlo*. Rap Solo, 2006.

◆ **Contributors**

Enric Bou is Professor of Hispanic Studies at Brown University. His teaching and research interests cover a broad range of twentieth-century Spanish Peninsular and Catalan literature involving poetry, autobiography, city and literature, and Spanish film. His latests books are *Daliccionario: Objetos, mitos y símbolos de Salvador Dalí* (2004) and the edition of Pedro Salinas' *Obras Completas* (2007).

Jennifer Duprey is Assistant Professor of Spanish in the Department of Classical and Modern Languages and Literatures at Rutgers University. Her areas of research and teaching are Modern and Contemporary Spanish Peninsular Literatures with a special interest in Spanish and Catalan Cultural Studies. Her work currently engages narratives of violence, justice, and memory in Peninsular Spanish literatures.

Gonzalo Goytisolo Gil, whose painting is shown on the cover, was born in Barcelona (1966), where he currently lives. He is the son of the novelist Luis Goytisolo, and a disciple of the realist painter Antonio López García. More information on his work is available at *www.gonzalogoytisolo.com*.

Kirsty Hooper teaches Galician and Spanish at the University of Liverpool, UK. She has published widely on Galician and Spanish literary and cultural studies. Her recent publications include *A Stranger in My Own Land: Sofía Casanova, a Spanish Writer in the European Fin de Siècle* (2008) and a co-edited volume: *Reading Iberia: Theory, History, Identity* (2007).

Stewart King is Senior Lecturer in Spanish and Catalan Studies at Monash University, Australia. He has published extensively on twentieth-century Spanish and Catalan authors. His most recent publications include *Escribir la catalanidad* (2005) ooand two edited volumes: *La cultura catalana de expresión castellana* (2005) and *Beyond the Periphery: Narratives of Identity in the Basque Country, Catalonia and Galicia*, a special issue of *Antípodas: Journal of Hispanic and Galician Studies* (2007). He is currently writing a book-length study on cultural and national identities in crime fiction from Spain.

Jon Kortazar is Professor of Basque Literature at the Universidad del País Vasco-Euskal Herriko Unibertsitatea. He is the author of several books on twentieth-century Basque literature, including *Euskal Literatura XX. mendean* (six editions, 1990–2003), *Teoría y práctica poética de Esteban Urkiaga, Lauaxeta* (1986), *Luma eta lurra* (1997), *La pluma y la tierra* (1999), *La literatura vasca en la transición: Bernardo Atxaga* (2003), and *La narrativa vasca, hoy: Una mirada desde la postmodernidad* (2003).

Germán Labrador Méndez is Assistant Professor of Modern and Contemporary Spanish Literature at Princeton University. His research interests include post-dictatorial Spanish cultural studies, the Avant-Garde and Modernity in Spain, and twentieth-century Spanish literature. His most recent publication is *Letras arrebatadas: Poesía y química en la transición española* (2008).

Laura Lonsdale is Fellow of The Queen's College, Oxford, where she teaches modern Spanish language and literature. Her forthcoming book *Fiction, Feminism and Form* is to be published by Tamesis (Boydell and Brewer) in 2010. Her research interests include contemporary narrative and the relationship between politics and literary criticism.

María del Pilar Lozano Mijares received her Ph.D. from the Universidad Complutense de Madrid and currently works at the BBVA Foundation. She has written articles on contemporary Spanish fiction and is the author of a book-length study, *La novela española posmoderna* (2007).

Luis Martín-Estudillo is Assistant Professor of Spanish Literature at the University of Iowa. His latest publications include *La mirada elíptica: El trasfondo barroco de la poesía española contemporánea* (2007) and the co-edited volumes *Hispanic Baroques: Reading Cultures in Context* (2005) and *Post-Authoritarian Cultures: Spain and Latin America's Southern Cone* (2008). He is currently working on a book-length study entitled *Europe Undreamt: Spanish Culture on the Edges of Modernity*. He is an Associate Editor of the Hispanic Issues series and *Hispanic Issues Online (HIOL)*.

Jonathan Mayhew is Professor of Spanish at the University of Kansas. He is the author of numerous articles and four books on Spanish poetry: *Claudio Rodríguez and the Language of Poetic Vision* (1990), *The Poetics of Self-Consciousness: Twentieth-Century Spanish Poetry* (1994), *The Twilight of the Avant-Garde: Spanish Poetry 1980–2000* (2009), and *Apocryphal Lorca: Translation, Parody, Kitsch* (2009). His current project is *Fragments of a Late Modernity: Spanish Poetry from García Lorca to García Valdés*.

Gonzalo Navajas is Professor of Modern Spanish Literature and Film at the University of California, Irvine. He has published more than one hundred essays on Spanish literature, film, and contemporary aesthetics and is the author of several books on modern and contemporary theory and culture, including *La utopía en las narrativas contemporáneas: Novela/cine/arquitectura* (2008). He has also written several novels, among them the recently published *En blanco y negro* (2007).

Mari Jose Olaziregi is Associate Professor with tenure at the University of the Basque Country and, since 2007, Assistant Professor at the University of Nevada. She is the editor of the Basque Literature Series in translation, created by the Center for Basque Studies (University of Nevada, Reno) and the director of *www.basqueliterature.com*. She has authored several books on Basque literature, including *Euskal eleberriaren historia* (History of the Basque novel, 2001) and *Waking the Hedgehog: The Literary Universe of Bernardo Atxaga* (2005), and has edited anthologies of Basque poetry and short stories. She is currently completing an edited volume titled *History of Basque Literature and Minority Languages in the Global Frame*.

Randolph D. Pope is Commonwealth Professor of Spanish and Comparative Literature at the University of Virginia, where he directs the Comparative Literature Program. His field of specialization is the Peninsular novel and autobiography, but he has also written extensively on other topics. He has published four books and over one hundred scholarly essays.

Cristián H. Ricci is Assistant Professor of Spanish at the University of California, Merced. He has authored articles on Spanish literature, from *Modernismo* to the Civil War, has edited two anthologies, including one on Israeli and Arabic writers of Spanish expression (*Caminos para la paz: Escritores israelíes y árabes en castellano*, 2008), and has recently published a book: *El espacio urbano en la narrativa del Madrid de la Edad de Plata, 1900–1938* (2009). He is presently completing a book on Moroccan Literature written in Spanish and Catalan (¡*Hay moros en la costa!*, forthcoming in 2010) and a new anthology of Moroccan writers of Castilian expression (*Letras Marruecas*, forthcoming in 2010).

Nicholas Spadaccini is Professor of Spanish and Comparative Literature at the University of Minnesota. He has published articles, books, critical editions and collective volumes with emphasis on early modern Spain and Latin America. He is Editor-in-Chief of Hispanic Issues and *Hispanic Issues Online (HIOL)*.

Maarten Steenmeijer is Professor of Modern Spanish and Spanish American Literature and Culture at Radboud University (Nijmegen, the Netherlands). His recent publications include *El columnismo de escritores españoles* (2006), *Más allá de Cervantes y Lorca: El éxito de la literatura española actual en el extranjero* (2006), and *Allí donde uno diría que ya no puede haber nada: "Tu rostro mañana" de Javier Marías* (2009).

Dolores Vilavedra is Associate Professor of Galician Literature at the University of Santiago de Compostela. She has authored several books on Galician literature, among them *Historia da literatura galega* (1999), *Sobre narrativa galega contemporánea* (2000), and *Un abrente teatral: As Mostras e o Concurso de Teatro de Ribadavia* (2002). She has also edited the correspondence of several Galician intellectuals, as well as the work of Rosalía de Castro.

◆ Index

Compiled by Isabela Varela

Abuín González, Anxo, 23n, 26, 39, 41, 132
Adams, Paul, 4, 24
Adriá, Ferran, 154
African borderland literatures, 206–15
African literature, 203, 215
African literature in Spanish, 217–18
African migration, 204–8, 212, 213, 216. *See also* migration
African women writers, 212, 213, 215, 219
African writers, xv, 104, 105, 217–19
Agirre, Domingo, 30
Agirre, José María (Pseud. Lizardi), 30–31. *See also* Lizardi
Aguilar, Paloma, 113n, 113
Agustí, Ignacio, 241
Akalay, Mohamed: *De Larache a Tánger*, 212
Al'Misnawi, Mustafa, 209; "*Tariq, aquel que no conquistó Al-Andalus,*" 205
Alas, Leopoldo, 169
Alcolea, Carlos, 184
Aldekoa, Iñaki, 29, 40
Aleixandre, Marilar, 127
Aleixandre, Vicente, 152
Al-Jabri, Mohammed Abd, 203, 206, 209, 212, 227
Allende, Isabel, 93n
Almodóvar, Pedro, 167, 168, 173, 178, 264, 273, 185; *¡Átame!* (1989), 167; *La mala educación* (2004), 178; *Pepi, Luci, Bom y otras chicas del montón* (1980), 167; *¿Qué he hecho yo para merecer esto?* (1984), 167; *Talk to Her*, 173; *Volver* (2006), 167
Alonso, Idurre, 144, 146

Alós, Ernest, 238, 243
Al-Sabbag, Muhammad, 227; *Tiempo de perlas of Al-Andalus*, 206
Altan, Ahmet, 40
Altisent, Marta E., 41
Álvarez Cáccamo, Xosé M., 132
Amat, Nuria, 233
Ameixeiras, Diego, 131n, 132
Amenábar, Alejandro, 275; *Mar adentro* (2004), 271, 273
Amor Blanco, Eduardo, 118, 120
Amrani, Muhammad, 207, 226n, 227
Amrouche, Taos, 227n, 228
Ancet, Jacques, 152, 161n
Anderson, Benedict, 14, 15, 24, 29, 40, 243
Anderson, Walter Truett, 112, 113
Aneiros, Rosa, 127
Anguerra, Joan, 78n
anti-Francoism, 262, 264, 265, 272
Antonioni, Michelangelo, 174
Arana Goiri, Sabino, 29, 31, 33
Aranguren, José Luis L., 185
Araquistáin, Luis, 29
Ararou, Ahmed, 208–12, 228; "Trabanxi," 210
Archivos y Bibliotecas del Ministerio de Cultura, 85
Aresti, Gabriel, 31, 40; *Harri eta herri*, xiii, 31
Arias, Santa, 45, 60
Arias, Xela, 123
Aribau, Bonaventura-Carles: "Oda a la pàtria," 236
Aristimuño, José (pseudonym, Aitzol), 31
Arkotxa, Aurelia, 28, 34, 40

Armstrong, Isobel, 254, 258
Arquillué, Pere, 78n
Arregi, Rikardo, 33
Arretxe, Jon, 144
Arriazu, Ascen, 113
Arthurian tradition, 124
Asensi, Matilde, 92
Asensi, Matilde, *El último Catón*, 90, 94
Ashbery, John, 152
Associació d'Actors i Directors Profesionals de Catalunya, 78n
Association of Galician Writers, xiii
Atencia, María Victoria, 150, 153
Atxaga, Bernardo (pseud. of José Irazu Garmendia), xiii, xiv, 36, 37, 40, 84, 139, 141, 144, 146, 175, 180; *Bi letter*, 34; *El hijo del acordeonista*, 172; *Obabakoak*, 36; *Soinujolearen semea*, 33, 34; *Zeru horiek*, 34
Augé, Marc, 201
Ávarez Cáccamo, Xosé Ma, 122, 132
Ávila Laurel, José Tomás, 228; *Avión de ricos, ladrón de cerdos* (2008), 221
Ayén, Xavi, 86, 94
Azaña, Manuel, 165, 166, 169, 170, 180; *El jardín de los frailes*, 165
Azancot, Nuria, 94, 91
Azcona, Rafael, 132
Aznarismo, 269, 270
Azorín, (José Martínez Ruiz), 174
Azzuz Hakim, Mohamed Ibn, 204, 228; *Cuentos populares marroquíes* (1955), 204; *Rihla por Andalucía* (1942), 204

Bachelard, Gaston, 258, 258n
Bada, Ricardo, 84, 94
Bagué Quílez, Luis, 48, 59
Balaguer, Víctor, 242n
Balboa Boneke, Juan, 218, 219
Balcells, Carmen, 82, 85. *See also* literary agents
Balzac, Honoré de, 113; *Cousin Bette*, 99
Barbal, Maria, 234
Barbal, Maria: *Pedra de Tartera*, 234
Barbeito, José Manuel, 33, 40, 42, 146n, 146
Barceló, Manel, 78n
Barceló, Miquel, 264, 184

Barcelona, 63–67, 69, 76
Bardem, Javier, 271
Baroja, Pío, 30, 39n, 169
Barral, Carlos, 82. *See also* editors
Barros, Tomás, 128
Barrutia, Pedro Ignacio, 38n, 40
Barthes, Roland, 68, 78
Barxas, López, 131n
Basque: historical memory, 141, 142
Basque Country, x, xii, xiii, xiv, 28, 30, 36, 270
Basque identity, 135, 136, 138, 139, 140–43, 145
Basque language, xiii, 138–44
Basque language and education, 140–41, 143–44
Basque language and nation, 138–39
Basque literary system, xiii, 31–34, 136, 140, 141, 143, 145
Basque literature, xiv, 28–31, 84, 135–39, 142, 143, 145
Basque literature promotion abroad, 36
Basque publishing houses, 35, 38, 141. *See also* publishing houses
Basque writers, xiii, 137, 138, 140, 141, 143–46
Bassi, Leo, 269
Batlle, Carles, 63, 78; *Temptació* (2004), 78n
Baudelaire, Charles, 52, 45, 152
Beckett, Samuel, 62
Belbel, Sergi, 63, 78; *Forasters* (2004), 78n
Ben Haddou, Halima, 227n, 228
Ben Jelloun, Tahar, 205
Benabdellatif, Abdelkader, 228; *El reto del Estrecho* (2005), 207; *Las columnas de Hércules* (2005), 207
Benet i Jornet, Josep María, 62–65, 67, 76, 79; *Olors* (2000), 63, 64, 78n
Benítez Reyes, Felipe, 48
Benjamin, Walter, 45, 46, 52, 73, 75, 79; "The Storyteller" (essay), 73
Benson, Ken, 201
Bergmann, Emilie, 251, 254, 258
Berman, Marshall, 268, 275
Bermúdez, Davies, 56
Bermúdez, Silvia, 43, 59
Bernhard, Thomas, 62

Bescós, Ramón: Bankinter (landmarks), 185
Bessiére, Bernard, 184, 201, 202
Besteiro, Julián, 170
Beyala, Calixte, 227n, 228
Bhabha, Homi K., 34, 40, 209, 211, 228, 239, 243
Biblioteca Virtual Cervantes, 102, 268
Bieito, Calixto, 63
Binebine, Mahi: *Cannibales* (1999), 205
Blasco Ibáñez, Vicente, 237, 177
Bloom, Harold, 176, 180
Boadella, Albert: *La torna,* 62
Bofill, Ricardo, 78n, 185
Bokesa, Cristino Bucriberi, 218, 219
Boladeras, Rosa, 78n
Bolaño, Roberto, 93n
Bollaín, Icíar, 273
Borges, Jorge Luis, 82, 84, 198
Bou, Enric, xii, 237, 238, 243, 267
Bouissef Rekab, Mohamed, 205, 228; *Aixa, el cielo de Pandora,* 207, 212; *El motín del silencio* (2006), 207; *La señora,* 207, 212
Bourdieu, Pierre, 81, 170, 176, 180, 264, 265, 275
Boym, Svetlana, 64, 79
Boyne, John, 100
Braudel, Ferdinand, 167
Brea, José Luis, 184
Brecht, Bertolt, 62, 61
Brines, Francisco, 113, 160n; "El regreso del mundo," 108
Broch, Alex, 250
Broto, José Manuel, 185
Browitt, Jeff, 23n, 25
Brown, Dan: *The Da Vinci Code,* 87, 88, 89, 90, 95
Bru de Sala, Xavier, 238, 239, 242, 243
Bruna, Sandra, 91. *See also* Literary agents
Buckley, Ramón, 264, 275
Buero Vallejo, Antonio, 62
Buffery, Helena, 259
Bugul, Ken, 227, 228
Burgueño, Jesús, 16, 24

Caballero Bonald, José María, 186
Caballero, Fernán, 103

Cabana, Darío Xohán, 132; *Galván en Saor,* 124
Cabanillas, Ramón, 49
Cabo Aseguinolaza, Fernando, 23n, 39n, 40
Cabré, Jaume, 234; *Les veus del Pamano,* 234
Cabrera, Ma Dolores, 131n, 132
Caeiro, Alberto (heteronym for Fernando Pessoa). *See* Pessoa, Fernando
Cajetani, Michele Angelo-Prince of Téano, 99
Calderón de la Barca, Pedro, 166, 175, 177
Calderón, Emilio, 90, 95; *El mapa del creador,* 90
Campo, Marica, 55, 59; *Memoria para Xoana* (2002), 109
Camus, Mario, 252, 178
Candau, Antonio, 161, 161n
Cano, Harkaitz, 33, 143
canon, xiv, 150, 152, 159, 160, 176, 177
canonization, 149, 154, 159
canonization in narrative, 120, 123, 124, 126, 127
canonization in poetry, 121, 122
canonization in theater, 129, 130
canonization of writers, 120, 125, 127, 130
canonizing institutions, 118, 127, 144, 151, 152, 159
Cardín, Alberto, 265, 275
Carlos, Helena de, 123
Carner, Josep, 14, 24; *Cor quiet,* 7
Carpentier, Alejo, 82
Carranza Font, Andreu, 95
Carrero Blanco, Luis, 117
Carvajal, Antonio, 114
Carvajal, Antonio: "Maitines" *Del viento en los jazmines,* 107
Casado, Miguel, 149, 153, 161n
Casani, Borja, 185
Casanova, Pascale, 81, 82, 84, 92, 95
Casares, Carlos, 120; *Deus sentado nun sillón azul* (1996), 131n; *Ilustrísima* (1980), 131n; *Os mortos daquel verán* (1987), 131n
Casas, Arturo, 39n, 40
Castaño, Yolanda, 123
Castelao (Rodríguez Castelao, Alfonso), 49, 118, 126, 128, 131n
Castellano, Ramón López, 242n

Castells, Ada, 243
Castile, 175
Castilla del Pino, Carlos, 184
Castillo, Johanna, 89
Castro, Luisa: *Viajes con mi padre* (2003), 109
Castro, Rosalía de, xi, 14, 24, 45, 49, 51, 52, 55, 56, 59, 109, 126; *Cantares Gallegos* (1863), 49; *Follas novas* (1880), 49; *en las orillas del Sar*, 12, 13
Catalá, Víctor, 227n, 228
Catalan culture, 61, 77, 84, 234, 241. See also culture
Catalan historiography, 252
Catalan identity, 236, 238, 251. See also identity
Catalan language, 251
Catalan literary canon, 237–39
Catalan literary studies, 233, 240–41. See also institutions
Catalan literature, xiv, 84, 110, 239, 250
Catalan literature: historiography, 235–39
Catalan literature and promotion, 234
Catalan nationalism, 242n, 249, 251, 252
Catalan society, 61, 64, 78n, 79, 238
Catalan theater, xv, 61–63, 70, 76–77, 77n, 78n. See also theater
Catalan women writers, 249
Catalan writers, 109–10, 248
Catalonia, x, xii–xiv, xiii, xiv, 248–49, 265, 270
Cava, Felipe Hernández, 185
Cavafy, Constantine, 151, 152
Cebreiro, María de, 43, 57, 271
Center for Basque Studies, 27, 37
Centro Dramático Galego (CDG), 128
Cercas, Javier, 180, 275; *Soldados de Salamina* (2001), 178, 272
Cerezales, Marta, 212, 228
Cernuda, Luis, 170, 180
Cervantes Saavedra, Miguel de, 167, 175
Céu e Silva, Joâo, 110, 114
Chaghmoum, Miloudi, 209; "*La quema de los barcos,*" 205
Chaho, Joseph Agustín, 29, 40
Chakor, Mohamed, 204, 212, 226n, 228

Chakor, Mohammad, 228
Chao, Manu, 268
Chicano literature, 274
Chija, Abraham Ben R., 237
Chirbes, Rafael, 84, 262, 275; *Crematorio* (2007), 274; *La larga marcha* (1996), 274
cinema, 167, 169–70, 173–75, 271–73
Cisneros, Sandra, 227n, 228
Civil War, 33, 72, 73, 76, 124, 137, 154, 155, 171, 189, 210, 241, 165–67, 178–80
Clarín (Alas, Leopoldo), 177
Cobo, Chema, 184
Coca, Jordi, 73, 78n, 79; *Antígona (Antigone*, 2002), 63, 70– 72, 78n; *Dies merdvellosos* (1996), 78n; *La japonesa* (1992), 78n; *Platja Negra (1999)*, 78n; Jordi: *Sota la pols* (2001), 78n
Cohen Mesonero, León, 205
Coixet, Isabel, 173, 174; *My Life Without Me*, 174; *The Secret Life of Words* (*La vida secreta de las palabras* 2005), 174
Colchie, Tom, 92. See also literary agents
Colinas, Antonio, 153
Colmeiro, José F., 43, 59
comics, 185
Conrad, Joseph: *Heart of Darkness*, 52, 59
Conrad, Josheph, 171
Consejería de la Cultura del Gobierno Vasco, 145
Consejo de Administración del Teatre Nacional de Catalunya, 77n
Constable, Marianne, 71, 79
contemporary Spain, xi, 85
Cornejo-Parriego, Rosalía V., 246, 258
Corrales, José Antonio: *Bankunión* (landmarks), 185
Cortázar, Julio, 82, 84
Cortezón, Daniel, 128
Costa, Joaquín, 165
Cots, Montserrat, 23n
Couceiro, Emma, 123
Crameri, Kathryn, 248, 249, 250, 251, 253, 258
criticism, 81, 82, 84, 88, 90, 92, 136–38, 140, 142, 143, 247
Cruz, Antonio, 185

INDEX   285

Cruz, Juan, 95
Crystal, David, 27, 40; *The Language Revolution,* 27
Cuerda, José Luis, 132
Cullell, Diana, 59n
cultural hybridization, 209
cultural memory, 63, 65, 66, 68, 69, 76, 220. *See also* memory
culture, 168, 169, 170, 173, 174, 176–80, 265, 274–75
culture and consumerism, xv, 186
Cunillé, Lluïsa, 63
Cunqueiro Mora, Álvaro, 120, 124, 128
Curros Enríquez, Manuel, 49

Dans, Raul, 128
Daoudi, Ahmed, 228; *El Diablo de Yudis,* 205
Darío, Rubén, 45
Dasconaguerre, Jean-Baptiste, 34, 40; *Les échos du pas de Roland* (1867), 34
Davidson, Robert A., 45, 59
Davies, Catherine, 56, 59
Davis, Stuart, 259
De la Iglesia, Álex, 267
De Toro, Suso, 175
Debicki, Andrew Peter, 150, 161
Decadència, 236, 240
Deleuze, Gilles, 6, 14, 24
Delgado, Luisa Elena, 24, 114
democracy, 183, 186, 189, 265, 268
Department of Culture of the Catalan Government, 77n
Derrida, Jacques, 34; and deconstruction, 154
Deutschlandlied, 13
Deyermond, Alan, 102, 114
diasporic poetry, 219
Dickens, Charles, 88
Diego, Gerardo, 11, 12, 14, 24
Dieste, Rafael, 120
Dirección General del Libro, 85
Djebar, Assia, 227n, 228
Dobler, Alexander, 86. *See also* literary agents
Domínguez Prieto, César, 23n
Domínguez, Mónica, 35, 39n, 40
D'Ors, Eugenio, 170

Duprey, Jennifer, xv, 269
Dussel, Enrique, 206, 209, 228

Eco, Umberto, 88; *The Name of the Rose,* 90
El árbol de la ciencia, 30
El Fathi, Abderrahman, 208, 228; *Abordaje,* 208; *África en versos mojados* (2002); *Abordaje* (2000); *Triana, imágenes y palabras* (1998); *Primavera en Ramallah y bagdad* (2003); *El cielo herido* (2003); *Desde la otra orilla* (2004); *Fantasías literarias* (2000), 207; *Desde la otra orilla,* 212
El Gamoun, Ahmed, 201, 208, 209, 210–12, 215, 228
El Gheryb, Mohamed, 213, 230
El Greco (Doménikos Theotokópoulos), 177
El Hachmi, Najat, xiv, 213, 215, 216, 228; *Jo també sóc catalana,* 213, 216; *L'últim patriarca* (2008), 213, 214, 220, 238; "Carta d'un immigrant," 215
El Harti, Larbi, 208–12, 215, 229; *Después de Tánger* (2003), 210–12
El Kadaoui, Saïd, 226n, 229
Eliot, T.S., 151
Elliott, John H., 3, 24
Elorriaga, Unai, 33, 34, 37, 146; *Unai: Sprako tranbia* (A Streetcar to SP), 144
Epaltza, Aingeru, 33
Epps, Bradley S., 23n, 24, 39n, 40
Equatorial Guinea and colonial literature, 217–21
Escola Superior de Arte Dramático (ESAD), 129
Escude, Beth, 63
Espriu, Salvador, 15, 109; *Antigone* (1947), 70, 79
Estopa, 114; "Malabares" in *Voces de ultraumba,* 107, 109
Etxeberria, Hasier, 32, 33, 36, 40
Etxepare Institute, 145
Etxepare, Bernard, 28, 30, 40; *debile principium melior fortuna sequatur,* 30
Europe, 3–5, 8, 15, 21–23, 62
Europe and geography, 5–7
Euska Idazleen Elkartea (EIE), 36
Euskadi, 265. *See also* Basque Country

Euskal Itzultzaile, Zuzentzaile eta Interpreteen Elkartea (EIZIE: the Association of Translators, Interpreters, and Correctors of the Basque Language), 35
Euskaltzaleak (Bascophile Association), 30
Evaristo, Bernardine: *Lara*, 54
Even-Zohar, Itamar, 30, 35, 39n, 41, 138, 139, 146; "semiotic subjects," 141
Evita, Leoncio, 229; *Cuando los Combes luchaban* (Novela de costumbres de la Guinea Española), 217
exile, 46–48, 50, 56–57
exile and intellectuals, 118, 169, 172, 180

Fabra, Pompeu, 243n
Falcones, Ildefonso, 91, 95, 114; *La catedral del mar*, 90, 91, 101
Fancelli, Agustí, 251
Fanon, Franz, 211, 218
Farah, Nuruddin, 222
Faulkner, William, 152
Feijoo, Jaime, 40, 42
Feixas, Daniela, 78n
Feldman, Sharon, 77n, 79
Felski, Rita, 104, 114
feminism, 122, 126, 127, 245
Feria, Luis, 153
Fernán Vello, Miguel Anxo, 122
Fernández Cifuentes, Luis, 23n, 24, 39, 40
Fernández Retamar, Roberto, 222, 229
Fernández, Josep-Anton, 251, 252, 258
Fernández, Miguel Anxo, 131n, 132
Fernández, Pura, 88, 95
Ferreiro, Celso Emilio, 120
Ferrero, Jesús, 95
Ferres, Antonio, 169
Fesser, Javier, 267
festivals, 63, 122, 129, 130
Figueroa, Antón, 29, 40–42, 136, 138, 142, 146; *Diglosia e texto (Diglossia and Text)*, 29
Fischer, Joschka, 87, 234
Fishkin, Shelley Fisher, 110, 114
Fitzmaurice-Kelly, James, 23n
Flaubert, Gustave, 170
Flesler, Daniela, 206, 229
Flotats, Josep Maria: *Sala Tallers*, 77n

Fokkema, Douwe W., 24, 24n
Fole, Ánxel, 118, 120
Follet, Ken: *The Pillars of the Earth*, 101; *World Without End (El mundo sin fin)*, 101; *Pillars of the Earth*, 90, 95
Fonte, Ramiro, 44, 59, 122; *A rocha dos proscritos* (2005), 44, 46, 59n; *As cidades da nada* (1983), 44; *O cazador de libros*, 44, 45, 59n
Forcadela, Manuel, 122, 131n, 132
Fortes, Belén, 44, 45, 59
Foucault, Michel, 22, 24, 24n, 186, 187, 198, 202
Fraga e Iribarne, Manuel, 6, 118
Fraga, Xesús, 58, 59
Fra-Molinero, Baltasar, 219, 225, 219, 229
Franco: death, 117, 136, 156
Franco, Francisco, 61, 62, 76
Franco's regime, xii, xv, 58, 74, 82, 83, 118, 156, 157, 166, 167, 169, 171, 175, 176, 177, 206, 238, 241, 250, 169, 249
Franco's regime: political prisoners, 13
Francoism (franquismo), xiii, xv, 22, 61, 76, 117, 129, 154, 166, 261, 262, 264
Frankfurt Book Fair, xiv, 233, 238, 240, 241, 242n, 267
Freixanes, Víctor F., 131n, 132
Frenk Alatorre, Margit, 106, 114; *Corpus de la Antigua lírica popular hispánica (siglos XV a XVII)*, 105
Friedman, Susan Stanford, 23n, 24
Fuentes, Carlos, 82, 84, 93n
Fuertes, Gloria, 169
Fusi, Juan Pablo, 132
Fuster, Joan, 237, 238, 240, 243

Gabilondo, Joseba, 43, 57, 60
Gala, Antonio, 267
Galá, Lola, 95
Galicia, x, xii, xiii, xiv, 265, 270
Galicia: historical memory, 118, 125
Galicia: history, 124, 117–21, 124
Galicia: publishing and publishers, 119, 120, 122, 128, 131n. *See also* publishing houses
Galician: experience of displacement, 46
Galician writers, 119, 120–26, 129
Galician Association of Publishers, 119

Galician cultural theory, 43
Galician culture, 110, 125, 129, 131n. *See also* culture
Galician diaspora, 56, 57, 58
Galician Federation of Booksellers, 119
Galician identity, 271
Galician identity, 118, 120, 123, 124, 127. *See also* identity
Galician language, 110, 118–21, 124–26
Galician literature, 44, 45, 47, 56–58, 60, 84, 117–30, 133, 135, 136
Galician narrative, 119, 123, 124, 126, 127
Galician Network of Theatres and Auditoria, 131n
Galician poetry, 119, 121–23, 127
Galician society, 118, 120, 125, 128
Galician Statute of Autonomy (1980), 118
Galician theater, 127, 128
Galician Virtual Library, 132
Galician women writers, 109, 122, 123, 126, 127, 271
Galician writers, 109, 112, 120, 121, 124, 126
Galicianness, 43, 58
Gallen, Enric, 61, 62, 79
Gamoneda, Amelia, 159, 160
Gamoneda, Antonio, xv, 149, 150, 150, 153, 154, 156, 158, 161, 160n, 269; *Arden las pérdidas*, 149; *Blues Castellano*, 157; *Descripción de la mentira* (1977), 150, 155, 158; *Edad* (1987), 149; *El cuerpo de los símbolos*, 158; *Esta luz*, 149; *Lápidas*, 158, 154; *Libro de los venenos*, 149; *Libro del frío*, 149, 158
Garcia Barba, Ignasi, 78n, 79; *Camino de Tombuctú*, 78n; *A trenc dàlba* (1997), 78n
García Berlanga, Luis, 169
García Canclini, Néstor, 209, 229
García Gómez, Emilio, 250, 258
García Jambrina, Luis, 150, 162
García Lorca, Federico, 14, 24, 82, 151–53, 159; "Cantiga do neno da tenda," 53, 60; "Seis poemas gallegos," 52, 53; *Poema del cante jondo*, 8, 9
Garciá Márquez, Gabriel, 82, 84, 88, 93n
García Montero, Luis, 48, 151, 154, 160n, 161n

García Ramírez, Paula, 217, 218, 229
García Rodrigo, María Luisa, 202
García Sevilla, Ferrán, 184
García Valdés, Olvido, 153
Garro, Lander, 137, 138
Gas, Mario, 64
Gawsworth, John, 171
Geel, Nelleke, 87
Gelí, Carles, 234, 243
Gelman, Juan, 157
gender, 173, 176, 180n, 214, 220, 221, 245, 247, 254, 264
gender and identity, 245
gender interpretations, 247
gender politics, 246, 247
Generalitat de Catalunya, 248
Generation of the 1950s, 149, 160n
Generation X, 265, 266, 268
geography, 7, 8, 10, 13–15, 17, 18, 19
geography and rivers, 4–14, 21–23
geography and Spain, 9, 18, 19, 20
geography and space, 10, 11, 14. *See also* space
George, David, 79
Gibson, Ian, 114; *Viento del sur: Memorias apócrifas de un inglés salvado por España*, 111
Gide, André, 24; *Voyage au Congo*, 12
Gil de Biedma, Jaime, 149
Ginzburg, Carlo, 72, 79
Gironella, José María, 95, 241; *Los cipreses creen en Dios*, 82
Glenn, Kathleen, 246, 258
Glissant, Édouard, 43, 58, 60
Gómez, Lupe, 271
Gómez-Jurado, Juan: *El espía de Dios*, 90
Gómez-Montero, Javier, 114, 133; *Cuando va a la ciudad, mi Poesía: Das Gedicht und die Stadt*, 111
Gomis, Ramon, 78n, 79; *El mercat de les Delícies* (1993), 78n
González Fernández, Helena, 122, 132, 136, 146
González, Ángel, 160n
González-Millán, Xoán, 118, 120, 132
Gordillo, Luis, 184, 185

Goytisolo, Juan, x, 110, 169, 170, 177, 180, 213, 229, 230, 266, 267; *Juan sin tierra*, 169; *La resaca*, 169; *Señas de identidad*, 169; *España y su ejidos* (2003), 213, 229
Goytisolo, Luis, 110
Gracia, Jordi, 83, 95, 264, 266, 275
Gramsci, Antonio, 206
Grandes, Almudena, 84, 160n, 266
Grandi, Óscar Mariné, 185
grants, 85
Grassi, Paolo, 62
Gréco, Juliette, 252, 253
Griffin, Wiliam, 82
Grohmann, Alexis, 95
Groot, Ger, 90, 95
Guattari, Félix, 6, 14, 24
Guelbenzu, José María, 82, 83
Guillén, Claudio, 4, 5, 24

Hadj Nasser, Badia, 227n, 229
Hamlet, 49, 51
Hart, Stephen M., 258
Heinze, Úrsula, 132; *Culpable de asasinato*, 126
Henseler, Christine, xvii, xv, 113n, 114
Herder, Johann G., 236
Herrera, Fernando de, 166
Hierro, José, 269, 275
Hispanic identity, 13, 22. See also identity
Hispanism, xi, xii, xiv, 4–6, 12, 14, 22, 25, 110, 113n, 268
historical memory, ix, xv, 151, 154, 157, 272
historical novel, 124
Hoelscher, Steven, 4, 24
Hoenjet, Hans, 95
Hoffmann von Fallersleben, August Heinrich, 14, 25
Homilies d'Organyà, 235
Homs, Marc, 78n
Hooft Comajuncosas, Andreu van, 37, 41
Hooper, John, xi, 95
Hooper, Kirsty, 43, 50, 58, 60, 109, 114, 259, 271
Horace: *Ars poetica*, 104
Hugo, Victor, 45–46, 88, 103, 104; *Actes et Paroles*, 46

Humboldt, Wilhelm von, 29
Humlebaek, Carsten, 113n, 113
Hutcheon, Linda, 235, 239, 243
hybrid discourses, xiii, 203, 213–15, 221. See also literary genres and hybridization

Ibáñez, Andrés, 184, 193, 202; *El mundo en la era de Varick*, 201; *La música del mundo*, 196–201; *La música del mundo o El efecto Montoliu (The Music of the World or the Montoliu Effect*, 1995), 183, 194, 195
Ibáñez, Jesús, 202
Ichiishi, Barbara F., 246, 259
identity, xiii, ix, xii, 6, 7, 12, 44, 49, 56–58, 60, 203, 213, 215, 216, 218, 219, 220, 265, 262
identity and femenine, 273
Identity and language, xiv, 237, 238
identity and maps, 21. See also maps
identity and rivers, 13
identity and space, 14. See also geography
Iglesias Laguna, Antonio, 82, 95
Iglesias, Amalia, 152
Ilonbé, Raquel, 229; *Ceiba* (1987), 219; *Leyendas guineanas*, 219
Iñiguez de Onzaño, José Luis, 185
Institut Ramon Llull (IRL), 233
Institutionalization, 119, 120
Institutions, ix, 100, 101, 104, 108, 109, 110, 112, 169, 170, 176, 265; academic, xii, 22, 99, 100–102, 104, 105, 112; academic and Languages, 112, 113n; academic and study of literature, xi, 3, 4, 100, 103, 104, 112
institutions and history, 165–68, 171, 173, 178, 179
Instituto Cervantes, xiv, 145, 152, 203
Instituto das Artes Escénicas y Musicais (IGAEM), 128
Israel, Nico, 57, 58, 60
Izagirre, Koldo, 33, 137, 139, 144, 146
Iztueta, Juan Ignacio, 28, 41

Jacob, Christian, 14, 16, 17, 25

Jameson, Fredric, 151, 152, 162, 187, 194, 202
Jatib, Abdul-Latif, 204
Jdidi, Said, 204
Jiménez Heffernan, Julián, 152
Joan de Malniu. *See* Antoni Ribera
Jolas, Maria, 258
Jones Mathama, Daniel, 217, 218, 229
Joyce, James, 171; *Ulysses*, 172
Juan i Arbó, Sebastià, 237, 240
Juaristi, Jon, 29, 41, 42

Kafka, Franz, 178
Kaplan, Temma, 6, 25
Kapuściński, Ryszard, 25; *Imperium (1993)*, 17, 21
Karrouch, Laila, xiv, 213, 215, 229; *de Nador a Vic*, 213, 216
Khatibi, Abdelkebir, 214, 229
King, Stewart, xiv, 23n, 25, 243n, 243, 267, 268, 272
Kingsley, Ben, 174
Klein, Naomi, 234
Knapp, Margit, 233, 243
Koltés, Bernard-Marie, 62
Kortazar, Jon, xi, xiii, 265
Kushner, Tony: *Angels in America*, 77n

La clave Gaudí, 90, 95
La Guinea Española, 217
Labrador, Germán, 265, 271, 272, 275
Lafuente y Alcántara, Miguel, 103
Lafuente, Isaías, 23n, 25
Lahchiri, Mohamed, 204, 208, 209, 210–12, 215, 229; *Pedacitos entrañables, Cuentos ceutíes, Una tumbita en Sidi Embarek*, 211
Lahrech, Ouama A., 207, 229
Lakoff, George, 263, 272, 276
Landa, Mariasun, 32, 34, 41,136, 146; *La fiesta en la habitación de al lado: París, 1968–1969*, 34, 137
languages, 105, 109, 110, 112, 113n, 264
Laroui, Abdellah, 213; *al-Gurba*, (*The Exile* or *The Loneliness*, 1971), 205, 211
Larra, Mariano José, 169, 180

Larruri, Eva, 139, 146
Larsson, Stieg, 100
Lasa, Jexux Mari, 137
Lasagabaster, Jesús María, 29, 38n, 41
Latin American "*Boom,*" 82, 93n
Lauaxeta (pseudonym for Esteban Urkiaga). *See* Urkiaga, Esteban
Law of Normalization of the Use of the Basque Language (1982), 32, 144
Lefebvre, Henri, 7, 14, 25
León, Fray Luis de, 12, 25
Lertxundi, Anjel, 30, 32, 36, 41, 144
Liarás, Ana. *See also* editors, 91
Liddell, Angelica, 269
Lifshey, Adam, 220, 229
Liking, Warewere, 214
Linazasoro, Abelin: "Bernardo Atxagari," 141
Linazasóro, José Ignacio, 185
Líneas de actuación para el Teatro Nacional, 77n
linguistic diversity, xii, xiv, 111
Lipovetsky, Gilles, 175, 180
Lipski, John, 218, 225, 229
literary agents, 82, 85, 86, 91, 92, 119
literary canon, 208, 209, 213. *See also* canon
literary creation and ideology, 135, 137, 138, 141, 143
literary creation and language, 138, 140, 141
literary genres, 183, 185–87, 194, 198
literary genres and police and court drama, 191
literary genres and hybridization, 191, 198. *See also* hybrid discourses
literary genres and plots, 187, 189
literary groups, 119, 122
literary histography, 128
literary journals, 204
literary prizes, 101, 105, 110, 111, 119, 123, 125–27, 129, 136, 144, 149, 154, 213, 238, 160n
literature, 99, 108, 109, 110, 112, 167, 169, 170, 171, 177
literature: world, 106, 110, 111
literature institutionalized, 166, 167, 169, 170, 171, 176–78. *See also* institutions
Lizardi, 30, 31; *Eusko-Bidaztiarena (Song of the Basque Traveler)*, 30

Llamazares, Julio, 153, 156, 157, 162
Llompart, Josep M., 238, 244
Llull, Ramon, 235
London, John, 79
Lonsdale, Laura, xiv, 246, 247, 259, 266
López Barxas, Francisco, 132
López-Calvo, Ignacio, 212, 231
López Gaseni, Manuel, 35, 41
López Gorgé, Jacinto, 228
López Silva, Inma, 127
Los Nikis, 276, 261, 262; *El imperio contraataca* (1985), 261, 262
Losada, Basilio, 132
Losada, Basilio, 131n
Lottman, Herbert R., 101, 114
Loureiro, Ángel, 268, 276
Lourenzo, Manuel, 129
Lozano Mijares, Ma del Pilar, xv, 202, 265
Lyotard, Jean-François, 187, 202
lyrics, 102, 105, 107, 108

Maalouf, Amin, 34, 41
Machado, Antonio, 174
Macías, Sergio, 212, 228
Maeztu, Ramiro de, 166
Magán, Agustín, 128
Magris, Claudio, 6, 7, 12, 21, 25; *Danubio*, 6
Mahfouz, Naguib, 211
Mamet, David, 62
Manguel, Alberto, 89
Mankel, Henning, 100
Mann, Thomas, 178
Manrique, Winston, 95
maps, 4–8, 10, 14–18, 21–23. *See also* geography
maps and language, 16, 20
March, Ausiás, 235, 236
Marco, Joaquín, 95
Marías, Javier, 84, 95, 170–73, 181, 267; *Corazón tan blanco*, 84; *Todas las almas*, 171; *Tu rostro mañana*, 171
Marin, Louis, 14
Marinhas del Valle, Jenaro, 128
Mariscal, George, 23n, 25
marketplace, xi, 100, 102
Marocco and historical identity, 208, 211

Marsé, Juan, 110, 233, 249, 250, 259, 266; *El amante bilingüe* (1990), 249; *Si te dicen que caí*, 240
Martín Gaite, Carmen, 38n, 41, 266
Martin, Esteban; Andreu Carranza Font–La clave Gaudí, 90, 95
Martínez Cachero, José María, 189, 202
Martín-Santos, Luis, x, 179, 202; *Tiempo de silencio*, 188
Martorell, Joanot, 235; *Tirant lo Blanc*, 234
material culture, 63, 64, 66–68, 79
Mathama, Daniel Jones: *Una lanza por el boabí* (1962), 217
Mayhew, Jonathan, xv, 48, 60, 162, 269
Mayoral, Marina, 126
Mba Abogo, César, 223, 226, 229
McBride, Jim, 84
McHale, Brian, 186, 202
McLeon, John, 54, 60
Meabe, Tomás, 33, 37
Mechakra, Yamina, 227n, 229
Mekuy, Guillermina, 229; *El llanto de la Perra* (2005), 220
Mekuy, Guillermina: *Las tres vírgenes de Santo Tomás* (2008), 220
memory, 61, 63–69, 71, 73–76, 78, 79, 78n
Mendelson, Jordana, 24
Méndez Ferrín, Xose Luís 141; *Antón e os inocentes*, 118; *Arnoia, Arnoia* (1985), 131n; *Bretaña Esmeraldina* (1987), 131n; *No ventre do silencio* (1999), 131n
Mendoza, Eduardo, 188, 193, 198, 202, 233, 241; *La ciudad de los prodigos*, 84; *La verdad sobre el caso Savolta (The Truth about the Savolta Case*, 1975), 183, 188–92
Menéndez Pidal, Ramón, 16
Menéndez y Pelayo, Marcelino, 166, 177
Mercero, Gorka, 34, 41
Mérimée, Prosper, 29
Merino, Ana, 114
Merino, José María, 153
Mernissi, Fatema, 227n, 229
Merolla, Daniela, 56, 60
Mesa de Coordinación Teatral, 77n
Mesbahi, Mohamed, 206, 209, 229
Mesquida, Biel, 240, 244

Messari, Larbi, 204
Mestre, Juan Carlos, 153
Metge, Bernat, 235
Meyer, Stephenie, 100
Miampika, Landry Wilfrid, 227n, 229
Middle Ages, 105, 106
Mignolo, Walter, 215, 230
migration, x, 46–57, 59n, 78n, 111, 238, 240, 248, 270, 274
migration and Latin America, 274
Miguélez-Carballeira, Helena, 43, 60, 246, 247, 259
Milán, Eudardo, 153, 162
mileurismo, 274
Ministerio de Cultura de España, 114
minority languages, ix, 135, 139, 140, 145
Mitteleuropa, 21
Mitxelena, Koldo, 31, 39n
Modernism, 151–54, 158, 159
Modernism and Avant-Garde, 151, 154
Modernist poets and poetry, 151–54, 158–60
modernity, 23n, 169, 179
modernization, 206, 208–11, 223
Mogel, Bizenta, 38n, 41
Mogel, Juan Antonio, 41
Moix, Ana María, 249
Moix, Terenci, 237
Molas, Joaquim, 235, 244
Molière, 109
Molina Foix, Antonio, 185
Molina, Carme, 78n
Molina, César Antonio, 131n, 132, 152
Molinaro, Nina L., 254, 259
Molinero, C., 25
Molins, Manuel, 62, 79
Molins, Manuel: *Abú Magrib* (1992), 78n
Monegal, Antonio, 22, 23n, 25
Moneo, Rafael: *Bankinter* (landmarks), 185
Monleón, José, 230; *Cuentos de las dos orillas*, 205
Monsó, Imma, 109
Montejo, Andrea, 95
Montero, Rosa, 84
Monzó, Quim, 234, 239, 244
Mora, Cristina, 234
Moraña, Mabel, 23n, 25

Moreiras, Cristina, 264, 276
Moreiras-Menor, Cristina, 43, 45, 60
Moreno Torregrosa, Pasqual, 213, 230
Moreta, Miguel A., 212, 228
Morgades Besari, Trinidad, 220
Morillo, Fernando, 144
Morin, Edgar, 5
Moroccan literature, 204–7, 211–12. *See also* African literature
Moroccan literature in Spanish, 206, 212. *See also* African literature in Spanish
Moroccan Television Network (RTM), 204
Moroccan writers, 204–10. *See also* African literature
Moure, Teresa: *Herba Moura*, 127, 132
Müller, Jan-Werner, 33, 41
multiculturalism, 274
multilingualism, ix, xii, 23
Munibe, Xabier Maria, 38n, 41
Muñoz Molina: *Ventanas de Manhattan*, 172
Muñoz Molina, Antonio, 84–86, 95, 171, 172, 181; *Beatus Ille*, 86, 171; *Beltenebros*, 171; *Carlota Feinberg*, 86; *El invierno en Lisboa*, 86; *El jinete polaco*, 86, 171; *Plenilunio*, 86; *Sefarad*, 171; *Ventanas de Manhattan*, 171
Muñoz, David, 107. *See also* Estopa
Muñoz, Jokin, 137, 147
Muntaner, Ramon, 235
Muraro, Heriberto, 268, 276
Muslim society, 214
Muslim women, 207, 213

Nabokov, Vladimir, 171
Naïr, Sami, 213, 230
narrator, 187, 190, 192, 194, 195, 200
National Crusade for Catholic Unity and Spanish Identity, 74
National identity, x, 117, 166, 172, 173, 270
national literature, xi
nationalism, xii, 109, 111
Navajas, Gonzalo, 181, 194, 202, 262
Navarro Baldeweg, Juan, 185
Navarro Villoslada, Francisco, 29
Navarro, Julia, 91, 92
Navarro, Nuria, 230
Ndongo, Antimo Esono, 218

Ndongo-Bidyogo, Donato, 203, 218, 219, 230; *El Metro* (2007), 219; *Las Tinieblas de tu memoria negra* (1987), 219; *Los hijos de la tribu*, 219; *Los Poderes de la Tempestad* (1997), 219
Neruda, Pablo, 82
New Criticism, 103
New Media, books on Internet, 101; Galician Virtual Library, 128; influence, 128; video clips, 261, 262; YouTube, 109
New Media and Cervantes Virtual Portal, 108
New media and promoting of Galician literature, 119
New Spain, 263, 265, 270, 272–75
N'gom, M'bare, 217, 219, 230
Nichols, Geraldina Cleary, 246, 249, 259
Nietzsche, Friedrich, 178, 179, 181
Nini, Rachid, 213, 230
Nini, Rachid: Yawmiyyat muhayir sirri, 205
Nistal Rosique, Gloria, 230
Nkogo Esono, Maximiliano, 230; *Adjá-Adjá y otros relatos* (1994), 221; *Nambula* (2000), 221, 222
Nolla Gual, Enric: *Tratado de Blancas*, 78n
Novo, Olga, 123, 271
Nsang, Marcelo Ensema, 218
Nsué Angüe, María, 230; *Ekomo* (1985), 220

Obiang, Teodoro, 219
Odriozola, Joxe Manuel, 147
Okri, Ben, 222
Olaziregi, Mari Jose, xiii, 39n, 41, 42, 265
Oñederra, Lourdes, 33
Orejudo, Antonio, 192, 202
Orozco, Lourdes, 78n, 79
Ors, Eugeni d', 8, 25
Ortega y Gasset, José, xiv, 82, 167, 170, 175
Ortiz, Antonio, 185
Ortiz, Lourdes, 185
Ortiz-Ceberio, Cristina, 245, 246, 259
Ortiz-Griffin, Julia L., 82, 95
Osborne, Thomas, 23, 25
Otaegi, Lourdes, 31, 41
Oteiza, Jorge, xiii, 41, 184; *Quosque tandem (1963)*, 32
Otero Pedrayo, Ramón, 120, 126, 131n

Otero, Blas de, 177
Otero, Carlos, 185
Oyharçabal, Beñat, 28, 40

Pasqual, Lluís, 63
Pato, Chus: *Uránia* (1991), 123
Paz, Octavio, 82, 152
Pazó, Cándido, 128
Pemán, José María, 166, 177
Perec, Georges, 25; *Espéce d'espaces*, 10, 11
Pereda, José María de, 177
Pérez Beltrán, Carmelo, 230
Pérez Galdós, Benito, 81, 85, 96, 169, 177; *Fortunata y Jacinta*, 81, 93n; *La Regenta*, 81
Pérez Villalta, Guillermo, 184
Pérez, Albert, 78n
Pérez, Alícia, 78n
Pérez-Reverte, Arturo, 84, 87, 88, 92, 96, 167, 168, 181; *El maestro de esgrima*, 168; *El sol de Breda*, 87; *La tabla de Flandes*, 87; *Las aventuras del capitán Alatriste*, 168
Perkins, David, 235, 244
Pernas, Gustavo, 129
Perse, St. John (pseud. of Alexis Léger), 158
Pessoa, Fernando (Alberto Caeiro), 11, 14, 45, 151, 152; *Guardador de Rebanhos*, 9, 10
photography, 76, 102
Pié-Jahn, Guillermo, 230
Piñol, Rosa María, 242n, 244
Piñol, Sánchez, 175
Pinter, Harold, 62
Pla, Xavier, 238
Plan Galego das Artes Escénicas, 129
playwrights, 62, 63, 70, 77n, 78n
Plutarch, 17, 18, 25
poetry, 106–9, 188
poetry of experience, 150, 154, 161n
Polanski, Roman, 84
Political apathy (pasotismo), 184
Polley, Sarah, 174
Pombo, Álvaro, 86
Ponzaresi, Sandra, 56, 60
Pope, Randolph D., xii, xv, xvii, 114, 268, 269, 275

popular culture, xii, 105–6
popular literature, 104, 105, 108
popular music, 103, 106, 108, 113n
popular music industry, 109
popular songs, 103–8
Porta, Carles: *Tor. Tretze cases i tres morts*, 234
post Civil War, 157, 177
postcolonial literature, 208, 216, 219
post-Franco era, ix, xiii, 109, 249, 127, 151, 157, 178
Postmodernism, 151, 154, 158–60, 209, 245, 265
postmodernity in Spain, 183–86
postmodernity in Spain: 1990s postmodernism, 193–201
postmodernity in Spain: postmodern Spanish literature, 186–88
postmodernity in Spain: early postmodern fiction, 188–93
Pott, Banda, 32
Pozo, Jesús del, 185
Prabhu, Anjali, 213, 215, 230
Prats, Llorenç, 236, 244
Proust, Marcel, 11
publications (newspapers, magazines, journals, etc.), 84, 85, 89, 90, 92, 94, 95, 99, 100, 101, 149, 152, 184, 204, 234, 77n
publishing: editorial, 85, 86, 90, 91
publishing and distribution, 84–92, 90, 93n, 100, 102, 105
publishing and editors, 82, 86, 87, 91
publishing houses, xiii, 56, 85, 86, 89, 91, 101, 102, 105, 111, 119, 129, 144, 145, 149, 153, 212, 216, 219, 234
Pujol, Jordi, 248

Queizán, Mª Xosé, 126, 132; *A orella no buraco* (1965), 126; *Metáfora da metáfora* (1991), 123
Quejido, Manuel, 184
Quevedo y Villegas, Francisco de, 166, 179
Quico, Cadaval, 269
Quintana, Lluís, 23n

R.[odríguez] de la Flor, Fernando, 158, 159, 160, 160n

Rábade-Villar, María do Cebreiro, 57, 60
Ramoncín, 186
Raphael, Sylvia, 113
readership, xv, 84–88, 91–92, 100, 102, 105, 108, 124, 187, 188, 190, 192, 195, 206, 209
Real Academia Española, 268
Redden, Elizabeth, 112, 115
Reductio ad Imperium, 262
Reich-Ranicki, Marcel, 84
Reigosa, Carlos G., 132; *Crime en Compostela*, 123
Reixa, Antón, 132
Renaixença, xiv, 236, 238, 242n
Renan, Ernest, 30
Resina, Joan Ramon, 4, 25, 236, 244
Ribera, Antoni, 62
Ricci, Cristián H., 230, 231, 274
Ricoeur, Paul, 181
Riechmann, Jorge, 153, 154
Riera, Carme, 109
Rigalt, Carmen, 140, 141, 147
Rilke, Rainer Maria, 151
Riloha, María Caridad, 220
Rimbaud, Arthur, 152
Ríos, Julián, 202; *Larva*, 184
Ríos-Font, Wadda C., 235, 244
Riquer, Martí de, 237, 238, 244
Ritsos, Ghiannis, 152
Rivas, Manuel, xiii, xiv, 84, 109, 125, 132; *¿Qué me queres, amor?*, 125; *A lingua das bolboretas*, 272
Robbins, Tim, 174
Rodoreda, Mercé, 109, 231
Rodrigo, García, 185
Rodríguez Baixeras, Xavier, 122, 131n, 132
Rodríguez Marín, Francisco, 114; *Cantos populares españoles*, 103–5
Rodríguez Zapatero, José Luis, 152, 153, 154, 264
Rodríguez, Claudio, 149, 160n
Rodríguez, Ildefonso, 153
Rodríguez, Luciano, 131n, 132
Roig, Montserrat, 109, 240, 244, 249, 254; *L'opera quotidiana*, 240
Romaní, Ana, 123

Romero, Eugenia, 43
Rosa Camacho, Issac, 276; *El país del miedo* (2008), 274
Rosales, Emili, 86, 87. See also editors; *La ciutat invisible*, 86
Rose, Gillian, 74, 79
Rose, Nikolas, 23, 25
Roth, Joseph, 25; *Die Flucht ohne Ende*, 21
Royal Seminary of Bergara, 28–29
Royo, Curro, 132
Rubert de Ventós, Xavier, 64, 79
Rubio i Balaguer, Jordi, 236, 240, 244
Rubió i Ors, Joaquim, 244; *Lo gayté de Llobregat. Poesies*, 236, 237
Ruibal, Euloxio, 129
Ruibal, Rubén, 129
Ruiz Zafón, Carlos, 90, 93n, 96, 114, 181, 233; *El juego del ángel (The Angel's Game)*, 92, 101; *EL palacio de la medianoche* (1994), 93n; *El príncipe de la niebla* (1993), 93n; *La sombra del viento*, 86–89, 178; *Las luces de septiembre* (1995), 93n; *Marina* (1999), 93n
Rusiñol, Santiago, 77n

Sabina, Joaquín, 108, 160n
Sacido, Jorge, 40, 42
Sádaba, Javier, 184, 186
Sáenz de Oiza, Francisco Javier, 185
Sagarra, Josep María de, 62; *Galatea* (1948), 62; *La fortuna de Silvia* (1947), 62
Sahagún, Carlos, 160n
Said, Edward, 231
Saint John of the Cross, 167
Saint Vicenç Ferrer, 235
Saint Teresa of Jesus, 175, 177
Saizarbitoria, Ramón, xiii, 31, 33, 35, 39n, 41, 42, 144, 147; *Egunero hasten delako* (1969), 137; *Ehun metro (100 Meters*, 1976), 142; *Gorde nazazu lurpean (Let Me Rest*, 2000), 33
Sala, M., 25
Salgado, Daniel, 45, 48, 60
Salgueiro, Roberto, 128
Salisachs, Mercedes, 250

Salvador, Espriu: *Primera história d'Esther* (1948), 62
Sampedro, Benita, 231, 219
Sampedro, José Luis, 267, 268
Sampedro, Ramón, 271
Sánchez Ferlosio, Rafael, 266
Sánchez Mazas, Rafael, 178
Sánchez Piñol, Albert, 96, 234; *La pell freda* (2002), 84
Sánchez Robayna, Andres, 153, 162
Sánchez sandoval, Juan José, 212
Sánchez-Conejero, Cristina, 23n
Sanchis Sinisterra, José, 63
Sant Jordi, Jordi de, 235
Santana, Mario, 240, 242n, 244
Santiago, Silvio: *O silencio redimido*, 118
Santos, Carles, 62, 63
Saramago, Jose, 100, 110, 111, 114; *O evangelho segundo Jesus Christo* (1991), 111
Sardá, Rosa Maria, 78n
Sarrionandia, Joseba, 144
Sastre, Alfonso, 169, 177, 184, 252
Saura, Antonio, 184
Saura, Carlos, 169
Savater, Fernando, 100, 115, 186; *La hermandad de la buena suerte*, 100
Scarparo, Susanna, 242n
Scharm, Heike, 23n
Schiller, Friedrich, 236
Scott, Walter, 236
Segura, Santiago, 267
Segura, Xisco, 78n
Sempere, Pedro, 276
Senghor, Léopold Sédar, 219
Seoane, Luís, 120
Seoane, Xavier, 122
Seregni, Alessandro, 96
Seremetakis, Nadia, 67, 79
Serra, G. C., 240, 244
Serra, Pedro, 271, 275
Serrano Izko, Bixente, 42
Shakespeare, William, 171, 176
Shell, Marc, 111, 115
Shem-Tov, Tami, 100
Shubert, Adrian, 113n, 115

INDEX   295

Siale Djangany, José Fernando, 221, 222, 231
Sibari, Mohamed, 207; *El caballo*, 205
Sicilia, José María, 185
Sierra, Javier, 91, 92, 96; *La cena secreta (The Secret Supper)*, 88–90, 92
Silva, Lorenzo, 212, 228
Silveira, Xabier, 147; *A las ocho en el Bule*, 137
Simó, Ramon, 70
Sirera, Rodolf, 62
Smith, Paul Julian, 259
Smith, Zadie, 227n, 231
Snider, Sara, 23n
Sobrequés, J., 25
Sociedad de Literatura General y Comparada (SELGYC), 23n
Soja, Edward W., 24n, 25
Solá-Morales, Manuel, 185
Sollors, Werner, 111, 115
Sontag, Susan, 68, 79
Sophocles: *Antigone*, 75
space, 3–7, 10–12, 14, 15, 22, 23, 248, 256. *See also* geography
Spain and historical amnesia, 187, 189
Spain and maps. *See* maps
Spain's youth, 261, 271, 274
Spanish American literature, 82–84, 93n
Spanish contemporary culture, 261–64, 267
Spanish culture, 268, 274
Spanish intellectual discourse, 166, 167, 173, 174, 176, 178
Spanish literary system, xii
Spanish literature, x, 81–88, 92
Spanish Ministry of Culture, 86
Spanish society, xv, 171, 175, 177, 179, 186, 188
Spanishness, 6, 23n
Spitzmesser, Ana Ma, 202
Steenmeijer, Maarten, 95, 266, 267
Stilgoe, John R., 258
Strehler, Giorgio, 62
subaltern populations, 204, 207, 213, 216, 275
Subirana, Jaume, 36, 42
Subirats, Eduardo, 154
Sumai, Anxos, 127
Suñén, Juan Carlos, 153
Susanna, Álex, 131n, 132

Talens, Manuel, 202; *La parábola de Carmen la Reina*, 192
Tàpies, Antoni, 152, 153, 161n, 184
Tarrío Varela, Anxo, 39, 41
Taylor, Claire, 59n
Teixidor, Jordi, 62
television, 268, 269; *Das Blaue Sofa*, 234; *Esta noche cruzamos el Mississipi*, 268; *Made in Spain: Cuéntame cómo pasó*, 269
Tensamani, Mohammad, 204
Terry, Arthur, 248, 259
theater: companies, 61–63, 77n, 78n, 128
theater houses, 62–63, 64, 77n–78n
thracul, 89, 90, 92, 93
Ticknor, George, 23n
Till, Karen E., 4, 24
Tomás y Valiente, Francisco, 4
Tombs, Robert, 111, 115
Tomps, Isabelle, 111, 115
Tono Martínez, José, 184
Toro, Suso de, 109, 126, 131n, 132; *Calzados Lola* (1997), 126; *non volvas* (2000), 126; *Polaroid* (1986), 126; *Tic-tac* (1993), 126; *Trece badaladas* (2002), 126
Torras i Bages, Josep, 237, 244
Torrealdai, Joan Mari, 31, 42
Torrente Ballester, Gonzalo, 188
Torres Amat, Feliz, 237, 244
Torres Villegas, Francisco Jorge, 25
Torres, Xohana, 132; *Adiós, María* (1971), 126
Toufali, Karima, 226n
Toufali, Mohamed, 226n, 231
tourism, 111
Transition period (to democracy), xv, 62, 74, 76, 117, 118, 151, 183, 186, 188, 262, 264, 272
translations, 84, 87, 93n, 109, 111, 137, 140, 141, 145, 234
translations and Basque literature, 34–38
translations and Euskadi Prizes, 35
translations and funding, 86
travesía del desierto, 62
Tree, Matthew, 238
Tsuchiya, Akiko, 259
Tusell, Javier, 132

Tusquets, Esther, xiv, 245–47, 254, 255, 257, 259, 266; biography, 247; *El amor es un juego solitario* (1979), 248; *El mismo mar de todos los veranos* (1978), 248, 254; *Habíamos ganado la guerra* (2007), 247; *Para no volver* (1985), 248, 252; *Siete miradas en un mismo paisaje* (1981), 254, 255, 256; *Varada tras el último naufragio* (1980), 248

Uariachi, Abdelkader, 231; *El despertar de los leones*, 205
Ugarte, Michael, 219
Umbral, Francisco, 202
Unamuno, Miguel de, 30, 82, 166, 167, 174, 175, 177, 266
urban cultures, 274
Uribe Imanol, Dir: *Bwana*, 267
Uribe, Imanol, 175, 276
Urkiaga, Esteban (Lauaxeta), 30, 31
Urkiza, Ana, 33, 42

Vaello Marco, Eloisa, 203, 231
Valdés, Mario J., 235, 243
Valente, José Ángel, 149, 150, 152–54, 158, 162, 160n
Valero, Vicente, 153
Valle-Inclán, Ramón María de, 159, 166, 179, 180
Vallejo, Juan Pablo: *Patera* (2003), 78n, 79
Varela, Anxo Tarrío, 23n, 26
Varela, Blanca, 153, 162
Vargas Llosa, Mario, 82, 84, 96; *La ciudad y los perros*, 82, 93n
Vattimo, Gianni, 175, 181
Vázquez de Castro, Antonio, 185
Vázquez Molezún, Ramón: *Bankunión* (landmarks), 185
Vázquez Montalbán, Manuel, 263, 264, 276
Vázquez, Oscar, 24
Vega, Rexina, 127

Velázquez, Diego, 87, 166, 167
Veneno, Kiko, 186
Verde, Cesário, 45
vernacular literature, xi
Vicente Pozuelo, Juan, 132
Vidal Bolaño, Robert, 129
Vidal Folch, Xavier, 239, 240, 244
Vieites, Manuel, 132
Viladecans, Joan-Pere, 185
Vila-Matas, Enrique, 84, 233
Vilarós, Teresa, 264, 276
Vila-Sanjuán, Sergio, 238, 239, 244
Vilavedra, Dolores, xiii, 132, 133, 265
Villar, Rafa, 122, 133
Villaverde, Xavier, 132
Violadores del Verso, 275, 276
von Chamisso, Adelbert, 29

Wallerstein, Immanuel, 181
Walters, D. Gareth, 15, 26
Warden, Rebecca, 102, 115
Warf, Barney, 45, 60
Wells, Caragh, 242n
White, Deborah Elise, 46, 60
Wordsworth, William, 29
World War II, 21, 171, 258n

Xirau, Joaquim, 5

Youth Department of the Madrid City Council, 185

Zafzaf, Mohamed, 213, 231
Zafzaf, Mohamed: *al-Mar'a wa-l-warda* (*The Woman and the Rose*, 1970), 205
Zaldua, Iban, 33, 34, 42, 39n, 144–47
Zamora Loboch, Francisco, 219, 231; *Cómo ser negro y no morir en Aravaca* (1994), 219; *Memoria de Laberinto* (1999), 219
Zola, Émile, 178
Zurbarán, Francisco de, 166, 177

VOLUMES IN THE HISPANIC ISSUES SERIES

37 *New Spain, New Literatures,*
    edited by Luis Martín-Estudillo and Nicholas Spadaccini
36 *Latin American Jewish Cultural Production,*
    edited by David William Foster
35 *Post-Authoritarian Cultures: Spain and Latin America's Southern Cone,*
    edited by Luis Martín-Estudillo and Roberto Ampuero
34 *Spanish and Empire,* edited by Nelsy Echávez-Solano
    and Kenya C. Dworkin y Méndez
33 *Generation X Rocks: Contemporary Peninsular Fiction, Film, and Rock
    Culture,* edited by Christine Henseler and Randolph D. Pope
32 *Reason and Its Others: Italy, Spain, and the New World,*
    edited by David Castillo and Massimo Lollini
31 *Hispanic Baroques: Reading Cultures in Context,*
    edited by Nicholas Spadaccini and Luis Martín-Estudillo
30 *Ideologies of Hispanism,* edited by Mabel Moraña
29 *The State of Latino Theater in the United States: Hybridity, Transculturation, and Identity,* edited by Luis A. Ramos-García
28 *Latin America Writes Back: Postmodernity in the Periphery
    (An Interdisciplinary Perspective),* edited by Emil Volek
27 *Women's Narrative and Film in Twentieth-Century Spain:
    A World of Difference(s),* edited by Ofelia Ferrán and Kathleen M. Glenn
26 *Marriage and Sexuality in Medieval and Early Modern Iberia,*
    edited by Eukene Lacarra Lanz
25 *Pablo Neruda and the U.S. Culture Industry,* edited by Teresa Longo
24 *Iberian Cities,* edited by Joan Ramon Resina
23 *National Identities and Sociopolitical Changes in Latin America,*
    edited by Mercedes F. Durán-Cogan and Antonio Gómez-Moriana
22 *Latin American Literature and Mass Media,*
    edited by Edmundo Paz-Soldán and Debra A. Castillo
21 *Charting Memory: Recalling Medieval Spain,* edited by Stacy N. Beckwith
20 *Culture and the State in Spain: 1550–1850,*
    edited by Tom Lewis and Francisco J. Sánchez
19 *Modernism and its Margins: Reinscribing Cultural Modernity from Spain
    and Latin America,* edited by Anthony L. Geist and José B. Monleón
18 *A Revisionary History of Portuguese Literature,*
    edited by Miguel Tamen and Helena C. Buescu

17 *Cervantes and his Postmodern Constituencies*,
    edited by Anne Cruz and Carroll B. Johnson
16 *Modes of Representation in Spanish Cinema*,
    edited by Jenaro Talens and Santos Zunzunegui
15 *Framing Latin American Cinema: Contemporary Critical Perspectives*, edited by Ann Marie Stock
14 *Rhetoric and Politics: Baltasar Gracián and the New World Order*,
    edited by Nicholas Spadaccini and Jenaro Talens
13 *Bodies and Biases: Sexualities in Hispanic Cultures and Literatures*,
    edited by David W. Foster and Roberto Reis
12 *The Picaresque: Tradition and Displacement*, edited by Giancarlo Maiorino
11 *Critical Practices in Post-Franco Spain*,
    edited by Silvia L. López, Jenaro Talens, and Dario Villanueva
10 *Latin American Identity and Constructions of Difference*,
    edited by Amaryll Chanady
9   *Amerindian Images and the Legacy of Columbus*,
    edited by René Jara and Nicholas Spadaccini
8   *The Politics of Editing*, edited by Nicholas Spadaccini and Jenaro Talens
7   *Culture and Control in Counter-Reformation Spain*,
    edited by Anne J. Cruz and Mary Elizabeth Perry
6   *Cervantes's Exemplary Novels and the Adventure of Writing*,
    edited by Michael Nerlich and Nicholas Spadaccini
5   *Ortega y Gasset and the Question of Modernity*, edited by Patrick H. Dust
4   *1492–1992: Re/Discovering Colonial Writing*,
    edited by René Jara and Nicholas Spadaccini
3   *The Crisis of Institutionalized Literature in Spain*,
    edited by Wlad Godzich and Nicholas Spadaccini
2   *Autobiography in Early Modern Spain*,
    edited by Nicholas Spadaccini and Jenaro Talens
1   *The Institutionalization of Literature in Spain*,
    edited by Wlad Godzich and Nicholas Spadaccini

www.ingramcontent.com/pod-product-compliance
Lightning Source LLC
Chambersburg PA
CBHW030107010526
44116CB00005B/132